THE CLASSICS OF WESTERN SPIRITUALITY

Carthusian Spirituality
THE WRITINGS OF HUGH OF BALMA AND GUIGO DE PONTE

TRANSLATED AND INTRODUCED BY
DENNIS D. MARTIN

PREFACE BY
JOHN VAN ENGEN

PAULIST PRESS
NEW YORK • MAHWAH

The translations in this volume are based on Hughes de Balma, *Théologie mystique,* edited by Francis Ruello and Jeanne Barbet, Sources Chrétiennes, vols. 408–409 (Paris: Éditions du Cerf, 1995–1996) and Guigues du Pont, *Traité sur la contemplation,* edited by Dom Philippe Dupont, Analecta Cartusiana, 72 (Salzburg: Institut für Anglistik und Amerikanistik, 1985).

Library of Congress Cataloging-in-Publication Data

Carthusian spirituality: the writings of Hugh of Balma and Guigo de
  Ponte/translated and introduced by Dennis D. Martin.
      p. cm. — (The classics of Western spirituality; #88)
    Includes bibliographical references and index.
    ISBN 0-8091-3664-3 (alk. paper) — ISBN 0-8091-0480-6 (alk. paper).
    1. Spiritual life — Catholic Church. 2. Carthusians — Spiritual life. 3. Mysticism —
  Catholic Church. 4. Contemplation. 5. Catholic Church — Doctrines. I. Hugh of
  Balma, 13th cent. Viae Sion lugent. English. II. Guigues, du Pont, d. 1297. De con-
  templatione. English. III. Martin, Dennis D., 1952–   . IV. Title: Roads to Zion
  mourn. V. Title: On contemplation. VI. Series.
  BX2349.C36 1996
  248'.09'02 — dc20   96-30281
                                                                              CIP

Published by Paulist Press
997 Macarthur Boulevard
Mahwah, New Jersey 07430

Printed and bound in the United States of America

Contents

vii

CONTENTS

Translator of This Volume

DENNIS D. MARTIN studied medieval and early modern religious history at Wheaton College (Illinois) and the Universities of Waterloo (Ontario, Ph.D., 1982), Marburg and Tübingen. In addition, he has received Fulbright and National Endowment for the Humanities fellowships. He was assistant editor of *The Brethren Encyclopedia* (1983) and *The Mennonite Encyclopedia*, volume 5 (1990), and taught church history at the Associated Mennonite Biblical Seminaries (Elkhart, Ind.). Since 1991 he has taught historical theology and church history at Loyola University, Chicago. His interest in Carthusian history and spirituality began in graduate school as an outgrowth of studies in Cistercian and Benedictine spirituality and led to a book on late-medieval Carthusian life, *Fifteenth-Century Carthusian Reform* (E. J. Brill, 1992). He is presently working on a study of royal and noble patronage of Carthusian monasteries in Austria, Styria, England, France, Aragon and the Holy Roman Empire during the twelfth to fourteenth centuries as well as on a general history of the Carthusian Order through the centuries.

Author of the Preface

JOHN VAN ENGEN is director of the Medieval Institute and professor of history at the University of Notre Dame. He is a specialist in the religious and intellectual history of the European Middle Ages. His first book, *Rupert of Deutz* (1983), treated the twelfth-century Benedictine author. In The Classics of Western Spirituality series, he edited and translated the volume *Devotio Moderna: Basic Writings* (1988). He is currently writing a general book on Christianization during the Middle Ages.

FOR DALE AND SYLVIA SCHROCK MARTIN

filiali pietate
cum fidelitate Christo

Foreword

As a graduate student twenty years ago I spent many fascinating hours with the works of Nicholas Cusanus, particularly his sermons, his early treatise *On Learned Ignorance*, and his mature work, *On the Vision of God*. These writings by a man whose mind was perhaps the most sophisticated in the fifteenth century were also expressions of the heart. They led me to the Tegernsee Benedictines and they, in turn, led me to the Carthusians. Indeed, behind nearly every edifice of late medieval spirituality I examined, I found Carthusian traces. Secondary sources frequently referred to them but seldom had anything substantive to say about them.

Carthusians were friends to Gerard Groote and the *Devotio moderna*, Blessed Jan van Ruusbroec, Jean Gerson, Nicholas Cusanus, and many other spiritual writers. They were patronized by Duke Philip the Good and Duchess Isabella of Burgundy (Dijon, Basel); counts Ulrich and Ludwig of Württemberg (Güterstein near Urach), dukes Friedrich the Fair and Albrecht II of Austria (Mauerbach near Vienna, Gaming near Melk) and Heinrich of Kärnten and Tirol (Schnals); Emperor Friedrich Barbarossa (Durbon, Silve-Bénite); kings Louis the Great of Hungary (Váröslöd [Leweld]), Henry II of England (Witham, Liget), Louis IX of France (Paris), Alfonso II of Aragon (Scala Dei), and John II of Castille (Miraflores); popes Nicholas V (Bologna) and Innocent VI (Villeneuve-les-Avignon), and many other medieval kings and nobles, popes, bishops, and burghers. They helped transmit Latin writings of diverse spiritual traditions from the Continent to England. Indigenous vernacular English spiritual literature of the fourteenth and fifteenth centuries is intimately connected with the English Carthusians. Sixteenth-century personalities of the stature of St. Thomas More, St. Ignatius of Loyola, and St. John of the Cross considered becoming Carthusians. Christopher Columbus was advised by a Carthusian and was initially buried at the charterhouse Las Cuevas at Seville.

FOREWORD

Thus, even though they deliberately remained hidden from view in order to preserve their strict discipline, they filled for the fourteenth, fifteenth, and sixteenth centuries the role played in the tenth and eleventh centuries by the Cluniac network, in the twelfth century by the Cistercians, and in the thirteenth century by the Franciscans and Dominicans: the role of the most respected religious order, of society's most outstanding professional intercessors before God's throne. Founded in the late eleventh century, a few years before the Cistercians, the Carthusians grew very slowly during their first two centuries, but were highly respected from the beginning. They inspired, among others, Bernard of Clairvaux, William of St. Thierry, Aelred of Rievaulx, and Peter the Venerable.

Yet the thirteenth century is an as-yet largely unexplored period of Carthusian history. The two authors whose writings make up this volume are situated at the end of the century, just before the order's flourishing growth of the fourteenth century (ninety-nine houses were founded between 1300 and 1400, compared with thirty-seven in the eleventh and twelfth centuries and twenty-five in the thirteenth). Both authors have basked in Carthusian anonymity. Some scholars even suggest that whoever wrote *The Roads to Zion*, it was not the prior of the Charterhouse of Meyriat named Hugh (who himself may not have been "of Balma"). Although this issue remains unresolved at present, and we shall continue to employ the conventional designation for the author ("Hugh of Balma"), the considerable influence of both works was nearly always indirect and undercover—under the name of Bonaventure or embedded in the writings of Hendrik Herp or Ludolf of Saxony. When *The Roads to Zion* was overtly cited as authoritative, in the fifteenth-century Tegernsee mystical theology controversy, it was badly misunderstood by one side in the debate. Guigo de Ponte's influence has remained almost completely hidden from view. In a recent volume of the Classics of Western Spirituality, George Ganss, S.J., attributed the "germ of many features" of Ignatius of Loyola's "spirituality in general" to Ludolf of Saxony, not realizing that most of the words he was quoting were from Guigo. May the translation of these two frequently cited but often misread or unacknowledged late medieval classics open up new paths of inspiration *ad maiorem Dei gloriam*.

It is my pleasure to thank those who have helped make this book possible: the members of the Institute for Research in the Humanities at the University of Wisconsin–Madison, where I spent a fruitful year as a visiting fellow; l'Abbé Francis Ruello of Solesmes, who, together with

FOREWORD

Père Dominique Bertrand, S.J., of the Institute des Sources Chrétiennes, gave access to the unpublished critical text of *The Roads to Zion;* Dom Philippe Dupont and Dr. James Hogg, who made Guigo de Ponte's *De Contemplatione* fully accessible to readers inside and outside the academy; to the College of Arts and Sciences of Loyola University in Chicago, whose summer research grant permitted me to finish the project; and to Professor Bernard McGinn of the University of Chicago Divinity School, who responded with interest to my suggestion that these two Carthusians be taken up into the remarkable series he now edits and whose acute Latinity and willingness to pore over both translation and Latin originals for hours saved me much embarrassment. I am grateful also to two of my Loyola colleagues: Fr. Earl Weis, S.J., who read the entire translation with the eye of a skilled editor and wise scholar, and Dr. Willemien Otten, now of Boston College, to whom I turned for help with several problem passages. Given such generosity, it should be clear that any defects that remain are my responsibility. My debt to my wife, Carol, is known to her *familiariter et penitus.*

This book is dedicated in heartfelt *pietas* to those who arranged for my first lessons in a second language while personally teaching me the language of faithfulness to Christ. *Cultores* both, they tended the products of the soil and nurtured body, mind, and soul, planting in hope and building better than they can possibly know. Together we await the vision face-to-face, when faith and hope arrive at simple charity.

Chicago, St. Athanasius, 1995

Note: While this volume was in press, the Sources Chrétiennes critical edition of Hugh of Balma's *The Roads to Zion Mourn,* by Francis Ruello and Jeanne Barbet, appeared in print. From the introduction, which was previously unavailable to me, I learned that the editors have found seventeen manuscripts containing translations of this treatise into Danish, Portuguese, German, Spanish, Catalan, Italian, English, Flemish, and French, dating from the fourteenth to the seventeenth century. This information augments that found in the introduction to the present translation and indicates a much more widespread impact of Hugh of Balma's treatise than heretofore recognized by scholars. The critical apparatus of this new edition contains many additional references to works by scholastic theologians, notably Thomas Aquinas, that may have been used by or known to the author of *The Roads to Zion Mourn.*

DDM

Preface

Mystical theology—these words resonate still in many contemporary minds and hearts. They suggest teachings at once systematic and attractive, a paradoxical effort to render verbally an ineffable human experience of the divine. The texts in this volume, two thirteenth-century Carthusian works ably translated by Dennis Martin, will probably surprise modern readers. They do not cater to vague modern notions of the "mystical," breathy intimations of an invisible or immaterial reality hawked in brightly colored paperbacks arrayed in the religious section of mass-market bookstores. These medieval Carthusian texts put down in writing, first of all, practices meant to discipline the spiritual life of a few hermits—and any others who could read the Latin prose or benefit from its teachings. The authors aimed, second, to render mentally intelligible an extraordinary human experience of the divine, however difficult their consequent exposition. This they did by way of commenting upon a difficult text ascribed to a figure from the apostolic age of the church, Pseudo-Dionysius's little work *On Mystical Theology*. For those few who both maintained the spiritual discipline and achieved the mental understanding, these texts held out, finally, the possibility of realizing this experience of God almost at will—a controversial notion that generated sparks still two hundred years later. Dennis Martin, the historian of that later controversy, has made these texts available in modern English for the first time, with an introduction that directs readers through the maze of their teachings. This preface may help to orient readers to the larger framework, both institutional and intellectual, within which these texts were first written down.

The absolute identity of both authors as Carthusian remains uncertain, though highly probable. Indeed such anonymity befits Carthusian practice. The order, called Carthusian after its motherhouse (La Grande Chartreuse), located in a narrow valley of the French Alps above Grenoble, originated in the 1080s. It proved one of the most remarkable and enduring experiments to come out of the late-eleventh-century religious revival in medieval Europe. Bruno of Cologne, a secular master at Reims, sought in 1084 a secluded site for a community of hermits. Each would live in a separate cell joined by a common cloister. Each would maintain a solitary contemplative life, interrupted by morning and evening prayers, mass, and some common meals. Their number was not to exceed the apostolic twelve, and they would gain material support from no more than sixteen lay brothers *(conversi)*, who occupied a house further down the valley. This extreme vision of the solitary life attracted few followers initially. The order's first general chapter met in 1140 with six of a possible nine priors present. Only thirty-three houses for monks and two for nuns had been founded by the year 1200 (compared to more than three hundred fifty for Cistercian monks), and at the end of the thirteenth century there still were just fifty-six houses for monks and seven for nuns. These Carthusian works on the mystical life were written, initially, for a small contemplative elite.

The motherhouse issued its first customary in the 1120s, drawn up by its remarkable fifth prior, Guigo I (1109–36), who had been named prior at age twenty-six, only three years after entering the mountain hermitage. In the nature of a customary, Guigo wrote out what he presented as the group's common practices, beginning with their form of keeping the divine office and proceeding through community offices and religious exercises. He was not content, however, to fill the entire customary with routine matters. At the end, driving home the point of all that he had prescribed, he concluded with a lengthy chapter entitled "A Commendation of the Solitary Life," replete with biblical and historical examples, including Jesus himself, who was tempted while alone in the desert prior to taking up his ministry and who regularly withdrew from his disciples to pray. This same Guigo, during his years in the hermitage, compiled a series of proverblike sayings and stories (numbered at 476 in a modern edition) that captured in writing the wisdom of the solitary life. These began with the frank recognition that human hearts were roused by powerful drives *(vehementes affectus)*, even preoccupied with impure desires, much more than they were focused on the Lord. The whole point of this solitary community was to focus hearts directly on the Lord.

At the heart of Carthusian life, as envisioned by its priors and its statutes, was the individual cell. For the twelfth century this represented a radical refocusing of the spiritual life away from community life and prayer (the emphasis also of Cistercians and canons regular) toward individual meditation. Guigo's statutes of the 1120s prescribed (c. 28) what utensils, clothing, and furniture a cell should contain in order to maintain exemplary poverty. Notably, a cell was also to have all the materials needed for writing, and hermits might take books from the common library cupboard to their individual cells. They were to guard these books most carefully as "the eternal food of our souls," and were themselves to produce books zealously so that, "since we cannot preach the Word of God with our mouths, we may do so with our hands," that is, by writing and copying. Guigo's own religious insights, and the inscribing of them into a codex as proverblike items, arose out of that same solitary religious striving combined with an injunction to teach and preach through writing.

At the same time that Carthusians cultivated eremetical cells in secluded sites, their form of retreat into the "desert," schoolmen gathered in unprecedented numbers in bustling urban centers where they eventually founded the medieval university. Critics, including the monk Bernard of Clairvaux, accused clerical schoolmen of being driven mostly by curiosity and ambition, vainly pursuing learning as the means to a higher career. Here was no solitude but bands of clerics joined in protectionist guilds, no contemplation but boisterous argument, no satisfied interior experience but restless mental reasoning—such at least is the stark contrast usually drawn between these two worlds, with some historical justice. Yet in the second half of the thirteenth century, in the generation that would yield the two works translated in this volume, these two worlds drew closer together. In the year 1257 Saint Louis founded a Carthusian house in Paris, the first such house located on the edges of a city rather than in a rural valley—and that the city that had become by then the chief theological center of medieval Europe. In the course of the fourteenth century, the Carthusians would undergo an astounding expansion of ninety-four new male and two new female houses, a nearly three-fold increase in the size of the order. Many of these houses were founded by devout princes on the model of Saint Louis, and not a few were placed at the edges of urban sites. Carthusian hermits could not entirely escape what went on in these cities, just as their writings and books found an immediate audience beyond their walls, despite the formal requirement of seclusion and silence. Our two authors, though working in less urban cloisters, wrote on the brink of this expansion and may even have foreseen a burgeoning wider interest in a fuller exposition of the mystical life. Just as importantly, the Carthusians' own passionate interest in books, attested by their surviving library catalogues, brought the fruits of theological enquiry into the heart of their contemplative solitude.

Since the founding of the Carthusians, the University of Paris had gradually put in place a new scholarly discipline, *theology*, or professionalized "God-talk." Bruno himself had been a teacher of Scripture before retiring to his mountain retreat, and a formalized teaching of Scripture remained at the heart of theology. But theologians now also imported philosophical method, as well as an Aristotelian metaphysics, and were schooled as intellectuals to think in terms of "disputed questions," endless topics explored by way of *pro* and *contra* authorities and reasons. The Carthusians, however isolated their solitary pursuit of God, could not proceed unaffected by these larger trends in European intellectual life. Indeed the first of the treatises translated here, that ascribed to Hugh of Balma, may have arisen first as a disputed question and only later been placed at the end of a work that proceeded in more accessible expository prose. Either way, this Carthusian author, knowing the method, language, and relevant school authors in the newer mode of theology, thought it relevant to append such a learned enquiry to a meditative treatise.

The works stand as an emblem in some ways to this in-between status, this drawing fully upon elements from two worlds that recent historians have tried to keep apart. To achieve their end more authoritatively, these authors seized upon a supposedly apostolic work that expounded a "mystical theology" that went beyond the modalities associated with explaining the creeds or naming God. Pseudo-Dionysius, in a short but difficult work, described a way of apprehending God that was animated primarily by a neo-Platonic negative theology. These Carthusian authors gained access to Pseudo-Dionysius by way of a commentary prepared by Thomas Gallus of Vercelli, a canon regular who had worked in the house of Saint-Victor in Paris during the first half of the thirteenth century. From its beginning in the early twelfth century, this Victorine house had sponsored approaches that combined the disciplinarily theological with the personally spiritual. Carthusian authors creatively transformed this "mystical theology" into an affective way.

The two treatises in this volume, however conscious of contemporary theological modes and arguments, affirmed, as Martin has insisted, an authentically Carthusian spiritual way. They presupposed, and insisted upon, practices befitting the solitary life: rigorous self-examination, a thoughtful and repeated praying of the Lord's Prayer, concern with the posture and times of prayer, a careful training of the affections. Above all, they strove toward, and defended the possibility of, an affective grasp of the divine apart from a parallel cognitive preparation. Martin has set out the possible theological sources and meanings of such an affective approach. Two points might be made to conclude this preface and frame his discussion.

Seeking an extraordinary spiritual experience of the divine had become widespread in the later thirteenth century, even, or perhaps especially, outside cloistered circles. Beguines were noted for it and often drew upon the language of spousal love. Marguerite of Porete, notably, was condemned for envisioning and teaching a kind of emptying into the divine—not without its parallels to these Carthusian works. In each case, spiritual persons sought the means to rise above, or leave behind, the ordinary routines of religious life—for some of the more daring Beguine authors, even the sacraments and charitable works. The teachings espoused may have assumed such practices as routine, even banal, but focused on achieving endpoint, an experience of the beatific vision. Churchmen intervened worriedly to reaffirm the distinction between Creator and creature, between the material manifestations of Christ's grace necessary in this life and the unmediated presence of Christ promised in the next.

These Carthusian authors, writing as solitaries and in Latin at the end of the thirteenth century, aimed for much the same kind of experiential knowledge, described in their terminology as "affective." They, too, presupposed, even enjoined, the ordinary practices required to exercise the religious person. For them, what needed to be transcended was the intellective faculty, the need to reason a person's way into the being of God. The affective upsurge into God should come as easily as breathing, as easily to an unlearned peasant as to a learned schoolman, to a woman as to a man. Here is the irony that underlies these works and may indirectly have contributed to their reception. Such a goal, stated in that way, made sense only in a world where the newer mode of theologizing already reigned supreme, where even Carthusian authors felt a need to find new ways to affirm the experiential end of the solitary life. These works would not be what they are, sophisticated introductions to the mystical life, without a resourceful drawing upon the ways and authorities familiar to theology in that mode. These works offer an exegesis of the biblical text, the first duty of a schooled theologian. But whereas the schoolmen focused first of all on the literal and historical senses to explain the basic text and then on the allegorical to expound

PREFACE

its theological meanings, these Carthusian authors offered an anagogical reading, drawing out of the text that which pointed to the ultimate end of things, the beatific vision of God. So they both aimed at, and aimed to transcend, a mental grasp of the human experience of the divine. Such an intersection befit that moment when the world of the solitary contemplative and of the disciplined schoolman grew closer together, influencing one another more and more, even at times overlapping. This ideal and mode of expression drew unprecedented numbers of followers in the later Middle Ages.

Abbreviations

Note: Works available in a wide variety of editions and translations, e.g., the Rule of St. Benedict and the *Summa Theologiae* of Thomas Aquinas, have not been cited in specific editions.

AC = Analecta Cartusiana. Salzburg: Institut für Englische Sprache und Literatur; Institut für Anglistik und Amerikanistik. Note: this monograph series is not to be confused with the semi-annual journal of the same name published between 1989 and 1994.

ACW = Ancient Christian Writers series. Westminster, Md.

ANF = Ante-Nicene Fathers series. 8 vols. and index vol. New York and Buffalo, 1885–1896; reprinted Grand Rapids: Eerdmans, 1954–

Bernardi Opera = *Sancti Bernardi Opera Omnis.* Edited by Jean Leclercq, H. M. Rochais, C. H. Talbot. 8 vols. Rome: Editiones Cistercienses, 1957–1977.

CCCM = Corpus Christianorum, Continuatio Mediaevalis. Turnhout: Brepols.

CCSL = Corpus Christianorum, Series Latina. Turnhout: Brepols.

CF = Cistercian Fathers series. Kalamazoo: Cistercian Publications. English translations of Bernard of Clairvaux, William of Saint Thierry, Aelred of Rievaulx, Gilbert of Hoyland.

CS = Cistercian Studies series. Kalamazoo: Cistercian Publications.

ABBREVIATIONS

CSEL = Corpus Scriptorum Ecclesiasticorum Latinorum. Vienna.

CWS = Classics of Western Spirituality. New York, N.Y., and Mahwah, N.J.: Paulist Press.

Denis of Rijkel, *Opera* = In *Doctoris ecstaticis Dionysii Cartusiensis Opera omnia*. 44 vols. Montreuil, Tournai, Parkminster: Charterhouse of Notre Dame de Près, 1896–1913.

Dionysiaca = Pseudo-Dionysius. *Dionysiaca. Recueil donnant l'ensemble des traductions latines des ouvrages attribués au Denys l'Aréopagite*. 2 vols. Edited by Ph. Chevallier et al. Paris: Desclée de Brouwer, 1937, 1950.

DS.1M = *Dictionnaire de spiritualité ascétique et mystique*, ed. Marcel Viller and others. 16 vols. Paris: Beauchesne, 1932–1995.

ET = English translation.

FC = Fathers of the Church series. Washington, D.C.: Catholic University of America, 1947.

Gregory the Great, *Moralia* = *Moralia in Job*. PL 76. CCSL 143-143B. ET by J. Bliss, *Moralia on in Book of Job*, Library of the Fathers of the Church, 18, 22, 23, 31. Oxford: J. H. Parker, 1844–1850.

Guigo I, *Consuetudines* = Guigo I, *Coutumes de Chartreuse* [Consuetudines Cartusienses], ed. and trans. by a Carthusian [Maurice Laporte], SC, 313. Paris: du Cerf, 1984. Reprinted in *The Evolution of the Carthusian Statutes from the Consuetudines Guigonis to the Tertia Compilatio, Documents*, vol. 1. AC, 99, Documents, 1. 1989. Pp. 7–56.

Hugh of Balma, *Viae Sion* = Hugh of Balma, *Viae Sion lugent* (cited by chapter [caput], and part [particula], with page numbers and column a or b in the Peltier edition given in parentheses). Critical edition in SC, 408–409. Paris, 1995–1996.

LCC = Library of Christian Classics (Philadelphia: Westminster, 1952–1969).

ABBREVIATIONS

Leonine edition = the Vatican edition of the *Opera Omnia* of Thomas Aquinas (Rome). See Weisheipl, p. 357.

Nicholas Kempf, *Mystica theologia* = Nicholas Kempf of Straßburg, *Tractatus de mystica theologia*, ed. Karl Jellouschek et al., Analecta Cartusiana, 9 (Salzburg: Institut für Englische Sprache und Literatur, 1973).

Nicholas of Lyra, *Postilla* = *Postilla super totam Bibliam,* various fifteenth- and sixteenth-century editions (some reprinted in the twentieth century).

NPNF-1 = Nicene and Post-Nicene Fathers, series 1, ed. Philip Schaff and others (New York and Buffalo, 1886–1900; reprinted Grand Rapids: Eerdmans, 1954–   ).

NPNF-2 = Nicene and Post-Nicene Fathers, series 2, ed. Philip Schaff and others (New York and Buffalo, 1886–1900; reprinted Grand Rapids: Eerdmans, 1954–   ).

PG = Patrologiae cursus completus, series Graeca. 168 vols. Ed. Jacques-Paul Migne and others. Paris: Migne, 1857–1868. Reprinted Turnhout: Brepols.

PL = Patrologiae cursus completus, series Latina. 217 vols. Ed. Jacques-Paul Migne and others. Paris: Migne, 1844–1864. Reprinted Turnhout: Brepols.

Richard of Saint-Victor, *Benjamin minor.* PL 196. Also known as *The Twelve Patriarchs.* ET by Grover Zinn in CWS series. Critical edition forthcoming from SC.

————. *Benjamin major.* PL 196. Also known as *The Mystical Ark.* ET by Grover Zinn in CWS series. Critical edition announced as forthcoming in SC.

SC = Sources Chrétiennes. Paris: Editions du Cerf.

STh = Thomas Aquinas, *Summa Theologiae.*

ABBREVIATIONS

Weisheipl = James A. Weisheipl, *Friar Thomas d'Aquino: His Life, Thought, and Works*. Garden City, N.Y.: Doubleday, 1974, Washington, D.C.: Catholic University of America Press, 1983. Pp. 355–405 contain a useful listing of editions and translations of Thomas's works.

William of Saint-Thierry, *Epistola* = *Epistola ad fratres de Monte Dei*. PL 184. SC 223. ET by Theodore Berkeley in CF 12.

INTRODUCTION

I. CARTHUSIANS ON LOVE OF GOD, LOVE OF NEIGHBOR, AND LOVE OF CREATION

Although Hugh of Balma has conventionally been understood as part of the stream of renewed interest in the mystical writings of Pseudo-Denis in the twelfth and thirteenth centuries (Hugh of Saint-Victor, Thomas Gallus, Robert Grosseteste, Albert the Great, Thomas Aquinas),[1] the present volume seeks to place both Hugh and Guigo de Ponte primarily in the context of Carthusian spirituality.[2] Several previous volumes in the Classics of Western Spirituality series have hinted at the importance of the Carthusians for a wide variety of late medieval spiritual literature,[3] and scholars are beginning to give some sustained attention to Carthusian spirituality in the twelfth century, a spirituality grounded in a theology of love of God, one's neighbor, and the world.[4] Hugh's importance for Spanish spirituality in the sixteenth century was considerable, but wherever his writings circulated they did so primarily under Franciscan auspices. Although Melquíades Andrès Martín has called *The Roads to Zion Mourn* a "fundamental book in the history of our [Spanish] spirituality" and referred to its author as "one of the keys of peninsular spirituality,"[5] Hugh of Balma has seldom been studied against the context of the Carthusian tradition.

The Carthusian Order traces its origins to 1082–1084,[6] when Bruno of Cologne,[7] a former cathedral canon and head of the schools at Reims, left his prestigious positions in the wake of the Gregorian reform party's failed efforts to eliminate ecclesiastical corruption in the diocese. He and six companions eventually found themselves in the Alpine wilderness near Grenoble, where Bishop Hugh of Grenoble welcomed them and helped them establish a monastery that became known as La Chartreuse (later the "Grande Chartreuse"). Their aim was to live a very simple, primitive monastic life along the lines of that lived by the Desert Fathers but retaining elements of the common life as it had developed in western monasticism. They drew on the the statutes of the canons regular of St. Ruf near Avignon, the home community of two of the seven companions, as well as the Rule of St. Benedict. To ensure that their strict regimen would not be relaxed, with Bishop Hugh's

INTRODUCTION

assistance they acquired a large tract of wilderness land as a "desert" (*eremus*) with clearly established boundaries. More than a century of episcopal and papal legislation forbade lay people from entering this preserve,[8] and the Carthusians put severe restrictions on themselves to ensure that the members of the community would seldom leave the bounds of the *eremus*. When, in the 1120s, several newly founded primitivist monastic communities asked the fifth head of the Chartreuse, Prior Guigo I (d. 1136), for a written summary of its pattern of life, he wrote down what became the *Customs* (*Consuetudines Guigonis*) of the Chartreuse. By mid-century several monasteries banded together formally under the authority of a General Chapter, with the prior of the Grande Chartreuse as their head. From that point onward one can legitimately speak of a Carthusian Order. Individual houses are known as charterhouses, an anglicized version of the Latin *Cartusia*.

As it developed during the twelfth century, the order's spirituality emphasized scriptural and patristic simplicity. The lessons at the night office were drawn exclusively from Scripture and, although reading at table included patristic resources, these were almost exclusively drawn from commentaries on the gospels by six main Church Fathers (Gregory the Great, Augustine, Leo the Great, Ambrose, Jerome, and Hilary of Poitiers). Initially they had no hymns in their daily office. They celebrated liturgical feasts, except for Easter, with austerity. This liturgical minimalism was based on the belief that the worship of God "is the fruit of single-minded attentiveness, an unconditional offering of the whole person to him. It follows that everything possible needs to be done in order to prevent the person from being distracted from this primary task."[9] Thus the austere liturgy served the same purpose as the immense and strictly enforced enclosure: to preserve the monk from any sort of distraction.[10]

Some of the original strictness (refusal to receive lay guests of any sort and limited hospitality even for monastic guests; infrequent conventual Masses; strict fast on bread, water, and salt three days a week, etc.) was slowly relaxed,[11] but in the later Middle Ages the order as a whole became famous, indeed notorious in some circles, for its success at retaining much of its original rigor. Part of the explanation for this lies with the system of visitations: The General Chapter named two priors in each province to serve as official visitors who were to visit each charterhouse in the province biennially. These visitors were expected to examine thoroughly the spiritual, liturgical, economic, and administrative health of the community and were empowered to mandate reforms, including the deposition of the prior.[12]

A thorough description of Carthusian life as it developed over several centuries to reach its golden age during the fourteenth and fifteenth centuries is beyond the scope of this brief introduction.[13] Instead, with the aid of Gordon Mursell's survey, we shall look briefly at the spirituality of the emerging order in the early twelfth century, as evident in the writings of Bruno, Guigo I, and others. Already in the twelfth century the Carthusians typified and symbolized to much of the rest of the church the monastic ideal in a remarkably thoroughgoing, earnest way. As the spiritual and intellectual dynamism of the church shifted toward the street-preaching and university-lecturing life of the mendicant friars (Franciscans, Dominicans, Augustinians, Carmelites), the Carthusians became the stalwart "Old Order" contemplative monastic holdovers from an earlier age. At the heart of their contemplative monastic life lay the love of God, nothing more, nothing less, a love of God that fully encapsulates human love. As Gordon Mursell has pointed out,

> the logical conclusion of their theology of love was the asceticism of the Chartreuse; and it was that theology, rather than (say) the imperatives of Gregorian reform or the inadequacies of contemporary monasticism, which ordered and invigorated the Carthusian life . . . . The Carthusian theology of love . . . included an approach to human love as profound and coherent as anything found in [the courtly love lyrics of] Provence or Champagne, or recovered from classical antiquity. Love, for the Carthusians, involved an unequivocal detachment from the world, but only as a means to an end; for they saw that detachment as setting them free to love both man and God as each should be loved. The Carthusian life, in the eyes of its founders, involved not a rejection of human love, but its transfiguration.[14]

In his *On Christian Teaching* (*De doctrina Christiana*) and in many other writings, Augustine taught that only God is to be enjoyed; all other things are to be utilized as vehicles for the love of God. Carthusian spirituality, as indeed all Christian monastic spirituality, understood ascetic detachment (solitude, poverty, chastity) from the good things of this world as a means to free oneself from the excessive, and thereby misdirected, attachment to good things that has plagued all humans since the

INTRODUCTION

Fall. Augustine called this misdirected attachment "concupiscence." Today we might call it an addictive proclivity. For the Carthusians and other contemplative monks, true security, or *securitas*, meaning freedom from cares and anxiety, comes only from perfect love of God; true rest can be found only in God. The best way to relate to the good things God created is not to flee from adversity in order to have enjoyment; rather, it is to confront adversity.[15] Asceticism is precisely the willingness to confront adversity for the sake of love of God. Only then can one regain a proper, measured, ordered relationship to other men and women and to created things. In Mursell's well-chosen phrase, monastic claustration is not a flight from the world so much as a flight for the world.

> The theology of the Carthusian life finds its fulfilment in a longing for the things of heaven that supremely exemplifies its nature as the antithesis of worldly living . . . . The Carthusian monk seeks . . . to be moved by the higher things, and thus to move the lower things: to love nothing more than God, and yet to love one's neighbour perfectly . . . . Only the person whose eyes are fixed on heaven is free to know God and the world as they are, and to love them as he should. In that perspective the hidden solitary reverses the world's wisdom: he lives in the desert, but on the threshold of paradise; and he alone becomes, in the grand scheme of Guigo the Carthusian, "the servant of God, the companion of man, the lord of the world."[16]

Against this background, then, certain central terms employed by Carthusian writers merit consideration. I shall refer repeatedly to the *affective* spiritual tradition and to the *affectus*. Although in a broad sense this refers to what psychiatrists now call the left brain rather than the more speculative, linear, right brain, it had a more specific meaning in spiritual literature. Derived from the past participle of the Latin verb *afficere* (*ad-facere*), it means "to do something to someone," "to exert an influence upon," "to be brought into a state," "to be affected." It is a passively dynamic verb that scarcely permits translation as a noun. The Latin noun form, *affectio*, does not really mean what the English cognate "affection" means; rather, *affectio* means "the relation to or disposition toward a thing produced in a person by some influence; state or condition of body or mind, frame of mind, state of feeling, favorable disposition toward, good-will, love, affection."[17] Various words have been employed by translators: feeling, sentiment, disposition, inclination, movement, devotion. Most of these call for the active voice in their accompanying verbs. "Movedness" rather than "movement," "devotedness" rather than "devotion," or "disposedness" rather than "disposition" would better capture the Latin noun's meaning, but they are all extremely awkward. Even more difficult is the Latin *affectus*, referring to the aspect of the human spirit in which one is affected, disposed, impacted upon toward God. The present translation resorts most often to "affection" where a noun must be employed and to past participle forms (affected by God, moved, disposed) where possible, hoping the reader will not forget the intended actively passive thrust of these words—the affected soul has been moved, swayed, impacted toward God.

Carthusian, contemplative, monastic spirituality is a receptive spirituality. The monk knows he is unable to cope with the addictive power of sin in his life and enters a structured, rule-bound setting in order to gain an extrinsic crutch that will help him convalesce. If sin is an addiction, then men and women will always be recovering rather than recovered sinners. In admitting this weakness, this inability to conquer sin by himself, the monk is set free from the false boundaries with which he formerly tried to construct a self, set free to receive himself back as the re-formed image of God. Genuine *securitas*, freedom from anxiety, is created by the ascetic limits. The boundaries established by the rule and the physically demarcated Carthusian *eremus* did not constrict real freedom; rather, they restricted a false freedom that was really an addiction, a false love of good creation. They restricted this false freedom in order to set the monk free to love God rightly and, derivatively, to live properly with other men and women and to use the good things of creation. By restricting his life to a particular place with his vow of *stabilitas*, by eliminating the need to move from place to place, the monk is free to find God in the place where he is. Instead of a speculating (out-thrusting, searching, exploring) dynamism, the monk enters into leisured quiet, sags back into what seems to the world to be lazy inactivity. Only there can he truly find—by refusing to seek (in the world's sense) and by seeking truly (in meek, restricted, ascetic, receptivity).

Self-mastery and ascetic self-control have nothing to do with ownership of oneself; rather, true knowledge of self involves a recognition of one's inabilities, a recognition that enables one to be united with the Lord.[18] Therefore, love of God is not so much something one has for God as it is a longing lacking of Perfect Presence. As Plato pointed out in the *Symposium*, one cannot love what one already has; love is precisely the yearning and longing one experiences for what one does not yet have. Yearning (*desiderium*) is utterly central to Augustine's theology: "Man can say nothing of what he is incapable of feeling, but he can feel what he is incapable of putting into words."[19] As Mursell points out, words like "to desire," "to gasp" (*appetere, inhiare*), recur again and again in Carthusian writings. Ultimately this is an eschatological yearning for heaven, which is merely another way of saying that it is a yearning for God himself. The same yearning, when misdirected toward God's good creation, becomes concupiscence. Thus longing, desire, yearning are fundamental to all aspects of Carthusian and monastic spirituality. In the present translation, the Latin word *desiderium* has usually been translated as "yearning" or "longing" rather than "desire," since "desire" often carries pejorative connotations (selfish, illicit desire) in English.

Not everything in Carthusian spirituality consists of affective, yearning receptivity. The active struggle against sin involves rational and intellectual discernment as well. Monastic Latin employed the words *intellectus* (and *intelligentia*) as well as *scientia* or *ratio* to express various shades of what we refer to generically as intellect, reason, and understanding. In the present translations, *intellectus* and *intelligentia* will normally be rendered as "understanding" rather than intellection or intelligence, since *intelligentia* in Latin spiritual writing often carried more of a sapiential element than did *ratio* (which will normally be rendered as "reason"). *Mens* could be translated as "mind," were it not for the cognitive-rational connotations that are normally attached to it in modern English. As a result, when it refers to the human person, *mens* is normally translated as "spirit" or "human spirit," occasionally as "heart." When it refers to an aspect of the human person, which occurs primarily in the discussions of mystical ascent found in the last section of the unitive way and in the *quaestio difficilis* of Hugh of Balma's *Roads to Zion*, it is translated as "mind." *Sapientia* will normally be translated as "wisdom." *Scientia* has generally been rendered as "knowledge," occasionally as "science"; *cognitio* as "cognition"; and *cogitatio* as "cogitation," "pondering," or "reflection." (Apart from the above terms, which have special bearing on monastic and Carthusian spirituality, the translation of other Latin terms is discussed at the end of this introduction.)

II. BIOGRAPHY AND AUTHORSHIP

A. *The Roads to Zion*

1. *Who Wrote* The Roads to Zion?

Despite important archival research in the surviving records of the Charterhouse of Meyriat, we still know very little about Hugh of Balma's life.[20] The seventeenth-century Carthusian historian Charles Le Couteulx identified the author of *The Roads to Zion* as a knight of the de Balmey or de Balmeto family who entered the Charterhouse of Meyriat in 1160 after the death of his wife.[21] (The charterhouse at Meyriat, in the Department of Ain, south of Nantua, between Geneva and Lyon, was destroyed in the French Revolution.[22]) Early twentieth-century research seemed to confirm this family connection,[23] that is, that a Hugh of Dorche (de Dorchiis) of the same family was indeed prior at Meyriat, 1293–1295 and 1303–1305.[24] But was this Hugh also the author of *The Roads to Zion*?

Research conducted by Harald Walach for his dissertation on the concept of experience in *Viae Sion lugent* challenges a number of the conventional assumptions about Hugh of Balma/Palma, including his presumed links to the noble family de Balmey/Dorche.[25]

Walach challenges the conventional identification of the author of *The Roads to Zion* with the prior of Meyriat because all of the scanty records related to this prior refer to him as "Hugo de Dorchiis" rather than as "Hugo de Balma."[26] He thinks it unlikely that the prior of an out-of-the-way charterhouse like Meyriat would have had the knowledge of scholastic philosophy and theology that Walach detects in *The Roads to Zion*. Walach conjectures that the author of *The Roads to Zion* studied at Paris in the 1250s (Walach finds evidence of some of the scholarly controversies of the day in *The Roads to Zion*), was originally a Spiritual Franciscan, and was probably associated with the newly founded Charterhouse of Paris (1257), located in the former palace of Vauvert (located where the Jardin du Luxembourg is found today) and one of the first urban charterhouses. A Hugo de Moriaston left the Paris charterhouse in 1311 for the Charterhouse of Padula near Salerno in southern Italy, where he died in 1313.[27] Walach dates the genesis of the core of the work (the scholastic *quaestio* at the end) to 1260–1270.

INTRODUCTION

While it is not entirely unreasonable to question the conventional identification of "Hugh of Balma/Palma" with Hugo de Dorchiis, none of Walach's arguments on this point are conclusive and some are highly doubtful. For the sake of convenience, the present translation and introduction, like Walach's monograph and translation, will continue to refer to this person as "Hugh of Balma."

However, even if the author of *Viae Sion lugent* was not the prior of Meyriat known as Hugo de Dorchiis, one need not assume an urban, university-trained author. Even out-of-the-way Carthusian houses could be well equipped with basic liberal arts and theology texts. Virtually all of Walach's claims for *Viae Sion*'s dependence on ideas from Aristotle, Peter Lombard, Thomas Aquinas, Bonaventure, Adam Marsh, Albert the Great, and Hugh of St. Cher and its influence on Peter John Olivi, Ramon Llull, Margarete Porete, and the anonymous *Stimulus Amoris* involve theological, philosophical, and spiritual commonplaces.[28] Many of them could be just as readily attributed to nonscholastic, patristic, and prescholastic sources, especially Augustine (of whom Walach has taken no account).[29] Walach's claims need to be studied against the background of patristic, monastic, and Carthusian spirituality and theology.[30] Hugh's doctrine of aspirative prayer and the idea of illustrating it by means of an exposition of the Our Father may well have come from John Cassian, a ubiquitous source in medieval monasteries of all types.[31] If one approaches the work solely from the university setting of the late thirteenth century, one might well glimpse what seem to be echoes of a university setting; however, if one approaches the work from the monastic and Carthusian context, the same psychological and theological assumptions are explicable from that monastic and Carthusian context.

Despite the critique of Walach found in the present pages, we owe him great gratitude for his unstinting detective work in thirteenth-century archival and literary sources. Among other contributions, he has located the source of a puzzling misattribution of a quotation to Augustine in the "Difficult Question" (par. 4), locating it in Pseudo-Thomas Aquinas (Helwicus Teutonicus).[32] His sleuthing has also located in a work by Bonaventure a puzzling quotation attributed by Hugh of Balma to Thomas Gallus.[33] Read critically, Walach's study can become an important starting point for future research into Hugh of Balma.

Walach hypothesizes that the original germ of the work was its concluding "*quaestio difficilis* (Difficult Question)," that is, that he believes the work originated as a scholastic disputation.[34] The other parts were originally separate treatises compiled by their own author late in the thirteenth century into the work we now know as *The Roads to Zion*, in an effort to amplify and undergird the conclusions in the polemical *quaestio*. Walach may be correct about *Viae Sion lugent*'s having originated as one or more distinct treatises, although even here I am inclined to see fewer parts than Walach does. But even if, for example, the commentary on Pseudo-Denis's *Mystical Theology* in *Viae Sion*'s *via unitiva*, par. 82–115, was written separately from the rest of the work, this does not mean the *quaestio* was the original core of the work. If one has already assumed that the author came from a university background, one might be inclined to see the *quaestio* as central. However, none of the instances of direct response to academic debates of the second half of the thirteenth century in Paris that Walach adduces in *Viae Sion* is convincing. Above all, Walach expects more consistency and step-by-step development in a manual on mystical theology than medieval monastic writers expected. This makes him overeager to see inconsistency and development as signs of redaction or interpolation.

Moreover, reading the work from beginning to end, with knowledge of the Carthusian and monastic tradition on the life of penitence and the tradition of *lectio divina*, one sees the first three sections each building on the other: Monastic life is essentially a life of repentance growing out of consciousness of sinfulness and of steady prayer. As set forth by Guigo II in his *Ladder of Monks*,[35] meditation on Scripture (the long exposition of the Our Father) in the illuminative way seamlessly overflows into aspirative, direct conversation with God (the short exposition of the Our Father). The unitive way simply takes that prayer to another level. The interweaving of Scripture and the meditative exposition found in the two expositions of the Lord's Prayer is thoroughly monastic, not scholastic.[36]

In short, I have little difficulty accepting at face value the author's explanation that he wrote the *quaestio* last, in response to challenges made against the teaching on aspirative prayer in the first three parts.[37] The commentary on Pseudo-Denis in *via unitiva*, par. 82–115, may well have been added later, after the "Difficult Question" was added to the presentation of the purgative way, illuminative way, and unitive way, par. 1–81. The reference to the expositions of the Lord's Prayer in the *quaestio* implies that the *quaestio* was added toward the end rather than at the beginning of the compilation process. Moreover, even Walach agrees that the compilation and redacting were probably done by the same person who wrote the original distinct components and that the

11

redacting took place soon after the individual parts were written. Thus all students of this work agree that it may be dealt with as the work of a single author.

Walach's work, combined with Francis Ruello's forthcoming critical edition, will shed much new light on this long-obscure yet influential work. In that light, a general introduction to Hugh of Balma sketched against his own Carthusian and monastic background is a necessary and complementary element in any full appreciation of the work. Such is the purpose of the pages that follow.

2. *The Curious Career of* The Roads to Zion

For the sake of clarity, the present translation employs as its title the opening words of Hugh of Balma's treatise: *The Roads to Zion.* Through the centuries it has been known as *De triplici via* (On the Threefold Way) and *De mystica theologia* (On Mystical Theology). These titles are common among late medieval devotional writings and have caused much of the confusion surrounding the identity of *The Roads to Zion*'s author.

More than one hundred full or partial manuscript copies of *The Roads to Zion* survive. Of the seventy manuscripts known to the editors of Bonaventure's complete writings in 1898, most did not name the author, a customary practice among Carthusians. Three manuscripts ascribed it to Bonaventure, while two assigned it to a John of Balma (variously identified as a Dominican or as a "prominent professor"). Fifteen copies identified the author as "a Carthusian," with some specifying further "Henricus" or "Hugo de Balma."[38] Over the centuries, writers have credited the work to the fourteenth-century Carthusian Heinrich Egher of Kalkar and to the Paris theologian Jean Gerson (d. 1429). Neither of the two last-mentioned writers can have written the work, since Guigo de Ponte quoted from *The Roads to Zion* at the end of the thirteenth century, long before either Heinrich Egher of Kalkar or Gerson was born.

The attribution to Bonaventure, based in part on the fact that he did indeed write a work titled *De triplici via* (On the Threefold Way), has been the most pernicious and pervasive of all of the misattributions. The editor of the 1495 Strasbourg edition of Bonaventure's collected works not only included Hugh's work under Bonaventure's name but also modified passages that referred to the Carthusian order, making them appear to refer to the Franciscans. Although Francis Lamata, editor of the 1588

Vatican edition of Bonaventure's writings, exposed this tampering with the text, the interpolations continued to be included in a number of later Bonaventure editions, including that by A. C. Peltier (Paris, 1866). The first major Bonaventure edition not to include *The Roads to Zion* at all was the Quaracchi critical edition (1898, 1902). Since the Quaracchi editors' careful survey of the manuscript evidence, little doubt remains regarding the Carthusian origins of the work.

The Roads to Zion was probably written before 1297, since the *On Contemplation* attributed to Guigo de Ponte (d. 1297) refers to it. As we shall see, the authority for connecting Guigo to the work *On Contemplation* rests on the fifteenth-century Carthusian author Denis of Rijkel. *The Roads to Zion* makes repeated references to writings by Thomas Gallus (d. 1246), the Victorine commentator on Pseudo-Denis. The evidence evaluated by Pierre Dubourg led him to place the origins of *The Roads to Zion* between 1230 and 1290.[39]

Apart from the numerous manuscript copies, Hugh of Balma's treatise on mystical theology has been printed many times.[40]

1. Latin editions: Under the title *De mystica theologia*, it was included in editions of Bonaventure's collected works as follows: Strasbourg, 1495; Venice, 1504, 1564, 1751; Rome, 1588; Mainz, 1609; Lyon, 1668; Paris, 1866. Under the title *De triplici via* it appeared in the 1534 Cologne edition of the works of Denis of Rijkel (Denis the Carthusian; Dionysius Cartusianus), under the title "De triplici via ad sapientiam et divinorum contemplationem" (reprinted in Munich, 1603). Edited by Abraham de Franckenberg (de Monte, d. 1652), it appeared as "Theologia mystica sive trivium sacrum," attributed to Hugh de Palma (Amsterdam, 1647). The portion dealing with the exercises of the purgative way was included in Gerhard Kalckbrenner's *Hortulus devotionis* (Cologne, 1541, 1577, 1579). A critical edition by Francis Ruello will appear in the Sources Chrétiennes series (Paris).

2. Translations include the medieval Italian version (before 1367), which was published by Barthélemy Sorio in *Opere ascetiche di San Bonaventura volgarizzate nel trecento* (Verona, 1852).

Spanish translations and summaries are numerous,[41] beginning with one at Toledo in 1514 under the title *Sol des Contemplativos*. This edition was attributed to "Hugh of Balma" (but the title page noted that some people thought it was written by Saint Bonaventure).[42] It appeared in a looser paraphrase intertwined with the work of Hendrik Herp, titled *Cruz de Cristo y Viae Sion lugent y preparatio mortis* (Seville, 1543).[43] Other editions appeared at Medina del Campo in 1553 and at Alcala in

1558 (first published in 1548?). The original Toledo edition reappeared in Mexico City in 1575 (1571?[44]). A very free translation-commentary by the Discalced Carmelite Jerónimo Gracian was published in 1607, with various editions at Brussels and Madrid (1607, 1609, 1617, 1635, possibly a 1601 edition at Madrid),[45] and in editions of Gracian's complete works, including one in 1932. However, Gracian's commentary was based not on the Latin text, but on the rather free-wheeling Spanish paraphrase of 1543, which lacked the "Difficult Question."[46] Jesuit missionaries took it with them to Japan in 1554.[47]

The Roads to Zion was partially translated into German already in the fifteenth century, probably for lay brethren or lay people associated with Benedictine and Franciscan monasteries in Bavaria and Salzburg.[48] According to Gottfried Arnold, the Lutheran pietist student of medieval mysticism, another German translation appeared at Amsterdam in 1696.[49] Harald Walach has now published a full translation into modern German.

A fifteenth-century translation into late medieval Dutch of most of the "purgative way" section has survived in a Berlin manuscript, and citations of Hugh's *Roads to Zion* in six late medieval Dutch spiritual writings have led one scholar to speculate on the existence of a complete translation into medieval Dutch that has not survived.[50]

Although a fifteenth-century French translation was never printed, a new French translation will accompany the Sources Chrétiennes edition. An English translation of an extract from the chapter on the unitive way was published by James Walsh.[51] Rosemary Lees reports that an English translation of parts of *The Roads to Zion* by Robert Bacon, dated 1676, is listed in the manuscript catalogue of the Offenbach library.[52] Jasper Hopkins translated the prologue and the "Difficult Question" in 1985.[53]

B. Guigo de Ponte

Even less is known about Guigo[54] than conventionally has been asserted about Hugh of Balma. Even the sort of scanty archival evidence we have for prior Hugh of Meyriat is absent in the case of Guigo. Charles Le Couteulx tells us that he died in 1297, was said to have made his monastic profession at the Grande Chartreuse in 1271, together with Boso, the future prior of the Grande Chartreuse (1277–1313), and was a learned and devout monk who wrote a treatise called *De vita contemplativa*, which some people have attributed to Guigo the fifth prior of the Grande Chartreuse (= Guigo I, d. 1136). Le Couteulx confirmed that the name, as given in the archives of the Grande Chartreuse, was indeed Guigo, not Guido, and he cited the records of the Carthusian General Chapter for his death date, October 29, 1297. Le Couteulx further pointed out that Denis of Rijkel cited Guigo under the name Guigo de Ponte of the Grande Chartreuse in the second book of his [Denis's] *De contemplatione*.[55] Yves Gourdel says Guigo was also prior of the Charterhouse of Mont Dieu, but James Hogg has found no confirmation of this.[56]

As Le Couteulx noted, *On Contemplation* has often been attributed to Guigo I, the twelfth-century prior of the Grande Chartreuse.[57] It cannot have been written by him, since it refers to several writings of thirteenth-century scholastic theology, as well as to Hugh of Balma's *The Roads to Zion*. Part of it was taken up nearly verbatim by the fourteenth-century Carthusian Ludolph of Saxony (d. 1377), permitting us to date its composition approximately. The ascription to Guigo de Ponte and thus the more precise dating to no later than 1297 rests on the authority of Denis of Rijkel.

Guigo's *On Contemplation* was not nearly so widely transmitted and translated as Hugh of Balma's *The Roads to Zion*. Although a number of late medieval Carthusians knew it and used it (Ludolph of Saxony, Denis of Rijkel [d. 1471], possibly Nicholas Kempf [d. 1497]), it survived in only five manuscripts until an Italian translation was published in 1979[58] and a critical edition of the Latin text by Dom Philippe Dupont appeared in 1985. The excerpts incorporated by Ludolf of Saxony in his *Vita Christi*, however, did have a wide circulation, including a Spanish version read by Ignatius of Loyola.

III. HUGH OF BALMA'S TEACHING ON THE SPIRITUAL LIFE

Even a cursory inspection of *The Roads to Zion* reveals that almost half the work deals with the unitive way.[59] In contrast, Guigo de Ponte intermingles unitive and purgative aspects throughout his *On Contemplation*.

A. Outline

Based in part on Hugh's own outline in his prologue (par. 8), we offer the following outline:

15

INTRODUCTION

Prologue
  A. True and false wisdom; mystical theology and human learning (par. 1–4)
  B. The three-fold path (par. 5–7)
  C. Outline of the present work (par. 8–9); praxis precedes theory (par. 9)

I. Via purgativa
  A. How the soul is cleansed by contrary medicine (par. 1–2)
    1. recall sins (par. 3)
    2. recall God's favors (par. 4)
      a. generally (par. 4–5)
      b. specifically—the Carthusian religious life (par. 5–7)
    3. total submission to God (par. 8)
  B. Preparing to ask forgiveness: begin by praising God (par. 9–10)
  C. Asking for full forgiveness of sins (par. 11–15)
    1. God's mercy on all (par. 11–15)
    2. calling on intermediaries at God's court, especially the Blessed Virgin Mary in the Rosary (par. 14)

II. Via illuminativa
  A. Introduction (par. 1–8)
    1. fogged and spotless mirrors (par. 1–2)
    2. the three material and spiritual rays (par. 3–8)
      a. in Scripture (= the via illuminativa)
      b. spirit to spirit (= the via unitiva)
      c. ecstasy, rapture, face-to-face vision, aspirative method; affective ascent (= quaestio difficilis)
  B. The first ray
    1. introduction: the anagogical method explained (par. 9–12)
    2. illustration: discursive meditation on the Lord's Prayer—the long anagogical exposition (par. 13–44)
      a. *Captatio benevolentiae* (13–18)
      b. first petition (par. 19–20)
      c. second petition (par. 21)
      d. third petition (par. 22–24)
      e. fourth petition (par. 25–28)
      f. fifth petition (par. 29–34)
      g. sixth petition (par. 35–40)

B. The Theology and Spirituality of *The Roads to Zion*

Hugh of Balma has generally been identified with the assertion that one can rise to God by love alone, without any cognition accompanying or leading the way. He has conventionally been approached from the appendix to his *Roads to Zion*, where he offers a defense of this assertion in the formal structure of a scholastic *quaestio*, and this assertion has earned him a place in most surveys of Christian spirituality. I believe this is a misleading rubric to place over Hugh's head, but the conventional image of Hugh is so pervasive that we will in fact make the question of the relative roles of cognition and love our entry into his theology and spirituality. However, before examining what Hugh actually has to say on this topic and how it fits in a much broader context in his work, we must first examine the circumstances a century and a half after his death that led to the conventional assessment of Hugh of Balma's significance.

Hugh has always been read through the eyes of those who used and abused him in later controversies. The first such instance, the "Tegernsee mystics" controversy of the 1450s, has dominated the horizon for twentieth-century scholars. Later, because the relative roles of grace and free will were the burning issues in Reformation Protestantism and Catholicism, Hugh's emphasis on affectivity and passivity also led to the indirect use and abuse of his work in early modern Catholicism in Spain and France: in the Molinist and Quietist controversies. For the sake of brevity, we shall look at solely the Tegernsee debate here.[60]

1. Love and Knowledge: Is an Entirely Affective Ascent Possible?

A. THE TEGERNSEE DEBATE

Sometime before September 22, 1452, the abbot of the Benedictine monastery of Tegernsee wrote to Cardinal Nicholas of Cusa ([Nicholas Cusanus], d. 1464), Bishop of Brixen (Bressanone) in South Tirol, to ask if it was possible for the devout soul to ascend to mystical union with God without any preceding or accompanying cognitive activity of the intellect, that is, by love alone.[61] Nicholas had written a book titled *On Learned Ignorance* in 1440, a book that aroused great enthusiasm among the Tegernsee monks. Their prior, Bernard of Waging (d. 1472), was particularly excited about it.[62] Nicholas replied in haste on September 22. He pointed out that one cannot love the good unless one knows it, but also repeated his earlier insistence in *On Learned Ignorance* and other writings that the wisdom of God is hidden from the learned of this world and revealed to the simple. Yet he also cautioned that the simple and unlearned are vulnerable to deception by false visions and imaginings. In other words, both cognition and devout affections are required.

We do not know how the Tegernsee monks came across Hugh of Balma's treatise and its question. Werner Höver points to Johannes Keck of Giengen.[63] Keck, who had studied at Vienna and served the bishop of Freising (near Munich) in various capacities, including acting as the bishop's representative at the Council of Basel, gives much attention to Hugh of Balma in his commentary on the Rule of St. Benedict (1448).[64] Where Keck acquired his interest in Hugh is uncertain. Jean Gerson (d. 1429)[65] and Nicholas of Cusa valued Hugh as a commentator on Pseudo-Denis, and this may have brought Hugh to Keck's attention, since Keck seems to have been responsible for bringing copies of Pseudo-Denis's writings to Melk and Tegernsee circles from Basel.[66] On the other hand, Hugh's *The Roads to Zion* was copied at the Carthusian monastery of Aggsbach by its prior, Johannes Span (prior 1422–1435) as early as 1424,[67] and it is conceivable that the Melk Benedictines learned to know it through their Carthusian neighbors at Aggsbach, a half-day's journey by foot from Melk.

Sometime during the first two weeks of June 1453, Vincent of Aggsbach, who had served as prior but was no longer head of the monastery, wrote a treatise attacking Jean Gerson's views of mystical theology.[68] In his cover letter to Johannes Schlitpacher, prior of the Benedictine Abbey of Melk, Vincent said he had erred to have once put Gerson on the same level as the other commentators on Pseudo-Denis (Thomas Gallus, Robert Grosseteste, Hugh of Balma, or even Hugh of St. Victor).[69]

This discussion had been incubating for some time and was rooted in Vincent's own dislike of Nicholas of Cusa. Nicholas had once been a leader at the Council of Basel (1431–1449), but had switched sides to support Pope Eugenius IV against the council. Nearly all German Carthusians and all academics at the University of Vienna, many of whom were now leaders at Benedictine and Carthusian monasteries in Bavaria and Austria, were enthusiastic conciliarists. Most eventually made their peace with the failure of the council and the political deals between the pope and the dukes and princes of Europe.[70] Vincent, however, never abandoned the conciliarist cause and he never forgave Nicholas of Cusa for his "betrayal" of the council. When Pope Nicholas V placed Nicholas of Cusa in charge of monastic reform in Germany and sent him off on a highly publicized tour of German monasteries in 1451–1452, Vincent was outraged. Against this background, he bitterly attacked Cusanus,[71] and, since one of the authorities Nicholas employed in his defense of a limited role for cognition in mystical union was Jean Gerson (d. 1429), Gerson also became the target of Vincent's animosity. Gerson's writings were extremely popular in monastic and lay circles in Bavaria and Austria.

In Vincent's eyes, the error of "Gerchumar" (Gerson, Cusanus, and Marquard Sprenger, a Munich priest and friend of the Tegernsee monks who also wrote a treatise on the controversial question) was to conflate contemplation (which employs the Holy Spirit's gift of wisdom given to all believers at baptism-confirmation) with the mystical theology of Pseudo-Denis. Contemplation is part cognitive and part affective, but mystical theology is not. Mystical theology's central characteristic is the ascent in complete ignorance. Vincent's proof comes from his Carthusian confrère, Hugh of Balma. Although everyone has heard of Jean Gerson, Vincent says, few have heard of Hugh of Balma ("especially few of you Benedictines," one can almost hear him saying under his breath), yet, in Vincent's eyes, it is Hugh who really understood Pseudo-Denis, and Pseudo-Denis is *the* authority on mystical theology, acknowledged by all the parties—Gerson, Nicholas of Cusa, the Benedictines, and Carthusians alike. In Vincent's view, Gerson had said contradictory things about mystical theology in his effort to reconcile scholastic and mystical theology. For Vincent, scholastic theology is the reading, study, and understanding of Scripture in the Old and New Testaments, while mystical theology is a certain kind of submission, a remarkable sort of spiritual extension toward God. Gerson's teaching is like cheap beer; Hugh of Balma's is like expensive *Malvasierwein* (Malmsey, Madeira).

Moreover, Gerson was trying to use mystical theology as a catchall solution for the church's ills. He had tried to convince all theology masters and students at Paris that it is the true way to pursue theology. In his university lectures *On the Spiritual Life of the Soul* (*De vita spirituali animae*) he had challenged them:

> Do you wish to know that which is hidden? Then move from intellectual theology to affectual theology, from knowledge to wisdom, from cognition to devotion. This is that theology of which the great Arsenius, a man learned in Greek and Latin, confessed himself ignorant; indeed he admitted that he had not learned so much as its ABCs. Would that this theology were as familiar to all of us who call ourselves theologians as, at this moment, it is strange and unknown to us.[72]

Had he been present, Vincent says, he would have told Gerson: "You're crazy. Writing so much has made you lose your mind."[73] Closer to home, Johannes Schlitpacher had employed Hugh of Balma to call on preachers and professors at Vienna to convert to a study of mystical theology. In another letter to the Melk Benedictine, Vincent expressed his astonishment that Schlitpacher addressed his call to academics rather than to monastics. The study of mystical theology, he insisted, requires first an "undergraduate" degree (the *via purgativa*); it cannot be pursued by leaps and bounds (*per saltum*, probably an allusion to the "leapfrog" honorary degrees granted by some medieval universities). Vincent apparently felt that some of the participants in the controversy were, like Gerson at Paris, attempting to use a watered-down, popular "mystical theology" as an easy intellectual cure-all for problems of the spiritual life without reckoning sufficiently with its arduous practical prerequisites.[74]

A passage from Hugh of Balma's concluding "Difficult Question" may well summarize the issue that stuck in Vincent's craw:

The Psalmist says, *Taste and see.* "Taste" refers to the *affectus* of love; "see" refers to the intellect's cogitation and meditation. Therefore one ought first to surge up in the movement of love before intellectually pondering in order to know the hidden God. For this is the general rule in mystical theology: one ought have practice before theory, that is, one ought be well practiced in the heart before one has knowledge of the things said about it. ("Difficult Question," par. 16)

Vincent was on the losing side in the debate. The Tegernsee Benedictines led by Bernard of Waging, their friend Nicholas of Cusa, and Marquard Sprenger had a simple response: To love anything one must have recognized it as good, which involves the intellect.[75] To be sure, Vincent was not exactly a likable character. He had been removed as prior at Aggsbach as a result of his caustic conciliarist and antipapal tongue. The new prior at Aggsbach, Thomas Papler of Zistersdorf (prior, 1448–1458), had made his novitiate and profession at Gaming and readily turned to his former prior for advice on how to handle his new pastoral charge. In a letter to Schlitpacher, Thomas Papler says that Vincent had sent many inquiries to Schlitpacher, requiring much time and effort from Schlitpacher in response. Thomas, who thought Vincent's preoccupation was "not very useful" and "bears only modest fruit or no fruit at all," asked Schlitpacher whether it would be wise to permit Vincent to pursue these matters. Then he commented that "an outstanding and religious prelate in our land" had admonished him that Vincent's preoccupations run the risk of succumbing to the sin of pride, urging that Thomas communicate this to Vincent as his pastoral duty.[76] The "outstanding and religious prelate" most certainly was Nicholas Kempf of Gaming (d. 1497).

However, despite his failings, Vincent read Hugh more carefully than his main opponents, Marquard Sprenger, Nicholas of Cusa, and

Bernard of Waging,[77] and he read Hugh in a manner very similar to the reading given below.[78]

Reduced to its essentials, the Tegernsee debate had to do with how broadly or narrowly one applies the label *mystical theology*, which for them was inextricably tied to Pseudo-Denis. Vincent did indeed insist that mystical theology is totally affective, that it takes place "without cogitation leading the way or accompanying." However, for Vincent, mystical theology applied solely to the aspirative upsurge described in greater detail below. Hugh of Balma himself clearly specified the aspirative upsurge as the locus of total affectivity in the very title of his "Difficult Question."[79] Despite this, Vincent's opponents insisted on a broad definition of mystical theology, merging it with "contemplation" and "learned ignorance": all movements toward union with God together make up mystical theology. When they heard Hugh of Balma and Vincent talking about mystical theology's being totally affective, it seemed incongruous with the various stages of ascent to God as they knew them and knew about them.

Vincent clearly told his opponents what he was doing. That cognition was involved in the broader picture, he never denied. He himself said that the debate was over the timing of the cognitive role: In contemplation (= meditation, the Holy Spirit gift of wisdom, Cusanus's "learned ignorance") cognition leads the way and yields to an increasingly affective, supra-intellectual thrust. In Pseudo-Denis's book on mystical theology, however, the affective upsurge is prior and yields cognition.[80] Moreover, he says, his opponents focus too much on a single passage of Pseudo-Denis (*On the Divine Names*, ch. 7) as interpreted by Hugh of Balma and on Hugh's *quaestio difficilis*, yet they fail to grasp the import of the rest of *The Roads to Zion*. Vincent is even willing to grant his opponents part of their point (namely that when Hugh cites Pseudo-Denis on an "irrational wisdom" he has thereby admitted some role for cognition since one cannot leave behind what was never there).[81] But, having granted that, Vincent sees this as admitting that his opponents have merely gained control of the outskirts. The city of mystical theology remains untouched.[82] Vincent realized, as Hugh of Balma did (*via unitiva*, par. 83), that he was giving an affective reading where Pseudo-Denis talked only about cognition and absence of cognition, not about love. He thought his reading was consistent with the mystical tradition strictly speaking and could see no reason why Pseudo-Denis could not effortlessly be assimilated to the Latin, affective contemplative tradition.[83] His opponents, like modern scholars, were in effect protesting Hugh's (and Vincent's and Thomas Gallus's) reading of Pseudo-Denis. In the process, everyone misses Hugh's and Vincent's point: Pseudo-Denis's mystical theology applies only to the brief aspirative upsurge. Denis did say "without intellect." Yes, that does mean that there has to have been some intellect, if it is now to be abandoned, but no, that abandoning does not extend to the entire quest for God.

In other words, Vincent insisted on "total affectivity" but only for a specific point (the crucial point, to be sure) in the soul's relationship with God. His "tactical error" may have been to employ the term "mystical theology" (which, as Vincent knew well, was a new term in the Latin West[84]), since others had already assimilated it to the older standard term in Latin, *contemplatio.* Vincent thus offers a fascinating glimpse into a subject much debated by scholars of late medieval spirituality: the impact of Pseudo-Denis in the Latin West and the shift from *contemplatio* to *mystica theologia.* Vincent is well aware that Pseudo-Denis's own term, "mystica theologia," was not in common use in the West throughout the Middle Ages, and he believes that this new term (the gift of the Latin commentators on Pseudo-Denis, especially Grosseteste and Thomas Gallus) should be employed as a technical term alongside rather than replacing the older umbrella term, "contemplation."[85]

The assumption that Hugh of Balma taught an anti-intellectual, totally affective ascent to God from start to finish thus stems from Vincent's opponents, Marquard Sprenger, Nicholas of Cusa, and Bernard of Waging.[86] They were the ones who were "intransigent" and "absolute" (terms that Vansteenberghe applies to Vincent[87]); Vincent is the one who is making subtle distinctions regarding the Latin contemplative tradition, even though he did not know when Robert Grosseteste or Thomas Gallus lived.[88] This is indicated by Vansteenberghe's concluding assessment of Vincent, which in turn echoes the condescending dismissal of Vincent by Sprenger found in the fifteenth-century correspondence itself, a condescension that Vincent himself felt keenly.[89] For Vansteenberghe, Vincent is the outsider, the one with the idiosyncratic interpretation of Pseudo-Denis,[90] the strange, exotic Carthusian, the uneducated country bumpkin—in comparison with the cultivated Cusanus and the humanist-inclined Tegernsee monks and their highly placed priest-friend, Sprenger. It is true that Vincent was not university trained. Even Johannes Schlitpacher, generally quite favorable to Vincent, while praising Vincent's thorough knowledge of the Scriptures, lamented that Vincent knew little logic and philosophy, which made a debate with the Carthusian most difficult.[91] Yet Marquard's and Bernard's misapprehension of what Hugh of Balma was all about has become the dominant interpretation for modern scholars.[92] The simple substitution of *mystical theology* or *mysticism* for the entire contemplative quest has so embedded itself in modern scholarship that Endre von Ivánka[93] and others can argue that Hugh of Balma isolated the affective, unitive way from the other portions of the *mystical* ascent.[94]

Perhaps it is time to look more closely at what Hugh actually said about the roles of love and knowledge in the mystical ascent and what he meant by what he said.

B. HUGH OF BALMA AND COGITATION AND LOVE

First, we need to be clear about what Hugh meant by *cogitatio* and *cognitio*, since these are key terms in his "Difficult Question." Jasper Hopkins suggests that Hugh meant by cogitation something more than mere thinking,[95] for thinking can be a passing thought or deep meditation. Even in modern English, cogitation implies the latter rather than the former. For Hugh, cogitation is an intensive, deliberate form of thought that leads to cognition and understanding. But "knowledge" for Hugh could involve both affective and cognitive elements. He continued to use the term "knowledge" even when referring to the unitive stage, insisting that the intellect cannot penetrate *to the highest knowledge (cognitio)*. Toward the end of his discussion of the illuminative way he refers to mystical *cognition* as the goal of the ascent. Even in the unitive stage, he quotes Pseudo-Denis's definition of unitive wisdom as "the most divine knowledge of God known through unknowing."[96] In paragraphs 36–37 and 41 of the "Difficult Question," and throughout the "To the Contrary" and "Solution" portions of that *quaestio*, he repeatedly refers to a supreme knowledge that comes after the affective upsurge, that is, a knowledge that is redeposited in the human spirit after the affective aspiration. According to Hugh, Pseudo-Denis considered this unitive wisdom to be the cause of "all human spirit and reason, and every sort of wisdom and prudence. Every decision, every knowledge and prudence, comes from it; in it are hidden all the treasures of wisdom and knowledge."[97] For Hugh, "the words *wisdom* and *cognition* denote the perfection of both powers of the soul, the *affectus* and the intellect." It may be irrational, foolish, and mindless, but it is still knowledge (*Roads to Zion, via unitiva*, par. 85). Even at the highest stage the *affectus* knows, yet it does so without any admixture of the intellect.[98] Rapture itself is a form of knowledge (*via unitiva*, par. 110–11).[99]

As to the upsurge itself, we have to keep in mind that there are in Hugh's treatise four stages. Two are intellective and two are affective ("acquired" and "infused" are my choice of terminology, imported from later mystical theologians as helpful shorthand for more clumsy circumlocutions that might be employed here):

A. Intellective (see *Quaestio Difficilis*, par. 25–26, 37–39):

1. Meditation—movement from lower to higher—allegorical or metaphorical meditation symbolizing spiritual progress (= acquired contemplation; illustrated by Hugh's long exposition of the Our Father)

2. Radiant Contemplation—movement from higher to lower—seeing things when they are bathed in light from on high (= infused contemplation of angels, celestial things, God, Trinity)

B. Affective (*Quaestio Difficilis*, par. 27–31, 34–36):

3. Scholastic, common affectivity—acquired love, aesthetic attraction employing creatures to rise to love of God (illustrated by the short exposition of the Our Father)

4. Mystical and hidden affectivity—pure love, coming from on high to sweep the aspirant up to God (the upsurge described in the unitive way section)

One could just as well arrange these differently:

A. Scholastic, acquired methods, from bottom to top:

1. Intellectual acquired meditation (long anagogic exposition of the Our Father)
3. Scholastic affectivity (short anagogy on the Our Father)

B. Mystical, infused methods, from top to bottom:

2. Irradiated, infused contemplation (contemplation of angels, celestial things, God, Trinity)

4. Mystical wisdom in aspirative upsurge (affective upsurge described in the unitive way section)

Cogitation and intellection are involved in the first three and knowledge and understanding, lofty forms of insight, result from the fourth, but the fourth proceeds by love alone, in aspirative thrusts. Even the scholastic modes involve affectivity. The *quaestio difficilis* itself interweaves rather than isolates affectivity in every stage but the fourth one.

> The ardor of love far excels these, is much more lovely, and easier to obtain. But there are also two means of attaining this ardor of love. One is the scholastic and common way, the other is mystical and hidden. The first proceeds by means of searching and elevation, beginning with lower things and ascending to the highest by long practice. For example, this is the method followed in loving God with meditation leading the way. (*Roads to Zion*, Quaestio Difficilis, par. 27–28)[100]

This does not seem like "isolating" love from knowledge; rather, it simply inverts the conventional order: Viewed from the top down, love and praxis precede knowledge and theory, but one still leads to the other. Given this ambiguity, can one insist that Hugh "isolated" the affective portion of the ascent from the other intellective-affective components?

Moreover, even the fourth "stage" applies both to the illuminative and unitive paths: In paragraph 33 of the "Difficult Question" Hugh explains that the totally affective ascent applies to both the proficient and the perfected. For the proficient, purgation followed by cogitation[101] leads to God descending from on high to meet the person who is meditating, and the aspirative anagogy of the short exposition of the Our Father follows. The same descent from on high to lift the meditator into affective aspiration takes place in the unitive way, for the perfected. It is explicitly described in paragraph 34 of the "Difficult Question."[102] The short exposition of the Our Father is thus for proficients, following on the long exposition's cogitation of Scripture and created things, whereas the affective upsurge of the chapter on the unitive way, following on cogitation on angels, celestial things, and God, is the unitive way's equivalent to the short exposition of the Our Father.

Just when we think we have Hugh reduced to a neat, four-stage schematization, we find Hugh talking, in paragraph 33 of the "Difficult Question," about the *affectus* exercising cogitation, before dismissing cogitation and meditation in order to begin its yearning upsurge by love alone. So much for our neat divisions between the affective and cogitative! If the *affectus* itself exercises cogitation, they must indeed be intertwined.[103]

This was not new. The Carthusian tradition offers a precedent. Guigo II's famous twelfth-century *Ladder for Monks* describes the shift from meditation to prayer as precisely this sort of sudden, unexpected passing from discursive meditation into praise and worship of God. From one perspective it may seem like the meditator has "ascended" into the next stage of prayer, but it is really God who comes down to the meditator, exciting in him an outpouring upsurge of praise and adoration.[104] Contemplation, with its genuine knowledge of God, then follows as a fourth "stage" on the prayer-adoration of "stage" three.

The intertwining of the human faculties becomes clear in paragraphs 34–35 of the "Difficult Question," where Hugh points out that, in the unitive affective upsurge (the "higher" of the two affective, aspirative upsurges), the Holy Spirit comes down and inflames the *affectus* to the point that no more rational discernment takes place, that is, the human spirit no longer makes the distinctions it has made up to this point.

> For this true Love, which is the Holy Spirit, . . . himself touches the soul's supreme affective apex with the fire of love and sets it ablaze, drawing it toward himself wordlessly, without any cogitation or rational running hither and yon. Just as a stone pulled by its own weight is naturally drawn down to its own center, so the apex of the *affectus* by its own weight is carried up to God directly and unmediatedly, without any oblique tangentiality, without any cogitation leading the way or keeping it company.

Much of the problem in interpreting Hugh stems from the *scholastic* tendency to read him and other mystics in a linear, sequential way, a tendency characteristic of Vincent of Aggsbach's opponents in the fifteenth century and of much modern scholarship on mysticism.[105] This permits *us* to do the isolating, to focus on Hugh's chapter three (the "unitive way") and the concluding "Difficult Question," permitting us to interpret *The Roads to Zion* as advocating a totally affective *state of union* with God. Hugh seems to work with more of a chiastic framework, an interpenetrating, interlocking set of "stages," one of which (the central but not ultimate one) involves short bursts of totally affective aspiration. And, as we shall see later, Hugh's notorious statement of total affectivity has to do primarily with dynamic movement, not with a state of "union."

Indeed, his method of aspirative, affective upsurge is present even in the purgative stage. In par. 10ff. of the *via purgativa*, after an exposition of God's favors to the sinner, Hugh proceeds to the actual method of repentance and purgation. As an introduction, he offers five names for God, expounding the "why" of each one briefly (par. 10): God is Good, Beautiful, Lord, Sweet, Merciful. Then he offers sample prayers that employ each of these names aspiratively. At the end of par. 10 he makes it clear that the names are simply succinct labels for the ideas that lie behind them, but that the succinctness is essential to the actual process of imploring God's forgiveness. One cannot pray well with long discursive, conceptual reasoning; one can pray with short outbursts if one has first meditated on why God is good, beautiful, Lord, sweet, merciful. Even in the purgative stage the God-directed soul can avoid wandering from God, because "she is completely integrated in herself" "in the pull of these [brief] words" rather than "dissipating herself in wordy narrations or prolonged chatter" (par. 11).

In other words, *The Roads to Zion*, like Guigo de Ponte's *On Contemplation* and other works on contemplative theology, sets forth stages and steps that are not intended to be understood merely sequentially, despite the use of sequential language. That Hugh belongs with the affective mystics is beyond dispute—with many others he gives pride of place to affective union. But that he wished to isolate it from the cognitive elements to the degree Vincent of Aggsbach's opponents claimed he did is true only from a linear, sequential reading. That is one legitimate way to read and think, but not the only way. Indeed, one might view Hugh as reading the stages of "mystical theology" intertextually.

For instance, in paragraphs 26–28 of the illuminative way, Hugh insists that "presence" is a single, undivided reality. Heaven is seeing God face-to-face, encountering God's unmediated presence. Mystical "union" in this life is the same "presence" but in the inchoate manner possible for those living in love.[106] He thus applies the petition of the Our Father for "our daily bread, today" to the presence of God. Hugh then applies a *locus classicus* for Christian mystical *union* to this theme of presence (1 Cor 6:17).[107]

One indication of this is found in the "Difficult Question," par. 15, after he has quoted the famous passage by Pseudo-Denis regarding mystical wisdom's mindless, irrational, and foolish character. Pseudo-

Denis would never have used those terms if "mystical theology were to proceed by first cogitating and meditating through reasonings, as we observe other sciences doing." Once the *affectus* has been set on fire, knowledge results.

Of course, Hugh does believe that meditation has taken place in the illuminative way, before the upsurge of the *affectus*. The pattern he thus assumes is cogitation, upsurge, knowledge; or scholastic, affective, scholastic. One could as easily see this as a circle, or a spiral: from cogitation through love to cogitative understanding, for there is cogitation both before and after.

Another way of looking at it is drawn from par. 26 of the "Difficult Question," where Hugh explains that the second type of contemplation, from above to below in light radiating from on high, also *terminates* in the *affectus*, for it would not be contemplation if it did not terminate in affection. In other words, for Hugh, all contemplation leads to *affectio*, whether from below or above.[108]

In other words, Hugh's treatise ends in the middle! Both its beginning and end point to the instances of aspirative upsurge found in each of the three paths.

Much the same point is made in par. 30 of the "Difficult Question": Cogitation coming from on high terminates in the *affectus*, even as cogitation of the beauty of the universe builds up from below to terminate in the *affectus*. Thus both of Hugh's "affective methods" are affective by virtue of where they lead. So much for his "without cogitation leading the way."

> Finally, all meditating or contemplating terminates in yearning affection. For any meditation or contemplation that is not followed by loving affection does little or no good at all. Hence Augustine says that, rather than let meditation flit about, one ought to cling lovingly, so that cogitation, or meditation, might always precede affectionate love. Now the second method proceeds without employing any other creatures, moving solely by cogitation sent from God, as the faithful soul is affected to God himself. ("Difficult Question," par. 30)

Yet, the fact remains that Hugh did use the language of separation, cutting off. In par. 98 and 105 of the unitive way, he talks about the total rescinding of the eye of the intellect. In par. 9, he talks about the human spirit cutting off at the roots all functions of reason and understanding (qualifying it, however, by saying that this takes place "when, however, the human spirit in this life is actively intent on the upsurge"); in paragraph 18, he refers to the intellect's being divided from the *affectus*, promising to explain later how such a thing can be—when he deals with "the theory of this practice" (par. 82–115, cf. "Difficult Question," par. 16).

What does Hugh mean by this language of "abscission" and "separation"? Hugh's concrete metaphor for "cutting away" is taken from the construction of a bridge. First one builds a wooden framework (cogitative stages) to support the stones of the bridge's arches until the final stone is in place. The wooden framework is then removed and the stones (affective aspiration) "support" themselves. Sequentially, within time, one has "stones (affect) alone." But we are also dealing here with a foretaste of eternity. The wooden framework is indispensable to the construction and its form is incorporated in the shape taken by the stones themselves. The final arched shape of the bridge owes itself to that wooden framework. There is no prevenient cognition anymore, and certainly no concomitant cognition, but that is true only at this point in time. As modern people we are often so fascinated by the brief flash of mystical union suspended marvelously in space just as the arches of the bridge span a chasm that we forget the continued "presence in absence" that makes the arch possible.[109]

The aspirative and affective stone arch that is left behind supports knowledge of God, mystical wisdom, by continually upthrusting. Knowledge of God, mystical wisdom walks along the bridge, while affective aspiration surges upward. The stones can support mystical knowledge because they stand in place by themselves, but they do that only because they were laid down on a wooden framework of cogitation (allegorical meditation on Scripture and loftier pondering of celestial things and God himself) that is now gone.

Hugh continues, in par. 41 of the *quaestio*:

> Moreover, knowledge is twofold. One kind precedes the *affectus* of love, in proceeding along the common and scholastic path. Here one first has knowledge of God through [sense perceptions of] the creatures or through the intellect, before the affection of love is kindled. It is in this light that the statement by Augustine that was quoted at the beginning of this paragraph should be understood. However, in following along

the mystical path, according to Denis, the *affectus* of love precedes understanding knowledge, as we have said.

Hugh nowhere spells out in so many words the interpretation of
his bridge metaphor that we are giving.[110] But he was a monk who lived
the active life of ascetic discipline, meditation, and liturgical prayer for
most of his waking hours. No one living under a monastic rule can abandon these structural elements entirely, indeed, Hugh took them for
granted, subsumed them under the purely affective theme. Yet precisely
in their absence they are present,[111] even as the empty space under the
bridge's arches speaks, to those with ears to hear, of the easily forgotten
"preliminaries."[112]

In short, Hugh's allegedly exotic total affectivity is actually rather
mundane and commonsensical: We begin to love God by meditating on
revelation, on Scripture, on all creatures, even those from the heart of
hell. That in turn incites love for God, which surges up in our hearts.
And that upsurge of love leaves behind a deposit of real knowledge of
God that Hugh identified as Pseudo-Denis's "sapientia Christianorum"—the wisdom of Christians.

Thus, in the debate at Tegernsee over the question of an ongoing
role for cognition in mystical union, Nicholas of Cusa and others believed that love and knowledge always played a role, even in the final
ascent. Hugh believed that, after long preparation, for the fleeting duration of the unitive upsurge alone, cogitation and intellection were "cut
away." There was a genuine controversy in the 1450s, but we are as
mistaken as Marquard Sprenger, Nicholas of Cusa, and Bernard of Waging were if we label Hugh of Balma "anti-intellectual" or even describe
his approach as "totally affective."[113] The discussion, since the fifteenth
century, has failed to progress beyond the phrase "without advance or
accompanying cogitation" taken out of context.

But why would fifteenth-century experts in mystical theology have
misunderstood Hugh? In part because the lines between learned, philosophical, quasi-academic study of "mystical theology" and a more
simpleminded monastic practice were already being drawn in the fifteenth century. Vincent seems to have resented the sudden surge of interest in "mystical spirituality" on the part of university-educated reformers. He resisted the facile harnessing of mystical spirituality to the
cause of church reform by ineffective papal and episcopal reformers.
Mystical theology is food for "real men," for well-trained monastic spiritual athletes, and not for dandified spiritual dilettantes. As a monk and a

Carthusian, Vincent understood something of the indispensable function of ascetic and intellectual structure, and he approached Hugh as a monk. He knew that Hugh's *quaestio difficilis* did not stand alone. Marquard Sprenger approached Hugh more academically and scholastically, and the "Difficult Question" obviously drew his attention. He seems to have assumed that it summarized the entire treatise, when in fact it is a restatement in *quaestio* format only of part of the *via unitiva* section. Bernard of Waging's problem was different. He may have been led astray by his eagerness to reconcile Cusanus's "learned ignorance" and the general affective, Latin mystical tradition. The problem was that Cusanus's *De Docta ignorantia* and *De Visione Dei* belonged to a different, nonmonastic, genre. Vincent perceived this. Bernard initially tried to read them in an affective, monastic context, but Nicholas of Cusa definitively ruled such a reading out of court.[114]

The reading of Hugh of Balma given in the present study is not far removed from at least one fifteenth-century Carthusian reading, that of Nicholas Kempf, prior of the nearby monastery at Gaming, 1451–1458. Conventionally, Kempf has been portrayed as taking a middle position in the Tegernsee debate. He describes the movement of the will by means of both acquired and infused perfect *habitus*, from cognition of one thing to love of another without previous or concomitant *actual* cognition of the thing to which it ascends. He interprets Hugh to be teaching that cognition is a necessary point of departure even if it follows rather than precedes the loved destination. He also points out that learned folk might ridicule this sort of affectivity but simple folk will know what he has in mind.[115] Kempf explicitly declared that his purpose was to show that there is no discord between scholastic *doctores* and the practitioners of mystical science. He does something of the same with Hugh of Balma's teaching on an affective upsurge without cogitation leading the way or accompanying. In book II, chapter 21, he says that, although the school doctors find it hard to believe that intellectual activity can ever be entirely cut off, it is in fact true that, "with great practice in the love of God [gained] through cognition leading the way, it is possible to surge up, whenever one wishes, into actual love of God without actual cognition of God in the strict sense either leading the way or accompanying." Note that Kempf repeats the word "actual" (*actualis*)— underscoring the point we have made about Hugh: The totally affective upsurge is a dynamic affair. Only during the actual upsurge do cogitation and cognition fall away. This was initially the way Bernard of Waging tried to reconcile Vincent with Cusanus.[116]

INTRODUCTION

Kempf emphasizes that this totally affective upsurge is a matter of long practice. The metaphor he uses is that of a blind man who remembers things he once could see and senses them by force of habit. Simple lay folk understand this and learn it by practice while the learned scoff at it. Not unlike Hugh of Balma's effort to explain it with the image of involuntary breathing in and out, Kempf understands it not to be some exotic feat but a very simple and natural outcome of long practice in loving God. Above all, no more than Hugh of Balma did Nicholas Kempf portray this affective upsurge as the endpoint of mystical theology or as a mystical state.

As detailed elsewhere,[117] Kempf distinguished two mystical unions. One, the *via unitiva*, is a life of affective longing for God. The second, the *unio sanctissima*, comes after the cessation of all powers of the soul, after the presence of the Trinity has poured itself into the human person. In between lies the affective upsurge of Hugh of Balma.[118] Unlike Hugh, Kempf does not always use the term "knowledge" or "understanding" for what follows on the affective upsurge, but he does refer to the *scientia sanctorum* (knowledge of God enjoyed by the saints in heaven) and God's presence in the human person. All of the person's "own acts" have ceased, but that does not leave a nihilist void; rather, the person is simply filled with the holiness of God.[119]

How carefully and at exactly which point the other participants in the controversy read Hugh of Balma himself should be carefully studied. We need critical editions of all the texts in the debate, especially of Sprenger's *Elucidatorium mysticae theologiae*,[120] and a thorough study of the exact chronology of the debate, paying close attention to exactly which parts of the works in question were known to which disputants at which stages. Some of the confusion may have resulted from dependence on summaries and second-hand acquaintance with key treatises and letters. The entire Franciscan tradition needs to be brought to bear here, since there is evidence that the Benedictines and secular clerics may have come at the question from knowledge of Bonaventure's spiritual teachings.[121] How well did they know Thomas Gallus before Vincent launched his attack on Gerson?

The strange case of Hugh of Balma in the hands of Marquard Sprenger, Bernard of Waging, and modern scholars reminds us that fifteenth-century scholars were as capable of reading out of context as we are. We turn now to a more careful look at Hugh's teaching on the totally affective aspirative upsurge.

C. HUGH ON ASPIRATIVE, AFFECTIVE PRAYER

Much of our problem, as alluded to above, stems from our tendency to focus on mystical union as a state.[122] This is a modern notion. The medieval, Latin contemplative tradition preferred to speak of God's visitation to the soul (as one can clearly see from Guigo de Ponte's *On Contemplation*). Such great "contemplative" writers as Bernard of Clairvaux and Aelred of Rievaulx rarely referred to direct, ecstatic, rapture or "union." Instead, Aelred speaks of God's visitation to the soul in the same breath as "compunction," a term most of us would associate with the "lower" stages in the spiritual life: repentance. What we all too often forget is that the monastic life was above all a life of repentance. "Compunction," meaning the stimulus, goading, prick of God's visitation, could be sweet or painful, consoling or convicting.[123] Moreover, aspirative prayer was part of monastic tradition long before Hugh's time.[124]

Hugh defines mystical theology as an outstretched longing of love toward God (Prologue, par. 2). Kurt Ruh has pointed to William of Saint-Thierry's spirituality of *amor deficiens* and *amor desiderii*—in the Bridegroom's absence the soul's lacking becomes the means to expand the soul, an expansiveness for which Gregory the Great employed the metaphor of a narrow window opening that expands toward the inside.[125]

If one views Hugh of Balma's teaching on aspirative prayer *and* his notorious teaching on totally affective upsurge to God in this light, a light begins to dawn. For clarity, we shall look at the way he deals with aspirative prayer in the illuminative way, before he has even touched on the unitive way. Perhaps the key paragraphs are nos. 45–47 of the illuminative way. In paragraph 45 he says that all cogitation and meditation is cut away (*abscinditur*), the key term cited by those who read him as putting a complete break between the intellective and affective ascent. But, as we have seen, this *abscinditur* concept comes from his bridge metaphor. Here we see how it applies. Only in the final, fleeting (but powerful) stage of the *via illuminativa*, in the transition from the long exposition of the Lord's Prayer (par. 13–44; the long exposition is itself an anagogy) to the unitive way, do we find interjected the means of transition: aspirative prayer, which Hugh illustrates in paragraphs 45–54 by means of his short exposition of the Lord's Prayer. He immediately shifts from third to second person. From discursive (yet anagogical, i.e., allegorical) meditation, the soul now shifts to direct, loving, sighing address of the Beloved. All of this has precedents in John Cassian.

Yet even this involves continued meditation. Hugh illustrates his aspirative method by a form of aspirative meditation on the same contents as had undergirded the long exposition. The *contents* of paragraphs 46–54 are a truncated version of the *contents* of paragraphs 13–44. For example, in paragraph 46 the idea that *Pater* is a begetter was the key idea in paragraph 14: The *proprietas* of a Father is to generate, beget. The difference is one of attitude: In a flash, the meditator realizes not just cognitively the meaning of Father/Begetter, but feels affected by that idea, senses, knows affectively, what it means to be a child of the Father. Likewise, in paragraph 47 ("who art in heaven"): Heaven is studded with various constellations—the same point made in the longer exposition, but a point that now comes home affectively. Or, in paragraph 48 ("Hallowed be thy name"), Hugh repeats the cognitive concept: The property of "be sanctified" is "without earth," that is, above the earth, that is, heavenly. The difference is that in this short, aspirative upsurge, one is affected by the concept into some kind of experience of heavenliness.

Both the long, discursive meditation and the nonmeditative, noncogitative exposition of the Our Father[126] are means to ascend *paulatim*, gradually, step-by-step to the unitive way. Both are anagogic, upward uses of Scripture,[127] but one is totally affective and the other is cogitative and meditative anagogy.[128]

In other words, what Hugh means by "without any cogitation leading the way or accompanying" is that, in these short, aspirative upsurges, whether already in the illuminative way or in the unitive way, for a fleeting moment one thrusts up to God, an upsurge that takes place in God's descent to visit the soul. What most of us might be most interested in—the state of "mystical union"—is for Hugh the knowledge or understanding (*intelligentia*, mystical wisdom, unitive wisdom) that is redeposited in the soul, left behind in the soul, after these aspirative upsurges.

Thus the totally affective part of Hugh's teaching on mystical theology is really a method for darts of longing love directed at God but bathed in God's descending illumination that permits one to carry the cognitive contents of Scripture, or any created thing, into the depths of one's heart, one's *affectus*—to take things to heart.[129] We might say it is a method for making Scripture come alive experientially, to move from pondering about Scripture or creation to direct address of God in heart-felt, longing love.[130]

Somehow, between the thirteenth and fifteenth centuries, this essentially hermeneutic understanding became confused with issues of mystical ontology, permitting Vincent of Aggsbach and others to employ "total affectivity" as a weapon against Gerson, Cusanus, and others. Hugh states clearly that his "affective upsurge" applies to both proficients and the perfected ("Difficult Question," par. 33), whereas most modern students of spiritual theology assume that "union" is a matter for the perfected alone.

That Hugh is not interested in a *state* of mystical union but, rather, in the deposit of true intellection of God left behind after the totally affective upsurge is clear from his pointed remarks in paragraph 46 of the "Difficult Question": "Should someone ask, 'How shall I ponder if I am not supposed to think about God or angels?', the reply is simply: 'You shall aspire rather than cogitate.' " If the human spirit has been prepared, she "can only surge upward . . . saying, 'O Lord, when shall I love you? When shall I constrain you with arms of love?' " Resorting to this frequently assures her that she is "being set on fire more rapidly than if she were to ponder a thousand times about celestial mysteries, the eternal birth [of the Son], or the procession [of the Holy Spirit]." At the very end of par. 48 he refers to a lasting beatific state—but this is the end of the treatise and the line between this life and the beatific vision has been deliberately blurred to provide the climax to his work.

The "totally affective" upsurge is a fleeting and practical movement. It does not refer to the entire ascent, merely to "*ista consurrectio*"—a quick glance of the eye of the bride, a glance exchanged between lovers (*via unitiva*, par. 83, quoted below), an arrow that wounds the Beloved, a dart of love as we find it later developed in the *Cloud of Unknowing*. "In the *actual practice* of this upsurge, speculative knowledge knows nothing" (*via unitiva*, par. 83; emphasis added).

Hugh's language of ascent is nearly always dynamic, rarely static. He is forever talking about being moved into God, being impelled into God, a staccato drumbeat of *movetur, consurgere, consurrectio, motio*.[131] Since we have no real equivalent in English, it is difficult for modern English-speaking readers to grasp that even the word "affective" is based on a past participle that describes something that has happened: One is affected, one is moved, swayed, impacted by something.

The metaphor of a bridge whose construction framework is cut away is not Hugh's sole metaphor for the affective upsurge. In par. 47 of the *via illuminativa* he compares the aspirative, affective upsurge to a wick that must first be dried out in the sun by long meditation (par. 14–44), so that it can suddenly burst into flame (par. 45–54). Thus the aspirative upsurge requires the arid preparation of discursive meditation if it is to be kindled, just as the fully freely suspended stone arch of a bridge requires the prosaic wooden framework to undergird its seemingly daring defiance of gravity.

In *via unitiva*, par. 100, Hugh compares the aspirative upsurge to breathing, to involuntary gasping that occurs without conscious direction, yet employs cogitation as a means *through which* affection might be kindled. The means is important, even crucial, as a transition, but it is not the end, and, because we ignore the medieval distinction between final and efficient cause, we easily become confused here.

It was Vincent of Aggsbach's opponents and Hendrik Herp who began this confusion and the Spanish spiritual writers who continued it. Hugh became known as the champion of an anti-intellectual, passive, even an allegedly proto-Quietist mysticism.[132] Exactly how this happened in the fifteenth and sixteenth centuries deserves more study, especially after we have critical editions of the writings of Thomas Gallus[133] and the writings of the various participants in the Tegernsee debate, the vernacular Spanish versions of Hugh and Hendrik Herp, detailed studies of Herp's massive corpus, and of several associated late medieval Carthusian and Franciscan spiritual writers (Jakob de Paradiso [Jakob of Jüterbog], Rudolf of Biberach, etc.).

For now, however, it is probably best to read *The Roads to Zion* primarily in the context of Carthusian, Cistercian, and Victorine spirituality of the twelfth and thirteenth centuries (we know far more about twelfth-century than thirteenth-century Carthusian spirituality).

D. HUGH AND THE AFFECTIVE TAMING OF PSEUDO-DENIS

Viae Sion lugent is commonly seen by scholars as part of an affective taming of the intellectualist continuum from unknowing to knowing that constitutes the purist reading of Pseudo-Denis. This affective taming of Denis takes on its proper character especially when viewed against the intellectualist reading of Pseudo-Denis found in the works of Thomas Aquinas and Albert the Great.[134] "Love" or "affectus" is absent from the Pseudo-Denis's *On Mystical Theology*, although it is found in *On Divine Names*.[135] Beginning with Hugh and Richard of Saint-Victor in the twelfth century, love began to be equated with the

38

"unknowing" ascent of Pseudo-Denis's *On Mystical Theology*. Hugh of Balma makes use of the key imagery from the twelfth-century Victorines: identifying the Cherubim with intellect and the Seraphim with love (*via unitiva*, par. 84). Hugh is aware of what he is doing; in par. 83, he acknowledges that Pseudo-Denis never talks about the *affectus*, rather, only about unknowing. Drawing on Thomas Gallus, Hugh then proceeds to show that the two are equivalent:

> Now this upsurge [*consurrectio*], which is said to take place through unknowing, is nothing other than to be directly moved through the ardor of love without any creaturely means, without knowledge [*cognitio*] leading the way, without even any accompanying movement of understanding [*intelligentia*], so that it has to do solely with movements of the *affectus*. In the actual practice of this [upsurge], speculative knowledge knows nothing. This is the eye with which the Bridegroom is said to have been wounded by the bride (Ca 4:9), and the Bridegroom by his own testimony says it is a single glance: *You have wounded my heart, my sister, my bride, with one of your eyes.* (Ca 4:9)

Francis Ruello, James Walsh, and Rosemary Ann Lees have rightly pointed to the role of the Victorine, Thomas Gallus, in creating a thoroughgoing affective epistemology.[136] On the one hand, Hugh of Saint-Victor, Richard of Saint-Victor, and Thomas Gallus of Vercelli brought to bear on contemplative theology early scholasticism's drive to systematize and resolve the *sic et non* contradictions of patristic authorities. Thomas Gallus had read all the works of Aristotle available and had great respect for the philosopher.[137] Yet, on the other hand, as Walsh points out, Thomas worked within the patristic and exegetical tradition of the early Middle Ages and within the early Victorine and Cistercian spiritual tradition of the twelfth century. His main concern was to reconcile and adapt Pseudo-Denis to the Western mystical tradition.[138]

We do not know how much scholastic training Hugh of Balma might have had. He very likely studied the liberal arts and must have had some exposure to university disputations (which were conducted in the arts faculties as well as theology faculties). Hence Walach's effort to show that he must have studied scholastic *theology* is not persuasive. Moreover, Hugh's Latin is not exactly superb,[139] and he knew how to employ the tools of rhetoric (*via unitiva*, par. 58–81) alongside the disputation form.

Perhaps the most illuminating statement comes as Hugh concludes the section on the anagogical exposition of the Lord's Prayer in the illuminative way, paragraph 44. He insists that not only Scripture, but all things, even things in hell, can by their higher (i.e., anagogical) properties denote things of heaven. This rather optimistic but common monastic statement of the sign-value of all of creation follows on a passage about the restoration of image of God in the human soul, another commonplace of monastic theology.[140]

Even as he declares that scholastic theology is inadequate to comprehend unitive wisdom, Hugh employs technical terms from scholastic philosophy—for example, wisdom *supposits* for knowledge of faith and the foundation of love, and no mortal, no matter how well trained in science or philosophy, can comprehend wisdom by rational investigation or intellectual effort.

> Only for the sons eager for consolation does the eternal Father, and he alone, unlock it by his merciful and fatherly affection. Therefore, since it is closed off and hidden, that is, known only by a few, it is called "mystical." ("Difficult Question," par. 22)

2. Rhetoric and Language in Mystical Theology

Hugh may have been using scholastic terminology here to mock scholasticism ever so subtly. In his *quaestio difficilis* he insists that scholastic teachers and mystical teachers have different notions of the *affectus* and of the mystical theology of the Pseudo-Denis. Secular philosophers proceed from knowledge of sensible things, indeed, even some of Pseudo-Denis's works proceed from sensible things, but not his *De mystica theologia*, which proceeds from the top down.

Thus, although he makes use of scholastic argumentation, Hugh of Balma is no scholastic theologian. Each chapter and many sections within chapters end with formal perorations.[141] The theoretical sections of his work are always brief, followed by much longer practical examples.[142] The heart of his method lies in his anagogical (upthrusting, uplifting) hermeneutic. His advocacy of heartfelt aspirative prayer (*via illuminativa*, par. 45–54), although not original with him,[143] and his longer exposition of the Lord's Prayer (ibid., par. 13–44) have the same aim: to lift the devout soul upward toward God from the text of Scripture and the forest of signs found in all created things and beings.[144] The one (aspirative prayer) is simply a more praxis-oriented explication of the other (meditation on Scripture, specifically the Lord's Prayer). His meditative approach to Scripture employs the monastic tradition of *lectio divina*, for which the Carthusians had the delicious words of guidance from the pen of Guigo II as their basic handbook: *Lectio* places the grape of Scripture in the mouth; *meditatio* crushes it; with *oratio* its sweetness begins to flow; in *contemplatio* its taste floods the palate.[145] What Hugh has done is to apply this method of reading and digesting to a particular passage in order to show practically how to meditate. "And deliver us from evil" stimulates thoughts of the body's earthiness, which in turn leads to the image of being mired in mud, from which one yearns to be set free; yearning pleas for freedom lead to the image of God as a father kindly disposed to his struggling child, which in turn leads to reflections on human birth and rebirth in the context of the creation in the image of God and the human longing for a true fatherland (*via illuminativa*, par. 14–44). The consideration of aspirative prayer in par. 45–54 simply intensifies the yearning and longing process of meditation until the literal texts of the Lord's Prayer are swept into the Christian's heart and soul in order to be breathed upward toward God.

In the middle of the chapter on the unitive way Hugh first discusses the various "persuasions" or "reasons" by which one can be moved and swayed to pursue unitive wisdom (par. 30–57). Then he turns to the really mundane practicalities: the various exercises or industries (including proper posture, proper timing, and proper subject matter, namely the Passion and earthly life of Christ) that assist one along the unitive path.

The reasons that should compel one to pursue unitive wisdom are, for Hugh, persuasions. He does not offer a compelling demonstrative logic; rather, he relies on a wide range of human realities that move a person's affective inclinations. Some individuals might think they are simply too frail and weak to scale the heights of mystical union. If so, let them look at people around themselves: People are willing, despite fear and trepidation, to risk themselves for commercial gain. Why should one not have the same courage in pursuit of a spiritual goal?[146] Trees put down deep roots so that their branches can resist stormy winds, roots that draw water from the earth so that the branches can burst into bloom; a farmer works the soil and sows his crops in hope, long before he can be certain of a harvest; even the hardship of poverty and human suffering can inspire one to seek that which lies beyond human and created things. Throughout this section Hugh uses metaphor-rich scriptural citations to inspire, to uplift. Indeed, his metaphors can be too rich, as is evident from the appallingly mixed metaphors found in *via unitiva*, par. 56: One of the two arms that increase the soul's upward movement scrapes out a cavity in herself, which fills with graces that skip over mountains and hills. Hugh insists that the loftiest (most anagogical) imagery of Scripture itself ("Beloved of the Prince of Life"; "King of angels") can be literally and properly applied to the beggarly human soul (*via unitiva*, par. 37).

Hugh's use of a scholastic *quaestio* to conclude his book, in order to argue logically with those who refuse anything short of logical, scholastic discourse, must be seen in the light of the chapter on the unitive way. As far as Hugh is concerned, the rhetorical persuasion he offers there should really suffice—as the passage from the end of the longer exposition of the Lord's Prayer (*via illuminativa*, par. 44) quoted earlier suggests: The text of all of Scripture, all created things, even things from the heart of hell itself, in the strictest sense leads to this unitive wisdom.

Not only does Hugh list the various persuasive arguments, he constructs the entire rhetorical section along traditional rhetorical lines: After describing the unitive way theoretically (*via unitiva*, par. 1–29), he, as it were, steps back and begins his treatise all over again, with an exordium outlining the content, purpose, and style of his book (*via unitiva*, par. 30–57). Essentially he views his treatise as nothing more than a commentary on Pseudo-Denis's *Mystical Theology*, a "book" whose few words contain infinite meanings, a book whose subject defies reduction to words, whose subject is inward wisdom. Yet, although Hugh nowhere states this explicitly, the "simple style" that he will employ in fact imitates the "hyper" style of Pseudo-Denis—paratactic concatenations, a piling up of words intended somehow to suggest the ineffability of his subject matter.

Hugh makes considerable use of courtly metaphors. In the *via purgativa*, paragraphs 7–8, he compares the penitent begging for mercy to a criminal pardoned by a king and thereby entering into a relationship of servitude. When he mentions the need to invoke assistence from the saints, he compares them not only to courtiers at the heavenly court (*via purgativa*, par. 13), but also to the role of the court jester (ibid., par. 9). Courtly skills are needed by the soul intent on mystical union. Indeed, the opening line of the Lord's Prayer ("Our Father who art in heaven"), Hugh says, is a *captatio benevolentiae*, the beginning of a speech or letter that aims at capturing the reader's or listener's goodwill. His commentary on that phrase (*via illuminativa*, par. 13–18) emphasizes that one gains God's ear by praising him with the skills of a wooer rather than those of an artisan. One ought to praise God as the origin of all life, as one who diffuses his goodness generously, and as the occupant of the most marvelous dwelling-place (see especially *via illuminativa*, par. 14).

When he introduces the Rosary at the end of the *via purgativa*, Hugh refers to it as homage, or tribute (par. 14). Throughout the treatise he prefers *amor* to *caritas*, except in a handful of technical instances. In one instance he explicitly points out that he is using *amor* as an equivalent to *caritas* (*via unitiva*, par. 25). The upsurge into God in the *affectus* for Hugh is a matter of passionate *amor* made possible by the *caritas* of God shed abroad through the work of Christ.[147]

Thus, despite a very thin scholastic veneer, Hugh's approach is fundamentally rhetorical, since its subject defies logical exposition. The first rhetorical reason, or persuasion, takes the attack directly to scholastic theology: It exposes the folly [*insipientia*] of many, especially of religious, who pretend to be learned and logical. Instead, it is the simple who are wise. The worldly activities he offers as springboards for anagogical (metaphorical) inspiration come from agriculture, commerce, and warfare, three common, vivid examples accessible to the simplest listener or reader. True to his purpose of illustrating the method by his own choice of words and syntax, he concludes the first persuasion with paratactic overkill—the passage from par. 37, quoted above, which concludes with a long sentence that has been left intact in this translation in an effort to illustrate his procedure.

Hugh's use of the spiritual sense follows a fixed pattern, one that almost seems mechanical to our way of thinking. Having established the anagogical (allegorical) meaning of a word or phrase, he does not hesitate simply to plug in that meaning at a later point as a sort of conceptual shorthand.

Thy will be done, as in heaven—which, to apply the phrase anagogically, means "let thy will be done" firmly, steadily in motion, adorned with various lights—*so on earth*, that is, "thy will be done" in sinners, who not unjustly and in a strict sense [*proprie*] are called earth, because they are fixed in a region far from the fire whose cleansing burning lightens the soul so that she might, by loving and yearning while still on earth, gain a heavenly dwelling-place: for where one loves, there one, in a strict sense, lives. (*via illuminativa*, par. 24)

Yet Hugh is also a contemplative and mystical writer. Precisely because words are inherently limiting, concealing, and determining, unitive wisdom must always spill over the boundaries of words and creatures. Thus he subverts even his own metonymy:

> Thus he [Peter, Jn 6:69] says, *To whom shall we go?* Speaking as lovers do, he gives the most compelling reason not to withdraw from him: *You have the words of eternal life.* You have, not the words of the outward mouth, but the words of the inward spirit, emitting a stream of word-droplets that reveal the unknown joys of eternal life to your lovers much more effectively than proofs or evidence from the creatures or any other sort of words. (*via unitiva*, par. 46)

In the *via illuminativa*, paragraphs 10–12, Hugh applies the anagogic method to Jerusalem. He gives three levels of exegesis, conflating the moral and allegorical to yield the literal, moral, and anagogical senses. Yet the third is anagogical in a strict sense, whereas the other two are also anagogical in a broader sense. Hugh simply assumes that all of Scripture raises the human spirit to God.

3. Grace and Human Yearning

Hugh also uses grammar itself to carry one of his main theological themes. The Latin translation of Pseudo-Denis that Hugh used (made by John Sarracenus in the twelfth century) shifted from the active to the passive voice in the crucial opening passage of *On Mystical Theology*. Pseudo-Denis instructs Timothy first to "rise up" and then to "be uplifted." In the first, the "rising up," Hugh insists, nature and grace cooperate in the pursuit of unitive wisdom. But there is a point at which even persuasive reasons, aspirative prayer, meditative reading, and attention to the soul's best industries must cease. For ultimately divine wisdom is taught by God alone, directly, immediately (*via unitiva*, par. 82–115). In this "learning" no medium of any sort is involved. It occurs by grace alone. Yet, Hugh insists, it is not passive. When the human person is acted on by grace, it is the human person who is activated but activated from beyond himself (*via unitiva*, par. 111). Hugh has already made this clear in his theoretical, that is, theological, discussion of unitive wisdom (*via unitiva*, par. 1–29). He clearly embeds unitive wisdom in the order of salvation, insisting that mystical wisdom brings about perfected righteousness, making one properly disposed to oneself (*via unitiva*, par. 11–12), to earthly things (par. 20), to the body, to one's enemies (par. 21), to the cardinal virtues (par. 23–26) and theological virtues (par. 27–29). Guigo I's teaching on the proper relation of the monk to God, to other people, to the created world, and to himself was part of Hugh's theological tool chest.

Nor is it accidental that Hugh addresses the grammar of grace and human effort precisely at the point where he has employed all the possible rhetorical skills and tools of human learning. The final persuasive reason, the final human industry, is simply to recognize one's poverty and humility, literally to toss oneself away, for that act is what gives free sway to an increased longing and yearning that in the end is all that a human being can *do* to be joined to God: yearn for what one still lacks. The disposing arm, the one arm by which the human spirit *does* something, is precisely to attribute nothing to herself but to return everything to the praise of the giver. The other arm is simply worship, since praise of God provokes a greater largesse of grace that enables greater praise. Thus thanksgiving is the ultimate persuasive reason. Hugh's discussion of the persuasive reasons in *via unitiva* par. 30–57 therefore concludes by invoking the ultimate scene of worship and praise found in Scripture—the worship of the enthroned Christ in heaven (Rv 4 and 7). No summary can do justice to Hugh's language here; the passage (*via unitiva*, par. 54) must be read ruminatively as he intended it to be read.

In what I have designated part D of the unitive way, Hugh concludes that the ascent to union with the Most High requires neither grace nor glory nor remission of penalty or anything else except yearning for the One to whom alone the human spirit aspires to be united for his own sake (*via unitiva*, par. 104).

Hugh uses the language of *facere quod in se est*, "merits," and "virtues." Indeed, Dieter Mertens claims that Hugh considered mystical union to be a meritorious act of the soul, based on a prooftext from the opening paragraph of the *via unitiva*.[148] But Hugh is so clear on these matters elsewhere that the text cited by Mertens can be understood only when placed into a broader context. The very call to the monastic life of purgation, the opening path of the ascent to mystical union, is by the pure grace of God. There is a sacramental path of cleansing available to all; the monastic path is for a few, for those who know their own weakness and inability, and who, like the "dove or turtledove in the wilderness, in contemplative retreat," try to fly higher despite their feebleness (*via purgativa*, par. 6). Hugh's imaginary monastic penitent knows well that "many who are guilty of lesser offenses in eyes of divine majesty nonetheless remain under the lasting penalty of divine malediction" while he (the monastic penitent), "who much more deserved the same penalty, has instead been summoned to radiance of grace in this present life and to the prize of eternal happiness in the life to come—not by his own merits, but by the Creator's free generosity." Hugh asks us to consider an analogy: An earthly king who hangs one thief while pardoning another who had committed greater crimes acts justly and in pure mercy, in "the mercy proper to an earthly king, a mercy that directly contradicts what the pardoned thief deserved" (*via purgativa*, par. 7).

Hugh does use the language of *facere quod in se est*, of "congruent merit,"[149] but in such a way that it is the congruence of begging for mercy by the sinner incapable of doing anything except falling on one's face, the congruence of a criminal pleading for pardon.[150] Then, congruently, sorrow for sin is granted. If the sinner finds himself unable to arrive at the proper degree of sorrow for sin, having prostrated himself abjectly, then, Hugh says, let him trust in God, because sometimes God tests a person's patience, strengthening and sustaining it in the process. Clearly God is the one who does this, in Hugh's view. The key for the penitent is patience, but what is patience except waiting on God to do the work while doing what is humanly possible: being prostrate?[151] Lest anyone think that this still depends on the sinner's capability, Hugh continues in paragraphs 8–9 by insisting that special grace is needed for repentance.

Even the passage cited by Mertens is followed by what Hugh calls the heart of his book, in which Hugh makes clear that the soul's disposing is nothing more than weak humility, for she can only have a foretaste of glory while living in this life's wretchedness. "In mystical theology a few words encompass endless meanings" and "the outstretched union of the spirit yearning to attain her Beloved increases by the Beloved's own free gift, which, in this unitive wisdom is not for someone who assembles external things into a set of writings, but for someone who perceives inwardly" (*via unitiva*, par. 30–31).

The soul must dispose herself. Yet in the end this disposing is nothing more than indigence (*via illuminativa*, par. 52), nothing more than hollowing out a cavity for God (*via unitiva*, par. 56). Speculative contemplation (out-thrusting *vision*) lacks the power to transform. Only outstretching, deifying-"defective" *love* can do this. *Amor deficiens*[152] is in fact *amor deificans*. "Therefore he alone grasps divine things who does not look at his feet in cognitive contemplation," Hugh says, citing Pseudo-Denis, but rather "stretches out to glimpse something at a distance" (*via unitiva*, par. 97). Be importunate, yearn so hard for God that your begging becomes obstinate and pertinacious (*via purgativa*, par. 8), but do not forget that you are still a beggar,[153] an importunate beggar, to be sure (*via unitiva*, par. 90), but a beggar just the same.[154]

Mystical union is nothing but God's work in the soul. God is the creditor, humans are the debtors, and God's work is forgiving the debt, which permits the human spirit to "bind" God in love and "freed of every sin, to know with experiential knowledge that God is pleasing" (*via illuminativa*, par. 52). In the Peltier text this sentence reads "make you, who were once an offense, pleasing to me." The Ruello text inverts the phrase at first (make me pleasing to you), then reverses it in the next sentence. Both make precisely the same point, the point that constituted Martin Luther's great discovery in relation to God's righteousness: Righteousness makes God pleasing to us, salvation reveals God's love and mercy to us, rather than being a process by which humans make themselves acceptable to God. Of course, this theology was present through medieval monastic theology. Bernard of Clairvaux's *On Grace and Free Will* is typical, not exceptional, as Protestant historians have portrayed it.[155]

Finally, so far we have referred frequently to the ascent to God. Equally important is the descent of wisdom from on high—a wisdom that cannot be known except by receiving. In the view of James Walsh, this is the main theme of Thomas Gallus's work.[156] We find similar claims in Hugh's *Roads to Zion*.

Contemplation as the importunate begging of an indigent human soul—the center of Hugh's spiritual theology is found in this striking image rather than in the scholastic *quaestio difficilis* for which he has become known.

IV. GUIGO DE PONTE'S TEACHING ON THE SPIRITUAL LIFE

A. Outline

The structure and style of Guigo's *On Contemplation* are, to modern tastes, convoluted and florid. While one could translate by paraphrasing Guigo in order to permit a more rapid reading, the translation offered here retains his clusters of images as reminders to twentieth-century readers that medieval treatises were meant to be read ruminatively, slowly. If approached this way, *On Contemplation* turns out to be quite readable. The following outline is offered for those seeking a quick grasp of the work.

Although Guigo offers his own recapitulation of the eleven steps of contemplation in book I, chapter 11, *On Contemplation* does not simply consist of a sequence of eleven steps, nor do his three books follow each other sequentially. Instead, the entire work consists of three different treatises that return to the same subject from different points of view.[157] The first book presents twelve degrees leading the soul consoled by these twelve divine consolations to the summit of contemplative union. Guigo covers the first seven steps rapidly (ch. 1–2), since the mystical life in a strict sense begins only with step seven. Guigo's stages are as follows:

Book I

1. The justification of the sinner (ch. 1).
2. Loving anxiety of soul, God's visit, the soul's desire to be purified through contrition (ch. 1).
3. The grace of compunction and sorrow (ch. 1).
4. Compassion and concern for neighbor (ch. 1).
5. Compassionate love for and meditation on the suffering of the Savior (ch. 2).
6. The desire to know Christ in his divinity (ch. 2).
7. The visit of the spouse who illuminates the soul's darkness (ch. 2).
8. Aspiration to be lifted up to contemplate the blessedness of saints in heaven; the beatitude of reason, of will, of memory; to consider God as source of all good, to return to oneself (ch. 3).
   [Chapters 4–6 continue step 8: sorrow for one's exile, purification of the conscience in preparation for the Eucharist (ch. 4); the need to recognize the reality of tears (ch. 5); obstacles (pride, love of earth, impiety, busyness, ignorance of oneself); the means of overcoming obstacles (humility, sorrow for sins, meditation on Christ, heaven) (ch. 6).]
9. Continual meditation on divine things (ch. 7), with information on the various faculties of the spirit and on movement toward God in the will, memory, and intellect.

10. The mask of obscurity in the secret of the heart (ch. 8); the spiral movement in exterior things; the circular movement in interior things.

11. The rectilinear movement in higher things (each of these spiral, circular, rectilinear movements has anagogical and speculative aspects [ch. 8]).

This leads to ecstasy of the spirit (ch. 9), which is still part of step eleven, and to the six manners of seeing God (ch. 10), the highest of which is rapture, or ecstasy, of spirit.

Step twelve is really a summary of the eleven degrees, organized according to two principles, two types, three movements, and four necessities (the necessities are reform of life, prayer, divine material, exercises [ch. 11]), two sets of five acts of preparation, four wings, four types of contemplation, and so forth (ch. 12).

Book II

Book II has three steps of mystical union, of which the first is introduced in chapter 1, while the second is discussed at length in chapters 1 through 5. The third step is dealt with in chapters 6 through 13. These three steps are:

1. Purification and listening to Christ (contrition, confession, etc.).
2. Intimate union with Christ by daily meditation on his life—again, the emphasis is on contrition, purification, joy, preparation, facility.
3. Contemplation of Christ's divinity.

For these three steps there are three necessary things:

1. Prayer of several kinds (ch. 6).
2. Spiritual matter (ch. 7).
   Guigo deals first with speculative contemplation (ch. 6–9), which has three degrees: attentive consideration, alluring meditation, inventive contemplation—that is, he deals with epistemological issues of truth, rational and suprarational knowledge.
3. Spiritual method (ch. 8–13).
   The method has three conditions (ch. 8): purity from exterior concerns, spiritual solicitude, humble devotion to godliness (chapter 9 is an excursus on devotion compared to oil).

Guigo addresses the method of *speculative contemplation* first (ch. 8–9), then turns to the method of *anagogical contemplation* (ch. 10–13)—by abnegation.

Anagogical contemplation also has three necessary things: prayer, matter, method (ch. 10); it also has three degrees: adhesion of the imagination to the humanity of Christ; adhesion of discernment to the divinity of Christ; adhesion of union, a life inflamed by devotion and affection.

Book III

This book, which deals with active and contemplative lives, is the longest of the three. It begins with the three degrees of the active life (ch. 1), then the degrees of the contemplative life (ch. 2). Four exercises follow, namely Guigo II's pattern of lectio, meditatio, oratio, and desiderium. Chapter 4 covers a sweeter, more intimate contemplation that is both speculative and anagogic. Chapter 5 then deals with speculative contemplation: physical, scholastic, infused (ch. 6ff). It has three degrees (partially repeating Book II): attentive consideration (ch. 6); alluring meditation (ch. 7–14); inventive contemplation (ch. 15).

This latter degree, inventive contemplation, is a rapid and rare vision, from which one falls rapidly back to an intermediate state (ch. 15–16). There one begins again by mortifying the old man and his vices—pride, vainglory, gluttony (ch. 17–20)—and acquiring virtues (ch. 21–22) such as sobriety, discretion, and fasting. In other words, the entire process is circular—at the end one returns again to the exercises of first degree (ch. 24). In the end, one must pursue the images of the intermediate degree (ch. 25), and guard patience as grace retreats (ch. 26).

Thus the third book, like the entire contemplative process, begins and ends with the active struggle against vices. The climax, mystical ecstasy, is in the middle. Although some have suggested that Guigo's treatise is not organized methodically,[158] it might be more accurate to say that its principle of methodical organization is not a linear or sequential one. Guigo has good spiritual and theological reasons for such a convoluted organization: Mystical theology is not sequential or linear-logical. Although mystical theology cannot be expressed in words, one can perhaps hint at its paradoxical complexity through a nonsequential structure of exposition.[159]

Guigo drew on a broad range of patristic and scholastic sources.[160]

He also alludes to Cicero and Seneca and incorporates an echo of Virgil (obtained via Bernard of Clairvaux, see I.13, n. 160), whom he juxtaposes with Saint Paul. Bernard, Aelred of Rievaulx, Anselm, Bonaventure, and Francis all contributed to his treatment of meditation on the Passion of Christ. In many ways he reflects the twelfth-century Carthusian tradition more fully than Hugh. His three books on contemplation are a web of Scripture texts of the sort written by Bernard of Clairvaux and other patristic writers.

B. The Theology and Spirituality of On Contemplation

1. Love and Knowledge

When Guigo reaches the third of the three steps of mystical union, namely contemplation of Christ's divinity, he points out that the third thing necessary is a method of anagogical contemplation (II.10–13), that is, a method of negation, of abandoning. Here Guigo bases himself explicitly on Hugh of Balma (he does not cite him by name but the identification cannot be doubted), for Hugh has written the definitive work on anagogical contemplation as far as Guigo is concerned. Admittedly, Hugh is not for beginners, Guigo cautions. Walach constructs an extended speculative argument, based on the notion that Guigo de Ponte is trying in this passage to clean up or tame Hugh of Balma's radicality. Walach believes that Guigo de Ponte was commissioned by the Carthusian Order to write a normative and safe treatise on contemplation that would counter Hugh's *Viae Sion*. The obscurity surrounding Hugh of Balma even within his own order thus indicates an embarrassed attempt to silence Hugh. By the same logic, the obscurity that surrounds Guigo de Ponte would militate against any notion that his work was authorized and favored by the order.[161]

For Guigo there can be no question that anagogical contemplation is truer than (II.10) and superior to (II.13) speculative contemplation, but he includes both. Guigo refers to the "Difficult Question" and the treatment of the unitive way without denying the importance of the long sections about meditation on the Lord's Prayer.

Guigo's primary treatment of speculative contemplation is found in Book III. The first degree of speculative contemplation is consideration of God's attributes, not in a wooden, abstract way, but in admiration and wonder. Thus even Guigo's treatment of speculative contemplation is put in anagogic, affective terms—just as we have seen in Hugh of Balma:

God's attributes give rise to marvel and gratitude in the soul's attentive consideration. In the second degree one is drawn in meditation to God (ch. 7–14), reaching the "contemplation that finds" in the third (ch. 15). In other words, into the lowest and most cognitive level Guigo weaves an affective element (see especially III.6).

Guigo draws on the monastic tradition of discretion and discernment,[162] more than on scholastic analysis. When he reaches the eleventh stage of being "affected toward God" (what is usually referred to as the "mystical ascent"), he describes it as "a direct and anagogical affected and utterly intimate clinging in both enjoyment and vision"—but then comments that it could also apply to the ninth stage.[163] The ascent is not merely linear and sequential; rather, a description of one stage can also apply to another. How does one know which is which?

> . . . if one wishes to understand these twelve steps, one must understand the individual steps and the meaning of words according to their characteristic implications. For in each of these steps there is some kind of meditation, affection, yearning, devotion, and clinging. For example, in penitence, or justification (which forms the first step), we find a penitent person expressing a sort of clinging in the words: *I have clung to your testimonies, Lord, let me not be put to shame* (Ps 118:31 [119:31]). One must take account of the words' properties according to their own specific import—otherwise it is easy to read something erroneously, especially if the one reading does not know how to employ spiritual experience to discern what he reads. (I.8)

Not linear analysis but the deft touch of long spiritual experience permits one to discern one stage from the other. Without *discretio,* the stages blur and blend into each other.

2. Grace and Yearning

As with Hugh of Balma, so too for Guigo the method employed in contemplation, the effort of the soul, consists in nothing more than yearning for God, in the work (*officium*) of imploring prayer that God will grant grace (II.6).

In Guigo's central chapter on "method," on the soul's "holy pursuits" (*sancta studia*), the very darts of aspirative prayer, the soul's devout exercises, are handed to the soul by the Lord, who "cracks open the cloud" so that the soul's aspirations, her "sharp arrows of godly affections," can penetrate. "Fed and formed in her in her infancy" she can attain the blessed vision only by longing which itself is given by God. "Ascending by clinging to God she is affected by thirst, and, being thus affected she clings to God all the more thirstily." God himself is the master who "teaches men holy knowledge by means of the grace of godly affections and devotions, showing them what things are to be sought from God" (II.8).

The soul can do nothing except wait on God like a lady-in-waiting (III.7), open herself to be penetrated by God, cling to him with wide-mouthed gaze, and hold on for dear life.

> The third step is the human spirit's yearning, unitive clinging in which she gently burns for God, . . . With love growing from her own fervor she opens herself to receive and in receiving is set on fire. Then with great longing she gazes wide-mouthed at celestial things and in some wondrous way tastes what she seeks to have. This tasting, moreover, is the clinging, the union, through which the pious spirit enjoys God, in whom she blissfully reposes. (II.10)

The human person is a beggar, devoid of any assets, completely empty-handed. He may press forward to his Lord, but he does so with the importunity of a beggar, completely empty-handed, utterly devoid of any confidence in his own merits. Precisely because of his empty-handedness, because of his needy wretchedness, he can beg importunately without being thought presumptuous. For corroboration, Guigo appeals to standard beggarly behavior in the mundane experience of his readers (II.5).

Guigo's words are strikingly reminiscent of Guigo I, prior of the Grande Chartreuse, and strikingly anticipatory of Martin Luther:

> By this alone are you just, that you acknowledge and proclaim you should be damned on account of your sins. If you say you are just, you are a liar, and are condemned by the Lord, the truth, as being contrary to Him. Say that you are a sinner, so that speaking the truth you may agree with the Lord, the truth, that you need liberation.[164]

3. Rapture and Presence

Guigo describes (I.9) four forms of overpowering of the human spirit (*excessus mentis*): (1) an extracorporal vision, (2) a rapture that exceeds the imagination, and (3) a rapture that surpasses human reason. For all of these he simply refers his reader to Richard of Saint-Victor. Then (4) there is a "rapture of otherness (*excessus alterationis*) in which the devout spirit passes beyond the bounds of bodily sensation and, raised on high in this matter, is taken up into God in a supernatural manner (*divinitus*)." This fourth term seems to have been invented by Guigo himself.[165] He reserves for heaven any sort of union of essence-with-essence (I.10), which implies that step eleven is not consummated until heaven. It may be experienced in some manner of foretaste here and now, but the wall of the flesh separates one from the blessed life (I.10).

Moreover, the overpowering of the spirit does not deprive the human spirit of her senses either actively or potentially; rather, "she is divinely abstracted from them and they are weakened so that she is neither held back by them from the vision of God nor separated from them, as noted above" (III.7).

Intellectual rapture cannot occur without affective rapture, nor vice versa, but the devout soul learns to discern between the two and employ each in its own way. Enjoyment of God, being affected into God, is nothing other than to have fruition of God's presence (*praesentialiter Deo frui*) (I.7).

V. HUGH'S AND GUIGO'S IMPACT ON CHRISTIAN SPIRITUALITY

A. Hugh

In surveying the later influence of these two texts, we can begin with the ways Hugh's fellow Carthusians employed *The Roads to Zion Mourn*. Guigo de Ponte's use of Hugh of Balma has been considered above (see section IV.B.1) and will be evident from the translation and notes that follow. One of the most convoluted paths taken by Hugh's treatise begins with Carthusians and ends in the heart of the fifteenth-century Devotio Moderna. A work variously titled *De via purgativa*, *Exercitatorium Cartusiense*, and *Exercitatorium monachale* has been attributed variously to the fourteenth-century Carthusian Heinrich Egher of Kalkar and to the fifteenth-century Carthusian Denis of Rijkel, who definitely wrote a work titled *De via purgativa*.[166] Unfortunately, the work has not survived. Denis's sixteenth-century editor at the Cologne Charterhouse, Dirk Loeher, published what we know as the *Exercitatorium Cartusiense* in 1532 under the title *De via purgativa*. Denis himself was familiar with the *Exercitatorium*, which was obviously circulating in his day.[167] The work is, in fact, based on Hugh of Balma's purgative way, and it circulated in longer and shorter versions. In the manuscripts it is most frequently attributed to Heinrich Egher van Kalkar, but the question cannot be settled.[168] The trail does not end, however, with the Carthusians. In several manuscripts we find the *Exercitatorium* inserted into Thomas a Kempis's *Imitation of Christ*, leading to the rather far-fetched hypothesis that Heinrich Egher van Kalkar played a role in the composition of the famous late medieval classic, the *Imitatio Christi*.[169] The meandering path taken by this portion of Hugh's treatise shows how much in the mainstream of late medieval piety Hugh's writings were.

The Carthusian Jakob of Jüterbog (Jacobus de Paradiso, d. 1465) at the Erfurt Charterhouse drew heavily on Hugh for his primer on mystical theology.[170] The Erfurt Charterhouse had two copies of Hugh's treatise.[171] The Austrian Carthusian Nicholas Kempf cites Hugh as a "more detailed" discussion of the linkage between the highest form of mystical union and the anagogical sense of Scripture in his *De ostensione regni Dei*, chapters 28 and 31 (Graz, Universitätsbibliothek, cod. 262),[172] and he makes use of Hugh throughout his *De mystica theologia*.[173] Kempf's reading of Hugh is discussed above. In 1516 Gregor Reisch, the learned prior of the Freiburg Charterhouse and confessor to Emperor Maximilian I, was asked by his former student, Johann Eck, professor at Ingolstadt and later Catholic reformer and apologist, to locate copies of the writings of Hugh of Balma and other writers during his travels as provincial visitator in the Rhineland.[174]

We have discussed Denis of Rijkel's use of an anonymous reworking of Hugh's *De via purgativa*. He made full use of Hugh's list of contemplative industries and shared his insistence that mystical contemplation is not as easy as some people think.[175] Regarding the contemplative ascent, however, in contrast with Kempf, who approved of Hugh's affective ascent, in much the same manner in which Vincent of Aggsbach interpreted it, Denis of Rijkel criticized any effort to separate the affective and intellective aspects. Yet he also expressly endorsed Hugh's aspirative method in its affectivity: "In grace as it is actually experienced, it is possible for the *affectus* to burn, seethe, and blaze up suddenly and unexpectedly toward God in a most ardent and marvelous manner, unaware of any cognition leading the way, especially when this briefly befalls the human spirit that has been distracted."[176] Richard Methley of Mount Grace Charterhouse in Yorkshire, who translated the *Cloud of Unknowing* from English into Latin in 1491, may also have known and used Hugh's work.[177]

Harald Walach's efforts to show influence by Hugh of Balma on various thirteenth- and fourteenth-century figures—Peter John Olivi (d. 1298),[178] the anonymous *Stimulus amoris* (written before 1300),[179] Margarete Porete (d. 1310),[180] Ramon Llull (d. ca. 1315),[181] Meister Eckhart (d. 1327),[182] Henry of Ghent (d. 1293),[183] and John of Kastl (fl. 1380-1400)[184]—are not persuasive.

Outside Carthusian circles, one of the frequently suggested uses of Hugh's work is the anonymous English devotional work, the *Cloud of Unknowing*. James Walsh and Rosemary Ann Lees have described in some detail the parallels between these two works, although direct influence is difficult to demonstrate and it is not easy to distinguish the impact of Thomas Gallus from that of Hugh.[185] While noting that many of the putative influences may well stem from a shared use of Thomas Gallus, John P. H. Clark also points out the remarkable similarity between the *Cloud*'s "teaching on unpremeditated and extremely brief prayer without distinct images" and Hugh of Balma's aspirative prayers.[186]

A popular anonymous devotional work of the late Middle Ages from Austrian-Bavarian circles, the early fifteenth-century *Alphabetum divini amoris*, draws directly from Hugh for its fourteenth chapter.[187] The great interest in Hugh among Benedictine monks at Tegernsee and Melk, together with the intervention in the controversy by the Carthusian Vincent of Aggsbach, is described above.

Jean Gerson was perhaps the most influential spiritual writer of the late Middle Ages. As noted in the discussion of the Tegernsee controversy above, André Combes ascribes a key role to Hugh of Balma as a commentator on Pseudo-Denis in the development of Jean Gerson's views on mystical theology during the period from 1420 to 1424. After October 1425, Combes argues, Gerson adopted a fully affective view of the mystical ascent along the lines of Hugh of Balma. On this last point Combes's views have not been universally accepted by scholars;[188] in any case, Hugh of Balma's status as a major commentator on Pseudo-

Denis was not limited to the Carthusians. (Still, Gerson's use of Hugh does not necessarily escape the Carthusian orbit, since Gerson may well have learned of Hugh's writings from his Carthusian contacts.)[189]

Quotations from Hugh by various fifteenth-century Dutch writers and a partial translation of *The Roads to Zion* into Dutch in the early fifteenth century (with the possibility that the entire treatise was translated into Dutch) also testify to Hugh's impact on late medieval spirituality. Hendrik Mande (d. 1431), one of the devotional and mystical writers of the Devotio Moderna movement, knew Hugh's treatise and drew from it for his teaching on aspirative prayer, including an emphasis on its unitive function (unlike other Modern Devout who wrote on this topic).[190] García de Cisneros, the Benedictine reformer of Valladolid and Montserrat, drew on the Latin text of Hugh of Balma for his *Ejercitatorio de la Vida espiritual* (1500).[191] A valuable testimony to the reception of Hugh of Balma among Carthusians in the late Middle Ages is Oxford Bodleian Douce 262, containing the *Cloud of Unknowing*, the *Epistle of Privy Counsel*, and the culminating portion of the *via unitiva* chapter of *The Roads to Zion Mourn*, together with selections from Thomas Gallus and Hendrik Herp.[192] At least part of Douce 262 seems to have been copied at the London Charterhouse within two decades of the heroic martyrdom of the London Carthusians, 1535–1537.

Hugh was not only popular among Benedictines and Carthusians. His more widespread influence in the fifteenth and sixteenth centuries probably owes more to two Franciscans: Rudolf of Biberach (fl. 1270–1326) and Hendrik Herp (d. 1477). Rudolf's *Septem itineribus in Deum* was, like Hugh of Balma's *Roads to Zion*, attributed to Bonaventure and published among Bonaventure's collected writings.[193] Whether Rudolf knew and used Hugh's work is unclear but doubtful; distinguishing the impact of Rudolf of Biberach from that of Hugh in the writings of Hendrik Herp is not easy. Anselm Stoelen[194] says he owed more to Jan Ruusbroec than to Hugh, but the prominent role Herp gives to aspirative prayer has led many scholars to assume he took it from Hugh.[195]

The fact that Hugh's treatise was published among the writings of Bonaventure, alongside Rudolf of Biberach, who may have used Hugh extensively, contributed to Hugh's impact on Spanish Catholic spirituality in the sixteenth century, together with Hendrik Herp (whose writings arrived in Spain after 1530).[196] As noted above, Melquíades Andrès Martín has called it a "fundamental book in the history of our [Spanish] spirituality" and "one of the keys of peninsular spirituality."[197] Andrès

Martín recognizes, however, that it played this role having been translated and modified under Franciscan auspices.[198]

In this guise it affected Francisco de Osuna (Franciscan, b. 1492; *The Third Spiritual Alphabet*,[199] available in a Classics of Western Spirituality translation).[200] Via Osuna it had an impact on later writers, for example, Francisco de Ortiz (Franciscan, 1497–1546).[201] *The Roads to Zion Mourn*, in Spanish dress, was cited by Bernardino de Laredo (1482–1540) for his *Subida del Monte Sion* (1535, 1538), whose impact, in turn, is seen in Teresa of Avila (ch. 23 of her autobiography). However, it is not easy to distinguish the impact of Balma from that of Herp.[202]

Other Spanish spiritual writers who used the Spanish version of Hugh of Balma include Juan de los Angeles (ca. 1536–1609), who reproduced the argument of the "Difficult Question" in his *Triunfos del Amor de Dios* and his *Lucha espiritual y amorosa de Dios*,[203] and Antonio Sobrino (Franciscan, 1536–1622).[204] Writings on mystical theology by the Franciscans Sánchez Ciruelo (1543), Gabriel de Toro (1548), and Francisco Ortiz Lucio (1608) also indicate influence from Hugh.[205] Nor was Hugh's influence unknown among Dominicans, despite the more intellectualist cast of that tradition—the Dominican Tomás de Vallgornera (ca. 1595–1665) made use of *Viae Sion lugent*.[206]

Jesuits also knew his work, for example, Jerome Nadal (1507–1580, secretary and biographer to Ignatius of Loyola and spiritual writer in his own right)[207] and Alvarez de Paz (1560–1620).[208] Ignatius himself briefly considered a vocation as a Carthusian lay brother at Seville, going so far as to have one of his household servants obtain a copy of the Carthusian rule.[209] Spaapen has argued at some length but not entirely convincingly for significant influence by Hugh on Ignatius via Guigo de Ponte (i.e., via Ludolf of Saxony), Garcia de Cisneros (see under Benedictines, above), and Denis of Rijkel.[210]

The Carmelite Jerónimo de Gracián (1545–1614) paraphrased and commented on Hugh (see p. 14 above, under editions), as did his confrère, Miguel de la Fuente (1573–1626?).[211] John of the Cross's use of aspirative prayer has also been linked indirectly to Hugh of Balma.[212]

Francisco de Osuna, Bernardino de Laredo, and other Spanish spiritual writers were interested both in Hugh's anagogical expositions of the Lord's Prayer (*via illuminativa*, par. 14–54) and in the question of total affectivity found in the *via unitiva* and the "Difficult Question."[213] As a result of the latter interest, Hugh was tarnished in the wake of controversies over the purported "quietism" (excessive passivity in the spiritual life) of the writings of John of the Cross. At the end of the seventeenth century, Hugh of Balma's treatise was denounced to Roman authorities by the Spanish Capuchin writer Félix Alamín.[214] In seventeenth-century France, the Capuchin Constantine of Barbanson, the English exile, Benedict of Canfield, and Lawrence of Paris all knew Hugh's work.[215]

In seventeenth- and early eighteenth-century Germany, Gottfried Arnold quotes Hugh of Balma more often than Bernard of Clairvaux.[216] Arnold's *Historie und Beschreibung der mystischen Theologie* (1703), a complete rewriting of his well-known *Die Erste Liebe*, marks a shift in his interest from patristic to medieval sources. He may have known Hugh indirectly, through the writings of Pierre de Poiret (d. 1719), who was very popular among Protestant and Catholic pietists in Germany and the Low Countries.

B. Guigo

Guigo de Ponte tells his reader to keep quiet about mystical union, and his caution seems to have been effective. His *On Contemplation* was not widely transmitted. But one of those who did use it, even if indirectly, was his fellow Carthusian of the Strasbourg Charterhouse, Ludolf of Saxony, who borrowed book II, chapters 1–5, for the prologue of his own *Vita Christi* meditations (partly via Michael of Massa [d. 1337], an Augustinian friar).[217] Since Ludolf did not cite Guigo by name, those who read Ludolf's book remained unaware of Guigo. One of those who read Ludolf was Ignatius Loyola;[218] by way of the Jesuits, Guigo's work made its silent way to Teresa of Avila and other early modern Catholic spiritual writers.[219] The hidden yet powerful influence of Guigo's *On Contemplation* continues to this very day: In his introduction to the Classics of Western Spirituality translation of Ignatius's writings, George E. Ganss, S.J., quotes several paragraphs from "Ludolph's own introduction" to the *Vita Christi* as particularly characteristic of Ludolf's influence on Ignatius. The paragraphs Ganss quotes in fact contain most of the first chapter of Guigo's book II, slightly modified by Ludolf.[220] Ganss argues for "striking" similarity between the spirituality of Ludolf (actually Guigo) and that of Ignatius, going so far as to say that Ludolf's words "may have been the germ of many features prominent in Ignatius' later Principle and Foundation [of the *Spiritual Exercises*], and his spirituality in general."

Denis of Rijkel[221] does appear to have used Guigo's work directly. Based on Dupont's description of the handwriting, Kent Emery even speculates that Denis may have been the copyist of the Stonyhurst manuscript of Guigo's *De contemplatione*, which Emery had not been able to study directly.[222] Dom Dupont cites one tangential point at which Nicholas Kempf shows some affinity to Guigo.[223] Richard Methley may also have known *On Contemplation*, although James Hogg remains skeptical of such claims.[224] John Mombaer (ca. 1460–1501), author of the *Rosetum*, another work of meditation on the life of Christ that had an impact on Ignatius of Loyola and others, also draws on Guigo in passing.[225]

VI. NOTES ON THE TRANSLATION
AND THE LATIN TEXTS

A. Manuscripts and Editions Used for the Present Translation

The present translation is the first complete translation into English of either work.[226] The translation of *Viae Sion lugent* is made from the text established by Francis Ruello for the critical edition in Sources Chrétiennes (Paris: Éditions du Cerf).[227] Scripture references have been supplied from the edition in *S. Bonaventurae Opera Omnia*, vol. 8, ed. A. C. Peltier (Paris: Vivès, 1866), 2–53, based on the Lyons Bonaventure edition of 1647, vol. 2:680 (other editions: Strasbourg, 1495; Vatican 1596, vol. 7:699; Venice, 1611, vol. 2; Venice 1754, vol. 22:344), supplemented by my own annotations at numerous points.

The following summary of the manuscripts and the editorial basis for Abbé Ruello's edition is drawn from the typescript summary he so graciously made available to me. The abortive effort at a critical edition by Pierre Dubourg, S.J., in the 1930s produced a manuscript census of seventy-one complete and twenty-one partial manuscripts of *Viae Sion lugent*. In addition, Dubourg knew of twelve manuscripts containing excerpts. Abbé Ruello has uncovered eighteen more fragments and glosses. Of the complete and partial manuscripts, Ruello used fifty-nine. The oldest manuscript is from the late fourteenth century, the majority are fifteenth-century copies. They fall into no special geographical concentration, apart from a distinct cluster of Austrian and Bavarian provenance in the fifteenth century. Ruello discerns two clear text families. One is quite close to the series of Franciscan editions derived from the 1495 Strasbourg first edition. This "A" family is remarkably homogenous. So too is the "B" family, which consists of the cluster of eighteen fifteenth-century Austrian-Bavarian manuscripts. The oldest manuscripts have the "A" text. Ruello faced a choice between basing his edition on (1) the "primitive" state of the work (the "A" family), or (2) a composite text based on an "A" manuscript combined with readings from the "B" family, or (3) the text as it circulated at the beginning of the fifteenth century in the Austrian-Bavarian circles where all the "Hugh of Balma scholars" seem to have been concentrated. He chose the third path.

Although one could argue that the present translation might best have been based on the "A" text, practically speaking the closest one can come to that "A" text prior to the publication of the Sources Chrétiennes edition[228] is the Peltier edition or one of the other early modern Franciscan editions. However, these are so full of transcription errors that in many cases the text is scarcely intelligible. Ruello's choice to follow the Austrian-Bavarian cluster of manuscripts has the virtue of being based on a real text that was actively used by people eager to make sense out of *The Roads to Zion*. This meant that they themselves had done some textual criticism and resolved some obscurities.

However, a comparison of Ruello's text (prior to publication and thus minus the critical apparatus) with the Peltier edition reveals a few instances in which the manuscripts in the Austrian-Bavarian text family were the victims of scribal omissions, largely due to eyeskips, earlier in the transmission of the text. That is a risk inherent in beginning farther down the chain of transmission. These may be supplied in the critical apparatus to the Ruello text when it appears; my notations to the effect that something is "missing in the Ruello text" refers to the text itself as he has assembled it from the Austrian cluster of manuscripts. I have not hesitated to fill in such omissions, drawing on the Peltier text. In a few instances where the Austrian-Bavarian manuscript tradition seems inferior in a word or two, I have likewise followed the Peltier text.

The situation with regard to Guigo de Ponte's *De contemplatione* is much simpler. The translation has been made from the critical edition by Dom Philippe Dupont, a monk of Solesmes Abbey, published as *Guigues du Pont, Traité sur la contemplation*, Analecta Cartusiana, 72 (Salzburg: Institut für Anglistik und Amerikanistik, 1985). Dupont's introduction gives descriptions of the five known manuscripts of Guigo's work: C = Charleville MS 56 (from the Charterhouse of Mont Dieu, fourteenth century); P = Paris, National Library MS Latin 14978 (from the Abbey of Saint-Victor in Paris, fifteenth century); M = Paris, Bibliothèque Mazarine cod. 960 (from the Celestine monastery at Sens, fifteenth century); S = Stonyhurst, England, Jesuit College, MS 68 (Charterhouse of Roermond in modern-day Belgium, fifteenth century); T = Tortosa, Cathedral Chapter Library, MS 252 (from the Charterhouse of Scala Dei in Spain, fifteenth century). The Charleville manuscript is really composed of excerpts from *De contemplatione*, rather than the full text; the two Paris copies are full of errors, with M having been copied from P (M lacks much of book III). Thus Dom Dupont chose the Stonyhurst and Tortosa manuscripts as the basis for his text.

I have had frequent resort to Dom Dupont's French translation, and most of the notes in the present volume are based on his notes identifying Guigo's sources.[229] While retaining the references to Migne's *Patrologia Latina*, I have added references to recent critical editions and have attempted to provide clear references to English translations wherever possible (with the exception of J. Bliss's translation of Gregory the Great's *Moralia in Job*, 4 vols. [1844–1850]). I have not attempted to give citations to any of the many editions and translations of the *Rule of Saint Benedict* and Thomas Aquinas's *Summa Theologiae*, or to the various English translations of Augustine's *Confessions* and *City of God*. Although the titles of patristic and medieval sources are normally given in Latin, the reader will find the titles of these works given in English in the bibliography.

B. Translation of Latin Terms

The way I have dealt with several Latin terms requires comment. Seldom is the word *virtus* translated by its misleading English cognate, "virtue"; rather, it has been rendered as "power," "strength," or "force." *Exercitium* was frequently employed by the two Carthusians translated here. It means "training," "practice," "endeavor," but for the sake of simplicity has also occasionally been translated by its cognate, "exercise." *Perfectus* is often translated as "completed," sometimes as "perfect." *Anima* and *animus* are normally both translated as "soul." Although in classical usage *animus* referred to the animating force that makes a body live and move, Hugh and Guigo seem to have used *animus* as essentially equivalent to *anima*. I have generally used feminine gender where Hugh or Guigo use either *anima, animus,* or *mens*. Where they use *peccator* or another noun with grammatically masculine gender to refer to the human person, I have used masculine gender pronouns in my translation. This provides some alternation between masculine and feminine pronouns in

INTRODUCTION

English without resorting to awkward "he/she" and "he or she" combinations or impersonal plurals or "one," "oneself," and so forth. The words *pius/a/um* and *pietas* are particularly nightmarish for the English translator. The cognates "pious" and "piety" have been ruined by generally pejorative connotations over the past several centuries. In Latin, these words carried meanings that ranged from "respectful," "loving," "worshipful," "devout," "good," "goodly," "godfearing," "godly," to "affectionate," "affected," "tender," "gentle," "kind," "benevolent," "dutiful," "faithful," "loyal." With trepidation I have resorted to "godly" as normal practice. *Purgatio* and *purgare* have frequently been rendered as "cleansing" and "to cleanse" rather than "purgation" and "to purge" ("cleansing," "cleansed," and "purified" are also used to translate *munditia, mundare,* and *mundus/a/um*), to remind us of connotations broader than those borne by "purgation" in modern English. Given the context of contemplative spirituality, I have occasionally translated *familiariter* and *familiaris* as "intimately" and "intimate," although in Latin they can also simply refer to belonging to the same household, to "being at home," which, of course, did not mean the same thing in an ancient or medieval household as in a modern Western household.

Gradus is translated as "step," occasionally as "stage" or "degree." *Suspiro, suspirium,* and so forth, have been translated as "to sigh" and "sigh," and so forth. *Excessus mentis* is usually rendered as "raptured," despite misgivings about potential misunderstandings. Its literal meaning is "carried away" or "carried beyond" oneself—which is what "rapture" should, but no longer does, mean in English. *Immediatus* and its variants have been translated either as "direct" and "directly" or as "unmediated" and "unmediatedly," since "immediately" and "immediate" are not commonly understood today as meaning "without mediation."

Anagogicus/a/um could best be translated as "uplifting" or "upwardly" rather than by its simple cognate, anagogic. The latter is not widely understood in English, but "uplifting" is probably too bland to capture the meaning of the Latin technical term. Guigo de Ponte defines what he means by *anagogical* in *On Contemplation,* book 2, chapter 10; Hugh of Balma defines and illustrates it in the *via illuminativa* portion of *The Roads to Zion.* Perhaps even more useful is the vivid and intimate scene sketched by Guigo in *On Contemplation,* I.7:

> Once she has discovered a drop of honeyed dew, the loving spirit can no longer appear before God empty-handed, so she

brings him rich sacrifices of pure and robust prayer, coated with the oil of the Holy Spirit and set on fire with darts of glowing charity. She feels as if she not merely touches but actually directly wounds her Lord's heart. Called by his voice, she clearly catches sight of his presence as she looks up at him while clinging yearningly to him. That is what it means to see God. Hence Bernard says: "To cling to God is nothing other than to see God, which is granted, with special joy, only to pure hearts."

The words here translated as "looks up at him" are *aspectum anagogicum,* literally, an "anagogic sight." In this context Guigo makes clear that it is really a very simple matter of looking up longingly from the midst of a tight embrace. He deliberately uses the imagery of human love with conventional gender roles: The woman (human soul) responds to her Lover's voice quite naturally and simply with an upward glance. (This is precisely Hugh of Balma's imagery in *via unitiva,* par. 83.) That upward glance is the "anagogical" ascent. The reader will do well to keep this scene in mind when encountering the term "anagogical" elsewhere in this volume.

Consurgere and *consurrectio* have not been translated as "ascent," for that word is less dynamic than what would seem to be required,[230] especially in Hugh of Balma's use. It has been rendered as "to surge up" or as "upsurge." Similarly, although *tendentia* and its variants could quite properly be translated by "tendency" or "inclination," these terms would not capture the dynamism intended by Hugh. I have resorted to "stretch," "thrust," "drive," and even "urge." *Extensio, extendere,* and so forth, are translated normally as either "outreach" or "to reach out"/ "to stretch," although, as Kurt Ruh points out, the term as used by medieval spiritual writers also carries the connotation of expansiveness.[231]

I have often translated *contemplatio* and *contemplare* as "gaze" and "to gaze," to avoid the generally bland connotation carried by "contemplation" in English. "Speculation" and "envisioning" are used interchangeably to translate *speculatio.*[232] *Meditatio* really means something more than what is implied by its English cognate: It connotes repetitive practicing, a mulling over until one has almost learned something by heart. However, in the absence of a convenient circumlocution, I have generally employed "meditation" to translate *meditatio.* (For *intelligentia, scientia, ratio, mens,* and *cogitatio,* see the first section of this Introduction.)

Phantasmata is translated as "phantasms," to avoid the misleading connotations of "fantasy" in modern English. Phantasms are simply images that appear in the human mind/soul/spirit as part of the process of perception, intellection, and reflection.

Iustitia has normally been translated as "righteousness" rather than as "justice," since the latter English term has taken on largely secular connotations, leaving "righteousness" to bear nearly all the freight once borne jointly by "justice" and "righteousness" in English. (Occasionally *iustitia* and *iudicium* have been translated as "justice" or "judgment" to preserve the alliterative wordplay of the Latin text.) The Douai-Rheims version of the Scriptures generally uses "justice" or "just" to translate *iustitia* and *iustus;* in the present translation, the relevant Scripture quotations have normally been modified to "righteousness" and "righteous" for the sake of consistency.

Some terms defy a single, uniform translation into English. *Sentire* is variously translated to "sense," "feel," or "perceive." Had "happy" retained the meaning of "blessed" in English, *miseria* and its variants could be rendered as "unhappy" or "unhappily." Instead, I have called on "sinfulness," "wretchedness," or "weakness," occasionally "hapless," depending on the context. In medieval spiritual writings "human weakness, or frailty" (*humana infirmitas, humana fragilitas*) effectively meant human sinfulness. It has been translated here as "weakness" or "frailty," and readers should keep its broader implications in mind.

Finally, although it seemed archaicizing to translate *caritas* consistently as "charity," nonetheless, because medieval theologians did generally distinguish between *caritas* and *amor/dilectio*, I have rendered *caritas* as "charity." It is perhaps noteworthy that Hugh of Balma distinctly prefers *amor* to describe the relation of the human spirit to God. The first instance of *caritas* in his work is in the purgative way, par. 10, where it refers to God's *caritas* enveloping the world, and he uses it sparingly thereafter. Guigo, in contrast, uses *caritas* frequently, although he occasionally employs *amor* or *dilectio* where one might expect to find *caritas*.

In Guigo's *On Contemplation*, III.16 consists entirely of verbatim quotation from Bernard of Clairvaux, but has been included here for the convenience of the reader. One paragraph of III.6, which repeats the conclusion of II.7, has been omitted, with an explanatory note to the reader. Ellipsis marks (. . .) indicate a repetitive clause that has been dropped (e.g., III.11, line 3).

Direct quotations from Scripture are italicized with references given in parentheses in the text. Indirect allusions to Scripture are not italicized, and the references are given in the notes. Scripture quotations are generally taken from the Douay-Rheims version, with the now archaic "thee," "thou," and "thine" modified to "you" and "your." References to the Psalms are given in the Vulgate numbering, with the Hebrew number following in brackets. Scripture references not already found in the Peltier edition have been added by the present editor, who did not have access to the critical apparatus of the forthcoming Sources Chrétiennes edition by Abbé Francis Ruello.

One manuscript of Guigo de Ponte's *De contemplatione* (Tortosa) adds a large number of explanatory glosses, which make its text very wordy. For the most part these have been ignored. Where the glosses seemed particularly helpful, they have been summarized, rather than translated, in the notes.

Hugh of Balma

The Roads to Zion Mourn

PROLOGUE

A. True and False Wisdom

1. *The roads to Zion mourn because no one comes to the solemn feast* ♦ (Lam 1:4). The prophet Jeremiah spoke these words while ceaselessly lamenting his people's captivity. The same words could, however, be pronounced by any perceptive person who sees how people everywhere stray from paths of righteousness and roads of justice and fall into spiritual captivity. *Roads* refers to the yearnings by which loving souls living in earthly bodies are raised beyond all reason and understanding to God and to the celestial city Jerusalem. These pathways are said to *mourn* because no one pays attention to the *solemn feast*, since clerics and layfolk alike have cast off true wisdom and immersed themselves in worldly delights and useless curiosities. Yet there is something even more deplorable and worthy of limitless lamentation with heartfelt tears: Just as the people of Israel once abandoned worship of their Creator to serve idols made with hands, so too, in our day and age, many religious, indeed, many well-known and respected men, have abandoned the true wisdom in which God alone is worshiped perfectly and inwardly and is adored by single-minded lovers. Instead they wretchedly fill themselves with all sorts of knowledge, as if to fabricate idols for themselves out of various newfound proofs.[1] Diabolically inspired, these ideas so absorb and take possession of the human spirit that they leave no place for true wisdom.

2. They have been so unhappily held captive by the *painful occupation that God gave the children of men* (Eccl 1:13) that they have no vent by which the soul's flaming affections of love might reach her Creator. For God did not intend that the soul he created should be stuffed so full of sheepskin copybooks that his goodness is pushed aside; rather, he intended the soul as the seat of wisdom where the heavenly city's king of peace, namely God the Most High, might reside. This wisdom—which is known as "mystical theology" and was set forth by Paul the Apostle and written down by Denis the Areopagite his disciple—is the same wisdom that stretches toward God by love's longing. As far as the east is from the west, so incomparably does mystical wisdom excel all

69

created knowledge. For the learned of this world teach other kinds of knowledge, but the human spirit can learn this wisdom only from God directly, not from any mortal man.

3. Mystical theology is written in the heart by divine illuminations and heavenly dews; creaturely knowledge is written on parchment with a goose quill and ink. Mystical theology says: "Enough!" for through this wisdom the human mind finds the source of everything, namely God the Creator, and rests most intimately in the one who is the fountain of all goodness and happiness. Creaturely knowledge, in truth, never says "Enough!" for we rightly conclude that the person who cares not for highest wisdom strays from highest truth, like a blind man enveloped in darkness. Thus the infatuated soul stuffed full of human discoveries takes many detours. Mystical wisdom warms the loving *affectus* and brightens the intellect; other knowledge, whenever it finds a heart devoid of true wisdom, inflates it and frequently darkens the intellect with varied opinions and diverse errors. Therefore, having left behind human curiosity, captive as it is to useless knowledge, proofs, and opinions, the religious soul ought to rise yearningly by love's ascent to the source of all, in whom alone she may find truth. To preserve more gladly this newfound precious jewel, which she once loved badly or not at all, she ought all the more carefully[2] to forsake other things.[3]

4. Yet although this highest wisdom cannot be taught by men, we set forth here how anyone who attends the school of God, even an [illiterate] layperson, can receive this wisdom directly from God. Through love's affectedness it so exceeds all understanding that no philosopher, scholar, or secular master, no matter how diligently he applies himself to human wisdom, can grasp it.

B. The Threefold Path

5. This way to God is threefold, consisting of a path of cleansing, in which the human spirit is disposed for learning true wisdom; an illuminative path, in which the pondering spirit is ignited with the fire of love; and a unitive path, in which the spirit carried aloft by God alone is led beyond every reason, knowledge, and understanding. For, when a bridge is being built, we note that the builders first construct a wooden framework, over which the solid stonework is assembled. When the structure is complete, the supporting wooden framework is removed completely. So it is with the human spirit, which, though at first imper-

fect in love, begins to rise to the perfection of love by meditation until, strengthened by much practice in unitive love, she is raised far beyond herself by love's fiery affections and aspirations to the right hand of her Creator. Faster than can be thought, without any cogitation leading the way or keeping her company, as often as she pleases, hundreds or thousands of times, day or night, the human spirit is divinely drawn by countless yearning aspirations to possess God alone.

6. Thus any new disciple may rise by stages to the perfection of this knowledge by applying himself zealously to the cleansing way, which is the beginner's or child's path. It begins with these words: *Justice and judgment are the preparation of your throne* (Ps 88:15 [89:14]). After a short while, perhaps a month or two, subject to expedience, he can rise to love by pondering, bathed in superradiant divine light. Should anyone think it presumptuous that a soul wrapped up in all sorts of sins dare ask Christ for love's union, she should remind herself that there is no danger as long as she first kisses his feet by recalling her sins, then kisses his hand by recognizing his favors to her, and finally, advances to the kiss of the mouth,[4] desiring Christ alone, clinging to him by fiery affections alone. Moreover, the human spirit can properly ascend by pondering as she says the Lord's Prayer, to which we shall return later. This is the illuminative way, which begins thus: *Night shall be my light in my delights* (Ps 138:11 [139:11]). Then the soul steps up to a much higher level, in which, as often as she wishes, without any cogitation leading the way, she is directly affected into God, something that cannot be taught by any sort of human effort.

7. Thus, through practice in the cleansing and illuminative ways and under the inward instruction and direction of God alone, the soul learns experientially what no mortal science or eloquence can unlock. For love alone teaches most inwardly what neither Aristotle nor Plato nor any other mortal philosophy or science ever could or ever can understand. This means that each rational soul can learn her knowledge from the loftiest and eternal Professor, knowledge in which all reason, knowledge, and understanding falls away, and the *affectus*, disposed by love and transcending all human understanding, soars above,[5] steering the spirit solely by the rule of unitive love toward him who is the source of all goodness. This, therefore, is *mystical theology*, that is, the hidden divine word with which the human spirit, disposed by ardor of love, converses secretly with Christ her Beloved in the language of the affections.

C. An Outline of the Present Work

8. We shall proceed in the following manner in our consideration of mystical theology: First the path of cleansing will be introduced under three headings: (a) how the soul ought to be cleansed; (b) how to obtain abundant grace by genuine prayer; (c) how a sinner should pursue complete forgiveness of sins. Second, we come to the path of illumination, under which two topics are set forth: (a) the usual manner of employing meditation on the Lord's Prayer to enable the human spirit to surge up in love, and (b) how the same path of spiritual exposition of the Lord's Prayer can be used anagogically[6] to refer all Scripture completely toward God. Third, we shall draw conclusions regarding the unitive path, which begins with the words "O Wisdom which proceeds from the mouth of the Most High,"[7] revealing how sublime a life and what consummate virtues are acquired through mystical wisdom, making those who train for it all the more hungry for it.

Should this seem too difficult for some readers, on account of the depth of knowledge or obscurity of language found on the third path, which transcends all understanding, let them keep training on the path of cleansing, followed by the illuminative path. For suddenly they will sense and glimpse within themselves, solely by God's inward working, something of the third path, either in written words or while listening to someone else.

9. Now this wisdom [in the third, unitive, path] requires, first, that one perceive truth experientially within oneself, after which one can readily evaluate the meaning of all the words that have to do with mystical wisdom by comparing them with other teaching. This wisdom differs from all other areas of knowledge, because it has to be put to use in oneself before its words can be understood. In short, the practical precedes the theoretical. In other sciences one must first understand words before one can know what is being learned. Now the more eminent the teacher, the faster one comes into possession of knowledge. It is better to be a learner in mystical wisdom, with God as teacher, than a master who perfectly understands one of the liberal arts, a skilled craftsman or practiced architect in one of the mechanical arts.[8]

Second, as the Scripture passage *Approach him and be enlightened* (Ps 33:6 [34:5]) indicates, we shall teach how the rational soul might be fully instructed through all the creatures, both higher and lower, about attaining love of the Creator.[9]

Third, the text of the *Mystical Theology* itself will be clearly expounded. Although it contains few words, nevertheless its meanings and knowledge are almost endless.[10] Through full understanding of the difficult passages of the books written by Blessed Denis as well as the entirety of the Old and New Testaments, the hidden sense will shine forth for true lovers. For just as many rivulets flow out of a single spring, trickling down into almost countless rivers, and just as an almost countless number of lines proceed from a single central point, so too from understanding these few words that are expounded here the spirit is thoroughly taught how to be united to God and how to be brought to her supreme apex, where she experientially discovers the source of all wisdom. From this conjunction the faithful disciple learns far more diversely and richly than knowledge of the lower sciences permits. Such learning comes by means of well-chosen words that expound sacred Scripture in preaching that aims to ignite the hearts of its hearers.[11]

Fourth, we set forth eight practices through which the soul is wisely taught to acquire this wisdom and, once acquired, to maintain it.[12]

Finally, in response to those little minds who attack this supreme wisdom and say that the one's *affectus* never ascends unless led by forethought and meditation, a disputation employing both authorities and reasons is offered to convince them of their error and effectively unravel the knotty confusion surrounding the truth of this wisdom. This disputation argues that, without being led by prior mediating discernment, the soul is experientially raised above herself, transported by love alone, as often as she wishes.[13] For neither does reason understand nor understanding see; rather, as it is said in Scripture: *Taste and see* (Ps 33:9 [34:8]).

I. CONCERNING THE PATH OF CLEANSING

A. How the Soul Is Cleansed by Recalling Sins and God's Favors

1. *Justice and judgment are the preparation of your throne* (Ps 88:15 [89:14], cf. 96:2 [97:2]). When the soul wishes to attain perfect union with the heavenly Bridegroom through an affected spirit, she hungers for the bread of angels that feeds the blessed spirits in glory. Since she dwells here below in wretchedness, she must be willing to be filled with a few falling crumbs (Mt 15:27; Mk 7:28; Lk 16:21), ascending step-by-step through the threefold angelic office and lifted up by divine infusion,

since both the Church Triumphant and Church Militant are restored, revived, and glorified by the same celestial bread and the same wisdom.[1] Angels[2] have a triple office: to cleanse, illuminate, and perfect. So too the soul who desires to ascend in this life to that which absorbs the angels in glory—to the Most High[3]—should imitate them. First she ought to be cleansed, then enlightened by divine lightning, and finally, be set in place on the highest peak, on the summit of unitive, affective love.

2. First we must talk about the first path, the path of purgation. It is something of a matter for children, for beginners. On it a spirit as yet unshaped by human or mortal example pursues nothing but heavenly teachings. Even a simple, uneducated layperson can be experientially raised up from a practical to a theoretical illumination[4]—but only through divine manifestation.

Yet before this can take place, let wisdom, that is, the most blessed God, make herself at home in the rational spirit, according to the Scripture: The soul of the just [righteous] is the seat of wisdom[5]—for the soul ought to pass judgment and bring justice [*justitia*] on herself. She should judge herself because, sadly enough, when she turns away from and abandons the Creator as she turns toward the creature (as occurs with every mortal sin), she despises the Creator. Therefore she ought to humble herself fully so that, just as her contempt for her Creator formerly called forth his verdict on her sins, now her beginner's humiliation might call forth equal mercy from him. Driven by her sins, the soul once transformed delight in the Creator into delight in the creature. Let righteousness now arrive: since she once so delighted in the creature, let her now sorrow, or at least sorrow at her inability to sorrow, so that what God judges to be an offense might mercifully be perceived to have been set right through human pain. For Scripture says: *As much as he once boasted of and enjoyed himself, so now grant him torment and sorrow* (Rv 18:7). Thus does the medical art employ two contraries, namely humility as a medicine for the original contempt, and sorrow over sins to counter the original enjoyment of them. Thus may the soul, putting forth new growth as it were, be joined through a unitive taste of burning love to him who is the highest majesty and never-failing goodness. Now, something must be said about the suitable and compelling means to acquire this humiliation and sorrow for sin.

3. Even if this purgative path seems to be somewhat childish (especially in light of what is to follow), unless the human spirit expectantly fixes her attention on divine things and advances with care, she will never in this life arrive in practice at either knowledge of God or divine

things or at the fire of unitive love, nor will she be kept safe from those lower things that devour their owners. The soul should humble herself in the following manner: First she should revisit her sins in some sort of hidden place, especially in the hidden silence of the night. She should review the main ones succinctly, lest the devil lead her to delight in what should be providing her with bitter medicine. With her face turned toward the heavens, let her enumerate ten or twelve of her main sins in God's sight, as if she were speaking directly to him. As she names them, let her sigh, exalting God in everything and putting herself down as much as she can. She might use the following words or whatever form seems best to her: "Lord Jesus Christ, I am a most wicked sinner, more hapless and abominable than everyone else. I have offended your majesty and mercy so greatly and in so many ways that I am no more able to list them than one can number the multitudinous sands of the sea." She should sigh and groan there as best she can, because, just as a file applied to iron pushes away a bit of the iron's rust with each grating stroke, so too any sort of sigh or groan removes something of the rust of sin, even that which remains after the infusion of grace. Cleansing herself more and more after this fashion, the soul is raised by divine aid[6] to perceive things which reason does not research and understanding does not glimpse.

4. To bring humility and consternation directly home to a person, let him, as best he can, recall before God, first generally and then specifically, the divine favors granted him from on high despite his ingratitude. First let him recall that great nobility in which God created him from nothing, in which God created him according to God's own form, saying: "Lord, have you not brought me forth after your image? Though I was nothing before that, you made me so noble that I might hold on to you by grace in this present life and contemplate you face-to-face in glory. Yet I so provoked your stern judgment that, apart from your help, it would have been better for a wretch like me never to have been born, never to have seen the light of this present life."

Second, let him reflect on the favor of the divine incarnation, saying, "Lord, are you not the highest King of angels, who nonetheless so thoroughly made yourself nothing for my sake that you took upon yourself our wretchedness and humbly took to the road like a beggar and tramp? And I? Far from humbling myself, Lord, I despised your majesty by impudently extolling myself, trading you, the fount of happiness, for the momentary misery of this life. Whereto then shall I flee? *If I ascend into the heavens, you are there; if I descend into hell, you are present* (Ps 138:8 [139:8]).

5. After persisting for a while in the second step, let him march on to the third, namely, to recollection of the Lord's Passion, saying, "It is not enough, Lord Jesus Christ, that you stoop so low as to take on the humanity of mortal flesh while remaining God; rather, in order to take away the misery of all mortals you endured such fearful blows, such innumerable wounds, that from the sole of your foot to the top of your head no part of your body remained unspattered by your most sacred blood. What then should a wretch like me do, when I—the cause of your death—not only do not repay your goodness but instead further provoke you with my stinking misdeeds? Everything in the world, from heaven's highest pivot to the deepest point of hell, would have every right to battle against me. Therefore let all creatures serve the Lord by rising up against me, vindicating their Lord and Creator on me." Reflect for a while on the Lord's Passion in this fashion, so that, by love's probing, the human soul might reach the wound in Christ's side and be rewarded in touching the hidden divinity that lies deep within.

These three steps make up the reflection on the general favors, those which the Most High grants not merely to some but to all. Their generality underscores the magnitude of divine mercy.

6. After this he should consider what the Father of all consolation confers not on everyone but specifically on him, on someone called by divine mercy to the priestly office or to the religious life of the Carthusian Order.[7] For this path of cleansing belongs solely to those who flock together far from the worldly path.[8] Like a dove or a turtledove in the wilderness, in contemplative retreat, feeble though they may be,[9] they strive to fly above themselves, undergirding by the verdict of conscience the process of the removal of all mortal guilt.

7. First let him ponder that the Most High has called him from his miserable darkness to God's unchangeable truth, while leaving behind, mired in misery and worldly morass, many who are more worthy, more powerful, and in many ways prepared for a more abundant influx of divine grace.

Second, the penitent should consider the favor of God's mercy less in light of this world's misery than in light of hell's misery. For many who are guilty of lesser offenses in the eyes of divine majesty nonetheless remain under the lasting penalty of divine malediction, while this penitent, who much more deserved the same penalty, has instead been summoned to radiance of grace in this present life and to the prize of eternal happiness in the life to come—not by his own merits, but by the Creator's free generosity. Consider the following analogy: An earthly king hangs a thief. To another thief guilty of greater crimes he then grants praise equal in measure to the ignominy meted out to the condemned man. Such a king acts justly and he acts solely in mercy—the mercy proper to an earthly king, a mercy that directly contradicts what the pardoned thief deserved.

Third, let the sinner consider to what he is called, for the Redeemer's grace does not call him to the rule of Saint Augustine or Saint Benedict, but rather to that most sacred rule that Christ himself chose when he was led into the desert and fasted constantly for forty days and nights,[10] taking up for himself his forerunner's rule and keeping that rule himself, thereby showing us how to keep it. This rule exceeds other ways of life to the same degree that the divine word surpasses human doctrine.

8. Persisting thus in prayer, the penitent thinks not of himself but aims his speech directly to God, humbly referring to God not only general and specific divine favors but also the sinner's sins, reviewing them according to an inward order taught to him by God himself. Disconcerted by recalling his sins and God's favors, he now may take to the path of humiliation, saying "Lord, Father of all compassion, I cannot right the wrongs that I have miserably perpetrated in your sight, and I am unable to respond to the favors you have conferred on me despite my unworthiness. Because I may not destroy myself, you ought to put an end to me in my misery; yet, should you deign otherwise,[11] then send your warrior angel to receive my servile submission.[12] In other words, if out of mercy you choose not to carry out my deserved punishment, and, since I cannot kill myself, I shall do what I can[13]—like a pardoned thief give myself to you in perpetual service, never to forsake your service for the rest of my days." Then let him fall on his face, lowering himself utterly to exalt the Most High, whom he has offended. A more abject humbling of oneself calls forth more rapid and abundant divine mercy.

Now the principle of divine congruence means that, when the most devoted Father sees the sinner prostrate before his face, God must grant him sorrow for his sins, or at least sorrow that he lacks sorrow, so that by these two aforementioned remedies[14] the cleansed soul might recover what he once forfeited and might be restored to something greater than he formerly was.[15] If, however, through the steps outlined above, he should be unable to arrive at an effective degree of sorrow, let him simply cling to these words: It is enough for the Creator if a man does what he can.[16] Sometimes, knowing the outcome of the matter, God himself withdraws, depriving the sinner of consolation of sorrow for sin and, by testing the sinner, divinely sustaining the sinner's patience. This means that he will ultimately receive more ample consolation when he is finally granted from on high even greater contrition than he would otherwise have known.

B. Preparing to Ask for Forgiveness: Praise God

9. Yet, since the aforementioned things cannot be accomplished without special grace, we must consider how someone on the path of purgation might go about imploring God for grace. With eyes of sense perception we notice how a court jester, eager to gain some temporal favor from a prince without risking refusal, first praises the prince in all sorts of ways, and only then asks him to grant the favor. So too a new spiritual jester, disdaining the deceitful world, ought to proceed forthrightly.

10. Although God in himself cannot be named, we do name him when we name the things he causes, and we extol his magnificence through them. We extol him, first, because he is the origin and beginning of every corporeal and spiritual creature. Second, and somewhat more sublimely, we praise him because angelic and human spirits in glory are made blessed and lack nothing as they contemplate God's inexpressible beauty in its fullness. Third, we have an even more lofty reason to praise God—because all creatures, whether rational or irrational, submit to his majesty as the Most High himself has commanded. Fourth, we praise him for his noble creature, humankind, especially with regard to those who serve him in charity as their Creator. To his children dwelling in a life subjected to misery, the Father offers many gifts of interior consolation as advance indications of future blessedness and blessing, indicating that those who seem to exist in [this world's] nothingness are sons, sons of the Most High. Fifth and finally, we extol him because of the way he treats sinners. No matter how great the sins they have vainly labored long to remove as they knock on the door of divine goodness, he gathers them by divine clemency into his bosom of charity and mercifully writes off the sins they have committed. Indeed, those who have offended him most abominably may find richer and more precious favors falling from heaven than do those who are more innocent. Thus divine goodness extends all the way from a primordial outpouring

of divine grace to those dwelling in the dregs of sin. These five praises are captured succinctly in the following five words: Good, Beautiful, Lord, Sweet, Merciful.

C. Asking for Full Forgiveness of Sins

11. Having praised in this way, the penitent now can pursue the real point at hand—with confidence he can beg God for full forgiveness of his sins. This form of prayer and petition is taught in the *Canticle* when the Bridegroom says to the Bride: *Your voice is sweet and your face is charming*[17] (Ca 2:14). "Your charming face" refers to the way cleansing from sins drives away the cloud that darkens the face, and "your sweet voice" refers to whatever words one uses to praise the Bridegroom in a special way. Such names of praise for God are properly called songs of songs and are so suited to the soul that she may find hidden sweetness when she directs herself to God with these words, becoming fully united within herself in the pull of these words, rather than dissipating herself in wordy narrations or prolonged chatter.

Therefore, as often as possible, say, "O Good, Beautiful, Lord, Sweet, and Merciful, have mercy on this sinner whom you redeemed with your precious blood." Concentrating solely on this (that the Redeemer's mercy might forgive the sins she has committed) and being careful not to lapse into mere wordiness, let her pray these or similar phrases with growing affectedness.

12. Now, if the human spirit is to see her yearning fulfilled, she ought to take a cue from the manner in which God pours himself out. For the Spiritual Sun, Jerusalem the Heavenly City, spreads her rays of goodness over the good and the bad alike. So too the human spirit ought to implore the Creator from the bottom of her heart to extend his forgiveness to everyone bearing the image of the most Blessed Trinity, not just to herself or to those close to her. May the Creator redeem all those he has created, coming to their aid mercifully, regardless of what they deserve. It cannot be doubted that the human spirit calls forth and obtains divine mercy more speedily when she seeks out the traces[18] of the Creator of all mankind and the Redeemer of all mortals as he generously showers his charity on all. In some instances she may restrict her petition to prayers for herself and for specific others, yet charity is always spreading itself more widely, and, as far as she can, she ought to employ the same solicitously affective manner that she uses for herself in her prayers for everyone else. And so she should

pray: "Good, Beautiful, Lord, Sweet, and Merciful, have mercy on all sinners, whom you have redeemed with your precious blood." And then, as far as possible, let her imagine, as she says, "Have mercy," that the entire world is bowing in genuine worship and fitting reverence toward its Creator.

13. Yet excessive carnality and fickleness keeps the human spirit from making the sort of entreaties that would be most helpful. Therefore, the spirit ought to take a cue from those of high standing at the court of a king or the pope. When someone of this rank sees that he cannot accomplish his purpose by himself, he approaches another magnate at court to ask him to intercede and to entreat reverently on his behalf. Should a poor man find a highly placed mediator at court who nonetheless is humbly ready to hear the poor man's prayer, and, beyond that, ready to find others to intercede alongside himself; someone so intimately beloved by the pope that the pope wishes to deny him nothing, then even a pauper can obtain his desire without being upbraided or rejected in any way.

14. Now, since the Blessed Virgin excels all other saints in these qualities, the human spirit ought to run to her, saying, "You are most merciful, more humble than anyone else, and most powerful toward those who turn to you. For you set right the ruin of the angels, through you the gate of life is opened to saints, and thus you who proclaimed yourself a pauper are acclaimed by all alongside the dearly beloved Eternal King, whom you suckled at your holy breasts, thereby joining him to you with the inexpressible bond of love. I ask that through you my destitution might be relieved, that through you I might obtain my own proper cleansing from my sins, and that I might at last hold him tight in that perfect love with which you loved him from the bottom of your heart." Then say "Ave Maria" to her forty or fifty times, or divide them up into particular units as seems best. Let the soul offer this tribute[19] to the Virgin daily as a sign of love and spiritual homage, greeting her intently and affectively not in a picture painted on the wall nor in an image carved in wood, but turning directly to her in heaven.

15. This is the way of cleansing, together with an explanation, a path that can be retraced much better and more rapidly in the heart than in writing or words. Recall this cleansing briefly and succinctly as a starting point, and the second, broader path will soon come into view.

II. CONCERNING THE ILLUMINATIVE WAY

A. Introduction: Fogged and Spotless Mirrors; Threefold Radiance

1. By the path of cleansing the human spirit is lifted directly to the path of illumination, according to the rule enunciated by the Psalmist: *In his heart he has disposed to ascend by steps in the vale of tears* (Ps 83:6–7a [84:5–6]).[1] For through groans and tears the soul dissolves the rust left behind by sins and is thereby directly prepared to receive divine rays of light. We want to see how necessary this preparation is, and we do so initially from the perspective of the recipient. When you place a physical mirror in front of your face, if the mirror is covered with fog from breath or some other obscurity, no amount of staring at it can produce an image. As soon as the mirror has been dried off, a human face appears. Now, if we lift up human reason as a spiritual mirror, we could catch sight of the mirror found in ourselves, the reflection of the One we resemble. When the obscuring fog is removed from a rational spirit, the Spiritual Sun can be seen to be transmitting his rays of grace. In and of himself, he pours himself into everyone equally. We can take this farther—the physical sun's rays stand steadily at a [shuttered] window, without receding or reflecting their natural goodness back upon the sun. When the window's shutters are opened,[2] the sun illuminates the formerly darkened room. So too the heavenly city's true Sun of Righteousness (of which the physical sun provides a dark image or resemblance) steadily stands in readiness at the heart's door, looking forward to nothing else, until some sort of cleansing clears enough away to create an opening. Then the Spiritual Sun can joyously rest in the human spirit as if on a bridal bed, sealing the soul betrothed to him with splendid rays of spiritual realities. Purgation is thus followed by spiritual illumination, not only from the perspective of the recipient but also from that of the incoming rays.

2. Second, the need for cleansing is brought to light by considering how two distant things are joined in union. For the Book of Wisdom says that wisdom herself is *the brightness of eternal light, and a spotless mirror* (Wis 7:26). Therefore there ought to be some sort of assimilative conformity when the human spirit is united to the brightness of eternal light through the union of true love. To this end, having removed from herself every obscuring cloud, the human spirit should be formed into a

spotless mirror, instantly ready to receive more divine splendors of light. Purified in this way, she is shaped to conform to eternal wisdom.

3. Yet, by which light is the human spirit to be raised in anagogical upsurge to the third path, the unitive path? One notes that the physical sun is visible when it terminates by striking a lower body, as, for example, when we see it strike a wall. We also see the sun in its own rays, shining through the air. And we see the sun in itself, in the solar source. So too the divine ray appears to the spirit in three ways.

4. It appears in Holy Scripture when one discovers the anagogical sense under the husk of the letter by means of a gift of understanding, by which the human spirit, trained in manifold and marvelous ways, is directed on a certain ray of light to love of her Creator. Blessed Denis refers to this ray, which makes the spirit superresplendent, in his book *On Divine Names*, when he says, "In pure silence we do honor the inexpressible and we strive for the splendors that shine on us in Holy Scriptures, letting ourselves be illuminated by them."[3]

5. The second ray sent from the Spiritual Sun shines forth in the Spirit. Caught up by these rays of the sun, the human spirit contemplates eternal sights and, with a certain meditative wonderment, is formed by supercelestial things, learning about the eternal reasons, the eternal begetting,[4] the way the Holy Spirit binds together [Father and Son], and so forth. For just as the physical eye is raised up to gaze on the sun by means of the rays of the sun shining in the air, rather than by any other perceptible light, so too the eye of understanding is lifted up to knowledge of hidden supercelestial things by rays sent forth from the Spiritual Sun and not by any other discipline or knowledge nor by the efforts of any mortal teacher. Blessed Denis writes to Titus about this, saying, "Turn toward the ray of light,"[5] as if to say: Take up no other teacher, no other archetype, to perceive divine things, but enter within yourself and through the rays of light given you from on high, exert yourself all the more stringently to contemplation of divine things. For just as the rational spirit is more noble than the other lower creatures, so divine wisdom[6] appears more nobly in the rational spirit through the rays of goodness that are sent forth.

6. I shall pass up the opportunity to say anything regarding the third ray, in which the fountain of all goodness[7] and blessedness himself appears (which happens by rapture). [In this third ray], by the free gift of the Creator, the human spirit is rapt away and removed as far as possible from the sense perceptions of the body, yet remaining in the body. Snatched away to supernal things, with grace leading nature, the human

spirit gazes on the Creator face-to-face, gazes on the glorious visage that delights the members of the heavenly court.

7. Our concern at present is the first ray, which lies hidden beneath Scripture. Through it one ascends to unitive love. [Yet, a word or two on the other two rays is in order.] The second ray more often accompanies unitive[8] love, for the closer the human spirit approaches through loving affections to the fount of light, the more powerfully she is filled with increasingly divine rays, just as the dawn sheds light first on the regions closest to it. On the third path, through insatiable sighing the human spirit gasps for complete union with her Beloved. More acted upon than acting, she is divinely raised up to receive the third ray of light. The Beloved then says to the one who has sighed so long, *Friend, go up higher* (Lk 14:10). In this regard Denis later said in the *Mystical Theology*, "Surge up unknowingly to that union which is above all cognition, spirit, and intellect,"[9] where the practice of unitive love is handed on, where the *affectus* surges upward toward that which the understanding knows not. Then he adds these words, speaking to Timothy: "Removing from yourself all these things, and completely freed from everything that restrains, you will be brought up on high in purity to the radiance of divine darkness."[10] In speaking of the uplifting of unitive love he says "Surge upward" [*consurge*] for grace and nature are at work here. After that he says, "You will be brought up on high" [*sursum ageris*], since here grace, not nature, lifts the human spirit to experiential and unmediated knowledge of celestial things and through grace the human soul is made ready for such experiential and direct knowledge.

8. But since our present concern is with the illuminative path, it is necessary to describe how light shines forth[11] in the Scriptures, and then, to describe how we might ascend by this light to the third path. Moreover, that it might be clear to all that this ray of light lies hidden everywhere in Scripture, like light in an oil lamp, we offer one example, namely the Lord's Prayer. One could test this in similar fashion by looking at any part of both the Old and New Testaments and by applying any of the disciplines of truth. For there is no word in any of these which is not filled with the inner colloquy of the bride and Bridegroom.

B. The First Ray

1. Introduction: The Anagogical Method Explained

9. *Night shall be my light in my pleasures* (Ps 138:11 [139:11]), and so forth. Here the darkened outer husk of Scripture is called "night"; indeed, this refers to all sense-perceptible creatures, through which the

light comes to shine on the human spirit so that she might find rest in the upward-leading delights of unitive love. The illuminative life[12] corresponds to that angelic order known as Cherubim. Now, the life of cleansing, the first path, corresponds to the celestial order of Thrones, for the soul is first cleansed so that God might dwell in her as in a clean place. As has been said,[13] the second path, that of illumination, corresponds to the Cherubim, for the word *Cherubim* means "fullness of knowledge." Through the art of this second path, the soul acquires such light of theological[14] knowledge and such an expanse of wisdom in the Scriptures that she can apply all words of the Old and New Testaments and all of this world's creatures to yield understanding, or language that directs all things toward God by making love the point of reference. The third path, the unitive way, corresponds to the *Seraphim*, a term meaning *glowing*. In this path the soul is carried into God with such great ardor that sometimes the body is utterly and marvelously overwhelmed as the person's *affects* and movements stretch out toward God.

10. Note therefore that anagogy, that is, upwardness, takes three forms. The first has to do with God as he is in himself, as in the case of the human spirits in heavenly bliss and glory. This form of anagogy applies to David. According to the letter,[15] David was described as a superb fighter, while according to the moral sense of Scripture, "David" represents the soul, who ought to fight manfully against the devil, attacking him in scorn and refusing to let herself be subjugated by such a vile lord, for such a subjugation would forever separate her from her sweetest Jesus Christ. David is also said to have struck down Goliath, and he thus allegorically represents the Lord Jesus Christ, who acquired peace for his people by conquering the proud devil. For the word *David* means "beautiful to look at" (1 Sm 16:12). This symbolizes the inestimable beauty of the divine essence, at the sight of which every human and angelic spirit at rest in eternal bliss rejoices with inexpressible joy. So the gospel of John says, *This is life eternal, that they know you, the only true God, and him whom you have sent, Jesus Christ* (Jn 17:3). That is the anagogic exposition based on the vision of God by the blessed ones in heaven.

11. A second anagogy has to do with the Church Militant,[16] which remains so completely and undistractedly in the embrace of the Bridegroom. Now in a literal sense Jerusalem is called a city, indeed, a city well fortified and surrounded with powerful walls, which, in the moral sense[17] represents the faithful soul, who ought to be fortified inwardly with the weapons of virtues, grace, and love, without which weapons

she can accomplish nothing and is unable to resist the devil's attacks. Outwardly she should be surrounded with the strong walls of upright living and mortification of the five exterior senses, which can preserve unassailed the wholeness of the unitive love that rules her. Secondly,[18] since Jerusalem is called the throne of the kingdom, she represents the future assembly of the faithful under Christ her prince, who himself reigns in her as the peaceful king. For Isaiah once said of this personage of the king: *Our God, our lawgiver, shall himself come and save us* (33:22), ruling the Church Militant by the example of his life and word of teaching. Thirdly, Jerusalem can be understood as "vision of peace," which is what the Church Triumphant designates, for her inhabitants are peaceful because they rejoice in their happy presence in her, celebrating as they admiringly exclaim over the superabundant rewards of the eternal city of joys: *Better is one day in your courts than thousands [elsewhere]* (Ps 83:11 [84:10]). That is [another] anagogic exposition.

12. However, in the strictest sense this anagogy is a synonym for *upward movement,* in which some distance must intervene between the upward act and that to which an ardently aspiring person is elevated. In a strict sense, no upward action takes place in our first example, since there is no upward movement between those who bless the Most High and those whom he himself blesses with true peace. They live with the King in the bridal chamber, happily taking their rest in that marvelous serenity, already living above themselves in their longed-for union with him, rather than aspiring to something higher. Instead, it is the bride who properly seeks her Bridegroom, who is off on a journey. For no matter how far removed from him she may be, with insatiable desire she longs to be united with him, a longing that will be fully achieved in the tranquillity of life that comes with separation from the body. The Song of Songs follows the course of this uplifting wisdom when the bride says, *Let him kiss me with the kiss of his mouth,* and so forth, and *Draw me: we will run after you,* and so forth, and again, *Come, my Beloved, let us go forth into the field,* and so forth (Ca 1:1, 1:3, 7:11 [1:2, 1:4, 7:11]). For these petitions are nothing other than inflamed yearnings and restless affections calling more ardently on the Beloved so that the bride might more joyously attain upwardness. The same applies to the Bridegroom's words to the bride: *Open up to me, my sister, my bride* (Ca 5:2), and then, *Come from Lebanon, come* (Ca 4:8) and *Arise, make haste, my love* (Ca 2:10). For these words of the Bridegroom are nothing other than the sparkling rays he emits, inciting the *affectus* all the more urgently to more ardent yearning and restless sighing. This anagogic skill

is best acquired through the union of love, and it will be our focus here, as we have said.

2. An Illustration: Discursive Meditation on the Lord's Prayer

A. CAPTATIO BENEVOLENTIAE

13. We shall show how this anagogy is contained everywhere in Scripture by giving an example of a single passage, from which one truly can proceed to discover similar examples elsewhere in Scripture. Without further delay, we shall begin with the example of the Lord's Prayer.

One has to proceed with skill whether working with the literal sense or the anagogical sense. The bride must first gain the goodwill of the grantor[19] before she unfolds her series of requests. Thus she begins with three main commendations of the Beloved, gaining his goodwill toward her petitions, because he will look more favorably on someone who recognizes him as the source of the favors she receives. First, she praises him as the origin of complete and spiritual life. Second, she praises him because he widely diffuses his goodness. Third, she commends the worth of his dwelling-place, for so excellent a King would not deign to dwell except where there is a firm abode, or tabernacle, variously and suitably furnished on the inside. The first of these three is addressed by the word *Father*, the second by *our*, and the third by *in heaven*. In this way, beginning with the strict sense of the word, we carry it anagogically up into the hidden sense, that is, the mystical sense.

14. For instance, in a literal sense *father* simply means the one who engenders a son by emitting something from himself. Transferring this to the anagogic sense, someone is most truly said to be a father when he engenders many sons adoptively, rather than naturally, from the seed of deifying love he has emitted. This seed of deifying love gives perfect nativity to the human spirit when she begins to live in true life on earth, this side of heaven. Without it she could by nature scarcely come to true being. For she progresses more truly and effectively when she is truly born in love of God, who is true life, than she could progress on the basis of her natural existence, in which her primordial creation out of nothing has turned into a birth in guilt. From this source, which richly radiates life from on high, the human spirit receives sensation and spiritual stirring that truly attest to the sources of life. More than that, she also receives crumbs of the bread of inner consolation and is fortified with love as God mercifully shapes and forms her out of his fatherly

affection—until in the end she sees him face-to-face. All of this is the hidden, or mystical, significance of saying *Father*—for he is the fountainhead of all life.

15. Next comes *our*, which praises the outward sharing of his own enclosed goodness, as if one were to say, "By reason of your widespread goodness, not only do you pay attention to individuals but you also do all you can to let your radiance draw all rational spirits to yourself. Thus more than just a few very eminent and outstanding religious people are able to appropriate you, the fountain and source of goodness. On the contrary, no human or angelic spirit can hide itself from your naturally attracting warmth." That is the thrust of *our* taken in an anagogic, that is, an uplifting, sense.

16. *Who art in heaven* follows. Here goodwill is gained by reason of a surpassing and lofty dwelling-place. There are three ways that heaven excels other things:[20] It is continuously in motion, it remains steadfast, and it is adorned with a variety of constellations shining brightly within it. To apply this anagogically, the bride should adorn herself with this threefold characteristic in the hidden storeroom of her heart, as she converses with the Bridegroom in her chamber.

First let her be steadfast, saying something like the following: "O Dearest, you who are in heaven, that is, you who inhabit the inward bedchamber of some human spirits, not merely in the present, potential, and essential way you indwell all other creatures, but truly in yourself. You are a guest who brings rejoicing and comfort, perceptibly making yourself at home with those who have given other vices and delights a writ of divorce[21] for the sake of gaining your love more effectively. For you, who alone are at rest, these souls live in love, set free from hindrances by sighs and bonded to you by the adhesive of gentlest love. They cling to you so tightly that they cannot be pried loose, so that *love* might be *as strong* in them *as death*" (Ca 8:6). Hence, in order to be more firmly rooted, the bride in the Song of Songs cries out for assistance from her bridesmaids, namely from the angels, her companions and aides. She exclaims, *sustain me with flowers, surround me with apples* (Ca 2:5). That is, I beg you, sustain me with affections that cannot be beaten back, with affections that come not from you but from the Beloved from whom I beg you to obtain them. You who see him face-to-face, *surround me* with your solaces, calling him forth to aid me more richly, for *I languish [with love]* (Ca 2:5)—seething with unitive heat I long to embrace him totally. For I, until now living as a miserable little beggar, know so joyous a Lord experientially.

17. The second property follows, namely continuous movement. For when the spirit is beset by the sluggish and laborious motion found at the outset of the beginning stage, as she strives to rouse herself toward the heights, the truest and eternal Bridegroom certainly does not visit the human spirit and dwell in her. Rather, he comes to her when, through long practice, she deserves, by the lavish Giver's grace and favor, to receive such agile affections that she can be ardently raised above whenever she wishes, affected by delight unmixed with yearningly restless uneasiness. Then it is that the God of virtues dwells in her spiritually, but not by the sort of ceaseless activity which surpasses the condition of human powers and requires that virtues cease; rather, God dwells in her as the movement of love, by steady habituation and drawn by her own alluring wish, easily becomes a constant, steady movement. Thus she who at first walked with a slow, unsteady step in the meandering and half-hearted manner of a tortoise now runs rapidly, as if bounding over hills and mountains (that is, discounting both worldly and ecclesiastical honors). This explains her petition, in the portion just heard, when she exclaims with inward voice and drawn-out sighing, *Draw me after you* (Ca 1:3 [4]). For she was drawn by the one who alone is able to raise her above herself, at first slowly, then running in the "odor of [his] perfumes" (Ca 1:3).[22] Indeed, she becomes accustomed to being taken up into the Bridegroom's embraces with more abundant ardent yearnings. It is as if she has tasted the banquet gifts of Jerusalem the heavenly city falling like "crumbs from their masters' table,"[23] from the tables of those who have preceded her in the experience. She does not open the door wide enough for the Bridegroom,[24] since for love of him she is ashamed of the worldly joys that sully her.[25] Yet he keeps on knocking at the door, eager to enter, and, when he finally approaches her, she surges up, arms outstretched in flaming affections. It is not for his own sake but on account of her that he enters and resides, bringing her the solid food of affections so that he might eat with her and she with him.[26] And that is how the Beloved rests in a place of steady movement.

18. Thirdly, heaven is *adorned with a variety of constellations*. No matter what virtues she already has, as long as the human spirit lacks the most efficacious virtue, that is, purgation, the splendidly blooming Beloved will not yet fully indwell her, since her disordered powers and her unbridled delight in the senses darken her with a cloudy mist. Because she has no sparkle in her eyes, Jacob (i.e., the Most High God under whose feet all things are subject) does not find her pleasing and acceptable as a bride to whom he might indivisibly join himself.[27] Why?

Because light has nothing to do with darkness.[28] With virtues cleansed from inner impurity by the still brighter Light of Virtues, the human spirit can sparkle with the splendor of virtues just as the heavens are resplendent with the constellations of stars. Likewise, the Bridegroom's appearance, the manifold brightness of his radiance, and his luminous nobility move one to gaze peacefully upon him. So too the luminous and manifold brightness of grace and virtues in the human spirit give the human countenance a pleasant[29] outer appearance, which incites the Beloved, so sublimely charming, to deign to make himself at home with her.[30] One must hasten to add that the Beloved himself desires this more than she—the Beloved wants this former beggar to become a queen; he wants the one who once pursued worldly delights and was miserable as she sat at his left to be brought over by the transformation of love to sit on his right hand[31]; he wants the one who once was muddied and mired in sin's lightheartedness[32] now to be clothed with a garment woven from love's most precious, heavy[33] cloth of gold; he wants the one once sullied by a variety of vices to show herself in the lovely colors of shining virtues, so that the groomsmen, the friends of the Bridegroom, that is, the angels, upon realizing[34] her triumphant cleansing, might say to the Bridegroom: *The Queen stood on your right hand in gilded clothing [surrounded by variety]* (Ps 44:10 [45:9]).[35]

B. THE FIRST PETITION

19. Having gained goodwill, she follows up with petitions, beginning with, *Hallowed be thy name*. Of her seven requests, the first four are requests to obtain something good, while the other three are requests for the removal of something bad. Her first petition is made so that she might possess her Beloved without contrary delay; her second that she might not turn aside to leap over the boundaries of the rules of truth. Her third petition asks that the most Blessed One not limit to her what she has now perceived of him, but that he mercifully make it known to all other sinners; and her fourth one asks that, as a result of the favors flowing from him, she might unflinchingly persevere in all things, sustained by his own guidance.

20. As we have said, our prime task is to take up the characteristic meaning [*proprietas*] of the word and transfer it into the anagogic sense. Anagogically, *holy* is the same thing as "apart from earth." Therefore "let your wonderful name be made apart from earth in me," is grounded on the following text: *Why do you ask my name, which is wonderful?* (Jgs

13:18). The soul who lives wickedly, imbued with earthly desires and disfiguring worldly delights, is unable to see in love the serene tranquillity of a heart full of joy or to sense anything else. For such a soul is human and not God, carnal and not divine. She is separated from deifying love by all human things, being pulled by earthly horses, that is, she is rendered unsuitable by her affections, sense perceptions, and fleshly yearnings, as Isaiah says: *Egypt is man and not God* (Is 31:3).

On the other hand, the spirit of a lover can attain something of experiential, divine rejoicing when, fired up, she reaches out, even though she knows she is not yet disentangled from earthly affections, because she knows her own strength is insufficient for that. Knowing that she cannot firmly possess two opposite things at once, being pulled down lower by the earthly weight of corruptible flesh, she begs the Beloved more insistently that he remove it. In light of the worthiness of the joy that follows, she despises her former delight; by the rule of opposites, spiritual joy lays bare the bitterness of former joys, and the inner ray of light, even if not revealed in perfect fullness, clearly exposes the world's or the flesh's[36] fraud and ugliness. Then, with her disfiguring mildew and excrescence[37] consumed, she is lightened by love's fire and, astonished, is raised on high on the wings of affection. Thus here and now she can sense with sureness the wonder unknown to a newcomer. When through many affections and long unbroken yearnings she finds what she desired, she can say with astonished joy: *Truly you are a hidden God* (Is 45:15). Thus may the marvelous name be made holy—when the soul's petition is heard and, removed from the earth (i.e., from the flesh), marvelously the bride is presented to the Bridegroom, leaving them alone with each other.

C. THE SECOND PETITION

21. The second petition follows: *Thy kingdom come.* The kingdom of God is established on its lasting throne in the soul when such ardent force of love prevails in the spirit that not only does the soul, quickly and manfully putting down the rebellion of the inordinate inner senses, step forth as the ruler of the whole spiritual realm, but, by the power of that same love, she also subjects all actions to the judgment of reason. She does this in order to strive by every action to do what she has discerned to be more pleasing to the Beloved, panting to subject her body entirely to the Beloved, through the light he radiates, recognizing in advance what pleases him, and unwaveringly carrying it out with dis-

90

cernment. Even when she is not in the midst of this activity, let her nonetheless make her prayer at the accustomed hour—unless some external matter or higher obedience hinders—so that her will might not seem vain and empty to her Beloved. No matter what, she ought not *seek her own interests* (1 Cor 13:5), but seek God's (Phil 2:21), as the Apostle Paul says. She does all this so that God alone can reign in her, in the one whose will he has already obtained by his own rich sacrifice.[38] For it is right that she should in the end come to rest in him by whom she was created, that he alone should reside in her, that she should be preserved intact under his rule, that she should find sweet refreshment in him, that she might say with joy, *I sat down under the shadow of him for whom I longed,* adding the reason for such joy: *and his fruit was sweet to my mouth* (Ca 2:3). For the kingdom of God truly comes when she is seated under the shadow of the Most High,[39] the King of kings and Lord of lords.[40] This kingdom she truly attains when her will, as far as human weakness permits, is completely consecrated to God and not at all subject to any creature.

D. THE THIRD PETITION

22. The third petition follows: *Thy will be done.* Since she does not truly love unless she desires that everyone honor the one she loves, the bride (signified by heaven) asks that what she experiences mercifully be made known to other sinners (denoted by the earth). In this way the One who alone ought to be worshiped and adored insatiably can, by revealing to sinners their sins, show that he is kind, imparting to their spirits the spark of truth and the drop of reason that are found only by attaining him. In this way every tongue burning with that inner affection which alone makes it possible for a created spirit to converse with Uncreated Spirit can know experientially and confess the inexpressible verdict: *Our Lord Jesus Christ in the glory of God the Father* (Phil 2:11) confers on those who love him and who abandon earthly joys gifts far more precious than any they have given up.

23. Another reason why one also confesses Christ to be in the glory of the Father is so that the Father might by yearning love lift up in mercy the one who truly loves him, bring her to unspoiled union, and establish her immovably in the solitude of his bosom, as the Lord says: *I have loved you with an everlasting love, therefore have I drawn you, taking pity on you* (Jer 31:3).

24. *Thy will be done, as in heaven*—which, to apply the phrase ana-

gogically, means "let thy will be done" firmly, steadily in motion, adorned with various lights[41]—*so on earth*, that is, "thy will be done" in sinners, who not unjustly and in a strict sense[42] are called earth, because they are fixed in a region far from the fire whose cleansing burning lightens the soul so that she might, by loving and yearning while still on earth, gain a heavenly dwelling-place: for where one loves, there one, in a strict sense, lives. This noun *earth* cannot be expounded anagogically in its essence, but rather through causation, for just as love is the cause by which the human spirit attains all good things in love, so the absence of love is the cause of all sin,[43] whether penal (i.e., venial) or culpable (i.e., mortal). So it is that the sinner is called earth, for he is farther removed from the lightening presence of ignited love. Thus we find another sort of anagogical exposition in addressing what we call guilt, or sin. For, although in themselves guilt and sin have no characteristic drive corresponding to that which draws the bride toward her Beloved, we can explain them as an absence of love's urgency. Just as a certain characteristic within a creature or in Scripture serves to raise the spouse to the Bridegroom, to make the transfer to the uplifting, or anagogical, sense, and just as the presence of fitting love becomes the cause of every good thing, so love's absence is the occasion for every evil. This does not mean that lack or absence is a "something" in the human spirit; rather, that, in the absence of love, the soul lacks a tether and runs unchecked and aimlessly down false paths, running into all kinds of misery. Nor is this undeserved, for *her face is made blacker than coals* (Lam 4:8) and, deprived of the royal diadem (namely of God Almighty, her lover), she is so despised that *all her friends* (i.e., the angels) *despised her and are become her enemies* (Lam 1:2). No longer does love's affinity make her resemble celestial spirits; rather, these spirits are said to be hostile to her because she is far from her source of help, God Almighty, and has lost her regal seal. Thus it is not wrong to say that the soul deprived of love lacks every good thing, for her evil deeds separate her from her God, from him whom *neither eye has seen nor ear heard* [*nor human heart thought of,* him whom *God prepares for those who love him*][44] (1 Cor 2:9; Is 64:4).[45]

These things should be minutely and carefully mulled over to achieve greater clarity about how one might enter into them. For what has been said here will be manifestly proven either by cause, by essence, or by love leaping into eternal life, drawing up joy [and] the fuller radiance of eternal brightness.

E. THE FOURTH PETITION

25. *Our daily bread.* For herself and for others she desires to be raised on high by an increase of love. Lifted up above herself and existing closer to the source of all happiness, she might then eat her fill of the invigorating word, which so unalterably strengthens her that she no longer begs for the wretched delights of lesser things, no matter what she lacks. For she knows that she would suddenly slip back toward seeking out creaturely and fleshly consolation unless she satisfies a bit of her hunger with supercelestial refreshment, that is, the food of love and the bread of angels, constantly drawing deep draughts from the fountain of eternal beatitude. Therefore she asks for bread, that is, for increased love, which alone can strengthen the sick, fortify the weak, and satisfy the starving.

26. And she asks for this bread *today*, but rightly precedes that word with *daily*. She calls it *daily* because the human spirit cannot live a true life for a day, for an hour, not even for an instant, unless constantly bathed by the life-giving drop of dew. For just as the soul is the life of bodies, so love is the life of spirits. In light of the soul's limitations, the groomsmen gratefully say to the Beloved, *Lord, he asked life of you and you have given it to him,* life not for a moment in time but for *length of days, for ever and ever* (Ps 20:5 [21:4]). For the love with which the bride, by living, wholly loves the Bridegroom will not fail in the future but will be increased, so that the prophetic word which the Most High spoke through the mouth of Isaiah might be fulfilled: *The Lord, whose fire is in Zion, and his furnace in Jerusalem* (Is 31:9).

Now this can be put differently, in keeping with our present purpose—to draw out the anagogical spirit of the text. Unless an animate body is fed once a day with physical food, it loses its bodily strength and vigor. Likewise, unless a human spirit underway in unitive love reaches out once a day, aspiring to the kiss, she will soon become lukewarm and give up some of the height she has attained. (The exception to this need for reaching out to aspire to the kiss is when she has to do some work in the fields,[46] whether for the sake of a bit of bodily rest or for some special[47] reason.) Not surprisingly, the Bridegroom stands waiting at the door, saying, *Arise, make haste, my love, and come* (Ca 2:10). Should she keep him waiting too long, he quite rightly would become indignant and more frequently absent himself for a while. Though she might love him as intensely as before, still she would find herself saying more often, *By night I sought him whom my soul loves; I sought him and I found him not*

(Ca 3:1). In a strict sense, to seek by night can mean to ascend through the creatures, or to seek the Beloved in them (as some would have it, for whom to seek by night is to seek through the creatures or through the traces of the creatures). But this does not suit the anagogic, or unitive, movement, since in the anagogic movement, one should cling to the very Fount of eternal goodness without any indirect mirror, affect, or uplifting love. Seeking by night refers to the situation in which, for some reason, the spirit is hindered in her upward action, as when, after initially being stirred lucidly, brightly, without hindrance or cloud, she then finds herself surrounded by fog, rendering her *affectus* scarcely able to free itself from the image-filled knowledge of the one into whom she is being moved. This sometimes happens out of the human spirit's negligence, or for other reasons, as will become clearer later on. In any case, such a situation leads her to say, "I sought and I found no such" ardent and agile affections as I was used to.

Moreover, she asks *today*, in this present life. In light of eternity the "present" is simple and undivided, and the eternal present thus begins for those living in love in this present life. For that love with which the Bridegroom is loved in this life is the same in number as that love with which, in glory's eternity, one will be united to the One who makes all things blessed. This is what *today* refers to, this is what unity and clarity signify. And so, the reference to presentness expresses a single principle of continuity.[48] For the soul who clings to God in love is more truly and more directly fed with living bread than one body is linked to other physical bodies by shared corporality, which acts as a sort of glue or material bonding. This is what the divine Apostle Paul meant when he praised the unitive sighs of an aspiring soul: *He who is joined to the Lord is one spirit* (1 Cor 6:17). Therefore one rightly speaks of a single presentness, for the bride not only attends upon the presence of the Beloved, but the hierarch[49] of this wisdom, the divine Apostle Paul, says she is *one* with the Beloved.

27. *Today* also carries the meaning "light," for now the Sun of Justice truly rises, raising up the soul on rays of the sun to be trained in higher things, meriting the label *dawn* as given in the Canticle: *Who is she who comes forth as the rising dawn* (Ca 6:9)? Now, like the rising dawn, she begins to be refreshed with the bread of life, experientially sensing that she is being raised up in love, coming forth by force of the movements of love to mount on high. Lest the unlearned and immature be led into error, we note that this experience simply frees up the soul's

movements, the means of ardent arousal. The practiced spirit perceives this no less fully than the physical eye perceives a visible cow passing by on a path. For now we simply make this assertion; later it will be confirmed by irrefutable proofs.

28. The fact that eternity, the Beloved's presence, and light begin to shine inwardly already here in this life is confirmed by what the great hierarch, the Apostle Paul, says: *Our dwelling place is in heaven*[50] (Phil 3:20). For already the ascending Sun of Justice spreads over the earth, that is, over the loving spirit, who, however, still remains allied with a terrestrial body. Even though much hindered by the body's inclinations and especially closed off by the orientation of the lower part of the spirit toward worldly delights, still the south wind, the guiding breath of divine inspiration, wafts divinely transmitted rays which open up the body to receive divine things from on high. This is the spirit's higher part, which is united to God and refreshed by the bread of life and love, even though it frequently senses much that is unwelcome and annoying—stemming from the lower, terrestrial, rather than skyward, part. As much as she can, she should close the door of the *affectus*, so that it cannot look down toward lower things but might faithfully aspire upward toward divine things, so that the Beloved, already feasting with her, might say to her, *My sister, my spouse, is a garden enclosed, a fountain sealed up* (Ca 4:12). This garden is called a sweet-smelling blooming rose; it is said to be enclosed so that no enemy or neighbor might obtain a bit of true love. For the garden is open only to him of whom it is said that he alone, by reason of his blooming dignity, refreshes rather than roots up, the one who joyfully testifies of himself in the Canticle of Canticles, saying, *I am the flower of the field and the lily of the valley* (Ca 2:1), the one who desires to dwell not merely outside but also inside the human spirit. This the Most High effectively accomplishes when he invites himself into the poverty-stricken human spirit to feed her with living bread, that is, with the consolation of divine joy, saying, *Open up to me, my sister, my love, my dove, for my head is full of dew* (Ca 5:2). He already establishes the stimulating state in which she sweetly and variously calls forth from him what is here referred to as fullness. For nothing would be established through him unless it fills her with profound favors, gifts, and splendors. This is what is meant by the "head" being "full of dew." For just as the movements and sensations that truly attest to life descend from the head to the lower members, so too the life of love and awareness of joy descend to unitive human spirits from the Most High, who is the head of all the church.

HUGH OF BALMA

29. The fifth petition follows: *And forgive us our debts.* Here the bride asks to be freed from three pressing things. First she asks to be freed from the evil of venial guilt, since by means of her Beloved she is so well rooted in God that mortal sins have been removed far from her. Second, she asks to be freed from the danger [of temptation], which has to do with both guilt and its punishment. Third, she asks to be freed from the evil of the punishment incurred by frequently falling into sin.[51]

30. First she anxiously asks to be liberated from the evil of venial sins, something fully attainable only by the gift of love. For the human spirit can have no light except insofar as she is prepared by the unstinting preparatory radiance of her own spiritual sun pouring into her. Indeed, when disordered inner forces or unsuitable delights of the senses lead her to seek repose somewhere other than in the fount of beatifying blessedness, she averts her glance from him and becomes unfocused, unless illuminated by the light of the fount of brilliance. For venial sins darken the soul to some degree. Likewise, should she seek her delight elsewhere, as if the One who alone feeds all angelic and human spirits with the vision of his beauty and the attraction of his sweetness were insufficient for her—such a soul deservedly would be slowed down in her yearning. Therefore she eagerly[52] asks to be set free, lest she be pulled away from the sweet words with which she yearningly calls upon the Bridegroom to come to her aid.[53] Thus the Book of Wisdom employs the figure of a lamenting person to describe someone unable to eradicate his deeply rooted earthly thoughts: *For the corruptible body is a load upon the soul, and the earthly habitation presses down the mind that muses upon many things* (Wis 9:15). If one thinks a lot about lower things and welcomes the inward affect of creaturely voices, one becomes all the more distant from heavenly help. For the more the human spirit is distracted by thinking about tangential things, so much less is she brought to union with the fount of happiness. And then the body is said to weigh down the soul, because each of these things naturally tends toward its own proper place. Thus a constant struggle burdens the spirit, since the soul tends toward God, who alone is the place adequate for her, but the body in truth, because of its weight, always wants to be delighted by earthly things.

31. This can be stated another way: She asks to be set free so that he need not judge her to be unattractive because, stained [by venial sins], she cowers from the graceful light found in the Bridegroom's presence,

the Bridegroom she yearns with all her heart to embrace. To him she would seem to be less attractive because his gaze focuses specifically and solely on the inner beauty of the bride he is taking to himself. Only when she conforms through inner beauty of spirit to supercelestial beauty are her words acceptable to him. More than anything else, this is what he reminds her of when he sweetly says in the Canticle: *For your voice is sweet, and your face is charming* (Ca 2:14), that is, your *affectus* is charming.[54] For "your voice" tastes nothing but heavenly things, and "your face" is not deformed by a multitude of venial sins, or fleshly affections. Therefore your words are sweet to me, when, calling to you, through the impulse of affections, I say such things. And *your charming face* is readied for the honor of nuptial rites because *there is not a blemish in you* (Ca 4:7)[55]—which can only be because all blemish has been eliminated by perfect love. Thus, in surging up to that union which is acquired directly by love's movement, the human spirit's tendency to avert her glance must first be straightened out. When the *affectus* is brought back into line and carried upward, venial guilt is in no way able to inflict rude harm to the soul, since it is like a drop of water that falls into the fire and instantly congeals and is absorbed by the fire.[56]

32. Moreover *debts* obligate. It is quite reasonable, then, that we should be made to owe a certain penalty when the spirit is less directly oriented toward him in whom true happiness is found; when she deliberately hungers to repose elsewhere than in him who alone fully and sufficiently consoles the human spirit's yearnings. Thus, so that the very truth of his fullness might point out to others what he supplies, he says, *Come to me you that labor and are burdened down* (Mt 11:28) with laborious yet sweet striving in the higher affections. For because you have lived so long in wretchedness and because glory is delayed, you can consider yourselves burdened and slowed down by lugging around the weight of the body's burden. [*Come to me*] *and I will refresh you,* I who am none other than the eternal wisdom rising from on high, the one who imparts to you, not only in the future but even here and now, the divine consolations that quiet your yearnings. For *I am meek and humble of heart* (Mt 11:29), and therefore I stoop down to those who call forth my riches through constant yearning. I despise not the poor, for "I am humble of heart"; thus the poorer the spirit is in earthly riches, the better she is shaped to suit the royal marriage feast and the more rapidly will I raise her above the limits of human nature to union with me.

Do not await this by envisioning [*speculatio*]; rather, see by means of the tasting that leads the way for sight. For you will not see unless you have put into action the word of the prophet which says, *Oh, taste and see, for the Lord is sweet* (Ps 33:9 [34:8]). For repose will come and the murmur of an aspiring soul will really cease when she herself senses the Creator resting in her to a greater degree, which is what our Lord went on to say: *And you shall find rest for your souls* (Mt 11:29). Then love's yoke will be sweet and the burden light* (Mt 11:30). For by its worthiness and joyful attractiveness the yoke of love binds the will inwardly, so that he who bends his neck to bear this sweetest yoke feels no pain.[57]

33. Unlike other yokes, this one clearly carries the approval of those who bear it. Those burdened with another yoke bend their necks low,[58] but this one so elevates its bearers that it makes earth-dwellers into heavenly inhabitants, extending them beyond themselves, and making them into fellow citizens with the supernal spirits.[59] And so the burden is truly said to be light, because it lifts the spirit from lower things and, in elevating her, establishes her on the level of things above herself. The yoke is described as sweet because the one bearing it lives the angelic[60] rather than human life—imperfectly for now, yet fully and felicitously when body and soul separate.[61]

34. Again, the yoke is said to be sweet because it makes the human spirit lead this bitter life with such interior joy and rejoicing that the life of glory begins already in this life, so that the superabundance of the soul's joy can totally overwhelm and absorb the body's punishments. The burden is also described as light because the richness of the inner soul, like a fat fowl, well basted while roasting on a spit over coals,[62] keeps winter's icy hunger or summer's insistent heat from causing any harm.[63] And thus what the Bridegroom formerly promised her, saying, *I am your protector*, rightly becomes a present reality. Since you are attracted to my sweet yoke, *I am your protector;* and, when you see me—and no other—in glory, *your reward shall be exceedingly great* (Gn 15:1), for then you shall be paid for your service in war, and you shall be paid *exceedingly well*, because I will no longer halt your joy short of full knowledge. If you bear my yoke for a little while in misery, I shall mercifully make you fully share my glory.

G. THE SIXTH PETITION

35. The sixth petition follows: *And lead us not into temptation.* The human spirit is led into temptation when she is so entangled and ensnared by enticements that she partially agrees to the wicked work that the crafty seducer has insistently urged on her. The bride therefore asks

to be spared this danger, not because she lacks confidence in the Beloved's constant aid, but because she is aware of the weakness of human flesh. She knows that she has been firmly freed from temptation when the most deeply rooted yearnings make her present to her kind protector. Therefore she intently strains upward, to be raised above by her loving affections so that she might deserve to attain him and to call him forth by her affected clamorings. Confident of his mercy,[64] she can contemptuously face down the enemy's pressing and powerful temptations, despising them out of confidence in her Beloved, who has long since promised her through the Psalmist: *Because he hoped in me, I will deliver him; I will protect him because he has known my name* (Ps 90:14 [91:14]).

36. Another reason she asks to be set free follows from the enemy's insolent deceits. For they rage against her insofar as they are permitted to attack, but the more she is directly subject to the Creator's control, the farther she is removed from their dominion. When even stronger, more frequent, more varied, and more importunate temptation fails to prevail, they pursue her with raging fury, hoping that *the Jordan might rush into their mouth* (Jb 40:18 [40:23]), and that *he shall strew gold under him like mud* (Jb 41:21 [41:30]).[65] For the Jordan rushes into the mouth of the demons when the stream of love flowing out of the fount of eternal beatitude, the stream by which life enters into the spirit, is diverted, as if by a hidden channel, to the body's streams of worldly cupidity, setting off rushing waves of earthly honors. These overwhelm the sweet balsam of affected love through which the soul expresses her yearnings, and they thus fill the soul with violent surges. "Gold is strewn like mud" when sweetest love of the Creator, which beautifies the soul by its graciousness and seals her with the loftiest honor, turns into love of the creature, which, lamentably, sullies the soul's higher face.

37. Thus she begs him to set her free, longingly challenging him, asking him not to fail to see that she gains his love now. She has trampled down earthly joys and the kingdoms of the devil, and the Beloved, through the prophet, has promised such a yearning one that he will not only hear her request, but, like a welcome leader and companion in battle, will liberate her completely through his joyous presence in the midst of her temptation and reward her with the crown of glory for her faithfulness and for her victory, as he says, *He shall cry to me and I will hear him; I am with him in tribulation* (Ps 90:15 [91:15]).

38. The third reason why she asks to be set free from temptation's danger is that the human spirit united to God no longer pursues her own

affairs but follows the happy master *who makes his sun to rise upon the good and bad, and rains upon the just and the unjust* (Mt 5:45), that is, he sends the rays of his goodness to good people and uses those rays to draw them to himself; even while his rays also shine expectantly outside evil people, like the sun's rays shining expectantly on a shuttered window. He retracts not one bit of his goodly nature, but keeps on knocking on the door,[66] lest any rational spirit, whether Christian, pagan, or Jewish, should lack divine love because God stopped sending it forth. Therefore she who loves faithfully should labor zealously, both in inner prayer and in spiritual exercise, so that, having seen endless spiritual battles,[67] all the [spiritually] dead might be raised to the life of love and so that the [spiritually] blind might penetrate to knowledge of the most lucid truth. A human spirit united to God in friendship can beg great favors for sinners from the Beloved; because she is the most faithful and truest of friends, agreeing completely with what he wants to do and wants not to do, she can take much booty from the enemy through prayer and entreaties directed to her Beloved. In this she incurs the raging indignation of the enemy and thus she asks on behalf of everyone for liberation from the enemy's snares.

39. We come to the final reason for such a petition, the one most central to the matters dealt with in the present treatise. Having already experienced how sweet it is to love such a kind Beloved, she considers it a most bitter death, something she can scarcely come to terms with, to be separated from her happy consort now or forever. Indeed, she counts it an unbearable disgrace that someone who in godly fashion knows the great joy of loving the Beloved should listen to the enemy's conversation, should think worldly joys or earthly riches of any worth—as if she never really knew whether something truly is good. If a human spirit has been well and happily trained, she will warn sinful souls who have miserably withdrawn from such a fount of goodness, saying, *Your own wickedness shall reprove you, and your apostasy shall rebuke you* (Jer 2:19).

40. The explanation follows: *Know, and see that it is an evil and a bitter thing for you to have left the Lord your God* (Jer 2:19), meaning that the spirit incurs a double unhappiness when she shamelessly clings to the lower creature for the sake of worldly delights. By God's just judgment she not only loses her pleasures but she is also loaded down with sorrows, so that the one who wanted to have her fill of creaturely delights is filled with endless bitterness. For the more deeply worldly delight penetrates the recesses of the human spirit, the more the soul, sad to say, is filled with noxious poisons. The evil by which she has spurned

the Creator and clings to the creature reveals less how low she has sunk than how far she has turned away from the fount of all goodness. Since he is the sole and supreme Good, all things are called good to the degree that they fully participate in him and that which does not participate in the Good ought not be called anything, though that would be impossible. That same fount of goodness, rejoicing, and delight imparts the streams of his happiness to human spirits, mercifully pouring himself into some more and into others less, according to their degree of preparation. When a soul is separated[68] from that wellspring without whom there can be no joy, since joy is derived from that source, it is not surprising that such a soul separated from him becomes depressed, for the aqueduct of love from which the soul joyfully experiences and obtains gladness from the Creator has been obstructed and broken off. Torpor immediately spreads from lower things over the spirit and assails her, for she is cut off from the one from whom all joyfulness emanates, cut off from the one who is surrounded by unheard-of gladness and unique joy.

Yet, through affections and yearnings for the Beloved, the spirit is completely disentangled and triumphantly set free. From what she knows, she can despise the delights to which she has been subject, escaping by virile resistance from enemies who were sure she was about to be reduced to ignominy and proceeding in triumph to greater grace from the Beloved, a closer union with him, and a crown of glory.

H. THE SEVENTH PETITION

41. The seventh petition follows: *But deliver us from evil.* Here she asks to be freed from arousal and inclination toward sin. For even though she has been trained beyond all expectation and even though she continues to aspire to a more intimate union and yearns to be raised up to her Beloved, nevertheless the human spirit's earthly body and the hostility of the flesh may sidetrack the spirit from aiming toward the heavens above, veering aside toward the things her senses desire. Indeed, although striving to raise herself up to live through love in heaven, she sometimes finds herself mired down by cogitation.

42. Because she utterly detests the thought that the spirit, the sanctuary of the entire Trinity, might listen to libidinous talk or deliberately stoop to something shameful—which would make her contemptible in the eyes of the Bridegroom—with manifold longing she asks to be set free from such things. She does this not that she might escape the punishment she deserves, but that she might not incur the darkening that would render her less desirable in her Beloved's eyes.

Thus she ought to bend her ear to the kind Father who has begotten her in the life of love, and she ought to open the eye of understanding inwardly, so that she might cling with all ardor of love to the spiritual Father and aspire to his dwelling-place. Then for love of him she can forget homeland and family, and, unstained by any sort of caused or created thing, be a charming and well-adorned virgin bride desired by the heavenly Bridegroom. For, desiring to share himself with her, the Most High himself created her to his image and marked her with the image of the entire Trinity. In other words, he created her so that she might depend solely on him in the obedience of ignited love, whether underway in this life or in the heavenly homeland.

43. Let her constantly hear him inviting her through the sweet admonition of David the prophet: *Hearken, O daughter, and see, and incline your ear; and forget your people and your father's house* (Ps 44:11 [45:10]). The efficacy of love will accomplish several things by means of repeated sighings. When her soul was infused in her first birth, she gained by way of the flesh the corruptions through which she frequently falls back toward lower things. Now, in the second birth, by which she is perfectly born in God, she reverses and retraces her steps, as the flesh is sprinkled with the oil of the inner spirit. That which wounded the soul in the first birth is now healed by contraries[69] in her second birth through anointing with lovedrops of fragrant sweet-smelling perfumes. With the lower powers now become obedient, the spirit is partly re-formed and her original harmony reigns again in the flesh. Having gained victory from on high, she gives the Bridegroom the praise he deserves, singing because her prayers have been answered with twofold favor, namely, the sending of fire into the spirit and dew into the flesh, extinguishing the flesh's disfiguring punishment of the soul. Now possessing the Bridegroom under the impact of having been set free, walking in the light,[70] raised from fleshly somnolence[71] by his aid, she surges up to him in attentive vigil, saying, *O God, my God, toward you do I watch at break of day; for you my soul has thirsted* (Ps 62:2 [63:1]). Moreover, since the soul is now freed from sins and penalties and is no longer subject to them, in more ardent affections she begins to hold eager vigil at his door, seeking to begin to quiet the flesh and to make what has always been hostile to the spirit agree to its thoughts and wishes.

I. CONCLUSION

44. Applied to other passages, this one example illustrates what marvelous, broad and deep, tasty, and noble knowledge is hidden in the Scriptures, knowledge, namely, by which the bride is taught to leave

behind lower things in order to possess lastingly as a betrothed and pleasing bride the bridal gifts. Therefore, let no one be unsure about how the entire text of the Old and New Testaments can, with love leading the way and light accompanying, be explained according to the anagogic path and applied to the conversations and colloquies of the bride and Bridegroom.[72] For not only Scripture, but indeed all creatures, whatever they may be—even those from the very heart of hell[73]—can be most strictly [*propriissime*] applied to this same purpose, since they possess hidden in themselves this very wisdom, according to their noblest characteristics [*proprietates*], characteristics which happily can be laid bare by light radiating from on high.

3. Another Illustration: Aspirative Meditation on the Lord's Prayer

45. Having[74] in fact discussed how the anagogical sense lies hidden in the Scriptures, it now remains to speak of how one ascends to the unitive way via the present illuminative path, based on the Psalmist's word, *In my meditation a fire shall flame out,* and so forth (Ps 38:4 [39:3]).[75] Because up to now the human spirit making progress[76] remained undisposed for that which clears the way to carry anagogic affections to the Beloved, it was, until now, useful first to employ a bit of the pondering method just described [par. 13–44], so that through guiding cogitation a bit of a spark in the spirit might begin to affect her toward him to whom, in the third stage, she will be raised as often as she wishes, unhindered and without any cogitation leading the way or keeping company. To eliminate obstacles to this elevation and to make its full attainment possible, all pondering and meditation will be cut away from this wisdom as it makes its upsurge. For cogitation is not present here except in order that through it the affection might be set on fire.[77]

46. Thus one customarily ought to make progress through the meditation we have just described: first, as we have noted, by transferring the characteristic of a word[78] into the anagogical sense; second, by drawing the word back into love; third, by being affected toward God himself by God's gift.[79] To give an example: *Father,* that is, you[80] are the one who begets spiritual sons by means of a living offshoot of love. Therefore, I shall truly be your son when I bind you by true love. Oh, when will I love you, when will I bind you with the innermost cords of my heart? Likewise, employing the word *our,* that is, you are the one who pours out goodness far and wide. If I were truly to love you, then you would drip drops of your broad effusion into me. Oh, when will I

love you so ardently that a bit of your vast goodness might appear in me? In a similar way the words *in heaven* and all the others should be transferred into their anagogical sense.

47. Thus, led by meditation and by means of the aspirative prayer discussed here, the *affectio* of love is kindled little by little.[81] Just as a bit of tow[82] is first exposed to the sun so that it can dry out and can be suddenly ignited, so by means of these aspirative prayers that call forth the Beloved, one's spirit is more affectedly elevated.[83] Thus one says, *who art in heaven:* O wretched soul of mine, when will you be made as clear as the heavens, bright and adorned with the various starry virtues?[84] Then indeed, kind Father, you will gladly dwell in me. When will I sense you, when will I constrain you with hotly burning love, when will my wretched soul so full of excrement be purged by the flames of love? Surely you will then steal quietly into me and will discover the tidy and purified guestroom of my conscience.

48. Next comes *Hallowed be thy name.* O kind Father, when will your knowledge be made holy, that is, when will it be accomplished in a wretch like me apart from earth?[85] Well, that will happen when, having repulsed everything fleshly, I love you alone more than anything. Oh, when will I grasp you? Indeed, to have you alone is to count myself as having all riches![86] For this world would have no place in a wretch like me if you, sweet Father, were to dwell in me through grace and love.

49. *Thy kingdom come.* Woe to me, a sinner! Sometimes vainglory, sometimes gluttony, sometimes lust, try to live and reign in me, but I wish no one except you, Father, to reign in me. Then will you truly reign in me if I truly and ardently love you, for only the love of an ardent soul can properly host your repose. Oh, when, therefore, will I hold on to you through the bond of the most ardent love, so that you can begin to hold sway in me, so that you alone can arrive[87] to reign in my dim realm?

50. *Thy will be done, on earth as in heaven.* Your will will be accomplished in its primordial character when I, wretched and earthly, consent[88] as much to your will (within the limits of my human weakness) as do the blessed spirits who gaze on you face-to-face in heaven. But what will make me of one mind with you, sweetest God, if not solely the passion of love, which joins contrary wills and knows how to conform a loving person to you who love; the love which wondrously knows how to transform a person from glory to glory?[89] When, therefore, O kind One, will I love you truly and with all my heart, and, united to you by the bond of love, be of one mind with you alone?

51. *Give us today our daily bread.* O bread of angels, when will I be fed by your sweetest refreshment? The angels and saints live in beatitude in heaven as they touch you with inflamed affections, O kind Father. When will I have the bread of love, so that in this present life I might feed on the same food that fills the angels and saints in glory, so that I might eat some of the crumbs that fall from my Lord's table? O kind Father, give me this bread today, not tomorrow or later, for my heart is restless until fortified by a bit of this heavenly bread, bread that is called *daily* bread because the more one eats of it the more one's appetite for it increases daily.

52. *And forgive us our debts.* O kind creditor, when shall I know that the debts of my sins have been forgiven me? For if I were truly to love you, then I would know by some deep tasting that they have been forgiven.[90] For just as my sin makes me your enemy, separating me in my misery from you, so love, uniting me to you, would compel the forgiveness of all debts and make me, who was once an offense to you, pleasing and gracious. When, therefore, will I bind[91] you in love and, freed of every sin, know with experiential knowledge that you are pleasing to me?[92]

53. *And lead us not into temptation.* O kind Father, this I ask, not unmindful of your goodness, but, since I am unable to escape the hidden snares and dangers of so many sins, I ask to be inseparably lashed to you with the bonds of love, knowing, wretch that I am, whence the sweet smell of your love draws me to you. May you readily bind and constrict me with such cords that I will despise anything contrary to you and, having discovered you alone, cling inseparably to you. Oh, who will help me to lash myself to you alone, you who alone are a kind and sweet host for my soul, you who now make my turmoil carefree?

54. *But deliver us from evil,* not so much from the evil of hell's punishment but from that of purgatory.[93] I ask this, Father, not so much that I might escape torments but because otherwise pain is everywhere: If I were in hell, I would never see you face-to-face, but if I should remain in purgatory long after my death, my yearning to see your face in fullness of glory—the sight the angels always long to see[94]—would be exceedingly prolonged. But if I should love you ardently here, then reconciling love would remove the hellish punishment owed for sins. If I should truly love you, the flame of love would burn away the corrosion of sins, so that cleansed by flaming affections in death's final departure my spirit might fly away without delay to you, her long-standing desire.

When, therefore, will I love you so hotly as to banish hell's punishment
and free me from purgatory's fiery delay?

III. CONCERNING THE UNITIVE WAY

A. The Character of Unitive Wisdom

1. Introduction

Having spoken of the illuminative way, its nature,[1] and how one
actually ascends on it to union, we turn next to the unitive way. We shall
consider first its nature; second, the ways people can be persuaded to
pursue it; and third, the industrious efforts that firmly establish the human spirit in this unitive way.[2] What we say here applies to the practice
of the unitive way. Even if an uneducated person knows not how to
make sense of these outlines, he at least can be sorrowful in some way.
Second, if he knows not how to ponder the Scriptures, as laid out above,
he can at least aspire to love, saying in his prayers constantly: "O Lord,
when shall I constrain you with sweetest love?" An uneducated layperson, untrained though he be, could, through sorrow for his sins (as if
kissing the Beloved's feet), through recalling God's favors (as if kissing
the hand), reach all the way to the kiss of the mouth, which takes place
in yearning love, saying, *Let him kiss me with the kiss of his mouth* (Ca
1:1). It is not presumptuous to aspire to the kiss of the mouth if one has
first gained practice in the kiss of the feet and hand.

2. For the unitive way draws on the words of the antiphon, *O wisdom, you who proceed from the mouth of the Most High, stretching with
strength from one end to the other and gently disposing everything, come to
teach us the way of prudence.*[3] These are indeed the words of the Church
aspiring for God and yearning to be well taught by the one who is the
fount and origin of all goodness. Even though these words could rightly
and properly be understood to apply to the uncreated wisdom who is the
Son of God, in whose eternal going forth the outflowing goodness of
the supreme Father appears, nonetheless the focus of the present writing
is this same wisdom within time and manifesting itself to the rational
spirit. That outstanding teacher, blessed Denis the Areopagite, describes
this wisdom in the seventh chapter of *On the Divine Names*, where he
says, "Wisdom, the most divine knowledge of God, is known through

106

unknowing according to the union that is above the human spirit, when the spirit, withdrawing from all other things and then dismissing even herself, illuminated by the inscrutable and profound light of wisdom, is united to superresplendent radiance."[4] This is that Christian wisdom, an encompassing and deifying diffusion coming from the entire Trinity on high to faithful Christians, suffusing loving spirits with heavenly dew. It is wisdom herself, the origin of all deiform emanation, who descends—not some temporal benefit or set of gifts from the Bridegroom (e.g., grace, virtue, glory). Those loving spirits affected solely by the desire to be united to this wisdom yearn with sparkling affections, insatiable yearnings, and unitive aspirations.

3. The wisdom we are concerned with here is a surging up through flaming affections of unitive love beyond all functions of the understanding, in order to be established at the highest summit of affectivity. It is the same as that mystical theology by which the enkindled human spirit converses secretly with the Beloved in the languages of the affections, the mystical theology which cannot be unlocked by any industrious effort of mortals but which emerges openly in the spirit by divine mercy alone. That this wisdom is eternal and measureless is praised when she is said *to reach from one end to the other* (Sir 24:5ff.), but so too is she praised within time, insofar as *she sweetly disposes everything*, namely, rational spirits.

2. The Sublimity of Unitive Wisdom

4. We shall show, therefore, how the rational spirit, faithfully instructed by wisdom, finds herself sweetly disposed toward all things through this wisdom which is mystical theology, by divine light radiating from on high.

First, with regard to supercelestial things. In the blessed Trinity, the Son goes forth from the Father, and the Holy Spirit, who is true love, proceeds from both and binds the Father and the Son. So too unitive wisdom proceeds from the fount of supernal goodness and descends to the human spirit living here below, joining her by uniting her with the Uncreated Spirit. Just as the Father and Son, even though distinct, are nevertheless called one because they are bound by Love, so through this wisdom (which alone permits the human spirit to inhere nobly in the supreme Spirit), though the human spirit is nothing, she deserves[5] to enjoy being called one with that supreme Spirit. As the Apostle Paul says, *He who is joined to the Lord is one spirit* (1 Cor 6:17). This ordering is clear not only because of the order of the Persons acquired through the wisdom of unitive love, but also because of the divine activities. To God most blessed two acts are coeternal and consubstantial, namely, knowing himself and loving himself. When the human spirit burns in God and knows ardently with unfailing knowledge, as if basking and burning in the midday heat of glowing love, she loves him with inexpressible ardor. Through this ardor she knows him more intimately than through a sense-perceptible creature, and she is conformed to him as far as possible and transformed into him by deifying love. A human spirit disposed like this is an utterly precise imitator of the eternal actions.

5. But the most blessed God is not only the fountainhead of the order of the Persons and of the eternity of divine activities, but he is the overflowing source of all creatures, of both angelic and human spirits, as well as of all sensate and insensate creatures. Hence the creature's excellence is enveloped solely in its return to that source from which it has its primordial origin. For the rational spirit, created directly by the Fashioner himself and bearing the impress of the image of the very Trinity as a seal, excels the other creatures in dignity and emerges perfected and reshaped by divine decree when, pushing to transcend natural limits by outstretched love, she is united in an ecstatic upsurge of love to the very one from whom she came forth primordially—that a circle might become apparent in him, a circle by which she now begins to return to him from whom she came forth primordially.

6. Moreover, in this eternal Fashioner, the beginning and origin of all creation, all things are regulated in an unshakable ordering by his eternal reasons[6] so that, regulated by divine providence, all things whatsoever might ultimately come to rest in his orderings.[7] Thus the human spirit rising through importunate, or intimate, affections, with her flesh somehow bathed in a wondrous watering, finds her inborn corruption slowly weakening in her—to the degree that she expands heavenward by ardent exercise. By divine compassion she enjoys this victory, so that the more the human spirit submits to her own Creator in undivided love, that much more is her flesh subject to the commands issued by her natural spirit. By divine decree love calls the human spirit forth into concord[8] with her Superior, and, consequently, the now submissive body finds concord with the human spirit as she presides in the realm of her own body. With the Psalmist she says, *For you my soul has thirsted; for you, my flesh, O how many ways* (Ps 62:2 [63:1]).

7. Yet that Most High Creator of all wished not only to be the head of the creation as its maker or to rule it as its governor. Indeed at the end

of time he set out, as it were, to take leave of his celestial majesty and go abroad to visit his creature in her misery, a pilgrimage that ended when he embarked for the heavenly dwelling-places. To this pilgrim in the flesh now returning to heaven, the human spirit disposed by ecstatic love is made to conform. Though the human spirit came forth in freedom in her primordial creation from her Creator, she has been joined to the corruption of bodily necessity and made subject to manifold beggarly servitude; yet in the wake of supercelestial outpouring, she somehow gains a down-payment on eternal felicity as she is raised by extended practice of ardent aspirations. For where she loves she lives, and the importunate reach of her yearnings finds something of a natural end-point, coming to rest in him toward whom she stretches herself. Thus he who in the beginning existed on high next turned to take up the beggarly worldly condition, and then, in a third step, was seen ascending, glorified, into heaven. To him the human spirit is conformed by unitive wisdom, as is rightly said in the Apocalypse of those who truly love him, of those to whom childlike innocence has somehow been restored by the purgation of flaming love: *These follow the lamb, wherever he goes* (Rv 14:4).

8. The human spirit living in love is disposed through wisdom (as described above) not only with regard to the Creator but also with regard to the jubilant saints in glory. For a single, utterly desirable, and direct goal is established for both—an eternal rest which is the same as God most blessed. Yet, although a glorified spirit reposes in him now as she attends him in his presence, insatiable yearning carries a human spirit [living here below] upward, as if absented in inexpressible ardor, that she might aspire to more intimate union with him, saying, *Draw me, we will run after you in the fragrance of your perfumes* (Ca 1:3). Meanwhile the glorified spirit in heaven says, *The king has brought me into his wine cellar* (ibid.). Likewise, the human spirit in heaven who is perfectly joined with her Bridegroom delights in the inexpressible happiness she has already gained, whereas the human spirit joined to the body, though she may strive upward with this wisdom, nonetheless for all her anagogic movements finds the actual exercise to be without any soothing oil or delights—indeed, in a surprising way she experiences bodily affliction. Still, she has this one joy, that her actual direction is straight up, not veering sideways at all. Like a stone tending directly toward a lower point, her direction is toward the most blessed One who alone is the place that corresponds naturally to her dignity.[9]

9. Thus many who are less expert in this philosophy are mistaken

when they think the spirit surging up in anagogic movements is showered with all sorts of celestial sweetness. On the contrary, the spirit is taken on high in laborious toil and a certain bodily weakening results from stretching to God, a spiritual sundering, indeed a tensing of the body's members that results from the impetuosity of the anagogic movements.[10] This is described by Job: *My soul would rather choose hanging, and my bones death* (Jb 7:15).[11] The body could only with great affliction put up with the anagogic thrust, were it not tempered by the spirit's joy at her direct trajectory.

The beatified spirit in heaven is affected unmediatedly by the supreme Good, by eternal sweetness, in undivided exercise, whereas it seems as if the human spirit on earth rises to him in an intense and step-by-step manner, a movement very much like the rays emitted by flashing stars (if these celestial motions are the result of free will). The human spirit's anagogic movements are almost instantaneous, yet she falls back into herself suddenly after her upsurge, then surges up again and falls back again into herself.

So too the glorified spirit in heaven is joined in a most ardent union with him whose beauty she contemplates face-to-face; even if cognition and love are found together there, still cognition naturally precedes love. When, however, the human spirit in this life is actively intent on the upsurge that concerns us here, she cuts off at the roots all functions of reason and understanding. Because the intellect shares the corrupt flesh, phantasms mix into the intellect, which must be shunted aside when the upsurge of love takes place. In heaven, however, the human spirit will be cleansed because the corruption of the flesh has been laid aside. The spirit is thus raised up solely in a surge of the kindled *affectus*, since in heaven the affective incomparably excels the intellective, as will soon be shown. Even if in these and other ways the glorified spirit incomparably surpasses the spirit surging anagogically, nonetheless, through this wisdom, both kinds of spirits are vivified by the same supercelestial life and fed by the same sought-after bread.

10. And by the same wisdom the wayfarer's spirit is ordered and arranged into conformity with the angelic spirit, insofar as this is possible for someone walking the road of this earthly life. For an angel is an intellectual, or spiritual, substance which is not weighed down by any sort of body and thus can be caught up into the unchangeable brilliance of the joys of eternal light. When the spirit living here below by means of experiential knowledge of her outstretched affections is met by divine

wisdom announcing her presence through the free gift of her inviolable goodness, the human spirit's eye of understanding is opened by the very approach of wisdom, who, in the strictest sense, is light and brilliance itself. Because the spirit is more tightly joined by love to that which is above, fleshly affection quite rightly is cut back. Thus, extended in the flesh above the flesh, the human spirit is more and more caught up to lead the angelic life through love's yearnings. As the Apostle Paul says, *To me to live is Christ and to die is gain* (Phil 1:21).

11. The more the human spirit ardently aspires with the feet of her affections to find repose in him who is true life, the less is she joined to fleshly affection, as she senses the things which are of the spirit and is increasingly absorbed in God. She thus somehow imitates the angelic life through that divine wisdom, even if wretchedly and at a distance, owing to the three sorts of differences mentioned above.

12. The very same wisdom arranges the fullest sort of inward order in the rational spirit. How much humans lack is confirmed unfailingly when, leaving herself and encountering other creatures outside herself, the human spirit expects to find repose for her drives and appetites. Now the human spirit, the image of God, is adjudged to be more excellent than the other visible creatures, which are the vestiges of God, and therefore supercelestial wisdom dwells in her more fully and eminently than in them. But when she senses that divine goodness has unlocked in her the hidden storehouse of divine wisdom, she is no longer poor yet is now sustained by her lack of other delights. Nor does the primordial nobility hidden in her degenerate; rather, with the joy left behind by this more intimate union with God, she rejoices steadily, as she says with Job (not wanting other things to separate her from God), *I shall die on my couch, and as a palm tree shall multiply my days*[12] (Jb 29:18). For wisdom arranges the soul not only by making her to come to rest in herself, rooting out all outwardly directed wants; rather, wisdom's own costliness brings order to the human spirit. The more noble and sound the *habitus*[13] of wisdom held by the soul, the more angelic her spirit. In view of that wisdom by which she alone possesses God in her heart, the human spirit counts as nothing all the treasures, all the valuables, all the delights that the eye can see, reason investigate, and intellect understand. She affirms with every wise person: *Gold is mud in comparison with [wisdom]* (Wis 7:9). Why? Because she has such great nobility, dignity, and attraction within herself that *all the things that are desired are not to be compared to her* (Prv 3:15, cf. 8:11).

3. Unitive Wisdom's Consummation of the Virtues

A. THE THEOLOGICAL VIRTUES: FAITH, HOPE, AND
CHARITY; PHILOSOPHY IN GENERAL

13. Such nobility is evident not only because wisdom exists in the human spirit, but also because of other acquired virtues and freely given charisms that are judged to be better than other licit things. Now it is through wisdom that faith is certified, hope is strengthened, and charity is inflamed.

14. For faith is made certain when, through the senses, the human spirit perceives herself drawn by unfailing knowledge into the One who alone quiets her longing, something she knows truly and more truly than any material thing viewed by physical eye. If therefore she unmistakably knows the one toward whom she reaches in these upsurges, then in some manner the human spirit already knows for sure that he is the true God, the true Lord, whom she worships by faith. Or if indeed beginners or intermediates must attain this wisdom through the benefits of the Incarnation and Passion of the Lord, and if the *affectus* is increasingly inflamed with divinity by consideration of these benefits, then the spirit that has already been elevated in this wisdom ought in due course win through to such favors and, as a result, come to know the binding of the divine and human.

15. And if the human spirit, no matter how miserable she was up to this point, is fully assured by wisdom about many things pertaining to faith, then let any faithful soul know that the human spirit presses on from this to wisdom herself. Even if all the wise men of the world and all philosophers testify against her by saying, "Your faith is not true faith, indeed, you are deceived," she should reply to the contrary: "All of you are deceived, and I alone most happily hold the true faith, more faithfully than by reasoning and investigating: by the loving union, by virtue of the undeceived firmament in my heart." With the Apostle Paul she can say, *I know whom I have believed, and I am certain . . .* (2 Tm 1:12).

16. Not only is faith certified through this wisdom, but hope is strengthened, for, since "hope is a sure expectation of future blessedness,"[14] it is strengthened so much through this wisdom that it almost lacks any fear of failure to gain future glory. For the household servants of a prince, over a long period of obediently carrying out their duties, gradually find that a certain sense of being-at-home replaces the fear that

initially sprang from awe of their lord's majesty; indeed, fear completely vanishes, replaced by confidence in his goodness and [in their] at-homeness, a confidence that cannot imagine anything coming between them and him. To apply this anagogically, the human spirit that was once lukewarm pursues a unitive at-homeness through yearnings and affections until by the Beloved's own gift a wondrous confidence is left behind in the human spirit, uprooting every prickly fear (except where it serves as a caution). Now she can say with the Apostle Paul, *What can separate me from the love of Christ? Shall hunger, sword, . . .* and so forth, whether indeed *now or in the future* (Rom 8:35)?

17. Charity is inflamed, made whole, and perfected through this wisdom. For, since the most blessed God himself is *a consuming fire* (Dt 4:24; Heb 12:29), the more he drives every sort of chill from the way-farer's spirit, the more she approaches him inwardly through love's out-stretchings. Because she thus aspires through anagogic movements to-ward a more intimate union with him, she exposes herself to the consuming rays of the Spiritual Sun and, like a wick exposed to the rays of the sun, is ignited by fire sent from on high.

Hence this sun is said to consume spirits in three ways. First, by itself it increases the spirit's ardor, and by means of ardor cuts out the obstacles to love, so that love might blaze more ardently. This sun then piles on the spiritual favors by which love itself is perfected in the Spiritual Sun. Second, the Spiritual Sun sets the human spirit ablaze to love God himself most ardently. Third, this wisdom fires up the human spirit to love of each of her neighbors as herself and she, in turn, sick with insatiable yearnings, does not relent from aspiring to the fullest possible union.

18. Not only do virtues find their preeminence through this per-fected wisdom, but the human spirit is advanced beyond all philosophy, all of reason's research, all theological speculation and inquiry. The nat-ural philosopher indeed knows the Creator, because he observes that all physical creatures have a cause. He thus affirms by infallible proof that the goodness, the marvelous order, and the immensity of created things could not have come into being except from a single omnipotent Cre-ator. In the words of the Apostle Paul, *For the invisible things of him, from the creation of the world, are clearly seen, being understood by the things that are made, his eternal power also, and divinity* (Rom 1:20). This is how the philosopher arrives at knowledge. Yet since the entire world is nothing in comparison to the rational spirit (as uncreated wisdom her-self proclaims: *Playing in the world: and my delights were to be with the*

children of men [Prv 8:31]), the entire world is like a little circus in which beauty makes a brief appearance, with "beauty" referring here to angelic and human spirits. Hence the philosopher's narrow and beggarly natural knowledge knows nothing of the deep states of the human spirit[15] and lies as incomparably far beneath this wisdom as the East is separated from the West. The same applies to metaphysical or theological[16] consideration, both of which apprehend the one, true, good God in his simplicity by considering being and its differentiations, potentialities, and tendencies. But through this wisdom the human spirit, apart from any of the reasoning mentioned above, without any cogitation leading the way for love's movement or keeping it company, is able to apprehend through the affective summit the One who is the supreme good in an inexpressible way. No understanding can rise up to and no intellect can speculate about this apprehension. How this can be and how the intellect can be divided from the *affectus* is shown below in the discussion of the theoretical practice of this wisdom, beginning with the words "Arise unknowing" from *On Mystical Theology*.[17]

B. THE CARDINAL VIRTUES: PRUDENCE, FORTITUDE, TEMPERANCE, JUSTICE

19. We must consider how the human spirit is gently disposed toward lower things. We have already discussed how the body becomes subject to her when she is conformed by this [unitive] wisdom to the highest wisdom that rules the world. Here we must add something else. Just as someone seated on an adequately broken and trained horse can, by force of the reins, turn that beast of burden to the right or to the left at will,[18] so too the spirit no longer cowers in the body but, through this same wisdom, stands tall, and uses the force [*virtus*] of love as a set of spiritual reins to control the otherwise unrestrained exterior senses. In this way, at the nod and command of that toward which it tends, each domain, whether of [psychological] powers or [physical] senses, can be better regulated. The human spirit thereby makes a tabernacle out of her subjugated body and mind, a tabernacle corresponding to the model revealed on the mountain, a model that divine wisdom commanded Saint Moses to follow, as we are told in the book of Exodus (25:40).

20. Moreover, the human spirit is disposed toward and in the truest sense rules all worldly things through this same wisdom. Now, if an earthly prince were placed over all the world and, possessing all the delights, riches, and honors that all mortals have had from the beginning

of the world, were disposed to delight in them, he would then be subject to them, for he would thereby eagerly seek to obtain from them some repose, happiness, or perfection he himself does not yet have. Whoever delights in certain things is truly subject to them. Only he who despises lower things to the point that nothing earthly can disrupt love's tranquillity, only he who can disdainfully trample all things under his feet, is lord over all things.

The soul thus rules this kingdom when, seeking no other repose, she stretches yearningly toward things on high, saying with Paul the Apostle, *I consider all things as dung that I may gain Christ* (Phil 3:8). That is why Peter and Paul are called *glorious princes of earth.*[19] This was prefigured when the same wisdom promised the children of Israel without hesitation: *Every place that your foot shall tread upon, shall be yours* (Dt 11:24; Jos 1:3). Therefore, anyone who despises all things rules all things more truly than the princes rule this world.

21. Through this wisdom the human spirit is also gently disposed toward the wiles of her enemies, needing wisdom as much because of their stealth as their fortitude. For the shrewd[20] are zealously on the lookout for the tricks of the enemy by which the spirit united to God might be separated from her Beloved. Wisdom frees the human spirit from these attacks because, as the spirit approaches the fountain of light to drink deep draughts of love, she cannot help but be lit up by divine rays. Quickly and sagely she can then see through even the trickiest and best-disguised temptations that might hold forth under the cover of goodness. She thereby confounds the enemy's own shrewdness for, as it says in Proverbs, *But a net is spread in vain before the eyes of them that have wings* (Prv 1:17), who, through yearning affections, *fly as clouds, and as doves fly to their windows* [i.e., to their dovecotes] (Is 60:8), as one reads in Isaiah.

22. Wisdom disposes to fortitude as well, because the human spirit clings with such vehemence to the one she loves, the one she truly knows, that she would rather let herself be slain a thousand times over than even once to sin deliberately against her Beloved. She has two aids in obtaining such ineradicable fortitude. First, she is protected like a member of God's own household by the guiding right hand of her beloved Creator, as it says in Wisdom: *The souls of the just are in the hand of God* (Wis 3:1). Then, for her own part, should she be pummeled more insistently by her enemies' mightiest temptations, like a timid child who runs to mother when he is afraid someone will hurt him, the human

spirit assailed by temptations breathlessly runs to him whom she loves, seeking help. This is by far the best way to conquer demons.

23. This wisdom also brings the virtue of temperance to perfection. For human intemperance comes about when a man who fails to delight in the union of God and the soul wretchedly takes pleasure in gluttony, lust, or other fleshly enticements. Now the enjoyment found in God is so much greater than that found in the flesh, since God is better than any creature delightful to men of flesh. The more the human spirit sensually experiences true delight, the more vehemently she disdains fleshly delight. When she discovers true pleasure in love's bed,[21] she says, *It is good for me to cling to my God* (Ps 72:28 [73:28]). Having possessed this pleasure, she finds it easy to despise the others.

24. Perfect justice is acquired through this mystical wisdom, for true justice is to render to God, to oneself, and to one's neighbor what belongs to each. Through unitive wisdom one first returns to God what is God's, for any movement of upsurge places the soul before God's face, and through the affection of love the soul seeks the things that are of God, not her own. There can be no true love unless the lover loves the beloved more than herself. Indeed, this love permits her no repose except in the one she loves. For just as a stone's weight will not permit the stone to come to rest short of earth, its natural place, so too spiritual love permits one to rest nowhere except in God, who is the natural terminus of every spirit, a goal beyond which nothing can be desired.

25. Through this unitive wisdom God not only receives his own, but the soul receives what belongs to her, that is, in this wisdom the soul is perfected in her own self. The human Philosopher [Aristotle] says that the soul is perfected by means of virtues and sciences. Therefore the supreme perfection of the soul takes place when he who is the fount of all wisdom (for all created wisdom or knowledge, whether above or below, emanated from him) deigns to dwell spiritually in the human spirit. Hence God's dwelling in the soul who loves him is a truer form of residence than that of any human dwelling in a physical place. God does this by taking up a spiritual residence, for *God himself is charity* and *he who abides in charity*, that is, in true love [*amor*],[22] *abides in God and God in him*, as one reads in John's letter (1 Jn 4:16).

26. Moreover, through this wisdom one also renders to one's neighbor what belongs to him, doing so in the same love with which the Father loves and the Son loves. For, with the same love she has for her Creator, the soul loves all rational creatures who are sealed with the image of the eternal Father himself. From the fact that she loves the

Father emerges a fervent love of souls, increasing her prayers for the liberation of lost souls. That very love multiplies groans so that souls might turn back toward their own Creator, so that those who are dead through sins might be revived through the life of divine grace. As Jeremiah exclaimed, *Who will give water to my head, and a fountain of tears to my eyes? And I will weep day and night for the slain of my people?* (Jer 9:1).[23]

27. How unitive wisdom disposes every contemplative affection[24] for merit is plain, since, as often as the human spirit moves directly into God, she merits[25] eternal life. As often as the soul disposed by wisdom wishes, she can actually be swept up by rapid movements that are more fleeting than tongue can tell. By merit she is thus raised up in glory by one of these surging motions. Since each merit corresponds to a particular glory (except for the essential crown, the crown of the vision of divine beauty), this confirms that the soul accumulates innumerable crowns through this wisdom.[26]

28. In conclusion, we return to the beginning: Set on fire, the human spirit is brought to completion through this wisdom, so that like a circle, the most complete[27] of all figures, the spirit that has gone forth from the most sublime turns again to the same sublimity both now and in the future. Like an arc extended all the way from a starting point around to the same point, the spirit returns in the most direct pattern possible.

29. Therefore,[28] O eternal Wisdom, because no mortal can manifest that marvelous and uncreated wisdom which proceeds unmediated from you, the fount of life, come to teach us the path of prudence,[29] since, contrary to the other sciences, in this wisdom, practice precedes theory. First[30] comes the practice, by which the human spirit is cleansed in the first path; in the second she is enlightened; in the third she is perfected—so that this wisdom's threefold path might correspond to the ultimate hierarchy, namely the purgative path to the Thrones, the illuminative path to the Cherubim, and the unitive path to the Seraphim. Because, as has been said,[31] a man can persuade to this wisdom but cannot teach it,[32] therefore most blessed and highest God—you who by your nature are invariable and unchangeable, you through whom the creative force of all good things principally perdures, you whose face feeds angels, you who are uncreated wisdom, you who shed your brilliance on celestial and angelic spirits—therefore, highest God, vivify virtue in order that it might fill up your lovers; so that, separated from lower things, we may be raised up by you to yearn for and know you, and,

removed from every distraction of spirit, we may be turned by you toward the unity of a harvesting Father who gathers together his scattered Israel into the granary of eternal light. Amen.[33]

B. Persuasions to Pursue Unitive Wisdom

1. Introduction

30. *Come to him and be enlightened*, and so forth (Ps 33:6 [34:5]).[34] Since God most blessed *inhabits light inaccessible* (1 Tm 6:16), as the Apostle Paul says, and since an infinite number of degrees separates every rational creature from him, if the soul is to be bathed by the superbeautiful brilliance of eternal light, she must, as it were, depart from herself and be raised above by the Creator's freely bestowed favor until an approximate similarity and conformity between the creature, who receives, and the benevolent Creator, who flows into her, is established. Therefore the divine prophet says, *Come to him and be enlightened*, so that this might precede and illumination might immediately follow. With this we fully enter upon the theme of the present book. For, by a roundabout path, contrary to all writers on matters of theology and divinity, it teaches that one attains unmediated cognition of the Creator not by the mirror of creatures nor by genius in research nor by exercise of intellect, but through flaming gasps of unitive love. By these, although living in sin and misery, we have an unfailing foretaste not only of the fact that God is but indeed of how the most blessed God himself is the beginning and origin of all beatitude. As we shall see later, this foretaste exceeds the knowledge gained by reason as much as the sun's beauty exceeds that of all the other planets and as much as the morning star outshines all the other gleaming stars. Unitive love reveals hidden things and unlocks secrets. Rather than making the lover pursue earthly and human things, these secrets make him (now raised above himself) push directly for divine and heavenly formation.

31. Because boiling love aspires to union with the Beloved, it more ardently carries the spirit on high so that she might draw close to the source of true light, and it alone gives access to the one who dawns from on high, *enlightening those that sit in darkness and in the shadow of death* (Lk 1:79). Through him things in motion and things known obtain their full and complete perfection, permitting the human spirit to be adorned by her merciful Beloved with the ardor of love and the beauty of light.

Unitive love not only brings the soul to possess the glory of eternal beatitude as she retreats from the body, not only brings her to live the celestial life on earth, not only do lower things no longer make the soul anxious and divert her from her actions stretching toward the heights—more than all that, the yearnings of unitive love leave behind in the soul a perfection of knowledge that is incomparably more complete than any sought out by study, hearing, or exercise of reason.

32. In the present work, which I have written in order to make the mystical theology of Blessed Denis more plain, my purpose is to reveal that work's theory of how the soul might inhere to her Creator and how she might be more effectively and heartily united to him, as to the sweetest Beloved. In mystical theology a few words encompass endless meanings, as will become apparent in what follows. For the outstretched union of the spirit yearning to attain her Beloved increases by the Beloved's own free gift, which, in this unitive wisdom, is not for someone who assembles external things into a set of writings but for someone who perceives inwardly.

33. This book's style, therefore, is purely and simply anagogical, except when it briefly stoops to explain lower things in order to make the anagogic sense clearer. It is anagogical in style so that only those who love this supreme unitive wisdom purely might perceive it in themselves, while the wise of this world, or lovers of worldly things, will fail to grasp it either by intellect or *affectus*.

34. This book aims to attend to how the soul might aspire with all her heart to union with the Bridegroom, fitting her to receive in this present life a down payment on glory and the bridal crown. Every rational spirit ought to seek her own beatitude for five persuasive reasons. So that the main matter may be more eagerly appropriated when discussed at length below (par. 35–57), we precede it here with these five reasons.

The first reason is drawn from a consideration of worldly activities and creaturely irrationalities. The next three have to do with the perfection of potencies that are so happily obtained in the present life through the union of love. The last reason has to do with the continued progress and expansion of the human spirit, which steadily strengthens her in her desire, out of love for the Beloved, to reach toward greater things—until in her departure from the body she shall rise up to see the Sun of righteousness face-to-face, as he is.

2. Reason One: People Endure Hardship for Lesser Gains

35. The first persuasion exposes the folly of all mortals, especially of those living the religious life. As a certain saint says, someone pursuing a craft energetically endures toils and dangers, even financial losses, with cheerful equanimity. This is confirmed by examples from agriculture, commerce, and warfare.[35]

First, neither heat of the sun nor frost, snow, and ice keep the farmer from tirelessly furrowing the earth, repeatedly working the recalcitrant clods of the field with the plowshare, ridding it of all briars and grass, laboring to reduce the field to loose and friable soil. In all of this he is intent on a single outcome: to receive from the soil a copious harvest and abundant crop, all in hope of leading a life free of anxiety or increasing his wealth.

Now, if a farmer lets himself be buffeted incessantly by such toils and losses in order to find peace of short duration in earthly things as a man of earth, so too each person sealed with the image of the whole Trinity, and especially each monk, who has limited himself more strictly than others for the sake of more effective union with God eternal, should let himself be similarly buffeted. Thus will they be able to haul up joy from the well of blessedness in this present life and drink up glory through unitive yearnings in the future. If at the outset some difficulty appears or something seems unbearable to the flesh, the soul will nonetheless soon find longed-for repose in her most pleasant Beloved. Though the path seems narrow at the outset, as Solomon says in the Book of Wisdom, *afflicted in a few things, in many they shall be well rewarded* (Wis 3:5). And he speaks rightly for she quickly discovers the one from whom all pleasure and all delight flows.

36. A second example comes from those who undertake commercial business. Neither the ocean's uncertainties nor any sort of danger intimidate them, for as long as they remain focused on their goal of making a profit, they cheerfully take on all such challenges. Now, if such people incessantly subject body and soul to dangers of this sort, ought not the rational spirit be much more fired up with unceasing eagerness to find him who is sweetest of all? For when the spirit has gained her Beloved's delightful presence through the union of love, he takes away all her want and lack, keeping her from wandering far from him or going begging to find counterfeit delights in other creatures. Received as her guest, this Blessed One quiets every urge completely. When the soul senses his presence, she says of him, *I shall die on my couch, and as a palm*

tree shall multiply my days (Jb 29:18). She no longer wishes to have recourse to her accustomed interests, for she is already united to him in whom all sickness of body or spirit finds health-giving medicine. She now needs no human consolation.

37. Third, we observe that those inflamed by lustful ambition for this world's wars (as long as honors or power are in prospect) take no notice of war's dangers, exiles, and wanderings, remaining unfazed by war's deprivations as long as they can imagine honor accruing to themselves. Now, if they are willing to put up with such misery in order to be wafted high by the wind of vainglory stirred up by fleeting human praise, and if they consider this sufficient reward for all manner of exhaustion of body and soul, what sort of honor might drive the rational spirit, the noblest of creatures yet a beggar in relation to her Creator, to attain a prize of such worth: namely, to be united to him from whom she had her primordial origin, being created from nothing, and to be judged so worthy in the eyes of her Creator that she, who is less than a fly, less than nothing, should in strictest terms be called the beloved of the Prince of Life, of the King of angels; that lowly though she be, she might still be called forth to such great honor by the Most High Creator, who says in the Canticle: *Open to me, my sister, my dove,* and so forth (Ca 5:2).[36]

3. Reason Two: Examples Offered by the Perfection of Potencies

38. Having described how worldly activity calls the human spirit forth to such great enjoyment of the Beloved, we now must speak of how rational and irrational creatures stimulate her to find repose in her Creator. We consider first the sensate and vegetative creatures, followed by the [in]animate creatures and then the rational creatures.

39. We observe that a brute animal, who salivates when he sees what he knows from experience to be tasty, rushes heedlessly toward it. Now the spirit gifted with reason has a single delightful object in which both true repose and the satisfying of every hunger are equally present. She would be robbed of such a great immutable and present delight and judged a wretch by divine justice if, like a brute animal, she were in such a hurry to obtain by her senses her delectable morsel that she fails even to lift her eyes to that true unitive wisdom spoken of by uncreated wisdom: *All good things came to me together with her* [namely with wisdom] (Wis 7:11).

40. Indeed, she says *all things* so that nothing might remain incomplete in the human spirit in the presence of wisdom. She says *good things*

rather than *a good* so that the multiplication of divine favors might be brought home to the loving spirit. She says *came* to signify that she is to obtain all these things not from herself but from the Most High, her Beloved, who mercifully pours them into her. She says *together* since the soul has nothing good in herself and, if she did, it was filled up with manifold bitterness. She says *with her* to indicate not merely that the possession of this unitive wisdom would inwardly soothe the spirit as with oil,[37] but also that many delightful presents and favors, namely, many gleaming and sparkling drops, accompany the presence of unitive wisdom, giving the human spirit an experiential taste of glory here and now through wisdom. We ought to consider ourselves wretched if, as rational creatures, we fail to do what we observe in sensate creatures and instead slothfully busy ourselves with momentary delights, lamentably concern ourselves with lower things, and imprudently and wretchedly put to sleep the human heart's nobility.

41. This is also apparent from vegetative things. For instance, if a tree is to stand its ground unmoved when buffeted by the winds, it must send out roots to take moisture and strengthening nourishment from the very earth in which it is fixed; and, sending its branches skyward, it must depend on its powerful rootage if it is to persevere firmly in place without breaking. So too the human spirit stands erected above herself through unitive love and, anchored by penetrating affections, is rooted in him to whom she is united in love. In such fixed union, the eternal raindrops brought down from the gushing fountain of all delights and plenitude by love, especially by importunate movements of love, descend [below the soil] to reach, by way of a sort of root system, the trunk of the *affectus*. Thus they strengthen the spirit in her trunk, so that she might ascend continuously to the Bridegroom without leaning to one side. Thus may the branches of the spirit's other faculties take on bulk through the strengthening of love's movements (which here are called roots), growing strong enough to avoid being blown about like reeds in the cyclone of spiritual winds.

42. The sap makes trees grow strong, flower, and bear fruit, and a material tree would achieve none of these without the strength her sap provides. So too the sap of love makes a variety of higher things flower, to the great pleasure of the Beloved, and it makes the leaves of words bring forth the fertile fruit of works that never run out. For love produces perpetual lush growth, not out of the aridity of worldly things (except by despising them) but from the things that please the one whom she loves, so that lovers might perceive in themselves by experiential

knowledge the truth of his promise, made while he was living joyfully on earth and dwelling with sinners: *Good measure and pressed down, and shaken together and running over, shall they give into your bosom* (Lk 6:38). Thus God promises the aspiring soul, who is implanted by fiery movements of love into God as firmly as an insensate material tree, that she will realize that what she sees in the creature is free of and insusceptible to the experience of delight and pleasure. This the wretched soul adapts to herself, for she is the one to whom all sorts of delightful rewards are promised by the Giver of all.

43. Now let us see what the Scripture quoted above brings home to us. Jesus uses the word *measure* because love—the perfect union of love, which strictly speaking is called *measure*—is given to someone who is careful about being firmly rooted in God. By this union alone the soul's capacity is measured, so that she might quickly and perfectly grasp the more perfect union she yearns for, that she might long to love more ardently. As he apportions festive gifts to her according to the measure of her yearnings, the Most High pours himself into this poor little one. Uniting[38] the loving human spirit's *affectus* to the eternal, uplifting God is truly *good* measure, for she is united not to someone who is good by participation but to someone who simply *is* the supreme Good. A more ample goodness deifies the human spirit who is united to it and thus God alone can be called *good.* Thus the human or angelic mind in which the love that transforms the creature into the Creator piles up all the more abundantly is better because of it. This love alone, by its very name, ought to be named the noblest good *habitus,* because it transforms the soul, by her own deifying outreach, into God, who alone is good by self-definition. Love's fruits then rain down with exuberant increase upon the faculties and virtues of the soul, coming in such abundance that no corner remains empty, which is why Jesus immediately adds, *packed down.*

44. Now the presence of unitive love splashing over the entire person causes a certain contest among the virtues, as one virtue desires to engage another's movement. This is what the *shaken down* measure refers to. And because true love so throbs with fire that it cannot be banked under ashes but constantly flames up to transmit heat to others, so too love overflows into exterior words, freely setting out in words that on which the human spirit's *affectus* has been focused. While the spirit bears the weight of love's verbal limitation, the mouth, which is the messenger by which the spirit expresses what she senses inside, brings forth divine, not human, celestial, not terrestrial, contents.

Thus it can be said that love, the measure according to which the *affectus* is directed, strengthens her faculties by a variety of resources and stimulates the virtues to active battle. The human spirit, drawing on her dignity, can speak and act deliberately to reach out toward external things, except for things not permitted her because they pertain to him who possesses her. And even the latter should serve to rouse the soul in sadness to zealous toil and encourage her to approach the starting point of unitive wisdom audaciously. (The starting point is the really difficult part.) Then, rapidly settling down to remain fixed in her natural place, naturally seeking out her primordial origin, she can become firmly rooted there.

4. Reason Three: Examples Offered by Inanimate Creatures

45. Having spoken of how the human spirit ought to be roused to her delightful goal through the examples of sensate and vegetative things, it is time to address how the spirit can be more effectively stirred up by the examples of inanimate things. For just as every physical body keeps to the places suited to them, so spiritual beings, whether angelic or human spirits, have their proper place—not after the fashion of corporal dimensions but after the fashion of their own vigorous inclination, kept by God's own right hand from returning to the nothingness [out of which he created them]. Just as a body, because of its weight, naturally moves rapidly to repose in its natural place, so the importunate urges of spirit will not let the human spirit rest until she completely constrains him who by his own worth cannot not be desired and thus lodges by the weight of love in loftier union with him. Wandering without repose and without food, the famished spirit keeps on begging despite being occupied with all sorts of outward delicacies or honors. Her hunger will never be satisfied until she has been led to him whose image she imitates, until through the touch of love she comes to him for whom alone her very nature hungers, until he signals his presence in her by steady joy.

46. And this is brought home to us in the gospel of John where blessed Peter—who loved more ardently than the others and, seeing want on all sides while still finding complete peace only in the One to whom he spoke—said: *Lord, to whom shall we go? You have the words of eternal life* (Jn 6:69). He calls him *Lord* because he worships him rather than any creature. He could indeed call him *Lord* because love does not carry one off in some other direction but turns one toward him from whom one has come forth as from a primordial fountain. Thus he says,

To whom shall we go? Speaking as lovers do, he gives the most compelling reason not to withdraw from him: *You have the words of eternal life.* You have, not the words of the outward mouth, but the words of the inward spirit, emitting a stream of word-droplets that reveal the unknown joys of eternal life to your lovers much more effectively than proofs or evidence from the creatures or any other sort of words. So effective are they that those who sense them, according to the Apostle Paul, count everything else as dung in order to gain you (cf. Phil 3:8).

5. Reason Four: Examples Offered by Rationality

47. Fourth, regarding [the persuasive reasons provided by] rational creatures. Since the soul wishes to be completed by objectives that fit her faculties, that is, by something truly lofty and delightful, she aspires to extend herself on high to be united to that inexpressible One who is supreme majesty, unchangeable truth, and never-failing goodness. We pass over this briefly here, since we shall deal with it more amply later (par. 82–115). Yet in the present life, the soul does not consider true loftiness to exist in the creature. Though she be raised above other things more excellently through the loftiest honors, for both her spirit and her body she must necessarily test herself by sensory means, undergoing various kinds of want and subjection.

48. But the spirit truly gains the heights full of rejoicing only when she enjoys the great freedom that comes with the intimate union of love, a freedom that cannot be known except through experiential knowledge by which she knows ahead of time that she need not fear the devil or be frightened in any way of mortal man, that she need not feel the pangs of eternal punishment, something which lets her embrace death's approach with joy. This foreknowledge means that she can be free in all things because she has directly submitted herself to her own Creator through true union, so that his promise spoken through John might come to pass: *If therefore the Son shall make you free, you shall be free indeed* (Jn 8:36). The Son of God truly liberates when he offers an extended right hand of love to her so that she might inhere in him, with every creature placed beneath. Then no painful experience under God rules the one who loves him in unitive yearnings.

49. Now love has firmly planted her in a safe place so that she might fear nothing outside herself nor fear him in whom she lives, since familiar love makes her forget the stern judgments of him whom she loves. Hence Truth himself says in John: *These things I have spoken to*

you that in me you may have peace. In the world, you shall have distress
(Jn 16:33). For indeed, when the Lord speaks to the human spirit and
announces his presence in colloquies of spiritual inpourings, peace follows immediately, because the spirit to whom the Most High promised
distress in worldly things is absolutely freed from every servitude. It is
right that whoever fails to submit through true love to the majesty worthy of veneration should be miserably trampled by every creature, since
each creature thereby vindicates its Creator, grinding down by various
afflictions such a person unwilling to submit to God in love. By abandoning his proper Lord to cast his lot with despicable things, such a
person despises his own Creator as if he were not the true God. Hence,
the more intimately the soul clings to God through burning love, the
more effectively is she free of all subjection and the more she rejoices in
her proper realm.

50. Having said that true love reposes in that union of love that
unites to the One who is subject to nothing, we must discuss how it is
that reason finds truth only in him. But because we are here assuming
the viewpoint that true enlightenment is the result of love, we must discuss how the will finds full satisfaction in him and him alone when the
wayfarer living in this present life arrives at happy union with him. (This
will be described at greater length later.) Although the spirit ought not
rest in anything less noble than herself and although earthly consolation
or fleshly delight are not enough for her, still, sometimes she busies
herself with such things, which is contrary to her natural urge toward
God. This is lamentable because every true delight stills the yearning or
striving of the person hungry for it, whereas earthly things, no matter
how sweet one might think them, after a time leave a famished and completely restless appetite behind, as is obvious in all sensory things.
Therefore the appetite's urges never find repose in earthly pleasures.
What then should our human spirit do? She needs to end up with the
one thing that can speed her way to present union with the only One she
discovered to be better than herself, the One who alone conceals within
himself the *treasury* of rejoicing. When she finds this treasure through
experiential knowledge, she *for joy thereof goes and sells all she has and
buys the field* (Mt 13:44).

51. The level surface of unitive love is called a *field* in which the
spirit runs on the feet of the affections with kindled[39] yearnings. One
finds the *buried treasure* in that field by exercise of love when the One
who is true rejoicing proves himself palpably present through spiritual
knowledge or some spiritual festive gift. To acquire this love the human

spirit gladly considers everything else to be of little worth, since she perceives in her *affectus* the person and character of him whom she loves. She stretches above and beyond herself directly toward him, raised above by her Beloved's right hand, so that the things she has already heard might prove to be truer than the things she physically sees so plainly. In this light the words of David are quite justified: *For better is one day in your courts above thousands* (Ps 83:11 [84:10]), for, as the spirit runs aspiringly through the courts of love's open plain, she senses more joy of spirit in one day than she could experience in a thousand days of unsuitable delighting in vain things. It is called a *day in the court* because as long as the spirit is not running through this open field, she knows that she is covered by a darkening cloud in a variety of ways.

52. Next we turn to the rational goal known as truth. The truth suited to the rational spirit will not be glimpsed through created truth, because every truth is far removed from falsehood, deception, and opinion. (But here we make no mention of uncreated truth, only of created truth.) For falsehood is accommodated, deception follows, and opinion is multiplied where truth is unknown. And this is because the hidden things of truth cannot be known except in the spirit illuminated by light shining from above. Now this light shining from above we understand to be the hidden divinity mediated by light, just as exterior, corporal sense-perceptions are received without deception when bodily sight employs the medium of light to direct the ray of vision toward the sense-perceptible object. Where divine light is lacking, created truth turns into deception, not because of some defect of truth but because of the darkness remaining in the blinded spirit unable to perceive the ray of intelligible truth within her.

53. Hence, even though we see through our senses, almost all truth ultimately concerns divine realities, except for things to which we once assented by faith but have since turned into doubt or opinion. And so the rational spirit does not apprehend truth purely through human teaching.

Therefore, in order to find truth, the human spirit should hasten toward the union of love. More closely than one body is joined to another body by physical chains or man-made adhesive,[40] the kiss of love joins her to him who, according to the divine Apostle Paul, *dwells in light inaccessible* (1 Tm 6:16). And then, to the one who in filial fear both loves and fears her Beloved in equal measure, comes the promise of the prophet Malachi, *Unto you that fear my name, the Sun of righteousness shall arise* (Mal 4:2).

54. Mercifully, the divine enlightenment mentioned above comes

to pass: *Come to him and be enlightened* (Ps 33:6 [34:5]). Denis explains this in the seventh book of *On the Divine Names*. When the human spirit, in learning things that have to do with created truth, submerges her *affectus*, she is ultimately united to the One who makes his sun to rise on the good and on the bad, in order that she might be adorned with his variegated splendor. Denis says, "When the human spirit draws back from all other things and thereafter even dismisses herself, she is united with superresplendant rays and enlightened by deep and inscrutable wisdom."[41] Now he says "united" before he says "enlightened by inscrutable wisdom," so that it might be brought home to every human spirit that though profound and inscrutable, truth is known inwardly by clouded eyes in supreme and inaccessible being, solely by the mediating union of love.[42]

6. Reason Five: The Loving Spirit's Progress by Two Arms

55. Next comes the final [persuasive] reason, namely the progress of the loving spirit eager to reach out for greater things out of love for her Beloved. This does not take place after the manner of human philosophers who, puffed up by proud scorn, disdainfully refuse to attribute anything that can in any way be grasped by human understanding to that fountainhead from which every ray of truth spreads over the minds of all rational spirits. Instead, as much as the human spirit blazes with greater desire based on sensory things, having been taught by true wisdom, she knows that she cannot by her own merits obtain understanding of the things she possesses. Therefore she overflows all the more with thankful praise to the Grantor of all things. The more amply she receives graces from him, the more humble she becomes in her own eyes, putting herself down lest divine judgment convict her of robbery because, giddy in her own soul, she attributed to herself things not her own.

56. There are, then, two arms by which the upward movement of the human spirit's affections is increased. On the one hand, she disposes herself in preparation for the ascent; on the other hand, she calls for the free gift of divine inpouring by which what she already has is made to merit greater and richer rewards.[43]

She employs the first arm by the very fact that she does not attribute what she has to herself but redirects everything into praise to the Bestower of all things. In this way she scrapes out a cavity in herself by more truly fighting against herself. As this cavity wells up with divine graces that skip over mountains and hills,[44] the humbler places within her are filled by the graces pouring into her. The more capacious the cavity of humility, the more grace she can hold. Now to the degree that any creature acknowledges its source, it denies itself, since the more something created from nothing attributes every good and all existence to its Creator, that much more does it recognize the magnificence of the Creator. Thus it is rightly said that *God resists the proud, but to the humble he gives grace* (1 Pt 5:5; Jas 4:6).

57. The human spirit employs the second arm—the right arm—in aid of her yearning, permitting her to practice her exercises even more ardently than usual. When, through the union of love, the soul senses what things belong to God, she breaks forth into all manner of praise of God, and this praise, more than anything else (except the exercises of love), calls forth from God the largesse that makes it possible to give God even greater praise. This is what John, playing the part of such a praisegiver, says in the *Apocalypse: Blessing, glory, wisdom, and thanksgiving [honor, and power and strength to our God for ever and ever]* (Rv 7:12). Frequent acknowledgement of God's favors is like a trumpet sounding in the ears of the Beloved, calling on him to give the soul even more ample blessings. This frequent meditation on divine favors rouses the spirit to pour herself out completely in even more zealously obedient service to the overflowing Creator. Hence David, playing her role, says, *My heart grew hot within me: and in my meditation a fire shall flame out* (Ps 38:4 [39:3]), because his meditation consists in repeated consideration of divine benefits, setting the mind on fire to embrace even greater things for love of the Giver.

C. Industrious Efforts by Which Unitive Wisdom Is Gained and Preserved

58. We have said that the rational spirit cannot find repose in anyone except in adhering to the highest Good. Now we must consider the industrious human efforts that kindle burning love and aid unitive yearning to the point that the Beloved might look [upon the human soul] with the eye of goodness.[45] Since becoming accustomed to a good thing is the first step toward peacefully possessing any lofty thing at its source, four things must concur to bring about this perfect gaze from on high so that the much-yearned-for union might come to pass. One of these is found within the human spirit, a second comes from the body, a third from time, and a fourth from place.[46]

1. *Warming Up Gradually*

59. First, we see that when the sun is shining at full strength at mid-day, our eyes wince at the rays of the sun and are darkened. Therefore, if one wants to look directly at the source of the sun, one must follow a certain order, namely looking first at something less brilliant or perhaps at the sun as it begins to rise at dawn, and then observe it again at mid-morning. Only after this, having become accustomed to it, can one look at the sun at mid-day. So too, after the human spirit has dismissed all earthly things, after she has completely cut herself off from worldly joys, she still remains enveloped in a cloud that darkens her in many ways, a cloud that keeps her from being carried by unfettered movements to her goal. No one gains the summit quickly, whether he has devotion or lacks it, whether he feels he is hot or cold. Therefore the soul must take up industrious efforts in order, as shall be seen in greater detail below, to knock at the door of divine goodness and entreat God to flood her with mercy, so that the love seething through her can bring her to sense her Beloved (who created her in his image) burning near her, drawn solely by her submissiveness. Let her therefore not back away from her purpose, but keep on knocking as best she can, given her small stature, until through quiet love she hears the Beloved's sweetly consoling voice saying, *Behold, I am he, I who speak with you* (Jn 4:26).

2. *Invoking Saints and Angels*

60. The second industry is when the soul at the outset perceives that she is far removed from the ardor of unitive love through which she should be joined to the Beloved (for this ardor is far beyond the ability of a mortal human, who hungers for such great union of love from a miserable distance). She must therefore turn prayerfully with all her heart toward those who rejoice with the Beloved in the bridal chamber in glory, so that she, who lacks yearning ardor for him, might in her misery, through the supplications of those who now do not merely love him but rather burn with ardor for him totally, merit a spark of ardor. She desires not so much the very ardor of these heavenly saints, but, like a puppy begging to be fed, merely wishes for a few crumbs from the Lord's table.[47] This accords especially with two bits of counsel from the Psalmist, who says, *I have lifted up my eyes to the mountains*, adding immediately, *from whence help shall come to me* (Ps 120:1 [121:1]). Moreover, let us not forget Job's counsel: *And turn to some of the saints* (Jb 5:1).

61. For even if, as royal consorts, all angelic minds and the more outstanding saints are to be invoked most attentively, still the soul ought to have one special saint to whom she should be specifically and particularly devoted, so that since she is not always able to attend to divine things, her special patron saint might supply what she lacks, for he constantly stands in celestial glory within sight of God, sees God's unveiled face, and praises God with unceasing jubilation. Thus aided by her saint's intercession, the human spirit, who by herself is scarcely worthy to raise her lips to kiss the sole of her Beloved's feet, can be visited by love for the Beloved.[48]

62. We have said that both angelic spirits and the blessed saints in glory should be especially implored, since that happy city consists of both human and angelic beings. And so, let us not neglect the angels here. Listen to the voice of Raphael as he speaks to Tobias before revealing his angelic identity: *I offered your prayer to the Lord* (Tb 12:12). He was speaking these words while still playing the role of a soul wishing to ascend to God. The angels are the bridal attendants who carry the godly affections of human spirits to the Beloved so that he might supply what the human spirits lack by drawing on the store of never-failing compassion enclosed within his natural goodness. To us they bear signal service, coming forth as peaceful mediators of our blessed redemption in the incarnation of the word, announcing to us from the heavens the return of peace between the Creator and the creature, peace now reformed through the prince of life, our Lord Jesus Christ, heaping praise upon him and giving him thanks on our behalf, festively announcing great joys to the human race, bearing glad tidings.

63. Let the soul have reverence for that particular angel God's goodness has assigned to watch over her from the very beginning of her creation. She ought to entreat her angel eagerly so that, pauper though she be, through love she might be able to attain the One in whom, absorbed in his embraces, she rejoices in the happy beatitude of light inaccessible. May she be able to hear said to her what is said [by Gabriel] to Daniel, playing the role of the loving soul: *For you are a man of desires* (Dn 9:23). How shall we be able to repay our blessed guide and consoler who so gently admonishes the soul so that she might cling perfectly to her own Creator, even though she is weak in charity or cut off from him by her sin? So that the soul already dead might return to the source of life, the perfected angelic spirit redirects to the human soul those things which he has perceived, irradiating her in many ways and letting his own exercises kindle hers. He gives her joy through his company, especially

when the human spirit, by desiring to taste what he is totally taken up with, has come to resemble him, even if in a lesser way suited to her lower rank. It is easy for the human spirit to receive those things which the angel has directed toward her when both in nature and in grace a fitting proportionality exists, when there is an affinity of the same love, even though one may be less well rooted than the other. For just as it is humanly impossible to count the sands of the sea and the stars of the sky, so angelic favors toward us are infinite, for angels stand by those who pray, accompany those who are under way, and protect and defend those who sleep.

3. Postures for Prayer

64. Next follows the third exercise, or industry, which has to do with the various bodily postures for those who pray as they live in unitive longing. Among the various modes of praying described for us in sacred Scripture, let us first look at Moses, who stood up straight and raised his outstretched hands to heaven (cf. Ex 27:11–12). Second, there is Solomon, who on bended knee turned his face toward the earth and directed his hands toward heaven (cf. 2 Chr 6:13). Third, in the New Testament, we find Mary Magdalene, who fell on her face, prostate on the ground, to shower the blessed feet of the kind Redeemer with tears (Lk 7:38). Fourth is a sitting posture, which we find described in Luke.[49] Once more it is the Magdalene who was sitting at the Lord's feet in silence, praying more in the inner yearnings of her heart than with the outward lips of her mouth (Lk 10:39). Fifth is the example of the Lord Jesus Christ who, on his knees, then falling on his face, in threefold repetition entreated the Father that he might avoid, if possible, the cup of his Passion (Mt 26:39; Lk 22:42).[50] The sixth example is Jesus' posture on the cross, as, with hands extended and body outstretched, he commended his spirit to the Father (Lk 23:46). Seventh, when the apostles saw Jesus ascending to the Father, in their desire that he might return to them, they prayed inwardly as they stood erect with their faces toward the sky (Acts 1:10–11).

65. Although various postures are found to be useful to people who pray, given the variety of affections and cogitations with which they come to prayer, one mode in particular [is suited to the unitive upsurge that concerns us here]. For the body should be completely directed upward, with the face toward heaven above, since the shape of the body must conform to the disposition of the soul's affections and to the dis-

position of the spirit's activity. Thus if the human spirit were to extend herself in ardent motion, yearning for union with the Beloved, while pointing her [bodily] face downward toward the ground, her actual thrust would be impeded, even virtually destroyed.[51] Her yearning is a hunger for him who is located inexpressibly above her,[52] as Blessed Denis says in the *Mystical Theology* (in response to the longed-for joys promised to him): "You will be raised upward to him who is above all substance and cognition."[53]

Whether one stands up straight or bows the knee, the spirit in any case must, for the sake of congruence, rise up by the anagogic movements noted above.[54] For, we see from those whose thinking has probed deeply and subtly into these matters and from those who speak of lofty matters that the disposition of the body must respond to inner action, since one always must configure the outer to the inner.[55]

66. However, in meditating or weeping for sins, the body may take up a different posture, in order to look down at the earth like the publican who had provoked his gentle Redeemer to anger against himself. Still other, different, postures may be assumed for other specific[56] forms of meditative or cogitation-filled exercises. What is necessary in anagogical activity is the sort of disposition described above—someone ardently yearning to be affected into union with the Beloved will speak to him intently as if she were seeing him face-to-face. Although he may be everywhere, nevertheless he is in heaven and the lover's speech is directed to him there. Since she is speaking to the One she adores in heaven on high, she must turn toward him by raising her face to him, for it is to him in heaven that she yearningly calls, asking him to transform her totally into himself.

4. Choosing the Proper Time

67. Having spoken of the effort to assume that bodily posture that can make the soul readily noticed by the only person she wishes to please, it is time to speak of the fourth industry, which has to do with time. Just as we observe that one necessarily feeds one's body once or twice a day,[57] so let the soul who longs to live in love prepare herself by girding her loins at the proper hour and fitting time, and then let the time of prayer take place, so that the human spirit's daily banquet may not lack bread and wine, the refreshment of living love. Let her thereby discover that her Lover gives her a much nobler and sweeter banquet than the refreshment she experiences in feeding the body's flesh. For it

would indeed be a shame if the lady [of the house] were to languish with empty stomach at the luncheon of honeyed love while a garrulous maidservant's carnal desire is satisfied at the proper hour or opportune time.[58]

68. We must clarify what sort of time is opportune. Now, by frequently doing good a *habitus* is left behind in the soul. So too, when the soul chooses to set aside time during the night as especially suited to prayer (as the prophet David says: *Night shall be my light in my pleasures* [Ps 138:11 (139:11)]), a certain comfortable pleasantness lingers in the spirit, so that she always carries out her exercise of raising herself toward God at that accustomed hour. If something keeps her from reaching out in prayer at the accustomed hour, it becomes apparent of its own accord and causes no small amount of stress (especially if the hindrance is an unimportant matter), for she has missed out on the hour in which she is accustomed to cling tightly to the Beloved, to the one who serves her the solid food of love and sets before her the fragrant cup of spiritual joy. Should there be any further question regarding the hour best suited for the human spirit to reach out in praise of God, listen to what the Lord says through the prophet: *In the daytime the Lord has commanded his mercy; and a canticle to him in the night* (Ps 41:9 [42:8]). This is said especially because by night one is less visible to other people, since at that time almost all tumult quiets and Christian people sleep. One ought to take up concern for these Christian neighbors for the sake of charity—not just concern for those to whom one is bound [by family ties, friendship, or acquaintance], but for all children of baptism. By protecting them in vigil through heartfelt prayers, the lion who prowls about seeking whom he may devour[59] will be unable to prevail over those whom the Father of all living has conformed to the image of his Son.[60] It is at night that the soul glows with a desire to surge up to her Lord's embrace. Let her rise to stand guard in vigil by night for all those for whom her own Lord sacrificed himself as a living victim to the Father.

5. Choosing the Proper Place

69. The fifth effort, which has to do with place, follows. When the ancient seducer sees from the human spirit's godly labors and other effects that she wishes to withdraw completely from his dominion, and that, longing to be sheltered under her Beloved's wings, she aspires to a much more noble realm under her Beloved's lordship, the seducer becomes envious of her happiness. He circles around her with his temp-

tations, and, knowing that he cannot deceive by means of an openly evil deed, he throws himself upon her as she aspires toward a good thing, employing the appearance of other good things to deceive her miserably. He tells her, "Truth himself admonishes his disciples in the Gospel: *So let your light shine before men, that they may see your good works and glorify your Father who is in heaven* (Mt 5:16). Therefore, you should persist in prayer in a public and open place, so that your example might attract simple lay folk and guide them to higher things. Why should you merely yearn to make progress for yourself in holiness, when through you no small multitude might be challenged to imitate your spiritual exercise, when you might call others to higher things by your living example far more than by words of doctrine?"[61]

70. Therefore a hidden location is required, so that, by eliminating onlookers, the soul can experience the glory that ought to follow upon unitive love, yet avoid falling into the trap of pride. Let her listen not to her own ideas but to those of the Creator, teaching faithfully in the gospel: *But when you shall pray, enter into your chamber, and having shut the door, pray to your Father who is in heaven* (Mt 6:6).[62] Now sometimes the evil enemy leaves her in peace for a while as she prays in a public place. But he does this so that his advice can more readily take root in her heart and so that she will later have no qualms about placing her prayer in the mouth of men and begin to think herself better than others, or even think she is holy. When this happens, she is beginning to waste away inwardly and will hear her Lord say to her, *Truly you have hated my discipline,* and abandoning the gospel's counsel, *you have cast my words behind you* (Ps 49:17 [50:17]). For you have cast behind you the multiple words of consolation that belong to someone eagerly praying, the words of consolation by which God alone announces his presence in the human spirit when he speaks with her. Instead of surging upward to reply gratefully and with varied actions to the Giver's freely given and unmerited favor, she turns her back on him to cheapen herself for the sake of human approval and the praise of men.

71. Although pressures and all sorts of dangers ought to cause one to practice this fifth industry with care, it is the new lover desiring to surge up anew who should keep this practice with great diligence on account of the slender reed of love that she has so far come to possess. Much greater danger looms over such a neophyte than over someone with long experience in the spiritual duel, since the latter, protected by the shield of love, recognizes with open eyes the enemy's wiles[63]—like an experienced soldier who shrewdly knows how to triumph over a hos-

tile attacker. Only the one who by weight of love has with great toil established his heart inwardly in the Lord his kind protector can without anxiety show himself to others.

6. Variety in Spiritual Foods

72. Having spoken of the fifth effort, by which the lover might from time to time merit[64] God's notice, we turn next to another industry, one that arises from the multiplication of spiritual foods. We can learn from the way animals naturally feed their bodies. If the same food, even though it may be very tasty, is set in front of an animal day after day, the animal's sense of taste grows tired from the constant repetition and becomes hungry for new foods. Even though the first food was undeniably tastier in and of itself, fresh and more varied repasts will satisfy hunger better and will be more deeply ingested. So too, if the human spirit spends the entire hour she has dedicated to divine colloquies in outstretched movements of aspiration to union with the Bridegroom, she will not be able to bear up under bodily fatigue. For, as we have said (par. 9, above), the stormy exertion of love brings more than a little stress, especially to the head and chest (in which the spirit is more fully rooted), but consequently the other parts of the body also suffer pain.

73. Let fresh repasts then be multiplied, three in particular, among which one stands out from its two side-dishes: the most devout prayer and most chaste affection by which the soul yearns to be united with the Bridegroom for his own sake.

First and foremost the beginner should ponder the Lord's Passion, that is, ponder how the glorious King offered himself in order to uproot our sins, being so obedient on our behalf to God the Father that he was condemned to the cruelest of deaths, which left no healthy place anywhere on his body, from the soles of his feet to the top of his head,[65] a death which left no part of him unspattered by his most sacred blood or hidden from the view of all.

Cogitation on the flesh is a gateway to enter into the divinity of love that is hidden inside. To symbolize this, he was willing to have his most sacred side opened up by the iron lance so that the wounds he suffered might become the indispensable means for the human spirit to be rooted in the depths of divinity. Still, as is said elsewhere, cogitation about the Passion and feeding on it by itself is not enough for the soul's dignity— only he who hid himself from human sight by the veil of the flesh can meet the soul's worth.

74. Therefore the divine Apostle [Peter] admonishes each soul to surge up above herself in aspiration: *Christ therefore having suffered in the flesh, be you also armed with the same thought*[66] (1 Pt 4:1). For great divine beatitude draws near to someone who is united to Christ's humanity through imitating his Passion in com-passion, who is conformed to him through bearing his precious wounds inwardly. After this she can dismiss all reflections on his suffering in the flesh, holding on to none of them, for the whole follows from the part, and she longs only to be more deeply rooted in him. It was to obtain this that she reflected on his wounds as a gateway. Such is the main starting point of spiritual exercise.

75. Next comes the second aspect,[67] which mercifully calls forth from God not a little divine mercy and divine notice. We refer to compassion for those whose sins are obvious, for those asleep in sins, for those blinded by their senses and deadened by delights. In compassion for them appears a filial and love-filled delight for those who were created in the image of their Father, so that those who imitate him in life might reign with him as saints in glory. Therefore have regard for those who are so miserably wounded and recognize those who are blinded, so that perhaps at least one out of a hundred adults might be found able to merit[68] in glory the sight of him *on whom the angels desire to look* (1 Pt 1:12) after he has issued the stupendous decree.[69]

If any man minister to me, let him follow me (Jn 12:26). For each living person will have offered zealous service, whether to God by doing good deeds or to the devil by sinning. After departing from the body, the soul will join the company of those she chose to belong to already during life, being assigned by God's just judgment either to the ranks of the glorious or the wretched.

76. If therefore I should see someone killed physically with a material sword or run through or crushed under the feet of the powerful, I have compassion for their misery by my natural *affectus*. How then can the human spirit say that she loves the Father of rational spirits when she sees so many sons sealed with his own image trampled under the feet of the cruelest of enemies and led away to a place where it would be easier to count each drop of water and each leaf of the trees than to avoid proclaiming mournfully those words that the Lord already said through Job, that man divine, *Let the day perish wherein I was born, and the night in which it was said, a man child is conceived*, continuing a bit later with, *Why received upon the knees? Why suckled at the breasts? Why did I not*

perish when I came out of the belly? (Jb 3:3, 12, 11b). The prophet Isaiah explains this in two ways.[70]

The first arises from observing the wretched torture in which body and soul, which have both sinned, are punished together as long as God is in glory. Isaiah says, *Their worm shall not die and their fire shall not be quenched* (Is 66:24). This worm is the remorseful conscience which deserves to bear eternally the punishment of sensory pain and damnation [i.e., separation from God], sorrowing for the things done in the world which, far from doing the person any good, now oppress him with sharp pain. Of such things the book of Wisdom testifies: *What has pride profited us? etc. [Or what advantage has the boasting of riches brought us?]* (Wis 5:8).[71]

77. And the Most High threatens eternal punishment for the damned through the mouth of Isaiah, who says, *Take away the wicked, that he might not see the glory of God* (Is 26:10).[72] And well does he call him *wicked*, for love alone can make the human spirit lead her life with that proper piety by which she offers true worship to her own Creator. By God's worthy judgment the one who, while she lived in the flesh, did not prepare and dispose herself to be chained by love to uncreated goodness is now carried off to be separated from happy enjoyment of God. For she is truly carried off as she delays and dies in darkness, separated from the happy vision of divine beauty by her pressing sins. Isaiah also says *That he* who lives the life of a brute beast on earth *shall not see the glory of God* (Is 26:10). It would be no just judgment if such a person were to exult in and enjoy the angelic life of knowledge of eternal truth and love of uncreated goodness that constitutes heavenly glory.

78. How could one be cheered by seeing so many gentle sons of one's own Father tortured with such unimaginable pain? Therefore, concerned not merely for one person but for the entire congregation of the faithful, the divine Apostle [Paul] said to the Corinthians: *Who is weak, and I am not weak? Who is made to stumble, and I am not incensed?* (2 Cor 11:29, cf. 11:28). For anyone insensitive to the pains and incurable wounds of his fellow members is no living and effective member united to Christ the head [of the church].

This industrious effort brings down from heaven no small mercy, and thus he who approaches it with his whole heart, with all his pleading, with his godly affections coated with compassion, with fiery words for widespread preaching,[73] and intense toil in all things will be covered with dawning wisdom from on high. In this way divine majesty mercifully stoops to send forth wisdom, teaching, and faith, so that every creature, from East to West, from North to South, Christian, Jew, or Gentile, for all of whom the Prince of Glory deigned to appear on earth, might come to true knowledge of truth;[74] so that no creature might miss out on the happy company of the one who gave himself not for one but for all as a priceless prize on the altar of the cross; so that no creature might lack the happy vision of him whom she was created to contemplate and love, the only fit object of her contemplation; so that the human spirit, longing to follow the gentle Father, and our Lord Jesus Christ, might employ her devout prayers and intense and ignited affections to help bear the sins of all the living, so that she might thereby be conformed to the one who carried the lost sheep on his own shoulders to the sheepfold of eternal brilliance,[75] restoring it to his own Father.

79. The divine prophet Jeremiah was indeed a living and effective, rather than dead, member, for as he saw his people atrociously trampled beneath a villainous king, he said, *Who will give water to my head, and a fountain of tears to my eyes? And I will weep day and night for the slain of my people* (Jer 9:1).[76] For Nebuchadnezzar designates the devil, Babylon's hellish consternation, while Jeremiah designates the soul united to God by love in its purest sense. Moses[77] raised his hands to heaven as a shield of fiery prayer and, having extended the mighty spear of love all the way to heaven, deserved[78] to reach the Lord of hosts so that the people of Israel might conquer Amalek by the Lord's strength. By force of the same love that united Moses to God, Moses shielded the people when the Lord said to him, *Let me alone . . . that I may destroy this people* (Ex 32:10). Because Moses bound the Lord[79] with such cords of affective prayer, the people of Israel did not suffer the real penalty their crimes deserved.[80]

Suppose a prince is served by two administrators, one of whom is constantly looking out for his own comfort, while the other truly wears himself out to do what is best for the prince's entire household. The second administrator would more readily be the recipient of his lord's choicest favors, since the first, lacking the godly concern for those who suffer that should be part of faithful service, is concerned only to procure his own profit.

80. If one gives consideration to these two types of suffering, they can, like two joyful companions, aid the yearning spirit in her striving, so that she is neither defrauded of her yearning nor cheated out of the goal she aims at. The primary one should take precedence, namely, being affected by the Passion and stripes of the Redeemer, for it is through him that we make our way toward perfect adherence to him. Sometimes

this process of individual meditation on the Passion comes to a halt, especially in people who travel the open and unimpeded path of ardent sighing and thus adhere to the Beloved in his own divineness more perfectly than most. Yet the prayer that grows out of compassion for one's neighbor, which is called forth by the sight of divine compassion, never stops; indeed, the more the human spirit is ardently affected, the more intently she prays to the Redeemer that he might apply his healing medicine of mercy and goodness to the wounded hearts of sinners. Living thus in consummate righteousness, she can then join Job in saying, *For from my infancy mercy grew up with me: and it came out with me from my mother's womb* (Jb 31:18). *Mercy grows* not when one constantly pays attention to one's own affections of spiritual joy, but rather when one stoops to attend to the misery of the unfortunate. *Mercy comes out of the womb,* that is, mercy proceeds from the moment when the human spirit receives living love from the emanation of divine fecundity, the living love in which at her primal begetting she appeared with angelic powers, the angelic life toward which she is now being transformed.

7. *Discernment*

81. The final effort is that which is discerned in anagogical wisdom, a discernment that ought to be embraced by those who love wisdom with all their strength. Now anything confused and disordered is considered to be corruptible and unstable; conversely, what is in order[81] and suited for its own ordering is judged to be completely stable. The disciples of truth ought to work wisely with lasting industry to establish in themselves the number of songs, hymns, or other things to be sung. What comes first, second, and third ought not be left to chance, and, unless some special need of fraternal love or of obedience to one's superior should intervene, one ought always strive to do things diligently and according to the established pattern. Through such happy exercises a certain habituation remains in the human spirit so that, should carelessness or inertia leave the accustomed exercises undone, the mind will notice it with a touch of sadness. What at first seemed laborious about such spiritual exercise is transformed by habitual practice into something almost attractive to the spirit. It is as if cold had been turned into heat and sluggishness into fleetness, something proven by unerring experience and carried by unitive love. Hence the bride says in the Song of Songs: *Draw me,* adding immediately, *We will run after you to the odor of your ointments* (Ca 1:3), for by means of love that draws and propels one

to the heights with a flaming *affectus*, the bride begins to run with amazing agility so that she can nestle in the longed-for bosom of her Beloved and, as often as she wishes, she can reach out to him most ardently by the yearning of unitive love that is sprinkled on her like perfume from on high.

D. How Divine Wisdom Is Taught by God Alone, Even to Simple Folk

82. Having spoken of the persuasive reasons and the efforts by which the human spirit reaches the perception of unitive wisdom beyond understanding, we turn to that wisdom which is taught without intermediary by God, handed down to the great hierarch, Paul the Apostle, written down in an anagogic and hidden style by Denis the Areopagite, and intended for Timothy, the fellow-disciple of truth, saying, "You, moreover, friend Timothy, for the sake of hidden sights leave behind with great, grinding effort[82] all sensory and intellectual operations, and everything perceivable and intelligible, and everything existent and nonexistent, and, as much as possible, surge up without knowing to that union with him who is above all substance and knowledge.[83] And indeed, in going out of yourself, freed and purified from every restraining thing, you will be uplifted to the supersubstantial ray of divine darkness, laying aside everything and separated from everything. See to it, moreover, that no uninstructed person hears these things."[84] These words of the Apostle Paul enfold supreme wisdom, the peak of all perfection possible in this earthly life, the utter depths of the writings of Denis the Areopagite. Once these words have been fully grasped, one can with unexpected ease make sense out of whatever in Denis's writings seems to surpass understanding.

83. Now this upsurge [*consurrectio*], which is said to take place through unknowing, is nothing other than to be directly moved through the ardor of love without any creaturely image, without knowledge [*cognitio*] leading the way, without even any accompanying movement of understanding [*intelligentia*], so that it has to do solely with movements of the *affectus*. In the actual practice of this [*upsurge*], speculative knowledge knows nothing. This is the eye with which the Bridegroom is said to have been wounded by the bride (Ca 4:9), and the Bridegroom by his own testimony says it is a single glance: *You have wounded my heart, my sister, my bride, with one of your eyes* (Ca 4:9).

141

HUGH OF BALMA

1. *Three Kinds of Knowledge*

84. Now knowledge is threefold. One type comes from looking at the mirror provided by sense-perceptible creatures. This is taught by Richard of Saint-Victor in the *Mystical Ark* [= *Benjamin major*],[85] where, in forty-two topics, he expressly teaches how the passage of the people of Israel from Egypt to the Promised Land offers a model for the ascent in six steps to the Creator of all things. A second type of knowledge exercises understanding through the sending of spiritual rays, teaching one to know the first cause through its effects and to arrive at unchanging truth by considering the exemplar from which each image comes. The great teacher Augustine gives no small attention to understanding this in his books *On the Teacher* and *On True Religion*. A third type of knowledge excels these other two by far. It takes place through the most ardent unitive love which actually, without any intermediary, disposes the mind [*animus*] and causes one to surge up most ardently, in one's extension, to the Beloved on high. As handed down in *On Mystical Theology*, this knowledge rises to the affective peak, in an upsurge said to take place in unknowing, or in ignorance, in order that, with all activity of the imagination, reason, intellect, or intelligence removed, through the union of most ardent love, the soul might perceive in this present life that which exceeds the grasp of the understanding. As far as the Seraphim surpass the nobility of the Cherubim, true love is more perfect than any *habitus* granted at the beginning of human creation and more perfect than justifying grace[86] or any special charism given for ministry to others.[87]

85. Just as the soul's powers of motivation excel those of cognition, so knowledge gained through unitive love, which penetrates divine secrets, outshines everything grasped cognitively. Blessed Denis defines this wisdom, which incomparably exceeds all others, as follows: "Wisdom is the most divine knowledge of God known through ignorance."[88] And this wisdom is said not only to outshine, but also to be more universal and more profitable than, other knowledge, cognitions, and learnings. For not only does this wisdom raise the *affectus* above itself and unite the creature perfectly to the Bridegroom in ecstatic love, but it elevates the eager intellect so that all prudence and cognition are far more flooded by divine flashes of lightning than could result from any enlightenment achieved by the exercise of human talent.

86. Thus, in book seven of *On the Divine Names*, Denis has the following to say: "We praise this irrational, mindless, foolish wisdom

exceedingly, saying that it is the cause of all mind[89] and reason, and every sort of wisdom and prudence. All counsel, knowledge, and prudence come from it; in it are hidden the treasures of wisdom and knowledge."[90] The words *wisdom* and *knowledge* denote the complete perfection of both powers of the soul [the *affectus* and the intellect]. Denis calls this wisdom "irrational" because reason can neither grasp it nor does it make use of it in rational inquiry. It is called "mindless" because it lacks mind or intellect and cannot make use of intellect in its exercise because the intellect is insufficient to reach all the way to the heights of perfect understanding [*intellectus*]. It is called "foolish" because this wisdom rises up in the *affectus* without making use of any sort of understanding; it is a wisdom that no understanding can grasp at all.

2. The Path of Abandoning

87. In the words cited above, Saint Denis has handed down this wisdom perfectly. First we shall consider what must be removed, then how one should surge up. Since in the upsurge the soul finds herself in a double state—both progressing and perfected[91]—we must first consider what must be removed, based on Denis's words *Leave behind sense perceptions*, before we come to the upsurge itself, when Denis says *rise up unknowing . . . raptured beyond yourself.*

88. In all of his philosophy, Denis employs "mystical sights" for that which transcends every consideration of being. This occurs when one knows intellectual things through preceding *affectus*, rather than the reverse order. This is the truest and most certain knowledge, far removed from every error, opinion, and image-based deception. Thus the things that have been said and will be said of the affective dimension of this wisdom, whether in theory or practice, are affirmed irrefutably, without doubt or opinion, in full view of the philosophers and professors of the whole world. Yet this knowledge is also said to be *mystical,* that is, "hidden," because few people dispose themselves to receive it and it hides within the heart where neither pen nor word can fully unravel its complexities.

A. ABANDONING INTELLIGIBLE AND SENSE-PERCEPTIBLE THINGS

89. In this mystical knowledge the *affectus* rules, commanding that the senses and intellect be utterly abandoned. First it insists that the powers of apprehension be relinquished (where Denis says to abandon

"sensory and intellectual operations"), and then that the objects apprehended by these intellectual and sensory powers be left behind (where Denis says to abandon "everything perceivable and intelligible"). Lest it seem absurd to abandon the senses, he gives the reason: "Because this wisdom is not like other knowledge, which comes from preexisting sensory cognition; rather, this wisdom is from above, according to the principle given in the words of Saint James, *Every best gift, and every perfect gift is from above, coming down from the Father of Lights* (Jas 1:17). If every gift comes from on high, then how much more would *this* wisdom come from above! For it is that part chosen by Mary,[92] who, kindled with fiery love for the Beloved, burned with desire.

90. This form of apprehending comes from above and not below, which explains the command to abandon the senses. For the office of understanding belongs not only to the outer senses but also to the inner senses. The most blessed God is not apprehended through his sweet fragrance or beauty or melodiousness or gentle touch, since all these things are directed by reason's prior apprehension, whereas unitive apprehension is above the mind and reason, as we have seen. A speculative learner must therefore draw up this wisdom from some source other than the objects of speculative knowledge's comprehension. In this one sees both the remarkable and much-prized nobility and divinity of this wisdom. For in his definition Denis labels it "most divine" because the soul virtually has to despoil herself and follow love's heavenly call to become a footservant to the *affectus*. Through this divine upward movement, the intellect is informed of the most divine things, having left behind at the touch of love habitual cognition. This informing of the intellect is not the mere learning gained through the senses, but involves the delights of the senses that move one to act on knowledge. The highest preparation for this wisdom takes place when inordinate delight in the creatures really is cut away from the exterior senses, so that God can be sought either mediately, immediately, or as final end. (The more one plunges into sensory things, the more weakly one rises up to divine things.) As the Psalmist says, *My soul refused to be comforted* (Ps 76:3 [77:2]), then adding an explanation of the reason for this rejection of delights, saying, *I was delighted, and was exercised, and my spirit swooned away,* meaning that, while the human spirit strives for divine things by means of anagogic movements and delights in her own direct thrust toward God, her spirit backs away from the delights offered by her exterior senses under devilish instigation. The same must be said of the delights of the interior senses, for sweetness ought not be loved nor gentleness desired by one who truly loves, but [God] alone

should be desired, except in some instances where one might love the sweetness or gentleness because they make the *affectus* burn more effectively and stubbornly for more intimate union. Hence this wisdom is located totally in ardent yearning, where every being or power and service of the power of understanding is commanded to be rooted out and relinquished. (Which does not deny that sometimes the intellectual power plays a large part in divine things, especially when flooded with light by divine insights.)

91. Yet there is another force in the human spirit that is much loftier than intellectual force and which, when its movements ignite the spirit, raises her to a more profound wisdom. This affective power gains primacy in the rational spirit because the affective apex of the spirit is higher and because of the ardor that raises the human spirit higher, an ardor surpassing all free charisms and infused habits [*habitus*] because of its stubborn extension and its own worthiness. Hence the commentator of Vercelli[93] says this about Denis's *Mystical Theology:*

> In this book he hands down a different and incomparably more profound means of knowing God, a superintellectual and supersubstantial method. Pagan philosophers did not grasp this because they did not seek it, nor did they even think it existed, nor did they catch hold of the power by which it is diffused into the soul. They thought the highest cognitive power was found in the intellect, when there is another power that exceeds the intellect no less than the intellect exceeds reason and the reason exceeds imagination. This power is the principal *affectio*, which is the spark of the *synderesis*[94] and which alone can be united to the Holy Spirit.[95]

And this is why, when the supreme *affectio* of the human spirit suspends the service of the entire intellect in an incomparable manner, not only are all operations that proceed from the sensory or intellective faculties ordered to be kept away from the intellect's power, but even the sensory and intelligible objects of these sensory and intellective faculties are left behind, beginning with those that are perceived by the exterior senses. Since the rational creature consists of two natures, the corporal and the spiritual, each has an object that corresponds to it, since each perceives eternal truth according to its own capacity.

92. Now there are humans who are merely sensory beings, who limit themselves to knowing only sense-perceptible things, as if the

sense they do have is merely an obtuse intellect and a twisted *affectus* and thus could not perceive goodness or divine truth in itself. Nevertheless, so that they might not lack experience of divine knowledge, God Most High established the sense-perceptible creatures, so that according to the Apostle [Paul], the *invisible things of God, being understood through the things which are made, are clearly seen* (Rom 1:20), and, according to the words of David, no one has any excuse by which he *might hide from God's heat* (Ps 18:7 [19:6]). Thus, having gone forth from his own goodness, he might be resplendent from height to height in every creature. Yet uncreated wisdom wants to remove such sensory things from the children so that, more happily and more truly fixed in the bridal chamber of the *affectus*, the children know that they have been brought to the secret inward bed of love, which the Jews and blind[96] philosophers begged for even as they made the rounds to learn from exterior creatures.

93. Hence someone truly praying in the spirit is commanded by truth to enter the chamber where hidden treasure can be found, a treasure not so much perceptible to the exterior as to the interior senses. Nor should this treasure be found by rational comprehension of the most blessed God, based on God's sweetness, beauty, and gentleness—which the soul, like a daughter who longs only to cling to her Fashioner, hungers for by anagogic yearnings—lest one seek one's supper in the manner of an impudent servant. The only exception to this is the one given above: that on occasion some sweet and refined food might entice the soul to burn more insatiably and intensely for God. Otherwise, we are admonished to cast out all intelligible things because, as discussed elsewhere, although all humans naturally desire to know, the thrust of the rational spirit can find no rest in any scientific knowledge or cognition except when rejoicing in joyful cognition of prime truth, which, we discover, is the only knowledge suited to the nobility of human understanding.

94. Though one might know all about the natural elements, all the components of bodies, and all the powers of the stars, yet because these are lowly things, instead of finding real rest in these the rational spirit would fall into wanton revelry as he becomes engrossed in creaturely idols that are weaker than himself—unless he returns to his ultimate purpose. Since, moreover, the human spirit is so noble that she can even look down on angelic beings, she remains nonetheless utterly garrulous and prone to error unless she somehow actually returns victorious and triumphant to knowledge of him from whom she originally went forth.

For even if one would try to know all created things in order to know the difference between them and the Creator of all by tracing them back to their proper limit, still, highest wisdom requires that all of this be abandoned, since the human spirit knows God without intermediary through inexpressible knowledge left behind by the union of love.

The third translation[97] of Denis's *On Mystical Theology* has this to say about knowledge in mystical contemplation [*theoria*]: "Through the union of love, which effects true knowledge, the soul is intellectually united to God unknown, in a knowledge that is much better than any intellectual knowledge."

B. ABANDONING EXISTENT AND NONEXISTENT THINGS

95. Then [Denis] adds, "[Abandon] not only intelligible objects but even all existent and nonexistent things."[98] Not only are we persuaded by the words of Denis that carrying out this exercise requires giving up any ultimate satisfaction in the creatures, whether lower or higher, but also that it requires giving up all existent and nonexistent things. Abandoning "existent" and "nonexistent" things means that any speculative form of apprehending the divine nature is excluded. Here "existing things" refers to the eternal reasons [archetypes] in the divine mind to which anything exemplified below, in the creatures, corresponds. When the human spirit is carried forth above herself and is moved directly into God her center, or final end, without admixture of any sort of creatures, whether lower or higher, then she has assuredly discovered a most orderly method of proceeding from human things to divine things.

When the human spirit reflects on how the creature comes forth from the eternal reasons, she draws in part on what is below herself and that means she is not completely and integrally raised above herself. Therefore in unitive wisdom she must leave behind all contemplation or reflection of the creature's own movements, aspiring to the single Intelligible above herself, and she is told to dismiss even contemplation of her own existence, no matter how noble it may be. For some sort of distortion and natural perception is present even there, and thus, in that sort of relative contemplation, the human spirit fails to abandon every sort of human apprehending for the sake of being taken up by another contemplation beyond her natural limits.

96. Yet the command comes to abandon even nonexisting things for the sake of the ascent of this wisdom. Abandoning "nonexisting

things" here refers to that which is not exemplified in creatures, such as all manner of ideas about the Trinity and the order of Persons in the Trinity. In the creatures we find no example of one Person generating another Person who is of the same essence as the generator, because, in creatures, whoever is the truly existing substance of some things is never equal to the love that connects them and the love of the existing substance is never equal with the lovers themselves. Therefore we are told to abandon this most excellent of all speculative contemplations [namely, of the relations within the Trinity], not because it is not good and noble, but because there is another higher means of apprehension in the human spirit, the only sort of learning through which one can reach the highest of spirits most excellently. This alone is what is called the "best part" chosen by Mary.[99]

97. Leah symbolizes the senses' contemplation of the creatures; another kind of contemplation is symbolized by Rachel. The reason that the wisdom requiring even the abandonment of contemplation of the Trinity is called the "best part" is that the more divinely and loftily the human spirit attains supercelestial things, the more she draws near to them, or the more intimately she is transformed into God himself; moreover, no speculative contemplation has this power to transform, since only outstretching, deifying love can do this. Therefore he alone grasps divine things who does not look at his feet in cognitive contemplation but rather stretches to glimpse something afar off. Thus Denis says in the seventh chapter of *On the Divine Names*, "Our mind needs to have that power of understanding through which she sees invisible[100] things, namely, moreover, it also ought to have that union which extends our spirit's nature, a union through which she is joined to those things which are above her. It is in this unitive way that divine words ought to be understood, not according to ourselves but according to ourselves established completely [outside][101] ourselves and totally deified."[102] To abandon these things is difficult, which is why we are commanded to cut them away with grinding effort and great striving of spirit.

3. The Upsurge [Consurrectio]

A. GENERAL

98. Having dealt with the things that must necessarily be abandoned, we turn now to the unitive upsurge. Here we note first the state of the person surging up—*through unknowing;* then we see that the in-

junction, *surge up*, indicates an extensive, that is, outstretching, upsurge; then we consider the single and central goal of the upsurge, namely *to that union with him who is [above all substance and knowledge]*.[103]

Since every form of apprehending discussed earlier is outside the mystical upsurge, in that upsurge one should be unknowing, that is, one should pull back [*rescindere*] the eye of the intellect altogether, for in this upsurge the intellect always aims to apprehend that toward which the *affectio* strives. Therefore the greatest adversary for this upsurge is the intellect's passionate clinging to the *affectus*, an adherence that must be peeled back [*rescindi*] with great effort. The causes of this are mentioned above[104] because one apprehends by phantasms, or by description and delimitation. How the clinging intellect can be pulled back is stated in *On Mystical Theology*, where it says *rise up unknowing*. Uplifting is a vehement thrust of the *affectus* that leaves the intellect behind. The upsurge is never purely affective unless the eye of the intellect is completely withdrawn [*rescindatur*], something stated at the outset of *On Mystical Theology*.

99. When altogether ignorant by virtue of having vacated every cognition,[105] the human spirit is united all the better because knowledge that is elevated above the mind knows nothing. This unknowing is the necessary condition for the most elevated form of apprehending, for all speculative cognition disappears in an upsurge that is unknown to the intellect, and speculative cognition *must* be left behind if one desires to proceed to knowledge above the mind. The more the intellect mixes herself into the *affectus* in this upsurge, the more impure is the upsurge; the more total the blindness of the intellective eye (which blindness only comes about by great toil and effort), so much more free and incomparably exalted is the upsurge of the affective eye's own extensions.

100. This can be seen in the physical example of breathing in and out, for just as respiration takes place from within a person without any preceding deliberation, so too the *affectus* is ignited without any deliberation and thus surpasses every kind of intellect. The *affectus* stretches toward him to whom it alone yearns to be united, and its action takes place completely separate from all understanding, at such great distance from the superior part [of the intellect] and aided by such suddenness that with surprising speed of movement, more rapidly than a thought, it surges straight up, like the process of breathing in and out. The *affectus* possesses such speed of movement, with importunately outstretched ardor, that the *affectus* pushes aside the nosy and pushy efforts of speculative cognition, as if rejecting a no-account beggar.

101. This cannot be expressed nor adequately explained by words, according to the passage from *On Mystical Theology*, chapter three: "Ascending now from lower things to the highest, one becomes more and more contracted at each degree of the ascent, until after the entire ascent one is completely without voice, totally united, speechless."[106] This is because uncreated wisdom wished to reserve the teaching of this outstanding wisdom to herself so that every mortal creature might know that there is a Professor in heaven who manifests the only true wisdom to his chosen scholars through celestial missives and rays of brightness.[107]

102. The second reason why this cannot be put into words is so that all this world's wise people might be ashamed when they see that a simple old woman or an unlettered herdsman can attain this upsurge to wisdom perfectly (provided they prepare themselves in the aforementioned manner), whereas the upsurge cannot be grasped by any natural science or human effort.

103. A third reason is found in the book of the Wisdom [of Sirach]: *by her own strength she trod the necks of all the haughty and proud* (Sir 24:11[108]). For no matter how much more glorious than everyone else a distinguished man or cleric may be, he cannot attain even the fringe of the robe worn by the wisdom that is known when one rises above every mind—unless he travels the childlike path of cleansing of his mortal sins, the path that prepares him for the unitive way, sorrowing and sighing that his former sins have provoked the wrath of the Grantor of all wisdom. For the necks of the proud and haughty must be bent to the humility of childlike beginners. Thus is fulfilled the prophetic word[109] in which wisdom reproves the wise and demands nothing except that they come down from their loftiness to the humility of lowly cleansing: *He has put down the mighty from their seat and has exalted the humble* (Lk 1:52).

104. Next we consider toward whom the upsurge enjoined with the words *rise up unknowing* aims, for it is in fact an upsurge to union with the Most High, an upsurge that is above the mind and knowledge. The reason for this has already been stated in part: The upsurge requires neither grace, nor glory, nor relief from punishment, or anything else for these yearnings for the upward action of surging up.[110] All that is necessary is the One who is the sole object of the human spirit's yearning to be united, a yearning that is found in a person who has turned his back on passionate desires. Within this sort of grasp, God is gained above every human mind and knowledge, insofar as he is perceived by a strain-

ing *affectus*—so that he is not seen in his absolute and unique being but is perceived by a mode of taking hold that leads the affected, touched soul above the mind and reason.

105. Hence this wisdom is completed only when the soul who has been affectively brought to her own supreme apex desires nothing other than to be united to God alone, having cut away all intellectual functioning. Because this is hard to do, Denis adds, "as much as possible"[111]—as the Psalmist says: *You have broken my bonds: I will sacrifice to you the sacrifice of praise* (Ps 115:16–17 [116:16b–17a]). When, aided by divine grace, the extension of unitive love manages to burst all the impediments of sensory and intelligible objects, and especially the interference on the part of intellective operations so constantly eager to apprehend what the *affectus* seeks, the affective spirit freed from her chains is like a bird carried aloft on the wings of ardent affection alone. She enjoys such great freedom that she can be moved ardently into God as often as she wishes, praying in the affectionate yearning of the mind's *affectus* that she might, as far as is possible this side of heaven, by her earnest entreaties see him face-to-face. Sometimes a human spirit lifted above herself in an upsurging motion like this appears to be almost entirely outside the body. Therefore Denis says, "as much as possible," for it is granted to no human spirit, unless by divine visitation, to perceive this. In the first chapter of *On the Divine Names* we find, "For it is fitting to ascribe to God supersubstantial knowledge of unknown supersubstantiality, which is above reason and intellect and substance itself. The more one looks on high, the more the ray of divine speech [*theoricum eloquium*] sends itself out in exalted splendors."[112]

106. This is the same as saying that the wisdom that comes by unknowing is perceived by God's teaching alone, as we have said already. The more this "divine speech" (which is the divine infusion in the midst of which the spirit chats joyously with the Beloved) is received by the *affectus*, the more intimately does God send himself into the human spirit. God does this so that he who is true wisdom might be known more brilliantly through rays that are more divine.

107. Next comes "And indeed in going beyond yourself."[113] For not only does Denis urge insistently that the creature be utterly uprooted by unitive wisdom, but also that one specifically put to death the intellect itself and make it submit to the divine inflow alone. The Apostle Paul referred to this going beyond itself when he wrote to the Corinthians: *If we are out of our minds, it is for God,* and so forth (2 Cor 5:13). Through this continued going beyond itself in ignited love, the soul

better merits[114] that more efficacious removal and purgation which follows upon her outstretched and blight-consuming flames than she did at first—as she begins to surge up through wisdom. For just as there are two kinds of cleansing of corporeal things—through water and fire—so it is in spiritual things, where the first purgative path passes through cleansing sorrows and frequent tearful remorse [*attritiones*], while the much more effective cleansing comes in ardor's upsurge.[115] Hence in this excess of ardor the spirit is held back far less than at the outset of the work of surging up,[116] since she is now free of the world's delights and purified of every alienating affection. Far removed from every obstacle and liberated from her chains, she is now carried nimbly aloft to the brilliance of divine incomprehensibility.[117]

B. THE ORDER OF THE UPSURGE

This, then, is the order of upsurge. First the *affectus* should abandon all reflection on and love of sensory things and all contemplation of intelligible things and rise up in purity, without any mixture of the intellect mixing in at all, so that the *affectus* might be more inwardly united to him in whom it knows its urgent yearnings will find their sole repose. Through this upsurge of longer-lasting anagogic movement, the *affectus* extends itself more and more, and the human spirit is cleansed more effectively by fiery sparks. The flesh no longer grumbles, since the spirit finds her repose outside love of fleshly things, from which she necessarily is now much more hidden away than before. Hence the *affectus* gains agility in pure movements, and as often as it wishes, is moved most ardently without any premeditation by the intellect.

108. That is why Denis first says "surge up unknowing" and after that says "be uplifted." He means to say that at first only with difficulty does the apex of the *affectus* surge as the human spirit exercises the anagogic upsurge, but then, through her own outstretched[118] love and through increasingly effective cleansing, she surges at will with little difficulty and is raised up in wondrously nimble movement. Even if love and nature run side-by-side for a while in this anagogic movement, still, as impediments are removed and under increased infusion of [grace] on high, the more efficacious ardor of love brings incomparably more scope and agility of movement than does the vigor of natural affection.

109. This is what is meant when Denis says "laying aside everything,"[119] and so forth, where he deals with the two principal things to be laid aside, namely: all restraints and every finite thing. The first refers

to the *affectus*—for to the degree that one is affected by any creature one is necessarily joined to it and as a result is ensnared by it,[120] thereby becoming less agile in the upsurge toward divine things. Yet Denis mentions not only every restraint but also every finite thing. By "finite thing" he means that which is known by its own form and having distinct being. Every speculation or contemplation of such things must be removed, because just as every restraint causes the *affectus* to delight in a less worthy creature and by itself renders the *affectus* impure, so too the intellect is made impure by finite things. To be made impure means that the intellect is darkened, for the human speculative knowledge that fills it is like an obscuring and obfuscating cloud in comparison to that wisdom which comes through superresplendent divine rays.

110. Still, this last quotation from Denis has more to do with the highest knowledge of understanding than with an increasingly nimble upsurge, since according to the wisdom of Blessed Denis the only true knowledge of divine things is that which is left behind for the sake of[121] the experiential knowledge of upsurging action. Hence the spirit's upsurge encounters divine mercy, according to her needs, so that after she has spent a long time aspiring to bind her Beloved more intimately with more ardent chains of love, for the brief time that her capacity can handle, she can by rapture be granted the beatific vision,[122] especially if she is cleansed from all restraints and finite things. She is then raised up to the ray of divine darkness, which is another name for the light of divine incomprehensibility, according to the words of Denis in his letter to Timothy [Dorotheus]: "The divine cloud is that unapproachable light in which God is said to dwell invisibly, on account of the surpassing brilliance."[123]

111. This wisdom comes directly before knowledge of rapture; thus the Beloved later says to the aspiring soul: *Friend, go up higher* (Lk 14:10). Hence Denis says "surge up" before he says "be uplifted,"[124] since nature and grace are at work in the ascent of unitive wisdom; yet in the highest elevation of the understanding, grace alone is at work, lifting up without any medium, lifting up in rapture, raising the spirit in the body, yet hidden away from bodily senses. In this final, affective-intellective uplifting of understanding the intellective and affective powers attain their consummate faithful service, not passively, but by being acted upon.

112. After this, Denis says, "See to it, moreover, that no uninstructed person hears these things." Indeed he gives the same admonition at the end of the first chapter of *On the Divine Names*, where he

speaks of knowledge through previous love: "We ordain that holy things be kept for the holy, in accord with divine tradition, and that they be kept from being used or derided by the uninstructed; better yet, if people are that bad, let us set them free from their hostility toward God."[125] He very frequently gives the same warning in his other works, and he immediately explains why: for such people think they can know the one *who places darkness around his hiding place* (Ps 17:12 [18:11]), the sort of thing they know as knowledge, when God can only be apprehended by means of the Good, the True, the Kind, and similar terms.

C. CONCLUSION

113. Yet this anagogic wisdom is a sort of contemplation that is distinct in itself and different from every speculative discipline of knowledge, entirely transcending reason's grasp. Because many of the wise and learned are manifestly unable to see this, they deride this highest wisdom and consequently impugn the Most High God who grants wisdom of this sort. Therefore, with Blessed Denis and, much more, with the Lord Jesus Christ, I ask anyone whose eye might fall on this treatise never to show a bit of it to untaught doctors and philosophers of this world who live the fleshly life. Show it only to such of them as wish to begin to take up the childish path of purgation. For hard-working artisans ascending step-by-step within themselves solely by divine influx will quickly test all that has been said much better and with far more joyful experiential knowledge than those who work the liberal arts.

114. I wished to write these things for this reason: that those who are less experienced in this wisdom, having confirmed their path, might direct their steps, knowing what they will soon find. Should they have unusual difficulty at the start or in the ecstatic upsurge, still *afflicted in a few things, in many they shall be well rewarded* (Wis 3:5),[126] that they might see experientially *what eye has not seen nor ear heard, what has not arisen in the heart of man* (1 Cor 2:9; Is 64:4).[127] Those who cling to him through love of his supreme wisdom [are able to see] this in the present life, as the human spirit now says, *I hold him and I shall not let him go* (Ca 3:4). Since this wisdom may seem almost foolish to the untaught, we propose next the theory, proceeding by reasons and arguments, of how the human spirit is able to surge up, how she can remove impediments, by what means the union takes place, and many other things that are relevant to the refutation of human philosophy. So that this ascent to such great wisdom might not appear irrational we shall now clearly dis-

cuss natural, theological, and anagogical arguments drawn from the eternal reasons.

115. For Denis's wisdom seems most difficult [to understand] because it proceeds by a method that stands above all reason and can only be perceived by the inflowing of the Holy Spirit. This is true especially of *On the Divine Names* and *On Mystical Theology*, where it is said at the outset that this teaching is not asserted *in the persuasive words of human wisdom but is proven by the power of the Holy Spirit* (1 Cor 2:4) inspiring the writers of Scripture,[128] by which we are joined inexpressibly and unknowingly to inexpressible and unknowable things in a better union than is possible in our intellectual ability and activity.[129] Thus, when the Holy Spirit sets in motion the affective apex of the soul (in the words of the Psalmist, *touch the mountains, and they smoke* [Ps 103:32 (104:32)]), then the entire depth of Denis's wisdom, as it surpasses understanding, proves to be far more certain and easier, and therefore far more lovely and love-worthy, than the best of all other types of learning. For it proceeds without any doubt or opinion and, since the practical is more easily[130] known, and thus ought to be known before the theoretical, theory follows implementation. Peace be to all lovers of true wisdom, and may divine goodness flow down. Amen.

A DIFFICULT QUESTION: WHETHER THE SOUL IN HER *AFFECTUS* CAN, BY ASPIRATION AND YEARNING, BE MOVED INTO GOD WITHOUT ANY OF THE INTELLECT'S COGITATION LEADING THE WAY OR KEEPING HER COMPANY

1. To bring into the open the truth of the hidden and mystical matters already discussed, a difficult question is posed, a question through which the truth of this wisdom will shine forth most clearly to anyone with understanding. We ask whether the soul in her *affectus* can, by aspiration, or yearning, be moved to God without any of the intellect's cogitation leading the way or keeping her company.

[A. The Affirmative Position]

2. It would seem that some cogitation must necessarily take place before the *affectus* can, by love's extension, be moved into God.

3. First we consider the authorities. (I) The Psalmist says *in my*

meditation a fire shall flame out (38:4b [39:3b]),[1] which would seem to say that the human spirit must first meditate reflectively before surging up in the fire of love to the Beloved himself through affection as the *affectus* glows inwardly.

4. (II) So too, Augustine says, "We can love what we cannot see, but we can by no means love what we do not know."[2] Therefore one must first know something by reasoning or by intellectual cogitation before one can love something with the *affectus* of love. Thus cogitation necessarily precedes the affection of love.

5. (III) [Alongside the authorities,] reason has its say, reasoning regarding the Deity. The soul actually extending herself through love's yearning into God, into the one she loves, is, in the seventh chapter of *On the Divine Names,* called "Godded," or "deified"[3]—to the degree that it is possible for a creature to be conformed to the superexcellent Trinity through love's stretching movement. Now, in the Trinity the Father comes first in the order of nature, for he is the highest power. The Son, who is knowledge of the Father, or highest wisdom, comes next. The Holy Spirit, who is true love in his procession, binding Father and Son, is third. Now "former" and "later" here have nothing to do with time, since all three Persons exist equally from eternity. Instead, these terms have to do with the nature [of the three Persons] and they are employed for the sake of our understanding. For the generation of the Son, who is the true and highest wisdom or knowledge, naturally precedes the procession of the Holy Spirit, who is true love.[4] Therefore in the soul who can strive in her own small way through outstretched love to imitate the Blessed Trinity, we would expect that there first be some sort of pondering about him toward whom she is tending or some sort of understanding knowledge, before she could by love's yearning surge up to him aspiratively. Therefore cogitative knowing always precedes the affection of love.

6. (IV) Likewise, Blessed Denis says that the Church Militant imitates the Church Triumphant, as far as this is possible. Therefore the faithful soul wishing to surge upward through love in degrees that correspond to the angelic order imitates above all the spirits of those who love in the last part of the hierarchy, where three orders are found: the Thrones, Cherubim, and Seraphim.[5] In imitation of these, there must necessarily be three properties, or offices, in the soul who actually wishes to surge up. First come the Thrones, symbolizing how the soul must utterly leave behind all other things, for example, worldly honors,

fleshly affections, and earthly delights, in order to prepare a place where God alone will dwell. Second are the Cherubim, a word that means *fullness of knowledge;* imitation of them would be mediated by light coming from above, a mediation through which the human spirit, pondering supraintellectually, would know and grasp divine and celestial things above human understanding. Third must come the Seraphim, the highest order. The human *affectus* now flames up with yearning for him whom the mind has already known cherubically, for *Seraphim* means "ardent," "burning."[6] Since the Cherubim, to whom the cogitating knowledge is proper, rightly precede the Seraphim, who must be understood as the ardor of love, if the soul is to try to imitate the triple angelic office, knowing through cogitation must precede any actual ardor through love. The affection of love should in no way surge up without cogitation leading the way.

7. (V) Likewise the soul surging up through love tries to be conformed to the blessed spirits of the saints who gaze on God face-to-face. For they see before they cling by love, since, unless they understood the inexpressible beauty, they simply could not cling unwaveringly with fired-up affections to the beatitude that makes their delight complete. Thus, unless we have knowledge before we have the affection of love we cannot be conformed to the spirits of the saints in glory, who see the divine beauty in order to delight in it with inner affections through love that surpasses all understanding. Thus understanding precedes love in the saints in heaven.

8. (VI) So too, the way the powers of the soul are arranged indicates a natural order for setting the soul in motion. I see that from the very beginning of her creation the soul has three powers that are naturally distinct, namely memory, understanding, and will. In us memory is nothing other than an extension of divine similitude. Understanding is the means by which, without investigating or reasoning, any soul naturally knows her Creator. Will is that power through which the soul loves her Creator and naturally stretches toward him, and it is because of the will that the human *affectus* is unable to be satisfied with the fullness of the earth's riches and honors, for she stretches toward God alone that she might in the end repose in him. Since the power of understanding, in which cogitation takes place, naturally precedes the power of will, in which is found ardor, or love's affection, therefore the movement of understanding, that is, cogitation, precedes the movement of will, that is, loving. No *affectus* is able to surge up by means of love's affection

without reflective intellection leading the way, no matter how much it might be raised with ignited affections to encounter what comes down from above.

9. (VII) The same appears to be true of the process of apprehending and the movements of the senses. For if I am to be moved to delight in something imagined, I would first have to know it in advance by sensory means. Before I can enjoy something, my external eye or another sense must apprehend it so that I might desire to have it. Movement toward cognition of things higher than the imagination is similar: I must first cognitively ponder God or some other delight if I am to be able to aspire to him with inward affections or to take delight in him in any way. Therefore cogitation in advance always precedes love's upsurge.

10. (VIII) Likewise, according to what Denis says in the first chapter of On Mystical Theology, all intellect and all cogitation on sense-perceptible creatures, even all pondering of God and the angels, must be left behind in love's upsurge. But to propose this is most foolish. What does the soul do if she may not think of God, or the Trinity, or the angels? She would seem to be in a cloud or in the ocean, since knowledge of understanding must always direct love itself—otherwise mystical wisdom would be folly and an abuse of wisdom, that is, no wisdom at all.

11. (IX) Likewise, everything that is apprehended is apprehended as some concept of being—whether related to the One, the True, or the Good. Therefore God, no matter how he be apprehended, is apprehended in relation to being, that is, as the supreme Unity, the supreme Truth, or indeed the supreme Good. Since none of these modes can be apprehended except through cogitation (for if I comprehend something as One, I must ponder unity; if as True, I must ponder truth; if as Good, I must ponder goodness), therefore since love's apprehension apprehends God insofar as he is good, there must necessarily have been some previous cogitation on goodness itself before the affection is actually moved toward God as good.

B. To the Contrary

12. But on the contrary: It seems that the *affectus* disposed in love can freely be moved into God without any of the intellect's cogitation leading the way or keeping her company.

(I) First there is the authority of the great hierarch Denis, in the first chapter of On Mystical Theology, where he says to Timothy: "You, moreover, friend Timothy, for the sake of hidden sights leave behind with great, grinding effort[7] all sensory and intellectual operations, and everything perceivable and intelligible, and everything existent and non-existent, and, as much as possible, surge up without knowing to that union with him who is above all substance and knowledge."[8] According to this, in the ascent of mystical love one ought to abandon every intellectual operation and all cogitation and surge up solely according to the union of affective love, which surpasses all understanding and knowledge. Therefore one does surge up, truly loving in love's affection, without cogitation leading the way.

13. (II) In the third translation of Denis's *On Mystical Theology*[9] we find the following: "Through the union of love, which effects true knowledge, the soul is intellectually united to God unknown, in a knowledge that is much more noble[10] than any intellectual knowledge. Because she leaves behind intellectual knowledge, she knows God above the intellect and the mind."[11] Therefore since, as this passage says, God cannot be known through intellectual thinking, he is known most truly through the touch[12] of love. Thus, to speak plainly, all intellect must be abandoned and one must surge up to God solely through the *affectus* of love.

14. (III) Likewise chapter seven of *On the Divine Names* says, "Our mind ought to seek to have that power of understanding through which she sees invisible things, namely, a union that exceeds our spirit's nature, a union through which she is joined to those things which are above her. It is in this [transcendent] way that divine words ought to be understood, not according to ourselves but according to ourselves totally, according to ourselves established completely [beyond] ourselves and totally deified."[13] Therefore, even if in human things one understands before being affected, in true and experiential knowledge of divine things, one ought first to sense through love before using understanding to ponder the One whom one has sensed. Therefore one must surge up through love so that this state of knowing [through love] might leave true knowledge behind in the human spirit. For that which the *affectus* senses experientially, namely her perception of divine names, she then truly understands in the intellect.

15. (IV) Likewise, in the same chapter he says the following: "We praise this irrational, mindless, foolish wisdom exceedingly, saying that it is the cause of all mind and reason, and every sort of wisdom and prudence. In it are found all counsel, knowledge, and prudence; hidden in it are the treasures of wisdom and knowledge."[14] Since he calls it "irrational," this wisdom cannot proceed by investigation of reasons,

and since he calls it "foolish," it cannot proceed like the other school sciences, in which the normal procedure is this: We first know everything that we understand.[15] If therefore mystical theology were to proceed by first cogitating and meditating through reasonings, as we observe other sciences doing, then it would not have been labeled "foolish" by Blessed Denis, nor would he have called it "mindless," that is, without mind. For the *affectus* of love is set on fire without any mental thought or meditation. Therefore, knowledge is left behind in the mind as a result of the *affectus* of love, and not vice versa.

16. (V) Likewise the Psalmist says, *Taste and see.* "Taste" refers to the *affectus* of love; "see" refers to the intellect's cogitation and meditation. Therefore one ought first to surge up in the movement of love before intellectually pondering in order to know the hidden God. For this is the general rule in mystical theology: One ought have practice before theory, that is, one ought to be well practiced in the heart before one has knowledge of the things said about it.

17. (VI) The same point can be made by authority of Thomas of Vercelli in his commentary on *Mystical Theology:* "The business of this wisdom suspends the use and services, both practical and theoretical, of the senses, imagination, reason, and intellectus and excludes every intellect and intelligible thing. It transcends all being and every individual thing and every enigma and representation. In the divine honor it unites the summit of the principal affection to the divine Spirit."[16] Therefore no sort of cogitation or cognition by the intellect is required in mystical affection.

18. (VII) This can also be proven by reasoning drawn from the deity. For the rational human spirit is perfected according to how she ascends by orderly stages to divine things. But I see that there are three Persons in the deity, namely Father, Son, and Holy Spirit. The Father is the highest power,[17] the Son is the highest wisdom, and the Holy Spirit is the love binding them. But the Holy Spirit, who is true love, is the last person of the Trinity according to nature and according to our understanding, but not according to time. For first one must understand the Father as the one who begets, then the Son as the begotten, and then the Holy Spirit as the one who proceeds from both. Now the Holy Spirit, as the last, is closer to us. Therefore since the soul progresses by ordered stages in the ascent, she must have love, which is appropriated to the Holy Spirit, because the Holy Spirit is closer to us, before having cogitative understanding or even wisdom, which is appropriated to the Son. The affection of love thus precedes knowing and not vice versa.

19. (VIII) Likewise, the soul is perfected in the image of the Church Triumphant to the degree that she receives an infusion from God, the source of all happiness. Yet Denis affirms that, since the order of the Seraphim (meaning "burning, ardent") is first in line, they receive this infusion more richly and perfectly than the order of Cherubim (meaning "fullness of knowledge"). Therefore the *affectus*, which corresponds to the Seraphim, is affected and moved prominently into God through the ardor of love before the intellect, which corresponds to the Cherubim, can cogitatively understand the object of the *affectus's* yearning. Therefore the *affectus* is first moved to God without prior pondering by the intellect, which follows behind the *affectus*.

20. (IX) So too the rational spirit receives an influx from God first and foremost in accord with its degree of affinity to God. The *affectus*, especially well disposed by love, is supreme in the rational spirit and is thus closer to the uncreated Spirit. The summit of the *affectus*, being closer, is thus touched by God through the radiant fire of love in the human spirit before the intellect can apprehend God, since the intellect is the power of the soul that is much farther from the supreme Creator than is the *affectus*. Therefore the *affectus* is always moved into God sooner than the intellect understands God by cogitation.[18]

21. (X) Likewise, since God is, as it were, infinitely distant from any creature, the soul must come closer to him if he is to be apprehended even slightly by the creature in her misery. Only love can make the soul extend herself and draw closer to God, and thus, the more ardently[19] the soul loves, the closer she approaches the fountain of light, and the closer she comes to the fountain of light through love, the more that fountain enlightens the intellect through knowledge. Therefore, as far as God is concerned, one must first love ardently before knowing understandingly.

C. Solution

22. We must agree with Blessed Denis, in the first chapter of *On Mystical Theology*, that mystical theology alone can be called the wisdom of Christians. For it undergirds knowledge of faith and is the foundation of charity. And no mortal, no matter how well trained in the sciences and philosophy[20] or how knowledgeable, has ever been able or ever will be able to apprehend by rational investigation or intellectual effort this wisdom found in the supreme *affectus*, far beyond the faculties of the human mind. The eternal Father, and he alone—in merciful and fatherly

affection—opens it up, solely for his children eager for consolation. That is why it is called "mystical," meaning hidden, closed off, known only to a few.

23. Now there are two ways of apprehending, corresponding to the twofold natural human faculty for reaching God. Every soul has a power of understanding, which is the faculty of the intellect, and a power of loving, which is called the *affectus*. With these we apprehend God, who is supreme Truth and supreme Good. With the intellect we grasp Truth, with the *affectus* we attain Good. A dual path of excellence fits these two. One path is called contemplation and is symbolized by Rachel, whose name means "charming to look at." On this path the human spirit, infused with divine light from on high, has what it takes to contemplate celestial things by meditation and cogitation. The other path is in the *affectus* and is called the love's ardor. It takes place in the fire of the Holy Spirit sent down from on high, as the soul aspires in flaming affections to God alone, yearning only to be more intimately united to him with tighter cords of love. This second path is called the "best part," the one chosen by Mary,[21] who ardently yearned, as the gospel of John says.[22]

24. Hence, just as the New Testament stands out in comparison to the Old Testament, so too the way of love, or perfection, which is found in ardent love and is designated by Mary, is nobler than all meditation or intellectual contemplation, which is designated by Rachel.

Now, we must also realize that contemplation itself takes two forms in the intellect, just as the ardor of love is acquired in a twofold way in the *affectus*.

25. The meditation, or contemplation, that moves from the lower to the higher is one type; the contemplation that in fact descends from the higher to the lower is the other. Richard of Saint-Victor, in his *Mystical Ark (Benjamin major)*,[23] draws conclusions concerning the former, employing forty-two examples of created things to show how the human spirit adorned by the light of understanding ought to arrive at knowledge of the supreme Creator. For just as the people of Israel proceeded from Egypt to the Land of Promise through forty-two stages, so the faithful soul, through these forty-two considerations, can attain to knowledge of the highest truth suited to every rational spirit.

26. The second type of contemplation proceeds in the reverse order: The human spirit makes judgments about the lower creatures aided by the light radiating from on high and according to the standards of truth and the eternal reasons, which she perceives as she meditates

within herself according to divine illumination. The more amply the soul is flooded with light radiating from on high, that much more unerringly can the mind [*animus*] scrutinize truth in the creatures and in all affects, doing so in accord with the causes and reasons that are identical with God, from whom every exemplified and conceived creature came forth in the very beginning. (One should not understand this to mean that this [second kind of] contemplation [from on high] does not terminate in the *affectus*, otherwise there would be no contemplation. But these two types of contemplation are not our present concern.)

27. The ardor of love far excels these, is much more lovely, and easier to obtain. But there are also two means of attaining this ardor of love. One is the scholastic and common way, the other is mystical and hidden.

28. The first proceeds by means of searching and elevation, beginning with lower things and ascending to the highest by long practice.[24] For example, this is the method followed in loving God with meditation leading the way. First the faithful learner views the external creatures with the external eye, or external sense. A bit later, ascending a bit higher, he retains in his imagination what he has already perceived with the external eye. Rising higher yet, by reasoning and comparing, he discovers a single, necessary, creating cause of everything. In this way the philosophers arrived at knowledge of God. For seeing such a magnitude of creatures, the beauty of the way they are ordered, and their usefulness, these philosophers and everyone else unerringly recognized a single, almighty, all-wise, and utterly good Creator. They knew this through the faculty that is higher than external sense or [internal] imagination, a faculty called reason.

29. Pondering the creatures in this way leaves a certain habit in the intellect.[25] Moving from viewing the creatures to being flooded by radiance and illumination somehow sent from God, the human spirit is raised to a much clearer contemplation of divine things. This [higher] faculty is called the faculty of understanding, or the intellect, and it consists solely in pure meditation.

30. Finally, all meditating or contemplating terminates in yearning affection. For any meditation or contemplation that is not followed by loving affection does little or no good at all. Hence Augustine says that, rather than let meditation flit about, one ought to cling lovingly, so that cogitation, or meditation, might always precede affectionate love.[26]

Now the second method proceeds without employing any other

creatures, moving solely by cogitation sent from God, as the faithful soul is drawn[27] to God himself.

31. This second way of surging up to God is nobler and easier to achieve than all the methods previously mentioned. Here unitive wisdom is found in love's yearning, which aspires on high through flaming affections. It is the same upward aspiring that Denis defines in the seventh chapter of *On Divine Names:* "Wisdom is the utterly divine knowledge of God known through ignorance, according to the union that is above the human spirit, when, withdrawing from all things and then even dismissing herself, the spirit is united to the Inscrutable through supersplendid rays, having been enlightened by deep wisdom."[28]

32. In this wisdom, according to what Denis says at the beginning of *On Mystical Theology,* "we are commanded to abandon all sense perception and sense-perceptible things, all intelligible and nonintelligible things."[29] Hence this wisdom draws the lover's *affectus* on high without any preceding investigation or meditation. There one ought not ponder about creatures, angels, God, or the Trinity, for, instead of being led by meditation, this wisdom surges up as it aspires by means of the yearning found in the *affectus.*

33. Note, however, that this wisdom is understood in one manner by those who have made progress and in another manner by those who are perfected. Those making progress must cleanse themselves in the cleansing path described above.[30] Somewhat later, as they cogitate, they encounter God himself inflaming them from on high. They encounter him, not by meditating on God or on the angels, but by surging up as they stick to the path that directly follows on the purgative path, that is, according to the second, shorter exposition of the Lord's Prayer given earlier (*via illuminativa,* par. 45–54), which is a prayer made in spirit and in truth. After the *affectus* has exerted itself for a long time, after the mind has carefully raised itself in cogitation in the manner described earlier, it dismisses cogitation and meditation, and, aspiring to union with the Beloved himself by yearning love alone, as often as it wishes, day or by night, inwardly or outwardly, the surging mind [*animus*] lifts itself upward. Now we find love's affection preceding cogitation, for what the *affectus* feels, the intellect truly understands.

34. Just as we said that contemplation takes two forms, descending and ascending, so too with the affection of love. In the scholastic path [mentioned above], the *affectus* ascends from [love for] the lower creatures to the *affectus* of love, but in mystical wisdom the opposite is true: for this true Love, which is the Holy Spirit, the third Person of the

Trinity and the last as far as the origin[31] of Persons is concerned, is closer to us and is the point of departure for the affective upsurge to God. The Holy Spirit himself touches the soul's supreme affective apex with the fire of love and sets it ablaze, drawing it toward himself wordlessly, without any cogitation or rational running hither and yon. Just as a stone pulled by its own weight is naturally drawn down to its own center, so the apex of the *affectus* by its own weight is carried up to God directly and unmediatedly, without any oblique tangentiality, without any cogitation leading the way or keeping it company.

35. Hence this highest power of the human spirit, this *affectus*, is capable of being joined directly to the Holy Spirit by chains of love. And this highest power of the human spirit is unknown to almost everyone, except those whose apex is being touched and moved directly, without mediation, by the fire of the Holy Spirit.

36. Hence Denis says that this force in the soul is directly moved by the touch of the Holy Spirit and it is according to this touch that all of *On Mystical Theology* proceeds. "Now there is a law predefined by us, teaching us to assert the truth of God's Words, not in persuasive words of human reason, but in the power by which the Holy Spirit inspired the writers of Scripture[32] according to which we are inexpressibly and unknowingly united to inexpressible and unknown things, according to the better power of our understanding and the operative union."[33] By this motive power of the Holy Spirit comes a much greater and direct knowledge of God than is possible through any sort of investigating intellect or reason.

37. When the apex of the *affectus*, in which our being moved by ardor to God takes place, is touched, God's touch leaves behind in the human spirit the truest of all understanding knowledge. For only in what the *affectus* senses of God can the intellect truly learn, or apprehend. That is why the conclusion to chapter one of *On Mystical Theology* says: "Through love's union, which is an effective[34] union of true knowledge, one is united to God in understanding ignorance that is far more noble than any understanding cognition."[35]

38. Out of this union the mind is given marvelous clarity for the investigation of hidden things, as the phantasms in the imagination burst open, restraining the disorder of the external sense by inward tether, mortifying even the flesh's sensuality and pestiferous corruption, which brings about an ignited *affectus* that simply overflows. The more the human spirit is raised up by aspiration, the more the corruption of evil fleshly inflammation abates.

39. These things help explain the difference between scholastic and mystical teachers, since their arguments proceed according to differing understandings.

D. Refutation of the Original Propositions

40. Regarding the first authority, we ought to say that the phrase *in my meditation a fire shall flame out* (38:4b [39:3b]) should be understood as referring to those who are becoming proficient. Now, since these people do not yet have an abundance of love's ardor, one ought to spend some time in meditation[36] according to the path explained in the second, shorter exposition of the Lord's Prayer (*via illuminativa*, par. 45–54), not in cogitation of angels, supercelestial matters, or of God and the Trinity which can most efficaciously stir up the *affectus* in the third state, that of the unitive way, where, the exercise of love having been perfected, cogitation can be dismissed from her service as a guide along the way.

It is something like the building of a bridge.[37] A framework of wood supports the stones during the earliest stage of building, but after the edifice is constructed and the stone walls have been completely fixed in place, the entire wooden framework is removed, since the structure of stone can stand immovably without the service provided by the wood. That is how cogitation is employed as a vanguard during the stage of gaining proficiency; when love's affection is perfectly attained, all the faithful service provided by reflection and meditation up to and through the proficients' stage is removed.

41. Regarding the second [authority], we readily concede that "we are able to love what we cannot see, but we cannot at all love what we do not know," for mystical wisdom undergirds knowledge of God. That is why mystical wisdom is called the "wisdom of Christians" in the opening lines of *On Mystical Theology*. Moreover, knowledge is twofold. One kind precedes the *affectus* of love, in proceeding along the common and scholastic path. Here one first has knowledge of God through [sense perceptions of] the creatures or through the intellect, before the affection of love is kindled. It is in this light that the statement by Augustine that was quoted at the beginning of this paragraph should be understood. However, in following along the mystical path, according to Denis, the *affectus* of love precedes understanding knowledge, as we have said. The prophet David speaks of both of these. Regarding the first he says, *in my meditation a fire shall flame out* (38:4b [39:3b]),[38] regarding the second,

DIFFICULT QUESTION

Approach him, namely, by steps of love, *and be enlightened* (Ps 33:6 [34:5]), that is, through knowledge of truth. This second kind of knowledge is more certain and unerring than the first—when something is recognized by certain signs seen in the object itself as being delightful to eat, the very knowledge of its delectability often inflames the appetite of the viewer, but afterward, when he has eaten the thing, the taste of it leaves behind a knowledge that is more sure and complete than the knowledge that preceded the tasting. So it is with the matters we are discussing.

42. Regarding the third argument, [which proceeded by reasons drawn] from deity,[39] one must say that the argument is true according to the [scholastic,] common path, as the soul actually ascends. Yet, the mystical process follows a pattern opposite to this argument, as our "contra" arguments revealed.

The Cherubim and Seraphim reveal the other procedure.[40] If one moves from lower to higher, then knowledge precedes love just as the Cherubim precede the Seraphim. But in the contrary pattern, descending from higher to lower, the Seraphim receive influence from God first and foremost, ahead of the Cherubim. In the same descending way the *affectus* is first moved by love to God before that which the *affectus* feels can be perceived by the intellect. This validates the reasoning in the second argument of the "To the Contrary" section.

43. Regarding the fourth and fifth propositions, one must say that there is no similarity between wayfarers on earth and the saints in heaven because the saints see the brilliance of eternal light face-to-face, without any phantasms or fleshly taint mixed into it, without the darkening cloud of an intervening medium. If this is the highest level, because no hindrance is present, then naturally one first has to apprehend divine beauty with the intellect before the *affectus* could enjoy it in an indivisible union. But with wayfarers on earth, even if they love while still living in the body, nevertheless, according to Aristotle, phantasms are mingled with the human intellect and thus every intelligible thing, including the supreme intelligible thing, namely God, is grasped by some mixture of intellect and phantasm, or imagination.[41] Even if greater[42] illumination from on high separates the phantasms from the intellect, still the intellect illuminated from heaven apprehends God in a finite and limited way, and thus all intellectual cogitation always remains impure and unclean. Therefore, if the mystical upsurge is to be true in this present life, Denis orders that cogitation[43] be completely isolated from love's *affectus* and that one rise up solely through love's ardor. For even though God is

wholly desirable, as is said in Canticles (5:6), he is nonetheless not wholly comprehensible, neither here and now nor in the future. Therefore, the more effectively every sort of intellectual knowledge is cut away in the upsurge, the more rapidly the human spirit apprehends, soaring freely on high,[44] the object of her yearning. Therefore one must be utterly vigilant to keep any intellectual cogitation from mixing into love's unitive upsurge.

44. The sixth point is resolved by taking account of the twofold form of the loving upsurge, as described above where we said that "one ought not think about angels or the Trinity."[45]

45. The same point refutes the seventh proposition.

46. In response to the eighth proposition, one must say that even though this mystical theology's method of rising up seems foolish or irrational to those who do not know this wisdom, nevertheless, it proceeds most wisely and according to a marvelous pattern. For, entirely by the weight and discernment of love, the soul's *affectus* is carried to the One she loves, and this happens more truly, surely, and unerringly than the physical eye can see any sense-perceptible object, indeed, more certainly than the intellect is able to comprehend any sort of truth about God through cogitation.

Should someone ask, "How shall I ponder if I am not supposed to think about God or angels?" the reply is simply: "You shall aspire rather than cogitate." For without any pondering on God or angels, if the human spirit has made some preparation along the path of purgation, she may indeed not know how to say anything and can only surge upward in this manner, saying, "O Lord, when shall I love you? When shall I constrain you with arms of love?"[46] If she resorts to this frequently and repeatedly, she will have experiential knowledge that she is being set on fire more rapidly than if she were to ponder a thousand times about celestial mysteries, the eternal birth [of the Son], or the procession [of the Holy Spirit]. So this is the best sort of foolishness, of which Blessed Denis says, "We praise this irrational, mindless, foolish wisdom exceedingly, saying that it is the cause of all mind and reason, and every sort of wisdom and prudence."[47]

47. To the ninth objection one must reply that, according to the method employed in this upsurge, God is not apprehended like all other things are, namely by the mode of being—of being one, true, or good. Rather, when the supreme strength of the soul, the apex of the *affectus*, is touched by the fire of love, by that motion and that touch the *affectus* sparks with aspiration for God. Thus Blessed Denis confounds all those

scholastic and speculative doctors because they think they know everything but know next to nothing (and even then can only conjecture and
opine) about this true wisdom by which the human spirit is drawn to
God. That is why this true wisdom should by no means be propounded
to such scholars, as Denis wrote to Timothy: "See to it that no uninstructed person hears these things. Moreover, by 'uninstructed' I mean
those who are formed by the things that exist in this world."[48] Deriding
them, he adds a little later, "Whoever thinks so highly of himself as to
think he can perceive divine things or the fullness of knowledge by his
own intellect, such a person I would say is uninstructed."[49] Later he
adds, "They think that they can, by their own sort of knowledge, know
him who makes darkness his hiding place (Ps 17:12 [18:11])."[50] They
are unlearned because mystical knowledge is found entirely above the
human mind, where every sort of intellect fails which apprehends only
by means of the One, the True, the Good, the Being. Through the summit of affection mystical theology in truth teaches the disciple of truth
to surge up through love, and, what is more, the human spirit can never
surge up in these sorts of loving movements if she is doing any sort of
cogitating as she surges; rather, whatever elevation of affection she
might have gained would, unhappily, be taken away. The intellective
power must be left behind, like a maidservant who has been dismissed,
and the soul must do without the intellect's loyal service as she surges in
active motions to union with the Beloved. Raised up so loftily, she is
then as far removed from her maid as midday is from sunrise. Let her do
this as often as she can, day or night, a hundred times or a thousand
times, as long as the body can endure it.[51]

    48. So she can understand how this should be done, we give the
following physical example. Consider the motion of a stone falling to its
center naturally by its own weight. Likewise, the *affectus* disposed by
the weight of love surges up to God without any cogitation or deliberation, as if it were stretching toward its center. By these movements the
affectus lifts itself up in a constant yearning, a yearning that will obtain
its fulfillment and peaceful gaze in eternal beatitude, unless for a short
time, as in a rapture, it is lofted above itself in divine elevation that comes
not by nature but by grace.

    49. If a speculative or scholastic teacher is unable to perceive this,
let him listen to the chief hierarch of this wisdom, the Apostle Paul,
who said that none of the wise Greeks could understand it because this
wisdom is known only by spiritual scrutiny—he told the Corinthians
that our spirit, united to the divine Spirit, has a feel for the things of

God.[52] This is the wisdom about which the spiritually mature converse. This is what the Lord promised the apostles when he said, *And you shall be clothed with power from on high* (Lk 24:49). Hence, just as a priest clothes himself from the head, that is, from the highest part, down, so the soul is clothed from her highest part, from the *affectus*, downward. Before any cogitation serves as guide, she is touched by the fire of the Holy Spirit. Thus the evidence is clear: The soul who truly loves is able to surge up to God through an *affectus* set afire by love's yearning, without any cogitation leading the way. Amen.

GUIGO DE PONTE

ON CONTEMPLATION

PROLOGUE

Here Begins the Prologue to the Books on Contemplation Compiled by Dom Guigo de Ponte, a Monk of Chartreuse.[1]

If, as you read this treatise, you read anything that comforts and strengthens you, thank God, the teacher of all good things. In this way you can evade the poisonous talk of envious people who, aware that they neither can have nor really wish to have any good thing, dislike in others what they themselves lack. Instead they grind away at others, denigrating them.[2] Sometimes they openly spew forth their evil's envy in public attacks. Sometimes, unable to gnaw away at the good, they deceptively conceal their envy with furtive and malign silence and elaborate disguise. Or they might commend something with cunningly faint praise and feigned delight while concealing even better things they have learned from other people. Sometimes, when others desire to learn of God by spiritual effort, they hold them back or divert them from their quest by presenting alternatives. By these and similar means, as the Scriptures say, detractors hateful to God,[3] whom Jerome calls "hounds,"[4] persist in trying to ruin the pursuit of good through all sorts of clever schemes, seeking to drive a wedge between people's hearts. That is true enough regarding the envious.

Note also that the hidden things of divine contemplation, especially at the level of tasting wisdom,[5] cannot be known in advance by anyone except those to whom God has granted this experience. Thus you are right not to believe what inexperienced and envious folk say about these things. The modest things found here are set forth so that you might beware of evil people who, as Augustine says,[6] should always be avoided. For even though today you are surrounded by good people, tomorrow you might find yourself among evil people. For the envious first try to keep others from the good, then to cover up and stifle the good. If they are unable to do either of the above, they seek to ruin them, either openly or deviously.

Thus ends the prologue.

HERE BEGINS THE FIRST BOOK
ON CONTEMPLATION

Chapter One: The Four Steps That Prepare for Contemplation: Justification of the Unrighteous (steps 1 and 2), the Lower Fountain (3), Compassion and Rejoicing with One's Neighbor (4)

As one whom the mother caresses, so will I comfort you, says the Lord in Isaiah sixty-six [Is 66:13]. In various ways[1] *the Father of mercies and God of all comfort* (2 Cor 1:3) and goodness sees fit to console, according to the multitude of his riches and mercies,[2] the soul he has predestined to be conformed to the image of his Son.[3]

In the first place, he sees fit to comfort by flooding the soul dead in sins with life-giving grace, justifying and raising her from the guilt that incurs eternal damnation. For this four things are needed: (1) an inpouring of grace itself, (2) the movement of a consenting free will that accepts the consolation of divine favor, the (3) contrition of a remorse-filled heart, through which contrition God (4) forgives guilt and forgets the sins.[4] Thus the prophet's word: Whenever the sinner groans, I shall remember none of his iniquities—if he laments so as not to return to the vomit he spewed out in genuine confession.[5] This step is the penitential state in which "he weeps for past sins and repeats not what he has bewailed."[6]

Second, if the sinner who has been raised up and justified by grace remains in the grace given him, the giver of all good things visits him in a variety of ways and renews him by the tender comforting of paternal providence. Then, desiring to cleanse the soul that is still soiled by the stains of sins remaining after the remission of guilt, God bestows on her the grace of anxiousness, namely, certain tender and anxious affections by which she strives *to labor in her groanings, to bathe her bed each night, to water her couch with tears* (Ps 6:7 [6:6]). Even so, her hardness and dryness of heart renders her unable to achieve this and the blight of sins must be consumed gradually by the fire of freshly infused charity.[7] Sometimes this occurs with a greater, sometimes with a lesser degree of sighing and not without continual and anxious affections. Even though this grace may appear arid, it is not sterile because God sees not so much what you are but what you desire to be—if you do what you are able to do.

At this stage, the sinner's soul should strive to know her faults before God in heartfelt sorrow. This goes a long way toward softening a heart of stone, for "he who senses sorrow soon finds tears and slips into lamentation."[8] Thus the soul ought to indict and condemn her past evils, and judge and examine also her present sins, vices, and infirmities, so that she might know what she lacks,[9] placing it carefully before her own eyes as one places manure around a vine in order to make it fruitful.[10] With the Psalmist she ought to say to her vinedresser: *Before you my soul is like earth without water* (Ps 142 [143]:6); and, *My spirit is in anguish within me, my heart within me is troubled* (Ps 142 [143]:4); likewise, *I am struck down like grass, and my heart has dried up, because I forgot to eat my bread* (Ps 101:5 [102:4]).[11] Likewise applicable are the words the daughter of Caleb said to her father when asking for his blessing: *You have given me a dry land, give me also a source of water* (Jgs 1:15, cf. Jos 15:19).

In this way the Father of godliness, who *is near to all who call on him in truth* (Ps 144 [145]:18), bestows on the thirsting soul sorrowing over her wretchedness, that is, on those who are converted at heart,[12] the upper spring and the lower spring.[13] He does this little by little and according to the will of his good pleasure; after the soul herself makes an effort to receive the grace of God with care and not in vain,[14] the Lord himself gives drink to the thirsty one and inebriates her. *Whoever asks receives, whoever seeks finds, and the door shall be opened for him who knocks* (Mt 7:8). Therefore, in the third step, if she zealously begs for the goodness of the Lord, the grace of more generous contrition and compunction is poured into her. Thus the one who has long burned with sorrow for her sins and has sought greater paternal confidence in the remission of her sins is filled with grace, after having first tasted the wine of compunction at the lower spring.[15]

In the fourth [step] she receives the grace of compassion and goodwill toward her neighbor, whom she formerly envied and in whom she found no holy joy. Now she yearns to make herself to *rejoice with those who rejoice and weep with those who weep* (Rom 12:15), constantly thanking God for all his benefits, whether given to herself or to her neighbor. These are the two breasts of the bride[16]—whoever lacks them is not worthy to suck the breasts of the Bridegroom (namely *honey out of the rock and oil out of the hardest stone* [Dt 32:13]), for one deserves to receive God according to the way one has treated one's neighbor. Thus Augustine says in a homily on *Blessed are the merciful* (Mt 5:7) and in a homily on St. Maurice: "As you treat those who ask of you, so God treats those who ask of him."[17] Likewise, *With that measure with which you have measured, it shall be measured out to you* (Mt 7:2; Lk 6:38). He who has no breasts available for his neighbor remains parched for the grace of God, as shown by many authorities and stories found in many places.

Chapter Two: Concerning the Fifth Step, Namely Affection toward Christ in His Holy and Incarnate Lovingkindness. Concerning the Sixth Step, Namely, the Upper Spring; Concerning the Seventh Step, Namely the Illumination of the Soul, the Kiss, and the Embrace

As a sick person convalesces, he slowly recovers strength in stages. So too, in the fifth degree, the spiritual soul affected by godliness is inflamed to love and compassion for her Redeemer, who gave himself for that very soul. As best she can, she occupies herself with diligent, frequent, and devout consideration of Christ's bitter suffering and the glorious mystery of the incarnation of the Word of God. As she clings to her Lord, she meditates over and over in godly love on Christ's entire life and way of life.

Sixth, such a soul, guided and watered by the lower spring, desires from time to time to drink the waters of the upper spring, namely, to know Christ but no longer according to the flesh. This yearning brings her much progress and prepares her for the Bridegroom's embrace. As Saint Bernard says, "For the soul to whom the Lord is about to come, the ardor of holy yearning ought to precede his face to consume all the rust of sins and thus to prepare a place for the Lord."[18] Likewise, Jeremiah says in Lamentations 1: *From above the Lord has sent fire into my bones and has chastised me* (Lam 1:13). Likewise Augustine: "The entire life of a good Christian is holy desire."[19]

In this stage sometimes she rushes to him in heaven, calling on him with the words, *"As the deer pants for fountains of water, so my soul pants for you, O God"* (Ps 41:2 [42:1]); sometimes indeed by her worthy spirit of godliness she attracts him[20] to herself, as Jeremiah says: *A wild ass accustomed to the wilderness in the desire of his heart, sniffs out the wind of his love* (Jer 2:24), that is, she draws *Christ to dwell through faith,* which works through love, *through the Holy Spirit* (Eph 3:16, 17; cf. Gal 5:6), which is called the south wind,[21] as it says in the Song of Songs, chapter four: *Arise, O north wind, and come, O south wind.*[22]

In the seventh degree, when the Bridegroom has been long sought after with sighs and tears and godly yearning, he sometimes sees fit to

brighten with his presence the soul seeking him. Like the sun at full
strength, he lights up the soul's darkness, enters her hidden house, and
descends into the soul with an inestimably sweet and utterly pleasant fall
from on high, like rain on a fleece.[23] In tranquil silence he inflames with
brilliance and renews and gladdens the devout spirit, whence Hugh of
Saint Victor, in his book *The Soul's Pledge* (*De arrha animae*), says:
"What is that sweetness that occasionally touches me as I reflect on him
and either vehemently or gently moves me until I am somehow a complete stranger to myself and know not where I left off? Suddenly I am
indeed something new, transformed completely, and I begin to feel so
fine that words to describe it fail me. My conscience is overjoyed, all the
wretchedness of past sorrows slips into oblivion, my spirit exults, my
understanding shines, my heart is full of light." Hugh replies to his own
seeking soul: "Truly it is your beloved who visits you, who comes and
touches you."[24] But because our merits are insufficient for us to receive
such a visitation, we ought to call on the saints for their intercession and
seek them out with diligent veneration.

Even though this inestimable consolation is rarely given to anyone,
not even to those who are more perfect, still, on occasion it is granted a
soul still covered with rust, unformed, and unworthy in every way, who
nonetheless is searching and thirsting for God the living spring.[25] She
receives this consolation as a foretaste of the sweetness of the marriage
union with the heavenly Bridegroom, as a foretaste of union of the word
of God and the faithful soul. This visitation, descent, and fall of the word
of God into the soul comes to the thirsting soul making progress as an
aid, pledge, and longing. To the careless, lazy, and slothful soul it comes
as a great judgment, because she knows not the time of his coming (Lk
19:44). In this longed-for union, mingling, embrace, and kiss of word
and soul, which is completely unknown and unknowable until experienced, there is found nothing corporeal, nothing of the imagination.[26]
For the devout spirit ascends not; rather, she receives the mercy of God
from on high in the midst of her temple,[27] no indeed, she receives God
and his mercy poured out into the innermost marrow of her heart. As
much as she might perceive her Bridegroom glowing and gently burning
in the bedchamber of her soul, still she does not see him as he is. For yet
another type, or degree, of contemplation, which yields a briefer and
more rapid glimpse than that of the aforementioned visitation, may
sometimes be had in this present life.[28] If anyone wishes to attain this
degree, let him faithfully seek and thirst for Christ the Lord as he pursues the aforementioned steps.

Chapter Three: The Eighth Step, Which Is the Gaze of the Human Spirit Aspiring on High. Angels and the Blessed Ones in Glory. The Soul's Inward Prayer

In the eighth place, having been thoroughly taught, embraced, and kissed by her Bridegroom, Christ the Lord, the godly spirit rises up by, as best she can, seeking out the place where he lies down, where he dwells at noonday.[29] That place is blessed eternity and undying happiness. In this stage the human spirit ought to exert herself in three ways: First, she should contemplate those who enjoy God, that is, the angels and saints reigning immortally in the happy life. Second, she should consider the source of all good things, that is, God, since the highest and most perfect abundance of complete happiness and eternal reward consists in enjoying God. Third, she should apply these things to herself [in prayer].[30]

First, the godly spirit should consider with humble and thirsty contemplation those who enjoy God, that is, the happy citizens of heavenly Jerusalem, who are filled with the finest wheat.[31] Like a spotless mirror,[32] they are able to reflect purely, completely, and clearly the inexpressible and most sublime blessed Trinity,[33] in whom they have all they need, namely, understanding eyes that gaze unblinking at indescribable light, at rays of eternal brightness and truth. For them this perfect regarding of truth, this perfect knowledge of truth, is a plenitude of enlightenment, brilliance, and light that dispels all ignorant darkness, error, and spiritual fog. In this way human understanding, or reason, created according to the image of God,[34] finds its complete happiness in a perfect and blessed illumination.

Second, their hearts blaze brightly like fiery coals[35] burning in the furnace of divine charity. This makes them replete with blissful enjoyment, sweetness, and peace, giving their will, or love, perfect happiness.

Third, because they thus consider divine light and enjoy eternal charity, they break forth into unbroken, harmonious praise, calling out without ceasing all day *Holy, Holy, Holy, Lord God of Hosts* (Is 6:3) and similar songs of praise to God. In this unending celebration in unbroken eternity, the memory possesses her complete and perfect bliss. Thus we see that the image and likeness [of God] in angels and saints finds perfect blessedness in the image's origin, namely God.[36]

Then let the soul consider that so great a Lord accepts with good pleasure the service they offer in seeing, praising, loving, and enjoying him in steady leisure[37] before his face, while he shows his sons and heirs, who sometimes knew or could have known his angered brow, a constant countenance of joyous satisfaction and acceptance. He carries on with them an unceasing conversation that clearly shows his complete will— but in varying degree, depending on how much each of them can handle. Likewise, he harbors for them a heart of fatherly charity glowing so immeasurably that he loves each of them singly more than all of them together love him, since he loves his own children out of himself, who is infinite and uncreated love, whereas the children love him with created love poured into them.

Finally, the devout spirit should return to herself, weeping for her wretchedness, thinking about her exile, and aspiring to the blessed life as she says: O Lord, Father of Mercies, you who are light inaccessible, purest brightness of eternal light, who alone possess immortality, the life by which all live, *the peace that surpasses all understanding* (Phil 4:7), immeasurable goodness and most sublime charity, wellspring of all good things, have pity on me, a captive and sickly sinner unable to take hold of you because I am blind, wretched, and bent over.[38] I am thus unable and unworthy to fix my gaze upon you or even to raise my eyes to you. Lord, you who give all things abundantly to those who call upon you[39] and do not scold us for our faults but with fatherly recompense wipe them away and forget them; you who from the beginning miraculously save even the greatest of sinners; you who choose sinners for your glorious, happy, joyful, and holy friends *so that they might sit with the princes and hold the throne of glory* (1 Sm 2:8); you, Lord, who illuminate with such marvelously abundant brilliance the thousands upon thousands who serve you and the millions who attend you;[40] you who fill and refresh them so richly, copiously, and superabundantly with your sweetness and fullness; yes, indeed, you who bless with immeasurable and unfathomable light, peace, and goodness a multitude that none of us can number, bestowing by your eternal happiness that which no one can describe; you see fit to offer me, your wretched, famished pup, some of the crumbs that fall from the lords' table.[41] With these crumbs you brighten my darkened understanding, form and reform my will, cleanse my memory of all the dregs of sin, so that I might understand you, love you, and recall you[42] as you alone restore to your image its lost similitude to you, reforming and renewing that same image.

When these things are thought with devout heart and in the spirit of wisdom, they draw to themselves sweet heavenly dewdrops from the Savior's fount, which gently reawaken the soul to life. Rejoicing in the drops of divine sweetness,[43] she sprouts spiritual fruits for salvation,

179

having been sweetly recreated and made fertile by the grace of the Holy Spirit as that same Spirit's anointing touch teaches the soul[44] what is necessary for her spiritual health,[45] drawing on the Spirit's knowledge of what is best for the soul. Such a soul knows for sure that she lives, and she knows intimately the one who prays for us with unspeakable groaning.[46]

Thus clinging to God she tastes tears of manifold flavors—here sorrow, there compassion, now devotion, then the delights and treats of eternal sweetness. Watered and fed in various ways by all sorts of tears, bedewed from on high, intoxicated with the heavenly wine, and anointed with perfume of costly balsam, she experiences[47] the word of the Bridegroom. As Song of Songs, chapter five, says, *My soul melted when my Beloved spoke* (Ca 5:6)—spoke, that is, to me with the voice of his sweet inspiration and grace. This indeed is the voice, the tongue, of the Bridegroom, with which he often speaks to and touches the self-surrendered soul in utterly secret conversation.

Chapter Four: How One Should Approach the Eucharist

With this water, that is, the water of tears, we should wash the hands of our conscience in order to approach the Lord's table—to approach the altar with a cleansed heart so that we might sense the reality, the spiritual force of this sacrament. For thus the Lord promised in Revelation, chapter two: *To the victor I shall give hidden manna, and I shall give him a gleaming white stone;*[48] *and on the stone is written a name that no one knows except the one who receives it* (Rv 2:17).[49] The reality of the sacrament is the power of unity and charity toward God. He who receives the sacrament eats judgment to himself[50] unless he receives through the Spirit's first-fruits at least a tiny bit of those seasoning herbs that are essential to bring out the taste of the reality of the sacrament.

When you are at the table, then, be sure to have in all things an attitude of devout reverence and awe toward Christ, because he is the Lord your God, or an attitude of godly and devoted love because he is your Father and Bridegroom—otherwise I would rather you did not receive at all. Whoever does not know Christ experientially in this way appears not to have been touched by Christ, indeed, appears to have been passed over. In such circumstances it is expedient for him to withdraw from that table rather than to treasure up the wrath of God against himself by eating judgment to himself.[51] Yet beyond that, no one other than God can or should judge a man—*only the spirit of man who is in him*

(1 Cor 2:11). *Let each one pay heed to how he builds thereupon* (1 Cor 3:10). He whom the Lord permits to handle this sacrament with frequent devotion will know by tasting how sweet the Lord is and can experience what Gregory said in his homily on the verse from Luke fourteen: *Sending an embassy he asks for peace terms* (Lk 14:32): "The sacrifice of the altar offered with tears and a generous spirit intercedes in a unique way for the forgiveness of our sins."[52]

Chapter Five: On the Many Types of Tears

There are many kinds of tears.[53] Those that flow on account of fear of damnation might be called servile tears; they do not suffice to recover one's eternal inheritance.

The tears that flow from human piety and emotion can be considered to be neutral: If they flow from good intentions, they are good, but if they flow freely under the impulse of inordinate human emotion, that is, from false piety, they are not good.

Then there are tears that flow on account of temporal and material adversity. These can be mortal sin if they indicate an impatience with divine judgment.

The tears that flow out of sorrow for having offended the Creator, as in the case of the woman accused publicly of sin (Lk 7:37–38), indicate a contrite heart.

Likewise, there are tears that flow from compassion for one's neighbor. Thus Samuel wept for Saul in First Kings;[54] thus too Paul says, *[I fear] that I might have to mourn for many who formerly sinned and have not repented* (2 Cor 12:21).

Then there are the tears that flow out of compassion for Christ crucified: thus *Mary stood weeping outside the tomb* (Jn 20:11). In Luke's gospel it likewise says that *a great multitude of people and of women followed him, weeping,* and so forth (Lk 23:27).

Likewise, there are tears that flow from a longing to draw close to God. Thus the Psalmist says, *My tears have been my bread day and night, while people said to me daily, "Where is your God?"* (Ps 41:4 [42:3]). These tears vary just as much as a thirsty soul's longings and God's inpourings vary.

In the same way there are as many varieties of tears connected with deploring one's wretched sinfulness, imploring God's grace, and giving thanks as there are ways to do all of the above, namely, to deplore one's sinfulness.

Likewise, one should realize that just as one fast differs from another fast, and silver differs from gold, so too one set of tears differs from another. Gregory says, "A good work that is not covered with tears is a lean sacrifice; but a good work greased with tears is a fat offering."[55] Bernard says, "Happy are those tears that the loving hand of the Creator wipes away, that is, from the eyes of his chosen ones [*electorum*]."[56] Jerome says, "With bitter tears Peter was restored to his place after thrice denying Christ."[57] And Gregory says that in contemplation it is the spirit baptized with tears that sees most clearly.[58]

Chapter Six: The Many Preparations for Tears. On Hearing and Seeing, Kissing and Embracing God

Many things prepare one to have tears. If you desire tears, first make an effort to expel six hindrances: pride; love of earthly things; callousness, or impiety; excessive busyness; ignorance of yourself; massive sinfulness.

Begin by pursuing humility to counter pride, for *God resists the proud, but gives grace to the humble* (Jas 4:6; cf. Prv 3:34). Avoid falling in love with your own excellence. Likewise, fear of hell goes a long way toward bringing tears. As Gregory says, "More than anything else, a preview of hell calls forth compunction"[59]—if one pays attention to it. Remorseful consideration of one's own faults also helps greatly, as Bernard [William of St. Thierry] says in his *Letter to the Brethren of Mont Dieu:* "He who senses sorrow soon finds tears and slips into lamentation,"[60] and as Gregory says in his first homily on Ezekiel: "When sung before God with eager heart, psalmody obtains from him the grace of tears."[61] So too devout meditation on Jesus Christ is powerful, as Bernard says, "Will not he whose well of tears has dried up find it bursting forth more abundantly and flowing more sweetly as soon as he calls on Jesus?"[62] Likewise a godly and earnest recollection of one's heavenly homeland helps prepare for tears, as the Psalmist says, *By the waters of Babylon, there we sat down and wept*, and so forth (Ps 136 [137]:1). The state of one's body also makes a difference, for, as is pointed out in Bernard's [William's] *Book on the Solitary Life*, in the chapter mentioned above, "physical weariness often gives rise to more forceful feelings of devotion."[63] The pure affectedness of glowing charity overcomes everything, as the Lord says in the gospel of John: *If anyone thirst, let him come [to me] and drink, . . . and from his belly shall flow rivers of living water* (Jn 7:37–38), and as the same Lord says in the Apocalypse, *To the thirsty I shall give of the fountain of life freely* (Rv 21:6),[64] which itself is the *fountain of gardens, the well of living waters,* (Ca 4:15), as the Canticle, chapter four, says. The sweet sound of good singing is also effective, even though Cassiodorus says that "a charming air delights the soul but does not compel it to fruitful tears."[65] He is right about this, although, if the heart is carefully focused on compunction or devotion, a charming air may compel it to fruitful tears.

Filial fear by which the devout spirit is constantly on guard lest she do something that would displease her Creator also avails much, as Bernard notes in Sermon Fifty-Four on the Song of Songs: "In truth I have learned that nothing is so effective in obtaining, retaining, and recovering grace as always to experience awe rather than becoming proud in God's presence. *Happy is he who always trembles.*[66] Therefore, fear when grace smiles, fear when it vanishes, fear when it returns again—that is what it means to tremble constantly."[67] Likewise, invocation of the saints, especially of the Blessed Virgin, is a most effective way to prepare for tears.[68] For Saint Bernard says of the Virgin: "By force of desire, fervor of devotion, and purity of prayer, she gains the fountain of faithful love so that, from a source higher than the angels, she might draw living water which then spills out over men." She herself is the aqueduct, the garden fountain, our neck.[69] Incessant and insistent prayer avails too, as Gregory says in the fourth [third] book of the *Dialogues:* "The grace of tears should be sought from our Creator with great groaning."[70] It also helps to keep company with and recall to mind devout people, according to one of Gregory's homilies: "As I think of Mary's penitence I would rather weep than speak."[71] Furthermore, guarding the gifts of grace is important, for whoever freely receives the blessing of God's heavenly grace loses it unless he eagerly shoulders the yoke of truth by avoiding evils, amending his life, and putting off the old man and his deeds.[72] In Bernard's words: "Just as God deals mercifully with us, so he desires that we deal truthfully with ourselves, accusing, punishing, and correcting ourselves."[73] Gregory says: "Compunction that comes from charity and arises from yearning is something like a kiss. Every time the soul kisses God, repentant remorse stirs within her in his love."[74] And Richard of Saint-Victor adds: "The Bridegroom is heard by recollection, seen by wonder, fondly kissed by love, embraced by delight; or, he is heard through a showing, seen through contemplation, fondly kissed by devotion, and held tight for an infusion of his sweetness."[75]

GUIGO DE PONTE

Chapter Seven: The Ninth Step, Which Is Constant Meditation on Divine Things; an Explanation of Clinging to and Enjoying God

The ninth step is constant meditation on divine things. When a practiced soul is able to ascend to that place where she tastes the dew-drops of divine things and delights all day long in her meditation on God and things of God—then she can rightly say with the Psalmist: *O how have I loved your law, O Lord! It is my meditation all day long* (Ps 118 [119]: 97).

In this stage she should seek often to be affected into God [*affici in Deum*] as she ascends. To be genuinely affected toward God means to thirst and yearn for God through a godly heart's earnest meditation, to ascend and linger as close as possible to his face, until in that meditation the fire of charity[76] that the Lord came to earth to impart[77] flames up. Right away her will is oiled with the fat of sweet devotion, producing that delicious love which flows from on high into the thirsty soul. The Holy Spirit instantly pours himself out in that love and through the path of love. As soon as he arrives, the Spirit turns water into wine, that is, he makes meditation which was formerly arid and cold, even insipid (even when done by exercising the mind), flame up with Uncreated Charity's longing. Just as a dry and shriveled piece of parchment is unfit for fine penwork until it has been oiled, so too, the unction of the Holy Spirit expands a dry and fearful heart so it can hasten to the Lord on out-stretched wings of devotion set in motion by godly affections. Then the remaining thoughts make festival to the Lord,[78] swallowing a divine portion, thanks to reason and godly yearning[79] and clinging in intimacy to his feet throughout a delectable sabbath.[80]

Once she has discovered a drop of honeyed dew, the loving spirit can no longer appear before God empty-handed, so she brings him rich sacrifices[81] of pure and robust prayer, coated with the oil of the Holy Spirit and set on fire with darts of glowing charity. She feels as if she not merely touches but actually directly wounds[82] her Lord's heart. Called by his voice, she clearly catches sight of his presence as she looks up at him while clinging yearningly to him.[83] That is what it means to see God. Hence Bernard says: "To cling to God is nothing other than to see God, which is granted, with special joy, only to pure hearts."[84]

When the soul has been in this state and the richness of devotion poured out on her has lasted for a while, then the memory of sweet felicity produces wisdom.[85] For whatever enters the memory, whether it be God's blessings, the happy heavenly homeland, a longing for virtues, a

184

captivated spirit, or even evils formerly committed, she reflects on and digests in her own way each of these things wisely, that is, with relish,[86] transforming them into the fragrance of God's sweetness.

Understanding [*intellectus*] truly brings about contemplation in the process of enjoying and seeing, as the human understanding is flooded with the light of the Holy Spirit, and the Holy Spirit's fire lights up, loosens up, and penetrates the cloud or fog we all endure because of our sins. This opens direct access to the Creator for the human understanding. Then, firmly focusing his yearning on the Creator he has found in this way, the understanding's acuteness rests sweetly and gently in the Creator.[87] He enjoys his treasure, that is, his God, in reality, not through faith or hope alone, but somehow through a sure line of vision, that is, a sure grasp. Indeed, if he does not reject God, God comes down to greet the understanding in a way scarcely imaginable, kissing him in humblest grandeur with an utterly hidden, inexpressible, and sublime kiss.

These three—will, memory, and understanding—are one and the same in the soul and work simultaneously.[88] Yet they can be distinguished so that when the soul senses herself to be affected toward God she can discern between her own faculties and what she has in union with God, so that she might somehow worthily receive and host her guest, her Creator.

Nevertheless, this manner of being affected in God does not happen daily. Just as rich folk give their sons two garments,[89] one for festive and one for daily wear, so too the Lord Jesus has two, and many more, garments, with which he sees fit to clothe the servants he has made into sons. The aforementioned manner of being affected toward God is granted the soul only rarely, for she cannot have her festive garment unless the abundant dew of the Holy Spirit freely precedes her, descends to her, and works with her. When the human spirit is in this sort of state, she certainly celebrates in ways that cannot be put into words.

This manner of being affected toward God is partly speculative and partly anagogical, that is, it is accomplished partly by affirmation and partly by renunciation. When the godly spirit has become a bit accustomed to contemplating and ascending by either way, as the fragrant Holy Spirit wafts and moves and showers her with celestial dew, she easily sends out the roots of her ascents—her willing meditation directed on God and the things discussed above (the wisdom brought about by memory, and so forth).

She is now able to turn easily from one manner [of ascent] to the other. Even though, as it seems, intellectual rapture cannot occur without affective rapture, nor affective rapture without an element of intellectual rapture, when she ascends in the aforementioned manner, the godly spirit has learned to discern between the two and to exercise and maintain each according to its characteristics. To be affected toward God is the same as to enjoy God in his presence.

Should you ask what it means to enjoy God, it is impossible to know this until we have spotlessly cleansed spirits. Thus Bernard says, "Whoever is curious to know what it is like to enjoy the Word of God should make ready not his ear but his spirit. This is taught not by tongue but by grace; these things are hidden from the wise and prudent and revealed to babes.[90] Great and lofty, brethren, is the virtue of humility that deserves what is not taught and is worthy to attain what it cannot learn, worthy to conceive from and by the word what it cannot explain with its own words."[91] Should you wish to hear more about enjoyment of God, it would seem that to enjoy God is to cling tightly to him through the holy longings of an upraised spirit, and, while clinging, to taste and see how sweet the Lord is.[92] For he descends to favor with his worthiness the one ascending in the spirit of wisdom. He gives himself to the gaze of the pure of heart alone, and those who thus see as they cling, having received the favor of divine worthiness, employ their yearnings and sweetly and happily put their famished jaws to work as they finish swallowing the repast.

There is another manner, or rather, another form, of being affected toward God, which takes place almost daily in an anagogically uplifted soul. You may find fuller truth about this elsewhere, in one of the two books that follow.[93]

Chapter Eight: The Tenth Step, The Three Movements of Contemplation (Spiral, Circular, and Straight), and the Difference between Contemplation and Speculation

In the tenth step, God, who loves those who seek him, sometimes calls from the midst of the cloud[94] to the godly spirit, who is now well trained in the Lord's commandments and constantly seeks his face, presence, and knowledge alone. God calls the loving soul to dwell with himself in that cloud, as it says in Exodus: *When the Lord called Moses out of the midst of the cloud, Moses went up into the dark cloud in which the Lord was* (Ex 24:16; 20:21). This takes place in the hidden tranquillity and loving abode of the heart, where the soul knows she lives at close quarters with the glory of the Lord, with God's majesty and indescribable worthiness, in the pillar of cloud and fire.[95]

To understand this, or at least to gain a sense of it, God permitting, note that there are three movements or three ways in which the loving spirit can be raised up to contemplate her Creator. The first spirals indirectly,[96] the second is by way of a closed circle, and the third [step 11] is straight and direct. These three steps of contemplating divine things are set forth by Blessed Denis. Although they could be expounded in various ways, it is best, for the sake of untrained minds, to simplify his exposition and talk about approaching one's Creator first in exterior things, then in interior things, and thirdly in superior things.

1. The Speculative and Anagogical Spiral Movements

One seeks the bountifully good Creator first in exterior things. There are two ways to do this—first, through attentive consideration of Scripture or certain creatures, which leads to the fragrance of the Spirit. For without the Spirit we can neither draw forth the love and godly affectedness required to turn what we ponder around so that it faces God, nor thirst for God in godly yearning. This is the speculative spiral movement.

Second, the spiral movement of affectedness toward God and thirsting for God takes place instantly, without discussion or consideration by the mind's faculty of understanding, when hearing, reading, or seeing something divine. When such godly affectedness is poured out from above, the soul senses the love of God growing in herself as a fire of godly devotion. This is the anagogical spiral movement. It is granted to lay people and to clerics alike, according to the measure of the gifts of Christ,[97] who blows where he will.[98] In this spiral movement divine thoughts brighten the soul rationally and broadly through rational knowledge and experienced graces.[99]

2. The Speculative and Anagogical Circular Movements

In the second movement, the circular one, the soul seeks and finds God in her heart's chamber. It also takes two forms. The first is to think and reflect on something divine (God's blessings to us, the Redeemer's deeds, or something similar) in the storeroom of one's heart until one senses by godly affections that God is present to pour out his celestial grace and until one has relocated the circle of one's meditations in God by godly affections that gasp for his presence. This is the circular and speculative movement.

In the second form of the second movement the godly spirit is affected[100] toward God in a circular manner. Inwardly collected and bound by chains of divine charity, unable to wander outside herself, she is readied for the outpouring of heavenly sweetness. In sweet intimacy she holds on tightly to God himself, whose presence is limited only by the cloud of divine darkness[101] placed between, yet not separating, them. There she has her longed-for sweet, intimate, and extended talk with him, conversing about whatever she wishes to tell him. When it takes place, this kind of divine contemplation is most pleasant and efficacious, but it is not within human power to have it at will or, when one has it, to hang on to it. God, who gives and sustains this contemplation, has mercy toward those on whom he wishes to have mercy. This method is circular and anagogical,[102] for by means of it the godly soul is called away from exterior things and back into herself as she is united to God in godly love. That is how one sets foot on the tenth step.

Sometimes, when divine assistance prepares those thirsting in the vale of tears for the ascent to God,[103] the Lord reveals to the soul thirsting for a living spring a sort of cloud of divine darkness in which he shows himself to be present, but not face-to-face as he really is,[104] rather, in a mirror, enigmatically and obscurely.[105] A blind man who stands facing the sun's warmth as it warms, soothes, consoles, and usefully delights him really senses the sun's presence, even if he cannot see it at all.[106] In the same way, in this step the godly spirit knows God is really present in the chamber of her heart because of the divine warmth that warms, soothes, attracts, invigorates, consoles, illuminates, and brightens like the fire in the burning bush.[107] The things beneath the sun [God], that is, the properties that flow from him to the soul so that she can speak to him and she can be affected toward him, fill the sanctuary[108] of the heart where they take place in its inner chamber. Some of these properties of God are his mercy, goodness, patience, gentleness, worthiness, and intimate forgiveness.

Through these properties, which are still uncharacteristic and far removed from the truth which is God, the soul is wondrously affected toward God himself in this step. This takes place not by speculative reasoning or discussion, but in sweet loving and a tight embrace as the soul remains with him in the cloud and catches a hidden and eminent glimpse of him through faith that works through love[109]—*he shows himself,* Scripture says, *to those who have faith in him* (Wis 1:2). It is not a vision face-to-face, which, however imperfectly, is granted at another stage.[110] According to Gregory, "No one makes such great progress in the virtue of contemplation that he might fasten the eyes of his spirit on the indescribable ray of light. Rather, the soul looks at something below it and, thus renewed, she makes progress."[111] This total inability to fasten the eyes of understanding and the extensive but less than total inability to fasten the eyes of affectivity on God is what is meant by the "cloud."[112] Within it, however, the godly spirit can indeed sense a clear and hidden attraction to God's presence and can thus say with immense joy: *He who created me is resting in my tent,*[113] that is, in the hidden chamber of my innermost heart. If you prefer, you could say that the cloud is a type of covering for the divine majesty and glory which somehow covers the thirsting soul so that she who could on no account see God or endure the sight of him as he is might cling to God intimately. In one sense, the inability and covering are the same, namely, together they are the blindness of an infirm soul called and accepted by God's mercy, a soul who thirsts and wishes for what she is too weak to have: to see him who lives in light inaccessible.[114] Like Moses she says in awe: *If I have found favor in your sight, show me your face* (Ex 33:13).

Saint Job found himself on this [tenth] step when he said: *If only I were as I was in the months past, according to the days when God watched over me, when his lamp shined over my head and I walked by his light in the darkness; as I was in the days of my youth, when God was secretly in my tent, when the Almighty was with me and my servants were round about me, when I washed my feet with butter and rivers of oil flowed for me from the rock* (Jb 29:2–6).[115] Christ the rock[116] pours out rivers of his oil, that is, rivers of his love, mercy, and grace which yield the gifts of the Holy Spirit: joy and happiness, godliness and goodwill, all of which are oil. The godly spirit is sweetly anointed with these when, in her hidden chamber, she touches and takes hold of the anointed one selected from among his companions.[117]

In the soul's hidden chamber, the utterly desirable Beloved[118] is sometimes sensed so strongly that the godly spirit blazes with a foretaste of God as a consuming fire,[119] that he is a living fountain, fire, charity, and spiritual anointing.[120] In that chamber, the soul somehow hears by spiritual understanding, which is the ear of the inner man, the words: *Hear, daughter, and see* (Ps 44:11 [45:10]). She not only hears but also tastes flavors that whet the spirit's eager appetite, as Scripture says, *They that eat me, shall still hunger,* and so forth (Sir 24:29 [24:21]). In that hidden chamber a burning desire permits the godly spirit to smell God, until she can say: *My soul has desired you in the night* (Is 26:9), that is, in the darkness of the aforementioned cloud. There, as already noted, she sees openly by a sort of hidden gaze, in an instructed ignorance;[121] by means of a godly love of wisdom, she knows intimately. Blessed Denis says: "Wisdom is utterly divine knowledge of God known through ignorance."[122] These are the interior senses.

Even though she grasps the Beloved sweetly in the aforementioned manner, the godly spirit perceives all too well that her eye and all her spiritual senses are held captive, repelled, and blinded. Her senses cannot perceive him more forcefully even though it is under his direction that they have already powerfully sensed him. Even though the godly spirit is unable to have him as powerfully as she wishes, still, in his presence she catches sweet sparks of varying intensity, depending on how much the Lord sees fit to offer the thirsty soul from the fountain of life[123] and depending on how transparently pure her heart is.[124] For unless she has a pure heart, she cannot perceive at face value what is said of God, except as so much foolishness. Without a pure heart she cannot understand things that require spiritual scrutiny.

And that is what the circular and anagogical movement is like.[125]

3. The Anagogical and Speculative Direct Movement [Step Eleven]

In the third movement, or path, namely the rectilinear one mentioned above, one enjoys and seeks God in higher things, reaching straight for him [step 11]. Like the first two motions, this movement of elevation toward God also takes two forms: the anagogical direct movement and the speculative direct movement.

The godly spirit is carried *anagogically* to God in this direct motion when, after godly consideration and devout meditation on the man-God and the God-man, the soul knows that the flamelet of fervent devotion has flickered toward God without consideration or meditation leading the way. Strengthened by God's hidden assistance, in this movement the godly soul knows that ardor has carried her to God, that she is ardently affected toward him, that she ascends repeatedly closer and closer, enjoys God, talks with God familiarly in his presence, and clings more audaciously to this divine fellowship in the spirit of wisdom while her faculties are completely overwhelmed. More will be said regarding this abandoning, that is, anagogical, exercise later (bk. II, ch. 10, 13).

Although this direct and anagogical motion has much in common with the circular and anagogical motion, they also differ in many ways.

190

The straight and anagogical movement rises directly upward to be firmly and all the more powerfully fixed in God. The movement is as direct and powerful as the soul's capacity permits, although God's good pleasure and will knows how to distribute, govern, and circumscribe his favors. In this circular motion the godly spirit receives the word of God as he drops into her innermost heart, holding out her arms as worthily, familiarly, and joyfully as Saint Simeon did when he received the same Savior in the temple.[126] Nothing we have said to this point is as desirable as this form of enjoyment of God. Moreover, when the godly spirit has become practiced in the aforementioned movement, God's hidden decree often permits her to find him in the straight movement, even though she can scarcely find him through the other movements anymore. The straight movement is so much more complete than the others and, it seems, so much more lofty. Only one who has direct enjoyment of God rises to contemplate God's face in the city of supernal citizens, since such a one gazes on God with the sort of direct sight they enjoy.[127] This movement is direct and anagogical, affected and utterly intimate, clinging in both enjoyment and vision.

These things also apply to the ninth step (constant meditation), where the godly spirit is already for the most part free from pressing and oppressive thoughts and experiences purity and tranquillity of heart. She is thus suited in a certain sense for steady meditation on the divine will and sometimes can taste and attain the affected, clinging fruition of God that most properly belongs to the eleventh step. For, if one wishes to understand these twelve steps, one must understand the individual steps and the meaning of words according to their characteristic implications. For in each of these steps there is some kind of meditation, affection, yearning, devotion, and clinging. For example, in penitence, or justification (which forms the first step), we find a penitent person expressing a sort of clinging in the words: *I have clung to your testimonies, Lord, let me not be put to shame* (Ps 118:31 [119:31]). One must take account of the words' properties according to their own specific import—otherwise it is easy to read something erroneously, especially if the one reading does not know how to employ spiritual experience to discern what he reads.

The direct movement also pursues ascent to God through *speculation*. Richard of Saint-Victor offers the following definition of the difference between contemplation and speculation: "As much as gazing (contemplation) and envisioning (*speculatio*) might seem to be interchangeable, it nonetheless seems clearly evident that we call something speculation when it is perceived in a mirror, while in contemplation we see truth in its purity, unveiled and free of any shadow."[128] In the speculative direct movement the godly spirit is moved toward God through vigils and prayers as she seeks him in the streets and squares[129] with great toil and showers of tears. When the godly spirit has washed away her weightier sins with much weeping,[130] senses inwardly wisdom's godly embrace, and feels herself sprinkled with holy longing and sweet love, then sometimes she sees the ineffable light that truly is God. You will find more regarding this vision later in the present work (II.8; III.7). She who glimpses this even as a mere nod or a blinking of the eye deserves "to receive ornaments of gold, filigreed with silver" (Ca 1:10 [1:11]), in Saint Bernard's words.[131] By this direct movement the godly spirit is raised to God in undivided contemplation and, beside herself in spiritual rapture, merits at least a bit of a visible taste of the true light radiantly and vibrantly flashing with divine brightness, the true light that is God himself.

Chapter Nine: The Various Forms Taken by the Rapture of the Spirit

Because the rapture of the spirit [excessus mentis] has been mentioned in connection with this step, it should be noted that it takes many forms. There is in fact a rapture of fear by which one vehemently fears punishment—as the Psalmist says: *I said in the excess of my mind: I am cast away from before your eyes,* and so forth (Ps 30:23 [31:22]).[132] Then there is an overwhelming devotion in enjoyment of God by which the godly spirit surpasses human cognition to reach God through anagogical, abandoning movement. Another type of rapture, in the enlightened understanding, carries the godly spirit beyond all human understanding. Saint Bernard discusses this and the aforementioned matters elsewhere.[133] Then there is the rapture of alienation,[134] which consists of three steps: first, extracorporal vision; second, a rapture that exceeds the imagination; and third, one that exceeds human reason. Richard [of Saint-Victor deals with these.[135]] Finally, there is a rapture of otherness [excessus alterationis[136]] in which the godly spirit passes beyond the bounds of bodily sensation. Elevated in this way, she is supernaturally taken up to God.[137]

As varied as the rapture of the spirit may be, two forms of rapture are more frequently experienced by the godly spirit looking at God. One takes place in fervent devotion, the other in enlightened understanding.

As the soul busies herself reaching toward God by practicing both of these, she learns how to thirst more eagerly for the gifts of perfect purity and perfect charity. Should she mercifully, perhaps even with ease, obtain these gifts from God, the source of all good things to whom nothing is difficult, she will also beg of him the rapture of otherness.

Chapter Ten: The Ten Ways of Seeing God, including the Eleventh and Twelfth Steps

As the Scriptures report copiously, God is seen, or is said to be seen, in ten ways. (1) He may be seen by *faith*, as Scripture says: *All the ends of the earth have seen the salvation of our God* (Ps 97:3 [98:3]). Saint Bernard agrees, saying, "To have believed is to have seen."[138] (2) God is also seen through the eye of *reason*—by philosophers—according to Romans, chapter one (1:20) and the discussion below (III.5). (3) The patriarchs saw God in *figures*,[139] as when Abraham saw Three and worshiped One.[140] (4) The apostles saw God in the *flesh: We saw his glory, the glory as it were of the only begotten of the Father* (Jn 1:14), and *that which was from the beginning, which we have heard, and which we have seen with our eyes* (1 Jn 1:1). (5) God is also seen in the sacrament of the altar—not only by faith, but also through the flashing affections of the pure in heart. Thus the Lord's words in Leviticus, *I shall appear in the cloud over the oracle [upon the mercy seat]* (Lv 16:2), have been applied to the sacrament of the altar, for the Lord appears in this sacrament in a powerfully sweet and lovely manner.[141] (6) He can be seen also by the eye of enlightened love through godly ascents and anagogical clingings. (7) Some see God through spiritual imagery, as did John in the Apocalypse.[142] (8) God is seen fleetingly through his own unimpaired light, as discussed below (III.8). (9) Moreover, God is seen in full rapture of spirit, which is how the angels see him, as explained below (III.8). (10) And in heaven's blessedness God is seen truly and perfectly, as he himself is, by those who are in the realm of the living.[143] Thus 1 John 3 says: *Beloved, we are now the children of God and it has not yet appeared what we shall be, . . . but . . . we shall see him as he is* (1 Jn 3:2).

Except for the last two, all these visions may be had now. In the rapture of the ninth form God is seen in essence, and thus the eleventh step remains unconsummated until the rapture of spirit is complete. Moreover, even when the godly spirit attains the rapture of spirit she is separated by the wall of the flesh from the blessed life. When she has put aside the body [step twelve], she shall enter unhindered into the joy of

193

her Lord[144]—in company with those who live in exile from the earth she shall be joined to the Lord God in eternity. Note that these various ways of seeing God are dealt with in the *Compendium of Theology,* book one, chapter sixteen, and in the last book, chapter thirty-one.[145]

Chapter Eleven: A Short Recapitulation and Expansion of the Preceding Material

The first step is the justification of the sinner, or repentance, which is the second board God gives us after the shipwreck of innocence.[146]

The second step is when the human spirit persistently and anxiously implores God to grant the divine anointing and grace without which the spirit is like grass shriveled with drought.

The third step is devout compunction of spirit in which love and sorrow reign—in which godly devotion reigns in love, and contrition, or compunction, reigns in sorrow.

The fourth step is to suffer with and rejoice with one's neighbor. These are the two breasts of the bride—should anyone lacking these be placed in leadership, he will benefit neither himself nor anyone else, as Bernard says in sermon ten on the Song of Songs.[147] These four steps are discussed in chapter one above.

The fifth step is suffering with Christ through diligent meditation, which is most useful for healing the spirit and sharpening her sight.

The sixth step is the flamelet of ardent yearning, that is, prayer that is powerful in God's sight. Gregory says: "It is not our words but our yearnings that speak to the hidden ears of God."[148]

The seventh step is the visitation of the Bridegroom, or the penetrating descent of the word of God into the thirsty soul, which flows down humbly like a river of peace and enters the godly spirit. These three steps are covered in chapter two.

The eighth step is the contemplation of a spirit striving upward. This contemplation is the death of carnal affections through the rejoicing of the spirit raised on high.[149] Chapter three deals with this step.

The ninth step is constant meditation on divine things, which makes the godly spirit happy because her *will is in the law of the Lord and on his law she shall meditate* day and night (Ps 1:2). This step is dealt with in chapter seven.

The tenth step is the overshadowing cloud in the heart's inner chamber where the godly spirit sits down, as it were, under the shadow of him for whom she longs, whose fruit is sweet to her taste.[150]

The eleventh step is the rapture of spirit by which the godly spirit is often carried aloft to mingle with the holy citizens of heaven and gaze on God's face close at hand. These two steps are discussed above in chapter eight; the eleventh step is covered in chapter ten as well.

The twelfth step is the falling away of the flesh, that is, a death which is happy, not horrible, about which Boethius could say in his first book on consolation: "Happy the human death that does not interrupt the sweetest years and often comes at the behest of sorrows."[151]

In holy contemplation there is thus one origin and foundation, namely the Author of life. The godly spirit thirstily seeks him, her origin, through contemplation. She does so first through reading and devout prayer or exercise, through godly meditation and single-minded yearning. There are two forms of contemplating God himself—speculative and anagogical—which raise the spirit on high as if on two wings. This is discussed below in book two, chapter three.[152] The godly spirit is brought to God through three movements: spiral, circular, and straight. These are discussed in chapter eight, above. Four things are necessary for the re-forming of the inner man: holy living, devout prayer, divine material, and practice. These are dealt with in book two, chapter two, below.[153]

Chapter Twelve: Five Things That Prepare for a Well-disposed Spirit; Five Things That Cleanse the Spirit (with Three Additions)

Five things prepare the spirit to be well disposed: separation from the cares of the world, trials of the flesh, contrition of heart, confession, and baptism in tears. Moreover, after the godly spirit has been cleansed and has made some progress in contemplation, with God's help she leads a happy life in five other things set forth by Saint Bernard (by the same token, should God so ordain, her path may also lead into misery and exile). In Saint Bernard's words, "Separation from worldly life, affliction of the flesh, contrition of heart, frequent confession, and bathing in tears all cleanse the eyes of the spirit so they can be elevated to the true light.[154] When all impurity has been banished outside, wondrous meditation on God's essence, the sight of chaste truth, pure and powerful prayer, jubilation of praise, and fervent yearning lift the eyes of the soul upward. Therefore, whoever yearns to attain the life of contemplation ought to strive to be cleansed as described above and to adorn himself with virtues. Otherwise he will neither have what he longs for nor understand the inner workings of divine contemplation, which cannot be known unless one takes hold of them."[155]

In addition to the aforementioned paths to purity of heart, there are three things that conserve purity of spirit when practiced spiritually alongside other virtues. These three are: to flee from human praise, to flee the concupiscent love of pleasure, and to scrutinize one's heart daily to purge it of sin's uninterrupted corruption. Augustine seems to touch on this in his book *On True Religion*, where he says, "O obstinate souls, give me a man who is repentant in his own chamber, who daily chisels away anew at his own spirit, who resists human praises, who does not give in to the lusts of pleasures."[156] Wisdom will flood out of his hidden chamber.

Chapter Thirteen: Contemplation Requires Four Wings, according to Gregory, and, according to Bernard, Contemplation Is Fourfold

The contemplative life through which the godly spirit often flies away to the heavenly Jerusalem requires the four wings that Gregory mentions in his second homily on Ezechiel: "*Their faces and their wings stretched upward: two wings of each of them touched, and two [wings] covered their bodies* (Ez 1:11). The wings that touch each other extend above because love and hope lift the spirit of the holy ones on high. To say they join each other is fitting, since the chosen ones certainly love the heavenly things they hope for and hope for what they love. The other two wings cover the body because fear and repentance hide their past sins from the eyes of almighty God."[157]

To renew her longing, the godly spirit occasionally ought to call to mind the holy and happy visions the holy fathers received from God. One example is that of Saint Jacob, who said, *I have seen God face to face yet my soul has been saved* (Gn 32:30).[158] Likewise Job: *By the hearing of the ear I have heard you, now my eye sees you* (Jb 42:5), and Isaiah: *I saw the Lord sitting on a high and elevated throne. The whole earth was full of his majesty, and those who were beneath him filled the temple; the Seraphim stood above him and each had six wings* (Is 6:1–2).

Bernard says: "The first and greatest contemplation is to marvel at majesty. This requires a clean heart so that freed from vices and unburdened of sins it may easily rise to heavenly things. Sometimes, too, the one who marvels is held suspended for a short time in wonder and ecstasy. The second thing necessary for him is to look upon the judgments of God, a fearful sight that surely shakes the viewer vehemently, routs vices, undergirds virtues, initiates wisdom, and preserves humility (for humility is the good and solid foundation of virtues; should it waver, the whole house of virtues collapses). The third contemplation is busy with (actually, has leisure in) recalling blessings so that, rather than depart in ingratitude, the person blessed remains eager to love the one who blesses. Fourth, *forgetting what lies behind* (Phil 3:13), the contemplator can rest only by awaiting the things promised. Since he meditates on eternal things, and indeed the things promised are eternal, such meditation nourishes patience." Bernard writes these things in his [fifth] book *On Consideration.*[159] Do not give up: Stubborn labor conquers all.[160]

Here Ends the First Book on Contemplation

HERE BEGINS BOOK TWO
ON CONTEMPLATION

Chapter One: Two Steps Pertaining to Contemplation, Namely, That the Sinner Comes to Christ and Meditates on His Life

For other foundation no man can lay, but that which is laid; which is Christ Jesus (1 Cor 3:11). Since, as Augustine says, God supplies to the utmost and man lacks to the utmost,[1] whoever wishes to escape the ruin of his own misdeeds and to replenish his spirit must stick to the aforementioned foundation in which he finds his needs met.[2]

The sinner who wants to lay down the burden of his sins ought first to listen to Christ's invitation: *Come to me, all you who labor* with the labor of vices *and are burdened* with the burden of sins, *and I will refresh you,* heal you, and revive you, *and you will find rest for your souls* (Mt 11: 28–29, excerpts). In the first book of his *Confessions* Augustine says: "Lord, you made us for yourself and our heart is restless until it finds rest in you."[3] Let the patient then hear the good and caring physician, let him come to him in deep contrition, caring confession, and earnest intent to leave off sinning and do good as long as he lives and has being.

Second, the sinful soul who has already been made a faithful believer in Christ and has been reconciled to him through repentance should strive scrupulously to stay close to her physician and become an intimate member of his household, thinking over his most holy life each and every day as devoutly as she can. But she must be on guard from the start not to read over quickly and curiously a large number of the chapters of his life; rather, she should take in sequence one chapter a day, and use it to celebrate for Christ a delightful sabbath[4] of godly meditation, relishing her repose in it as she sweetly slumbers oblivious to outer tumult and worldly hindrances. No matter where she may be, she should return to it frequently as a secure and godly refuge from vice-filled vicissitudes of human weakness that constantly attack the servants of God. For the sake of spiritual recollection, recreation, consolation, and practice, she does well to return from time to time to the central memories of Christ, namely the incarnation, birth, circumcision, epiphany, passion, resurrection, ascension, outpouring of the Holy Spirit, and return in judgment. But let her make festive fare out of a single chapter per day.

Chapter Two: The Many Reasons Why This Spiritual Life Is Highly Desired

There are many reasons why a life of recalling Christ's life ought to be a sinful man's greatest longing. First, because of the forgiveness of his sins—for when he has passed judgment on himself, accusing himself in confession[5] and justice and freely accepting his penance, he is so clean and free of the filth of sin that he walks attentively with God and meditates in the aforementioned manner. God is a consuming fire[6] to those who cling to him, purging their sins.

Second, this life is desirable because of illumination, for the one who comes to his aid is a light shining in darkness.[7] Illumined by his light, one is taught to set proper priorities—to place Christ and heavenly things first, followed by oneself, one's neighbor, and earthly things.

Third, this life is longed for on account of the grace of tears so necessary for a sinner in this valley of misery, a grace which Christ, the *fountain of gardens and well of living waters* (Ca 4:15), likes to give to sinners who cling closely to him. For Christ is the one who calls out: *If anyone thirst, let him come to me and drink, and out of his belly shall flow rivers of living water* (Jn 7:37–38). But let the faithful sinner maintain a true and eternal goal in view no matter what he does, lest he take hold of a merely transitory reward in the tears that come from time to time.[8]

Fourth, this life is desirable as a renewal after sinful lapses in daily matters. For the Lord raises from failure those who steadfastly cling to him, as the Scripture says: *Make a bronze serpent and set it up as a sign; anyone who has been bitten, if he looks at it, shall live* (Nm 21:8; cf. Jn 3:14).

Fifth, this life is desired for its sweet, pleasant, and much-sought-after taste, as the Psalmist says: *Taste and see that the Lord is sweet* (Ps 33:9 [34:8]); as the Canticle of Canticles declares: *Under the shadow of him whom I desired I sat down and his fruit was sweet to my mouth* (Ca 2:3); as Isaiah says: *Your name and remembering you [are] the desire of the soul* (Is 26:8); and as the Canticle proclaims: *Your name is as oil poured out* (Ca 1:2). In all these ways his name is the soul's desire. The more the faithful sinner is inwardly renewed day-by-day, so much more eagerly he adores and cultivates again and again the life of his Savior, as it is said: *They that eat me shall still hunger and they that drink me shall still thirst* (Sir 24:29 [21]). The soul's eagerness has no end so long as the Savior's sweetness keeps condensing into dewdrops for her.

Sixth, this life is desirable because it brings knowledge of fatherly majesty, knowledge which can be had only through Christ, as the Scripture says: *No one knows the Father except the Son and he to whom the Son reveals him* (Mt 11:27).

Seventh, it is desirable because it makes departure from this dangerous life safe and free of anxiety. For the faithful sinner who in this life gives Christ daily hospitality in his heart, making up from sweet meditations a verdant couch for Christ[9]—the faithful sinner who, at night on his bed, seeks him whom his soul loves[10]—such a one, in turn, will be sought and received by Christ after death that he might have in eternity what he craved, wished for, and became accustomed to in this life: to be with Christ.

Chapter Three: In Praise of a Life of Contemplation on Christ's Humanity

This life is a good, peaceful, holy, charitable, pious, well-watered life that cleanses sinners and renews those who hold on to it, making them citizens with the saints and members of God's household.[11] To lead this life is sweet and lovely: *For her conversation has no bitterness, nor her company any tediousness* (Wis 8:16); rather, it is *joy and gladness* (Wis 8:16). It is indeed a delicious life of grazing and feeding on consoling solitude with an intimate and optimal companion of constant joy, strength, and comfort, a *tower of strength against the face of the enemy* (Ps 60:4 [61:4]) and against the trials and temptations of the sinner.

This life enlightens and teaches a man holy knowledge;[12] *for she teaches moderation and prudence, righteousness and fortitude, which are more useful in the life of men than anything else* (Wis 8:7). This life is the "best part" chosen by Mary.[13] As Gregory says: "Why Mary's part should be the best part is indicated when the Scripture adds that her part cannot be taken away from her. The active life ceases to be when the body disappears—will anyone give bread to a hungry person in the eternal homeland where no one hungers?" A little later in the same passage he adds: "The contemplative life begins here in order to be completed in the heavenly homeland, since the fire of love that begins to burn here will be fueled there by the very love of the one the soul loves. Thus the contemplative life is never taken away because the loss of the light of this present life merely brings the contemplative life to completion." That is what Gregory says in the second book [of his homilies] on Ezekiel, where he has much to say on the active and contemplative life.[14]

No one can excuse himself from this pleasant [*suavis*] and easy life of contemplating the Creator—for contemplation of the loftiest majesty begins simply enough by making one's way through the human life of our Redeemer. Whether one is a beginner, an intermediate making progress, or someone who has reached a degree of completion, all are able to possess this life and to find in it a good nest where their own chicks can roost.

No tongue is adequate to praise this life so good and so worthy above all lives, for it is the beginning of eternal life and of any loftier contemplation and angelic life. Is it enough for you to be with Christ uninterruptedly, to be with him *on whom the angels desire to look* (1 Pt 1:12)? If you wish to reign with Christ in eternity, begin now to reign and do not desert him whom to serve is to reign.[15]

Therefore approach with godly heart the one descending from the Father's bosom to the Virgin's womb. Come forth in pure faith as a witness with the angel to the holy conception. Rejoice with the Virgin Mother made fertile for your sake. With his good guardian Joseph attend his birth and circumcision and adore the infant King with the Magi. With the apostles accompany the good shepherd, Christ, as he performs glorious miracles. Be present at his dying to suffer and sorrow with his blessed Mother and blessed John the Apostle, and, with a certain godly curiosity, touch and feel with your hand each of the wounds your dead Savior suffered for you. Seek the risen one until you find him with the blessed Magdalene. Stand with the disciples on the Mount of Olives and marvel as he ascends into heaven. And, if you have followed him for a while on earth with godly, humble, and devout heart, he himself will lift you up to himself, seated at the right hand of God the Father, just as he promised the faithful sinner clinging to him: *Whoever serves me, let him follow me; that where I am, there my minister shall be also* (Jn 12:26). As the Lord says through Isaiah: *If you turn away your foot from the sabbath, from doing your own will on my holy day, and if you call the sabbath a delight and the Lord's holy [day] glorious; if you honor it by not following your own ways nor finding your own will in [idle[16]] words, then you shall delight in the Lord and I shall raise you up above the heights of the earth and I shall feed you with the inheritance of Jacob your father. The mouth of the Lord has spoken it* (Is 58:13–14).

Chapter Four: Praise of This Life with Respect to the Saints in Glory

This life makes the holy household of God good and kind toward those who invoke their aid, because of the joy we share with them. For example, could the Virgin Mother of mercy, godliness, and grace possibly despise you or avert her eyes from you, no matter how great a sinner you are, when she sees you take into your arms and cradle between your breasts (Ca 1:12)[17] her Son whom she loves above all—not merely once a day but frequently? Having seen you accompany her Son so attentively in each detail and having seen you offer him the office of godliness and service of devotion each and every day, could she possibly abandon you and her Son whom you thus carry? Not at all. So too the other saints are glad to look kindly upon those with whom the Lord is pleased to dwell, for the life of meditation on Christ's humanity makes his worshipers into their companions—they share a common life.

Clearly this life is the life of the apostles who clung intimately to Christ. This is the life of the blessed Mother of Christ, who clung even more intimately to him and served him in the years of his childhood. This is the life of the supernal citizens who enjoy Christ and are awed at his marvelous works, reverently attending him in eternity. It is right that this life not be taken[18] from someone who possesses it—who lives it and possesses it here below by grace—for it is the very reward which is promised to the wise and faithful servant,[19] and eternal life begins here on earth. For anyone who believes in him by imitating him shall not die eternally but shall cross over from death into life.[20] Nor shall he who by grace has completed a novitiate in this life (by celebrating here below the worship that is perfectly accomplished in the company of heavenly citizens), he who has had a master here below and has learned from him how to know him whom heaven's host contemplate clearly and perpetually face-to-face, become a mere novice in the order of heavenly monks.

If any faithful sinner has embraced this life lovingly, let him not doubt that Christ has taken him as his adopted son, for, as Saint Bernard says, "He to whom God is pleasing cannot displease God."[21] And certainly this life, as has been said, is a delightful one, for it makes other activities that have no part in this life of meditation on Christ's humanity seem loathsome, should the godly heart have to attend to them. May God grant this life to us. Amen.[22]

Chapter Five: Let the Servant of Christ Not Count on His Own Merits but Know That He Is a Mere Pauper

Let the faithful sinner wisely beware lest, no matter what state he finds himself in, he place his confidence in his own merits. Rather, let him approach empty-handed, like a mere pauper [*pauperculum*], stripped of everything, begging alms from his Lord. And let him not do this out of false humility, hiding his confidence in merits;[23] rather, let him know without a doubt that *no living person shall be justified in the Lord's sight* (Ps 142:2b [143:2b]), indeed, we are not even able to render an account of our thoughts, should the Lord wish to enter into judgment with us.[24] In this way, even the one who presses forward urgently toward the good Lord who calls sinners[25] will not be thought presumptuous. In the world, when beggars step forward to beg alms of the rich, they are considered more wretched, not more worthy, in proportion to their neediness; far from being considered presumptuous or proud, the greater their need, the greater is the pity with which good-hearted rich folk view them.[26]

Chapter Six: Regarding the Third Step, Which Is Contemplation of the Highest Deity and the First of Its Three Requirements: Prayer

The third step [cf. II.1] is the contemplation of the highest divinity. The person who aspires to contemplation of the highest Good should do so out of yearning for the Creator based on a re-formed inner man rather than confidence in merits. Such an aspirant requires three things: prayer, subject matter, and a method of implementation.

Since the service[27] of contemplation, which is the work of angels,[28] surpasses human knowledge and power, and since no one can attain it except with the aid and enabling of abundant grace, it would seem to be obvious that continual prayer imploring God to grant constant grace is most necessary. We can do nothing without it.[29] This prayer should not be spoken aloud with abundance of words[30] but should occur spiritually in the soul, raising up and holding out the spirit to God, as the Psalmist says: *Within me [I make] prayer to the God of my life* (Ps 41:9 [42:8]). Such prayer procures good affections; in the course of time it rises toward God like a plume of smoke,[31] according to the Scripture: *The sweet-smelling smoke rose from the angel's hand in God's eyes* (Rv 8:4). In the course of time such prayer brings about a pious and intimate talk with God, who seeks us out rather than disdaining intimacy with us—for he is meek and humble-hearted,[32] patient and full of mercy,[33] and thus he enjoys being with the sons of men.[34] Such prayer is a good contemplation that goes a long way toward gaining knowledge and love of God. Nevertheless, this kind of prayer is not quickly attained. This is the prayer described in the *Book on the Solitary Life*, namely in Bernard's [William of St. Thierry's] letter to the brothers of Mont Dieu: "Prayer, he says, is the affection of a man clinging to God, a sort of intimate and godly conversation, a state in which the enlightened spirit enjoys [God] as long as she can."[35] Should you not yet have this prayer, persist as hard as you can in earnest prayer to God until he rewards you with greater things.

Chapter Seven: Regarding the Second Requirement for Contemplation, Namely, Most Sacred Subject Matter; Regarding Speculative Contemplation and Its Three Steps

Second, contemplation of God requires spiritual material in which the human spirit acts and is acted upon. Note, moreover, that contemplation of God is twofold: speculative and anagogical, or intellectual and affective, or affirmative and negative.

Speculative contemplation has three steps: The first is careful considering, the second is meditation, the third is contemplation.[36] The first step, consideration, is "the focused thinking of a soul seeking what is true."[37] It involves standard ways of knowing and could be called the knowing stage. The second step, alluring meditation, is the "far-seeing glimpse of a soul engaged passionately in the pursuit of truth."[38] It is situated within wisdom and might be called the wise stage. It cannot be had except through the Holy Spirit's teaching, as Wisdom, chapter nine, says: *With difficulty we form an estimation of the things that are on the earth and we toil to discover the things within our sight; but who shall know your conclusions unless you grant wisdom and unless you send forth your*

Spirit from on high? (Wis 9:16–17). The third step, inventive contemplation, takes place in the awe-inspiring presence of highest truth.[39]

The first type of contemplation (speculative) is partly within reason and partly above reason. The other type (anagogical) is not only above reason but indeed seems to be apart from reason.[40] Speculative contemplation proceeds by affirmation, while the other contemplation proceeds by renunciation. The first makes use of affirmation and of the properties of certain words, as when it is said that God is the first and highest essence, the highest and perfect nature; the highest majesty, authority, good, knowledge, and energy; the force holding all things together; the highest truth, wisdom, justice, mercy, sweetness, godliness, glory, light, happiness, peace, eternity, charity; the fountain of all life; the highest and perfect Creator, sustainer, and lover of all good things visible and invisible; the origin of all existence, the best and eternal end of the good life—these and others like them are the sort of spiritual and holy material worthwhile for meditation on the highest Good, in accord with each person's capacity based on the measure of Christ's gift.[41]

Chapter Eight: The Third Requirement, Namely, a Method of Implementation: Avoiding Exterior Affairs; with Some Additional Comments on the Vision of God

The third requirement for contemplation is a method for exercising it. This method in turn requires three things: purity, attentive concern, and godliness.

To make the image of God (the human soul) pure and free to wait in attendance on her Creator, she must abstain as much she legitimately can from exterior actions. As Gregory says, "The spirit cannot be led away to contemplate heavenly[42] things unless she earnestly withdraws from the things that entangle her externally."[43] Thus the person thirsting for contemplation of God should avoid external matters, for, unless he does he will be so full of the spectrum of worldly fantasies that he will never have a heart quieted and serene, ready with a pure, spiritual taste to receive the purest subject matter mentioned above. As the Scripture says, *A satiated soul will despise honey* (Prv 27:7). A satiated soul despises honey when, having fallen for and being full of external cares and busyness, she tastes no spiritual sweetness in the divine things she handles, reads, or listens to. Soon the loathing she feels in her spirit tramples down divine delights. For this reason it is essential, as far as human necessity permits, to abstain from all other preoccupations whatsoever.

Constant spiritual solicitude is also essential so that, filled with the gift of knowledge and understanding and invigorated by the vital flow of grace, we might persist in learning the aforementioned divine material subtly and spiritually—according to each person's potential.

Finally, a person gazing on God in the hidden tranquillity of the spirit's eye needs humble and godly devotion so that, having taken up with godly yearning a single word of divine material, he can with utmost devotion, goodness, and simplicity of heart work more wisely at a God-given taste of what God is like.[44] This always takes place, according to the soul's capacity, on the path of sweetness and love in the dewdrops of the Holy Spirit.

When by God's grace the godly spirit is in the aforementioned state, the understanding follows behind a thirsty *affectus* quickened by the Spirit, striving to discover a ray of purest truth. If the coarser worldly fog be dispersed from the viewer's heart, she sometimes sees ineffably that ineffable light which truly is God. Two things are altogether necessary if this blessed vision is to be seen: The spirit must become even purer and, in her growing purity, let the innermost sprinkling of celestial dew make her fecund.

Moreover, this blessed vision occurs with wavering and unsteady sight, not with a fixed or firm gaze. It takes place in a fleeting transit in which the pious spirit hurriedly and momentarily glimpses the light of divine glory, the flash of blessed and divine reflection. This occurs by means of the sweetness of godly devotion and of burning, envisioning love. Indeed, to be more accurate, she sees that she is unable to see[45] on account of her great weakness and incapacity, an incapacity which ineffably stretches almost but not quite to the point of seeing—she sees within her limits as she is lifted up in spirit.[46] How absolutely lucid this most brilliant brightness is, and, as the Scriptures say,[47] how far removed it is from every thought of human effort, understanding, prudence, investigation, and estimation. Christ alone reveals it to whomever he wishes and when he wishes, for he hides it from the wise and prudent and reveals it to infants as he pleases.[48] Whoever wishes to attain this unspeakable light, which really is God, should strive to be cleansed, clinging all the more attentively to the Mediator between God and man who unites the lowest to the highest.

Gregory speaks of this blessed vision as follows: "By first burning off listlessness from the spirit's vision, the cloud of sins that covers the spirit is dissipated, and the soul is suddenly flooded by the resplendent flash of indescribable light and sprinkled with heavenly dew flowing from the limitless fountain. Perceiving truth, she sees yet sees not the greatness of that very truth."[49] He also says that, though she extends herself to the utmost, the human spirit scarcely knows the innermost limits, "for it is true that we know something of God when we sense that we are unable to know anything fully."[50] Likewise, the *Book on the Solitary Life* as cited above says: "Whatever God imparts of the vision and knowledge of God to the faithful here below, it is an enigmatic vision as if in a mirror[51] and is so far removed from the future vision and knowledge as faith is from truth and time from eternity—except when God on occasion reveals his face to his chosen and beloved in a sort of intermittent light, just as a candle enclosed in someone's hands sheds light and conceals light according to the will of the person holding it. Permitted thus to glimpse the fleeting and passing light, the mind can then blaze with ardent longing for full possession of eternal light. Sometimes, to give one a sense of what he lacks, the lover's consciousness is, as it were, briefly seized by grace, snatched away from him, carried off to the light of reality, away from the tumult of affairs into silent joys. There, in a manner suited to his capacity, for a moment, for an instant, utter reality as it is in itself is revealed to him. For a time indeed he may be transformed, in his own way, into something like that ultimate reality. When he has thus learned the difference between clean and unclean,[52] he is returned to himself and returned to the task of cleansing his heart for vision, to the task of fitting his mind for likeness, so that, should he be granted another glimpse, he might see in greater purity and enjoy it more steadily."[53]

Gregory of Nazianzus says of this blessed vision that "God can only be contemplated with a most subtle gaze of the spirit, and by a brief glance that takes place not in those things which are in God himself but in those things that surround him. In this way the face of truth is contemplated not from within truth itself but by means of those things that are close to truth. Before it can be held it flees, before it can be grasped it slips away. It offers itself to the heart, if the heart is pure, much as a stroke of flashing light illuminates human eyes by stunning them and then quickly passing away."[54]

As another example of this blessed vision of God, we note that some cannot see this world's sun because it has not yet risen for them. In the same way, sinners dead in their sins cannot see nor sense the Sun of righteousness.[55] These the Apostle rouses with the words: *Awake, you sleeper! Arise from death, and Christ shall give you light* (Eph 5:14). Some cannot see the sun because of a very opaque cloud that comes between their eyes and the sun. In the same way a spirit that has not been cleansed is completely obscured and clouded over by the fog of the world's ever-changing variety and cannot see God until she is cleansed. Still others openly see the sun brightly shining, yet its brilliant rays pulse so power-fully into their weak eyes that they see that they are unable to see the rays' source. In this case it is not the absence of the sun but merely the eyes' weakness that incapacitates.[56] One can indeed see the sun clearly without being blinded by its brilliance—if one is in open country early in the morning. That is how God is seen in heaven.

The more the cloud covering the sun thins out, the closer to the sun one's line of sight is. To this end the godly spirit energetically wipes away the clouds of sins and bends her effort to cleansing—through re-pentance, mourning, confession, groans, asking pardon, yearning for grace and glory, bathing her couch with her tears, freeing herself for divine blessings through thirsting solicitude and varied longings, and busying herself in the practice of other virtues. Such holy pursuits seek out not only the flowers but also the roots of virtues[57] as the godly spirit approaches the Sun of Righteousness. Just as a cloud covering the sun sometimes divides for an instant, permitting the sun to be seen every-where, so sometimes (with God's help) the darkness and fog of the spirit that afflict every man in one degree or another dissolve or disintegrate, and the Sun of Righteousness, the true light who illumines every light in heaven and on earth, can be seen in a godly rapture of spirit.[58]

Indeed, God, the Father of mercies and bestower of complete and holy consolation,[59] who is kind and good to the soul who seeks him,[60] often cracks open the cloud a bit for that seeking soul.[61] Through these little cracks she can reach God's goodness through certain hidden aspi-rations of the soul. That is, the Lord imparts to the soul certain sharp arrows of godly affections that penetrate her own cloud.[62] In the process, she spiritually and sweetly tastes divine things without seeing them. This feeds and forms her in her infancy so that she might attain the aforementioned blessed vision and other divine things. With his face invisible, God assists the soul gazing in godly longing and moves and advances,[63] attracts and restores her so that she delights in carrying out these daily exercises of a godly spirit. That is how a godly spirit thirsting for contemplation, knowledge, and love of her Creator, Redeemer, Ruler, and Savior gets started.

As the godly spirit perseveres, surrounded by roses and lilies of the valley,[64] God teaches her how to ascend above to the rivers of waters,[65] that is, to prepare her heart's ascents in the vale of tears[66] and to seek God, thirst for God, glimpse God, and cling more closely to God through both speculative and anagogical contemplation. Ascending by clinging to God she is affected by thirst, and, being thus affected, she clings to God all the more thirstily.[67] For the Master of all things is the one who is enthroned[68] in heaven and on earth and teaches men holy knowledge by means of the grace of godly affections and devotions, showing them what things are to be sought from God.

Chapter Nine: What Is Devotion?

Without oil all spiritual food—namely prayer, reading, meditation, fasting, and other religious exercises—remains dry. The oil of devotion, as it flows over and flavors the other spiritual foods, anoints the spirit and makes her rejoice in God's presence. As the *Summa Virtutum* says, devotion "is the tenderness of heart that makes it easy to dissolve into tears. It is the fervor of good will which becomes obvious to others because the spirit is unable to hold it in."[69]

This is the path of our cleansing, restoration, and enlightenment, the spiritual ladder by which the clean and godly spirit ascends to God. Should faults force its removal, no one, not even the fellow-citizens of the saints,[70] who are accustomed to climb it frequently, would be able to find the way.[71]

Chapter Ten: Regarding Anagogical Contemplation and the Book "Viae Sion." What Is Clinging to God? Let the Contemplative Be Fearfully Awed

The other type of divine contemplation, anagogical contemplation, is carried out through renunciation or removal of all things.[72] It is truer than the speculative type of contemplation discussed in detail above. Although any contemplation that raises the purified spirit to Jerusalem on high, whether through affirmation or through negation, can be called anagogical,[73] nevertheless there are differences between the two types in what precedes and what follows this goal. "Anagogical" can thus be applied to the contemplation that is achieved through renunciation of all things, which is said to be truer than speculative contemplation.

For in truth God surpasses everything visible, imaginable, and understandable, that is, he is above the three types of seeing God in this

life[74] that God occasionally granted according to his wish and good pleasure to the holy fathers: seeing with physical eyes,[75] seeing with the
imagination,[76] and seeing with human understanding as was the case
with Paul.[77] But the other type of contemplation, anagogical contemplation, is based on another way of reaching God. This is the contemplation
which the excellent booklet beginning with the words *Viae Sion lugent*
(*The Roads to Zion Mourn*)[78] discusses—anyone who wishes to attain
this kind of contemplation should read it assiduously.

Nevertheless, the author of this book, fine cleric and most sublime
contemplator that he is, has woven together much material, perhaps too
much material, best suited to those who are eager to advance rapidly. It
is too lofty and obscure for those looking for a path better suited to
and more manageable by their more limited capacity. Thus, to provide a
pattern for the spirit who finds herself at a lower level, who has never
understood the more sublime things of the Holy Spirit, three things
seem necessary as the starting point for this highest, that is, anagogical,
contemplation. They are the same as those mentioned under speculative
contemplation: prayer, subject matter, and method—yet they proceed in
a different manner.

First, prayer is necessary, in the same manner as described above.
The subject matter of this contemplation is not suited for weaving discussions and discourses about investigations and inquiries, argumen-
tations and conclusions, all of which anagogical contemplation most assiduously avoids. Instead the subject matter of anagogical contemplation
tries to entice and nurture the devotion of godly affections toward
Christ, who is the richly flowing fountain of all graces.

The exercise of anagogical contemplation has three steps. The first
is the godly spirit's imaginative clinging to Christ's humanity through
devout affection, saying: *My soul clings to you* (Ps 62:9 [63:8]). The second step is the godly spirit's clinging of discernment in which she discerns but does not separate God from man as she clings in godly love to
the divinity clothed with humanity, saying: *It is good for me to cling to
God* (Ps 72:28 [73:28]). The third step is the human spirit's yearning,
unitive clinging in which she gently burns for God, knowing experientially that one who clings to God in this way is one spirit with him.[79] In
this step, as the godly spirit leaves behind mental and anagogical prayers
and, inflamed with divine longing, pants for the face of her own Author,
she is joined to heavenly things and separated from earthly things. With
love growing from her own fervor she opens herself to receive and in
receiving is set on fire. Then with great longing she gazes wide-mouthed

at celestial things and in some wondrous way tastes what she seeks to have. This tasting, moreover, is the clinging, the union, through which the pious spirit enjoys God, in whom she blissfully reposes.

Note that the entire path of this contemplation consists in holy devotion and godly affection, and that it cannot be had otherwise. Hence the godly spirit must of necessity thirst for God, the living fountain, already in the first stage of the exercise. As devoutly as she can she must busy herself in being affected by Christ's sweetest humanity, approaching him humbly and familiarly through daily attentiveness. For better than anywhere else, it is in Christ's humanity that a weak spirit who loves even a little bit can be affected with devotion. By doing this the spirit is cleansed, which is most necessary, and she gains more and more intimacy with Christ. For when the spirit offers Christ humility, Christ extends intimacy to her, because he is meek and gentle and humble of heart,[80] nor shall the humble be put to shame over the expectancy with which they seek him alone.[81]

Second, just as the rising sun[82] slowly grows into the clear light of day, so let the godly spirit, with her godly longing, fear, and reverence, slowly strive through godly meditations on the humanity of Christ to cross over to his divinity. Just as in the first stage she paid more attention to the man than God, that is, to the humanity of Christ than his divinity (even though she somehow includes both at once), so now let her be as zealous as she can to place his divinity ahead of his humanity, and, grasping God by the handle of humanity, embrace the feet of God more devoutly. Let the godly spirit daily strive to exercise herself and progress in these two steps, for in the first she is cleansed and attracted, in the second she is purged and enlightened and well disposed to receive more potent blessings.

Third, when she has often become accustomed to draw on devotions sparked by the God-man, let her begin to turn them directly upward toward God, permitting herself to take on no other thought or meditation except a burning devotion inspired from Christ or given her by the Lord from whatever source. Then, as soon as she begins to be kindled, let her strive to burn as purely and broadly as possible before God.[83] Set on fire with her own small measure of godly yearning for God, she herself burns in imitation of the angels. In the book of Judges one reads that the angel of the Lord ascends in the flame from the altar that rises into the sky;[84] so too in the flame of ardent devotion that rises softly to God by intention and love the spirit herself makes a fiery ascent to her Creator and Lord by means of love itself. This the fellow citizens of the saints[85] do often, flying with flaming wings before him most frequently.

By persevering daily in this manner, the godly spirit gradually becomes so well trained that she can bypass the preparatory path and present herself directly to God, where she can stand face-to-face before God while meditating and drinking in the honeyed outpourings of supercelestial blessing—although occasionally not without fervent effort. Fed by the taste of these outpourings, she flies directly and rapidly upward to God if he so wills. She thirsts to be affected toward God almost daily, for, after a long time, the trained soul becomes accustomed to look for these anagogic movements nearly every day.[86]

This presentation—in which the pious spirit places herself before God and becomes fascinated by his face in thirsty yearning—takes place mysteriously through a sort of teaching impressed on the heart from above. It is like learning to write—after long practice one can write by heart. These anagogic movements are not learned suddenly, for no one is ready right away, but after long practice a sort of spiritual pattern is impressed on the soul. This patterning, at its highest level, constitutes the celestial skill of anagogical ascent. It is partly an ascent and partly an activity. As long as sin does not fritter away this ingrained skill, it forms a disposition in the spirit that makes her virtually always able to place herself before God, thirst to be affected by him, and cling directly to divine charity.

The godly spirit is said to cling to God when, as much as her frailty permits, she follows the example of the angelic host on fire with perfect charity before God as she burns with the glowing flame of godliness close to God. More than that, she is inflamed in God himself with lively yearnings that taste nothing except God himself or something of him that points toward possessing him.[87] By this exercise the godly spirit turned angelic citizen is taught and even divinely forced to prepare for repeated ascents in her heart and to dwell in the presence of God often, full of praise and fiery prayer. When she has become accustomed enough to being there, she calls to herself some of the heavenly citizens—first one, then another, now individually, then a group, then all of them, calling on them to intercede before God for her, in her wretchedness, and for other sinners.

This is accomplished not by putting in place a yearning that silently glows in God but by drawing on the yearning that steadfastly entreats, knocks on the door, and forces God's kindness to look upon her and upon sinners like her in the presence of his saints. The godly spirit ought especially to bend every ascendant desire to attain this, with God's help, to carry this out before her Lord's face. Like a man speaking to his friend,[88] or, if it seems more appropriate, like a household servant speaking familiarly with his master, surely the spirit raised on high in this way expresses herself spiritually in a variety of languages, that is, she multiplies the variety of her yearnings, petitions, and wishes. She speaks familiarly and unspeakably in new tongues, she expresses surely and openly before God. *For when he left the land of Egypt, he heard a voice he had not known* (Ps 80:6 [81:5]), that is, when she moves from captivity to liberty of spirit she recognizes a new language.[89]

Finally, since the judgments of God are a great abyss,[90] completely incomprehensible[91] and hidden, and since human sinfulness, captive to great weakness, is utterly frail and surrounded by countless visible and invisible pitfalls, the soul must strive most diligently to remain in godly awe and deep humility. For even if now she freely receives from God's hand the things described above, in the future God's just judgment might withhold them from her because she has become ungrateful or careless or puffed up, or she may fail to recognize what she has already received, whence they come, or the criteria by which the just Judge denies her them. "For as the gifts increase so too does accountability for the gifts."[92] More than anything else, the godly spirit who is in grace should fear being bereft of the works of grace and left to the weakness of nature, thus forced to feed her flock[93] in the flesh, that is, in the tumult of her carnal senses.

Chapter Eleven: Spiritual Grace Comes and Goes

It cannot be doubted that the Holy Spirit blows,[94] sometimes more, sometimes less vigorously, through the garden of the spirit, blowing as he will, when he will, as much as he will,[95] and on whom he will. Without the Holy Spirit a man can do nothing, nothing, I say—he can neither repent, nor control himself, nor raise himself on high. Note also that the Holy Spirit occasionally withdraws so that he might be recalled more eagerly,[96] or, be more eagerly received and more alertly anticipated when he returns. He makes both frequent withdrawals from and visits to those whom he indwells.[97] Even with those who have become spiritual the Spirit alternates his presence and absence, visiting at dawn and suddenly testing them.[98] The Holy Spirit withdraws whenever he wishes, according to the disposition of his hidden counsels, establishing and fixing in advance definite limits to a person's progress according to what the Spirit knows and wills. Whoever lacks the Spirit will not recognize the Spirit's withdrawal.

Chapter Twelve: A Review of the Three Steps in the Method Described in Chapter Ten Above

To instruct and console her for her lack of training in the first two steps, the godly spirit should have at hand some meditations so that, should the milk be taken away from her, she will not lack some solid food[99] to eat and transform into godly devotion. In the third step, as described above, she should strive, as purely as she is able, to submit herself directly to God's goodness in order to receive anagogical blessings, enkindlings, and ascents.

In the first step the spirit is cleansed, attracted, and enkindled. In the second step she is cleansed, attracted, enlightened and properly disposed. In the third step she is cleansed, enlightened, and elevated so that she can proceed to more divine things. If she tastes rightly, she always knows herself to be a beginner in such excellent and unsearchably profound things. Even though we have come a long way, we still perceive our progress to be nothing, on account of our blind, sinful, and wretched weakness, nakedness, sluggishness, bondage, distortion, perversion, and ingratitude.

Chapter Thirteen: That the Anagogical Practice of Contemplation through Renunciation Seems to Be Better in Many Ways Than the Speculative Method

The anagogical method of practicing contemplation by renunciation seems to be better in many ways than the method that proceeds through affirmation. For it appears to be easier, purer, and more useful, eager, certain, lovely, lasting, humble, and intimate. It is indeed easier to put into practice because, once one has been shaped by the aforementioned impress on the heart, it is much easier to arrive at and ascend to God using this method. Likewise, it is more useful for cleansing and healing the spirit, because in this method the spirit herself is more completely consumed by the fire of charity.[100] It permits purer enjoyment of God because the bright flamelet drives away the fantasies and darkness of the spirit more fully than in the other methods. In this method one ascends more eagerly, for the spirit rejoices in the presence of her Creator more copiously and richly. This is a more certain and safe way to find and possess God himself, because someone looking at God in this manner will scarcely find all her yearning deceived. This method is more lovely because a godly love burning for God lets the human spirit bring her efforts to a greater completion. Moreover, anagogical contemplation fixes the human spirit in God more firmly and holds on to God himself with godly yearnings. It is also a more humble way of ascending to God, for in this anagogical method the human spirit, as it were, shyly prostrates herself with veiled face before God. It is also, as we have seen, more intimate, because the spirit is much more frequently permitted to possess God by this method than to see God by the other method.

In the speculative method, the soul sees what she sees more clearly, elegantly, transparently, loftily, worthily, gently, sweetly, and joyfully— but she sees God only to a small degree and this blessed vision is only rarely granted in this life. Indeed, it is not surprising that the Lord wished to be seen transfigured before the apostles only once. If indeed you should be granted this vision once in this life, it is enough for you.

I believe that when the good Lord grants either method of contemplation to you, you will be pleased to practice the anagogic method more often than the other method. In the anagogic method you neither see nor understand, yet with eyes closed and your face veiled before God's face[101] you nonetheless certainly see the Creator's presence through the outstretched eagerness of humble yearning. You will strive to embrace him more eagerly with his own trustworthiness, clinging, as it were, to his feet in enjoyment— more eagerly, that is, than in the other method of contemplation, in which, as noted above, the spirit cannot see what she sees.[102]

In this anagogical exercise the clinging sometimes proceeds from the affection, as when the human spirit begins to cling to God in the aforementioned manner. Sometimes the affection proceeds from the clinging, as will be apparent in what follows. The clinging cannot happen without affection, for, as true as it may be that the clinging takes place in complete enjoyment, still the disposition, or the mode of ascent and clinging described above, often precedes one's actual standing before God in real affection and clinging. In this second manner, the ascent and clinging is a certain hidden, spiritual clinging that is godly and desirous yet cold—until, like a candle catching fire from being placed close to a flame, the soul can drink directly from God (the living fountain and fiery charity) that living water which flows back into him and can be set on fire from the fire of passionate and pleasurable clinging. Thus one sometimes refers to the first clinging [which proceeds from warm affection] and sometimes to the second clinging [which precedes the warmth of affection].

Here Ends the Second Book on Contemplation

HERE BEGINS BOOK THREE
ON CONTEMPLATION

Chapter One: The Active Life Has Three Steps

Let us all together hear the conclusion of the discourse: Fear God and observe his commandments; this is the whole [duty of] man (Eccl 12:13). "The Church knows of two lives commended to her from on high":[1] the active and the contemplative lives. Hence, after taking on roles[2] ranging from that of the foolish lover of the world to that of the philosopher or wise man of this world,[3] from that of the pauper to that of the rich, Solomon concluded in the end that there is nothing truly good outside of these two lives. His words *fear God* (i.e., love God with respectful awe) refer to the contemplative life, which concentrates on seeking God's face in chaste fear and holy love, and, having found God's face, clings to him as much as God grants. *Observe his commandments* gives figurative expression to the active life, which is of three types: reforming the self, caring for one's neighbor, and heavenly preaching or spiritual concern about the salvation of souls.

The first type of active life chokes off the passions of vices and acquires virtues by keeping divine commandments. In the process it frees one to strive for a reshaping of one's behavior. This type of active life is utterly necessary and an essential preparation for the contemplative life.

The second type of active life sets one free for, or concerns itself with, the physical needs of one's neighbors. The seven works of mercy and ministry to one's neighbors—to the hungry, naked, thirsty, sick, alien, dead, imprisoned—as mentioned in two verses of Scripture[4]— these are the works of godliness.

The third type of active life seeks to offer to one's neighbors healthful teaching and saving, discerning preaching, all done in God's charity.[5]

The first type applies to beginners and to all who thirst for contemplation. The second type applies to those who have made progress but are still much hindered in their contemplative practice and, with the eyes of the heart still veiled, are unable to gaze at heavenly things. The third type is especially applicable to prelates and the spiritually mature, whose disciplined preaching and zealous care of souls should arise more out of experience of the contemplative life and of heavenly graces than from study or learning acquired solely through knowledge.[6]

The first type of active life quiets the inner passions of the soul from which phantasms arise, images that impede contemplation.[7] Although human contemplation[8] is never completely free of phantasms, still it is one thing to be overwhelmed or weighed down by them and quite another thing to let them pass easily and not hold on to them. "Contemplative men," as Gregory says, "do not carry around with them the shadows of corporal things,"[9] "because their contemplation rests not on these things but on consideration of intelligible truth."[10] Gregory says of the first type of active life: "He who wishes to draw the bow of contemplation must first prove himself in the field of works."[11] Of the second type he says: "The active life means giving bread to the hungry and dispensing to each person what helps him most."[12] Likewise, of the third type he says: "The active life means giving bread to the hungry and teaching the ignorant with a word of wisdom,"[13] and also: "Just as a well-ordered life reaches from the active life toward contemplative life, so too it is most useful to direct the mind back toward the active life from the contemplative life."[14]

Whoever yearns to attain the sweetness of contemplation ought to prepare himself earnestly through these exercises of the active life.

Chapter Two: Why the Contemplative Life's Favors Are Granted Only to a Few

As Gregory says in his homilies on Ezekiel, book two, homily two: "The contemplative life consists in holding on to charity toward God and neighbor with all of one's spirit and in clinging to nothing except a yearning for the Creator. All exterior activity is quieted, so that one takes no pleasure in any action, but rather, having spurned all cares, the mind is inflamed by the prospect of seeing the face of his Creator. As much as he has been aware that he bears with sorrow the weight of corruptible flesh, so much more eagerly he longs to be part of that angelic chorus of praise and to mingle with the celestial citizens, rejoicing eternally and unchangeably in God's sight."[15] This life is peaceful and charming, gentle and lovable, hidden and desirable. It seeks God, thirsts for God, and clings to God. As Augustine says, "I owe myself more to myself than to others, yet I owe myself to God much more than to myself."[16]

Lest the contemplative life's comeliness be sullied by the vice of indiscretion, contemplatives should not lightly offer this life to public view. Thus it was that Christ—whose every action is instructive for us[17] and whose transfiguration most manifestly prefigures the contemplative life—did not wish to be transfigured within sight of the populace, nor even in front of all of the apostles. Instead he chose to reveal his hidden glory to a few of them, three in number.[18] In this example spiritual men apparently are admonished and instructed not merely to keep the hidden benefits of divine blessings from being broadcast generally but even to keep them hidden from members of their own household and from their companions.[19]

There are many reasons for this. First, because in revealing divine things the human spirit might become insolent and absorbed with her own light-headed and airy thoughts. The beauty of a godly spirit before God and men ought to consist in her simple and upright intention, even more so in her motives and her upright life, but her greatest beauty should be shown only in her hiding place in God's presence, as the Bridegroom says in the Canticle: *How beautiful you are, my love, how beautiful and comely you are, your eyes are doves that reveal not what lies veiled inside* (Ca 4:1).[20] Moreover, the godly spirit ought to conceal her secret things because such things are not commonly understood by men—God alone must teach them how to discover them, as the word of the Lord says: *No one knows the Father except the Son and he to whom the Son wishes to reveal him* (Mt 11:27). Bernard says much the same: "What holy contemplation experiences with God she cannot at all make known to others."[21] There are many other reasons why the hidden favors of divine contemplation should be concealed.

Nonetheless, such favors are revealed to a few who are fit for contemplation and who are more ready to profit by contemplation than to be obstructed by it, to receive than to spurn, to taste than to belittle, to love than to envy, to desire than to loathe. Contemplative men can demonstrate these things, not merely faultlessly but even wisely and meritoriously, to the glory of God and growth of charity, by scrutinizing themselves to ensure that no presumption, error, inordinateness, or undue humility lurks or looms large in their spiritual exercise. Although spiritual men ought to discuss their own situation with suitable spiritual friends, they should beware of presumptuously revealing their secrets to outsiders. Contemplatives who progress from strength to strength and daily merit seeing the God of gods in Zion,[22] both by speculation and anagogy, should have a godly fear of wastefully and unwisely casting the precious pearls of their hidden ascents to God (purchased by selling all they have[23]) before the inexperienced and unfit—for by such scattering, they lead people to a place where they do not belong. Those of us who profess the contemplative life but who lack the aforementioned favors can and should apply ourselves to the task frequently, thirsting and longing for the spiritual exercises of this life.

We can pursue this with that much assurance and prudence if we give ourselves little occasion for vainglory and make no excuse for neglecting our duty—which is simply to make ourselves free and empty for God in holy contemplation. For contemplation is not far from any one of us who seeks it with a true heart. The goodness of our Lord Jesus Christ arouses us to do this, for he is ready to kindle our hearts and to be with us and to offer us his word as the object of our attention and his grace as the object of our discovery and enjoyment. For that is what he did for the two disciples talking to one another on their way to Emmaus[24] and that is what he promised when he said, *For wherever two or three shall have gathered together in my name, there am I in the midst of them* (Mt 18:20).

Chapter Three: On Reading, Meditation, Prayer, and Especially Yearning, by Which the Godly Spirit Presses Forward to Rest in God

The holy life of contemplation is possessed in yearning by many but in practice and reality by only a few[25] who have forgotten or left behind the cares and concerns not only of vices but of everything pertaining to love of this world. This contemplative life strives earnestly to know, thirst for, love, and yearn for the one thing necessary,[26] namely, her creator, redeemer, ruler, and generous giver of all good things; her end and her beginning: Father, Son, and Holy Spirit, one God. Thus Gregory says, "In contemplation one seeks the source, which is God."[27]

This life is lived one way by beginners and another way by those who are making progress. Renouncing this world's yearnings and beginning to thirst for an inward stimulus toward God the living fountain, the godly spirit first joyously presses forward and endeavors to rest in God her savior, making use of four means: reading, meditation, prayer, and especially yearning.[28]

BOOK THREE

[First], the godly spirit surely rests in God through devout reading, seeking more to be educated and taught than to teach, inquiring as to what might please or displease God, seeking God's commandments in order to do them, seeking the taste of Scripture in the sight of God instead of knowledge in the sight of men.

Second, the godly spirit rests in God when she repeatedly meditates godly and attentive meditations. Sometimes she does this in sorrow for her sins and her faults; sometimes in renewed gratitude for divine favors; sometimes in celebration and godly imitation, if he grants it to her, of Christ's holy life lived for each individual; and sometimes in unbroken yearning for heavenly promises.

To this end she does what Richard of Saint-Victor talks about in his third book on contemplation regarding the fourth form of contemplation: "First you should return to yourself, enter into your heart, and learn to assess your spirit. Analyze what you are, have been, ought to be, are able to be; what you are by nature, what you are now by sin, what you ought to be by effort, what you yet could be by grace. Abundant riches grow from this practice, knowledge is multiplied, wisdom expands, the eye of the heart is purified, abilities are honed, and understanding broadens. He who knows not himself cannot properly assess anything. She who does not weigh the worthiness of her own condition does not realize that all worldly glory should lie beneath her feet. He who does not think about his own spirit first knows not at all what to think of the angelic or divine spirit. If you are unfit to enter into yourself, how shall you ever be fit to explore the things that are above you? If you are unsuited to enter the first tabernacle, by what impudence do you presume to enter the second tabernacle, which is the Holy of Holies?[29] If you wish to fly away to the second or third heaven, you must go by way of the first."[30] Our meditation ought to consist in these and similar things.

Third, the godly spirit rests in God through holy prayer prayed intently and movingly. She rests by repeatedly seeking out God's face, praying, praising, singing psalms, exulting, and blessing *with hymns and thanksgiving* (2 Mc 10:38).[31] Many of these exercises represent the condition of heaven's inhabitants, whose office is to praise God and to entreat him for mercy on our behalf. As Bernard says in the eleventh sermon on the Canticle: "Nothing on earth so appropriately represents the condition of those dwelling in heaven as does their eager praise of God. For Scripture says: *Blessed are they who dwell in your house, O Lord; they shall praise you for ever and ever* (Ps 83:5 [84:4])."[32]

Fourth, the godly spirit rests in God through godly and single-minded yearning that hungers to please God, single-mindedly mortifying and captivating all her other yearnings. And this yearning gives color and taste to the other three practices—the taste of divine sweetness and the scarlet color of twin charity.[33] Whenever human weakness causes her to stray from the true path the godly spirit always employs this yearning in order to redirect herself.

The godly spirit ought to progress in these four things from day to day and to practice her skills incessantly, for through them she is cleansed of many of her stains and is well disposed to receive higher favors.

Chapter Four: What Are Contemplation and Speculation? The Two Types of Contemplation

Afterward, should it please God, who rules and governs all our good works, the godly spirit is called to a more hidden contemplation of divine things and to a richer taste of the inner, lofty, and eternal sweetness. Held aloft by a heavenly cord, she learns by new experience another way to savor with divine joy what, as a beginner, she previously possessed through yearning. Thus Bernard [Guigo II] says, "Contemplation is when the upraised spirit is lifted up to God as she tastes the joys of eternal sweetness."[34] Or again, "Contemplation is an uplifting of the spirit to God through simple ascents."[35]

This contemplation, which few know from experience, has two forms, namely, speculative, affirmative, and intellective, on the one hand, and anagogical, denying, and affective on the other. To envision or speculate is, in this regard, to seek the Creator by looking through a medium, for whatever the godly soul employs as a medium between herself and God, whatever she seeks him with, serves as a mirror for her. When the soul begins to consider the characteristics she shares with God in whose image she is created, she is a mirror to herself—and the clearer that mirror is, the more she excels the other creatures of the world in more nearly reflecting God.

Chapter Five: The Three Types of Speculative Contemplation, Especially the Contemplation of Creatures and of Scripture

Speculative contemplation takes three forms, namely physical, scholastic, and divinely infused contemplation.[36]

Physical speculation, or envisioning, seeks God through the mirror of the creatures[37]—by considering the creatures [natural] philosophers[38] understand the Creator. *For God has manifested it unto them,* as the Apostle says: *For the invisible things of him, from the creation of the world, are clearly seen, being understood by the things that are made* (Rom 1:19–20). Thus Augustine admonishes in his book *On True Religion,* "In considering the creatures one should not exercise vain and short-lived curiosity, but should advance toward things immortal and everlasting."[39] Saint Thomas writes of the same thing in the *Summa Theologiae,* IIa. IIae. qu. 180, art. 4. This sort of envisioning is not well-suited nor helpful to someone who has little scientific learning, [for it requires someone trained in sensory observation] just as someone who desires to have the third kind of contemplation, infused contemplation, must close his senses to all visible things. Visible things distract and dissipate weak spirits, filling them with empty phantasms.

The second type of speculation, namely scholastic envisioning, seeks God through the mirror of the Scriptures. It is indeed useful and necessary, but nonetheless it often hinders the heavenly inflow, since exaggerated preoccupation with the Scriptures can hold the spirit in wretched captivity, keeping her far from fellowship with the Lord. That is what the Bridegroom says in the Canticle, chapter six, as he converses with the devout soul, who, after holding him tight with her devotions, turns to the study of the Scriptures: *Turn away your eyes from me, for they have made me flee away* (Ca 6:4 [6:5]). For, through curiosity and presumption regarding the Scriptures, she thinks she can carry out the contemplation which he alone can teach her to penetrate. God alone, as noted above, teaches the soul to find herself.

Chapter Six: The Third Form of Speculation, Namely Divinely Infused Envisioning, Has Three Steps. The First of These Is Consideration of the Divine Characteristics: What God Is, How God Is Known, and How Man Was Made according to the Image and Likeness of God

Divinely infused envisioning seeks God through the mirror of divine inpourings that direct the reason toward God. The three degrees of this speculation are attentive consideration, alluring meditation, and inventive contemplation.[40] These three steps are often found in Holy Scripture—sometimes in hidden form, sometimes openly.

In the first step attentive consideration concentrates on the divine characteristics. Although speculative and anagogical contemplation each have their own paths of ascent and although both are comprehensible to the inexperienced as they enjoy God at closer range, their beginnings are well within reach. Hence it is that this stage—attentive consideration—forms something of a point of departure for divinely infused speculation. One can strive to discover it clearly and rationally enough, as the holy authorities plainly teach. For example, sometimes the godly spirit takes counsel with herself, saying longingly, "What is God?" Then she replies to herself, "If you wish to consider what God is, you must call yourself away from exterior things and back to yourself. Then, when you have recalled and recollected yourself, you must strive diligently to eject all phantasms of visible things from your soul, something that can be done well only after you have had a long rest from all exterior things."[41]

Since God is spirit (Jn 4:24) and must be considered in a most spiritual manner, no soul is at all suited for inner spiritual reflection on God unless she has the wherewithal to keep out visible phantasms—otherwise her consideration might focus on them. When by God's grace she has called herself back to herself and shut out all phantasms, she can employ much greater godly thirst as she inquires within herself and says, "What is God?" Again she replies to herself, "If you wish to consider what God is, just as a good copyist planning to write in a fancy book first tries out his pen on a scrap piece to see how well it writes before beginning to write on expensive parchment, you must first consider spiritually the characteristics of your own soul—those characteristics that you share with God according to whose image you were created, so that you might perceive with discernment the spiritual affinity[42] you have with him."

For example, God is a supreme reality, invisible, and altogether simple, yet he acts in diverse ways among his creatures, mercifully saving some and justly abandoning others. So too the soul is in a certain sense a most noble thing, invisible and altogether simple in her nature, yet she deals with the body entrusted to her in various ways: for although seeing is one thing and hearing is another, and although speaking differs from smelling, nonetheless a single soul does all these things through the instrument of her body.

Likewise, just as God is eternally immortal, so the soul, once she has been infused, or created, endures forever in her immortal essence. Moreover, just as God wisely governs all he created—some things by grace or mercy, others by justice or nature—with nothing escaping his rule and direction, so too the soul is fit to govern what has been entrusted to her—the inner and outer man. This may take place through grace bestowed from on high to prepare the inner man to accept God's blessings or through the severe justice with which the soul punishes her own sins out of respect for God. It may also involve a mercy that prudently has compassion on her, keeping her from vices and sins which, in the end, would not go unpunished—whoever does this truly is merciful, as Ecclesiasticus says, *Have pity on your own soul, pleasing God* (Sir 30:24 [23]). Governing the inner man may also take place through the natural course of things. He who is not readily transformed by God has no business governing himself.

Likewise, just as God is fully present everywhere and in all creatures, sustaining and vivifying them, so too the soul is complete in each and every part and particle of her own body, enlivening and invigorating all of the body—as Saint Augustine wrote to Saint Jerome.[43] Even though these things cannot be fully known, as is true of other matters pertaining to the soul's knowledge of herself, still, as Gregory says, spiritual reflection on such matters greatly distances the mind [*animus*] from corporal things and corporal phantasms.[44] Hence this stage of contemplation—spiritual consideration—is grounded and rooted in the mind [*animus*] itself so that the soul might more easily rise to divine things.

Moreover, just as God is three Persons in one essence, so too the soul has three powers that correspond to the three Persons: memory, reason, and will. These three powers of the soul are equal to each other, as distinction three of the first book of the *Sentences* says: "Just like the persons of the Trinity, these three powers are a single human spirit [*mens*] and each of these three is the soul"[45] (see the *Compendium of Theology*, bk. II, ch. 31, 62).[46] As Augustine says,[47] what we in a strict sense call the human spirit [*mens*] is not the soul herself but that which is more excellent in the soul (see *Sentences*, book one, distinction three).[48]

Likewise, just as God is the supreme power whom no one can resist[49] nor coerce, so too the soul has power from God to rule not only herself but also other things, whether inferior or equal, and to help her direct her powers, abilities, and strengths against all adverse things. She also has a spiritual power, which, like divine power, is completely invincible—this is the power of the free will which nothing human, nothing short of God, can overpower. As Master Hugh says, the free will is an uncoerced appetite for good in the rational will; it can neither be forced to yield nor can it be removed unwillingly.[50] Bernard also says in his sermons on the Canticle that the soul is similar to God in the simplicity of her essence, the perpetuity of her life, and the freedom of her will.[51]

Moreover, just as God is supreme wisdom, so too he grants that the human soul has wisdom in his presence so that she might love and fear him, which is the beginning of wisdom, as Proverbs one says: *The fear of the Lord is the beginning of wisdom* (Prv 1:7), and likewise Psalm 110 [111] [verse 10]. Proverbs, chapter two, says: *The Lord gives wisdom and out of his mouth come prudence and knowledge* (Prv 2:6). This likeness of God given to the soul makes her blessed, as Proverbs, chapter three, says: *Blessed is he who finds wisdom and is rich in prudence* (Prv 3:13).

Likewise, just as God is good in his nature, indeed, is the source of goodness, so too the soul is originally and naturally good, not merely in the image [of God], by which she is always good, but even in her active likeness and imitation—so long as she does not undo the dignity of her creation and reformation by devising depravity. Thus she is similar in many ways to her Creator and, as noted above, God seems to extend a share of nearly all of the characteristics of divine goodness and generosity to his rational creature. By these she is enlarged and he ennobles and leaves his mark on her by his utter liberality. Hence Ecclesiasticus says, *God created man from the earth and made him according to his own image and clothed him with strength like himself* (Sir 17:1–2 [1–3]).[52] And Genesis, chapter one, says, *Let us make man according to our image and likeness* (Gn 1:26). We are created in God's image by nature and in his likeness by grace; to put it another way, we are created in God's image as far as the power of knowing is concerned, in his likeness as far as the power of loving God is concerned. Or, one might say, we are created in his image with regard to the ability not to die, in his likeness with regard to holiness of behavior; or, we are created in his image in regard to innocence, in his likeness in regard to righteousness. Thus man is made according to God's image so that he might imitate him in innocence and become like him in righteousness, in short, so that he might know and love God. The aforesaid items are taken from a glossed copy of the Bible.[53]

Furthermore, although the Creator made the heavens and the earth and all that is in them, among all these things only the rational spirit is fit for God. Only the rational angelic and human spirits are fitted for their blessed Creator by means of holy purity, knowledge, and love. It is for this that we were created, and, as [Pseudo-] Saint Bernard says, "The entire good of man is to know and love his creator."[54]

[The next paragraph, omitted here, repeats largely verbatim the

224

concluding paragraph of II.7, with the addition of a doxology. It deals with God's superlative attributes as material for contemplation in the first degree, i.e., in attentive consideration.]

In a literal sense this stage is entirely scholastic or cognitive and is nearly always at hand for godly consideration by a soul at rest and free of exterior concerns. The godly spirit is better served by considering these divine characteristics that are common to the entire Trinity with aroused godliness than by presumptuously puzzling out the properties, concepts, and distinctions of the three Persons.[55] For the latter are more deeply hidden and burden the human spirit intent on godly meditation of God more than the things which are applicable to the one supreme divinity. You can try this out in your own godly meditating.

As long as one remains on the level of consideration alone, this stage is burdensome and arid, since for the incompletely cleansed soul it is not merely dull of taste but actually loathsome. Such a soul has no real delight in eating the celestial manna; indeed, she loathes it and flees from it. But for the soul who has somehow freed herself a bit from the yoke of sinful tyranny and of oppressive thoughts and accusations, even though this stage may not seem very sweet compared to some of the others, nonetheless it is pleasant to embrace.

This step in the soul's exercise is not a great necessity for the soul accustomed to frequent devotions, for one who often hears the voice of her Beloved as he knocks on the door.[56] Of course, the soul seeking God cannot move up to the second step, that of alluring meditation, unless she has been called thereto by the Holy Spirit, as discussed below. Instead, she must remain on the first level or return to herself thinking common thoughts. But when the godly spirit hears the voice of the same Holy Spirit, who blows where he will and when he will, that voice makes her fertile and immediately fit to ascend to the second stage, without the [cognitive] consideration that marks the first stage. That is because the second step is one of wisdom, not of knowledge.

Chapter Seven: The Second Degree of Divinely Infused Speculation; the Rapture of the Spirit, and So Forth

The second step, which is alluring meditation, is sweet and delightful, lovely and desirable. Although it can require much effort, such labor is restful. It cannot be had in any way apart from the special inspiration and infusion of the Holy Spirit, who makes an otherwise arid spirit fertile by means of heavenly dew. When the godly spirit feels that she has been drenched with a new and unaccustomed sweetness of heavenly dew, as if with rich marrow and fat,[57] when she clearly senses her spirit opening wide for this inpouring and being enlarged to receive divine things, then in the tranquil spirit's more deeply hidden eye and summit she should take up one word of the aforementioned divine subject matter. As devoutly as possible, with godly yearning, she should strive wisely, sapiently instructed[58] by tasting spiritual inpourings, to breathe deeply of the Holy Spirit's fragrance with her inner nostrils and to chew thoroughly with her spiritual mouth this morsel of the divine. She cannot do or understand this except insofar as the Holy Spirit himself leads her, shaping and training the human *affectus* and understanding to be able to sense something of the Lord in goodness and simplicity of heart.[59] Thus, according to her capacity, she can sample what God is like on the shining and ardent path of sweetness and love that lights up the darkness and somehow shines upon the animal nature of human weakness.

A great struggle takes place at this stage, a struggle between the grace that leads the inner man and the human animal nature that powerfully oppresses the inner man by vigorously, even importunately, weighing down with obstacles posed by phantasms and the burden of her own heaviness the spirit who wishes to depart toward God. If by divine governance grace should be withdrawn or held back,[60] in this spiritual wrestling match the godly spirit is often forced to return to herself, unable sometimes to press forward to a means of attaining contemplation. Often she is compelled to say devoutly and plaintively: *I sought him and found [him] not; I called and he did not answer me* (Ca 5:6).

But when the godly spirit senses that she abounds more richly in grace and sees herself powerfully swept by the Spirit, who leads forth to overcome her animal nature and gloom, she may realize that she is in a spiritual state in which the understanding strives to find a ray of purest truth by following the thirsting *affectus* invigorated by the Spirit. If the coarse worldly cloud is wiped away from the envisioning heart, she sometimes sees ineffably that unspeakable light that truly is God. This occurs in a small way and most imperfectly because of the powerful reverberation and fleeting transit of the divine light of truth and because her capacity is so limited as to be like blindness. Held back by the animal nature of human weakness, she sees something but she never sees the light as it really is, and she always knows that she is inestimably distant from that supreme light. Hence Gregory says, "The cloud of our corruption hides the light incorruptible from us. Though the light may be seen in some manner, nevertheless it cannot be seen as it is. This itself shows us how far away that light is. For if the soul could not make out the light at all, she would not know that it is far away; on the other hand, if she discerned it perfectly, she would certainly not be seeing it as if through a cloud. Since one neither perceives it perfectly nor fails to see it at all, it is rightly said that God is seen from afar."[61]

Thus it is clear that the godly spirit receives in this second stage discretion and knowledge by means of a certain hidden intuition, a discretion that permits her to discern between human and divine. She sees how much she is stuck in her own darknesses and senses how much she fights off the grace that is drawing her out, how far she is from the full perfection of eternal light that she sometimes hopes might be given her. Although she hardly knows anything of the light's heights, she is not entirely ignorant of its foundation. For now she sees that just as the heavens are high above the earth, so too the Lord's paths are far above our paths and the Lord's thoughts are far above our thoughts.[62] This does not mean that she cannot attain in some fashion some part of the divine subject matter she contemplates.

Regarding the way in which this second stage is consummated in light, Saint Bernard says, "When a heavenly vision's flash of lightning suddenly floods a spirit beside herself in rapture, immediately—but whence I know not—certain imagined likenesses of earthly things appear, either to temper the extreme brightness or to assist learning. Well adapted to the divinely anointed senses, their shadow somehow makes the purest and most brilliant ray of truth more bearable to the soul and more capable of being communicated to others."[63] In this rapture of the spirit her own goodwill does not lead the way but is like a lady-in-waiting attendant upon the leading of the grace of God. She withdraws from or is actively removed from all exterior things that can be perceived by the senses or seen with the eyes and, with a certain gentle and tranquil sweetness, turns herself as completely as she can toward divine and interior inpourings. She thus transcends sinful and idle thoughts that lack understanding; she transcends necessary thoughts, imaginary thoughts, and the rational and reasonable thoughts which may be had in the previously discussed first stage, and she transcends all phantasms, reaching the current or at least a drop of the divine river that makes glad the city of God.[64]

Nevertheless, in the spirit's rapture she is not deprived inherently [habitualiter] or potentially of her bodily senses; rather, she is divinely abstracted from them and they are weakened so that she is neither held back by them from the vision of God nor separated from them, as noted above.[65]

Chapter Eight: That God Can Be Seen in Three Ways

Should someone say that God cannot be seen by mortal man, according to God's own words in Exodus, *Man shall not see me and live* (Ex 33:20), this would be true. A man really should die before he sees God. But note that there are three ways in which the light of divine brilliance may be seen. First there are those who see God perfectly, as he is, in the beatific life of heaven, as First John, chapter three, says: *Beloved, we are now the sons of God and it has not yet appeared what we shall be*, and a little later, *We shall see him as he is* (1 Jn 3:2). God's elect are not able to attain this blessed vision until after they have been released from *the body of this death* (Rom 7:24) through corporal, or natural, death.

Likewise, the light of eternal truth is seen through a complete rapture of spirit, just as the Apostle Paul, as described in the gloss on Second Corinthians, chapter thirteen (2 Cor 12:2), saw it: "He contemplated God in that overpowering, or rapture, of spirit just as the highest order of angels who contemplate God at closer range than the other angels."[66] No one can attain this vision unless he has died to himself, that is, to his corporal senses, as the *Gloss* says in the same place: "The apostle did not live as a man at that point, that is, he did not live according to body's senses, rather, every human sense was taken from him."[67]

The divine light can also be seen through an incomplete rapture of spirit, in a sudden stabbing or pricking intuition of heavenly contemplation. Thus Gregory the Great in his *Moralia on Job* says, "By first burning off listlessness from the spirit's vision, the cloud of sins that covers the spirit is dissipated, and the soul is suddenly flooded by the resplendent flash of indescribable light."[68] No one can achieve this vision of God without first dying to the world, as Gregory says in the *Moralia:* "He who sees the wisdom that is God dies totally to this life and is no longer bound by love of this life."[69] So too the gloss on the words of Matthew, *Blessed are the pure in heart* (Mt 5:8), says, "Let a man divest himself of the world, love eternal things, and embrace God as much as possible—for how much one sees of him is proportional to how much one dies to the world."[70] Likewise a gloss on Exodus, *Man shall not see me and live* (Ex 33:20), says, "Anyone who by keen con-

228

templation would gaze on the brightness of God while in this mortal flesh, must die completely to this life and no longer be bound by love of this life."[71]

Chapter Nine: Three Requirements for Seeing God's Face

Three things are required for seeing God's face: genuine purity of heart, death to this world, and a spiritual fecundity growing from the spiritual inpourings by which the godly spirit is raised to knowledge and love of God and separated from her animal nature—even if she still remains in some sense in her body. *For the word of God is living and effectual and more piercing than any two-edged sword, reaching unto the division of soul and spirit, of the joints also and the marrow, and is a discerner of the thoughts and intentions of the heart* (Heb 4:12). This word, moreover, is easily able to make two into one,[72] join the lowest with the highest, and to make all one in itself. These three things cannot be had by a spirit who lacks experience of spiritual affections fervently thirsting for God, affections rising ardently, like fire, on high.

The affection of worldly cupidity is a fire that burns cruelly, devouring and laying waste, shattering with fire the bonds[73] of human judgments, decisions, shame, reason, and, worst of all, shattering the bonds of divine commandments (as the Psalmist says, *fire has overwhelmed them and they have not seen the sun* [Ps 57:9 (58:8)]); so too holy affection is a fire that absolutely refuses restraint and rejects consolation,[74] taking no rest until it can rest in him whom it fervently desires. Thus Sirach says, *A hot soul is a burning fire, it will never be quenched until it devours something* (Sir 23:22 [23:16]). With God's help, this really takes place, as was mentioned above (I.8). The spirit is born aloft to the vision of divine light, a vision rarely granted to any mortal. The sudden flash of divine light which illuminates the eyes of the heart is perceived like a flash of lightning that suddenly stabs one's physical eyes.

Yet this blessed light is seen most imperfectly. It would be more accurate to say that the godly spirit sees that she is unable to see what she sees[75] rather than saying that she might see it; and it would be more true to say that she sees in a mirror enigmatically[76] rather than face-to-face, through similes rather than in truth, in a cloud rather than in broad daylight, through conjecture rather than in certainty and full view, through a flashing reflection rather than a fixed radiance. Although the blessed life, a spark or ray of divine brightness, the light of eternal brightness which truly is God, is seen unveiled,[77] this does not take place without great impediments that hobble the godly spirit. One might say that the spirit sees the blessed life but much less completely than it might be seen. This should surprise no one, for the highest *wisdom is easily seen by those who love her and she is found by those who seek her; she is quick to show herself to those who desire her* (Wis 6:13–14 [6:12–13]). But when she reveals herself, as was noted above (I.10), she gives herself to us not as a present possession but as a prize of eternal reward to console us and make us joyful as we toil here below. In revealing herself she strengthens us for and attracts and invites us to that prize, but the full possession of it awaits us in our blessed homeland.

Chapter Ten: The Obscurity of the Holy Fathers' Statements Regarding the Vision of God; Manifold Miseries of the Soul

It is also noteworthy that the holy fathers speak of the vision of God at various places with words that are not easily understood. For some seem to say that the essence of God may be seen in the present life,[78] while others deny this.[79] Then too, some appear to say that God is seen in this present life enigmatically, through a mirror,[80] while others actually say that he is seen without such a medium.[81] Some seem to say that the vision of God lasts for a while, others clearly that it does not.[82] And it would not be wrong to complain that a clear sense of the meaning of many authors is hard to come by.

Yet I believe and trust the Lord that, after granting the soul two or three experiences of this vision, God will also grant a resolution of apparently conflicting statements. Moreover, in his book on the Trinity, Augustine clearly states who is able to see God: "The Father, Son, and Holy Spirit, whom we call, believe, and understand to be a Trinity of one and the same substance, or essence, is the supreme good discerned by the completely cleansed spirit. For the human spirit's sight is indeed too weak to be fixed on such a surpassing light, unless she has been cleansed by the righteousness of faith."[83] Later he adds, "Divinity cannot be seen by human vision at all, but by the vision of those who are no longer human but have passed beyond the human."[84] Saint Gregory says that "no one is able fix the eyes of his spirit on the ray of indescribable light that is God."[85] Yet these and similar statements can be reconciled if one takes account of the way in which the holy Doctors of the Church and the writers of sacred Scripture respected diversity. If we do not grasp some of what they say, let us leave it to the Holy Spirit. In that vein, we note that the flame of love that the Lord came to cast upon the earth[86] ascends by hidden ascents *like a pillar of smoke perfumed with myrrh and frankincense and all perfumer's powders* (Ca 3:6) to God. This created column [of smoke] clings to its Creator who nonetheless is a consuming fire,[87] immeasurable and uncreated. In the same way, I say, the godly spirit attains some experience of the beatific life, of true happiness, of true delights, of divine peace, of truth and charity.

Yet here and now the wretched soul is held captive, blind, twisted and deformed by various diseases, and is so ensnared by many chains that she cannot at all grasp divine things with proper understanding. She is so mired in her sins, misery, and necessities that even the things she can grasp and understand have little or no flavor for her.

Chapter Eleven: Three Aspects of the Second Stage of Speculative Contemplation (Alluring Meditation); the Differences between Wisdom and Contemplation; Concerning Worldly and Lazy Contemplatives

Just as the first step had to do especially with the gift of understanding, the second step has to do primarily with the gift of wisdom, which has three divisions. The first is knowledge of things through a true taste of them. Bernard speaks of this in the following words: "You have fully found wisdom if you weep away the sins of your former life, if you think little of the desirable things of this world, if you desire eternal beatitude with all your longing. You have found wisdom if each of these things taste to you just as they are."[88] That is what is meant by calling wisdom a tasting knowledge.[89]

The second division is knowledge of eternal things. As Augustine says, "This is the correct distinction between wisdom and knowledge: understanding cognition of eternal things belongs to wisdom and rational cognition of temporal things belongs to knowledge."[90] According to this reading, wisdom is not completely different from the gift of understanding, but the gift of understanding knows as if by seeing, while the other two know as if by tasting.[91]

The third division is experiential knowledge of divine sweetness, which directs all one's powers toward divine contemplation, delighting eagerly not only in known things but in unknown things. This type of wisdom is what Augustine had in mind when he said, "Sometimes you send me into an unaccustomed affectedness sweeter than any I know."[92]

Only this second, sapiential degree of alluring meditation, which makes the spirit fertile, tranquil, refreshed, and joyful, can lead from the first to the third degree [of speculative contemplation]. And this second degree is most profound and hidden, for its wisdom truly is drawn from the hidden depths. This second degree, which remains unknown to the extent that it has not been experienced, employs hidden exercises to draw the gift of wisdom from the Holy Spirit's penetrable depths in order to form and reform itself. It is like drinking a good wine straight from the cask of someone who has just let you into the cellar where he has kept good wine for himself. Thus the godly spirit, when she arrives jubilantly and exultant at this stage, sweetly sings and copiously expresses, or wishes to express, her thanks. In the words of the Canticle, *The king brought me into his wine cellar* (Ca 2:4) and into heavenly wisdom or into knowledge of supernal joys—by the grace of contemplation.

But this should be understood to apply to a soul of long-standing ascendant experience, who knows how to offer herself to God in steady sacrifice as a burnt offering of holy ascents in a consuming flame, who has offered her body in virile and austere repentance and in earnest discipline. For whoever gives himself to contemplation in one way or another but does not make the aforementioned sacrifice of his own body, no matter how much one might call him a contemplative, cannot compare himself to those active men who constantly mortify the flesh with this sacrifice, or martyrdom.[93] Thus it is said in Sirach, *Better is the iniquity of a man than a woman doing a good turn* (Sir 42:14)[94] Such an unmortified contemplative is no man but would be better called a woman, who nonetheless does a good work in the Savior. Just as many seculars are better than many monks,[95] so the perfect active life is better and more powerful than a contemplative life lived lazily.

Chapter Twelve: Sinful as She May Be, the Soul Is Praised in Many Ways When, by the Grace of God, She Is Truly Active and Contemplative, though She Must Avoid Pride by Considering Her Sinfulness

A soul which truly has both the contemplative and the active is not unjustly called a temple of God, a royal court, angelic, divine, the bride of Christ, and similar things. Saint Anthony was such a person. Discipline is especially pertinent to the active life, and, as Hugh of Saint Victor says, "Discipline of God consists in three things, namely in commandments, in temptations, and in afflictions. In commandments God tests your obedience, in temptations he tests your steadiness, and in afflictions he tests your patience."[96] Then too the godly spirit herself, shut off from exterior concerns and thoughts and adorned inwardly with holy virtues, is a temple of God, a royal court, a nuptial chamber, and a regal and fragrant apartment. Because she invisibly receives the good wine poured into her, the wine of divine graces flowing into her from on high, she is beyond doubt also a wine cellar: *The king brought me into his wine cellar* (Ca 2:4), that is, he gives the grace of returning to one's heart[97] so that one's inward ears might *hear what the Lord God will speak within me, for he will speak peace to his people and to those who are converted to the heart* (Ps 84:9 [85:9]).

Yet the godly spirit is called a temple of God or wine cellar and the like not out of arrogance or presumption but because of the unspeakable dignity of the heavenly king. Far from diminishing that dignity, God's application of these names to man (who in his own right, as Bernard says, is stinking seed,[98] a pot of excrement, worm-bait[99]) actually highlights God's glory. To keep from becoming proud, the faithful soul should always remain aware of and keep in view what she is in her own right, using discipline to own up to these lowly things even while she renders to God the things of God[100] that God has given her. For just as the tent of Kedar,[101] as far as she is concerned, is sinful, weak, muddy, given to vices, deserving the punishment of eternal damnation, subject to countless traps, so also by grace of divine dignity and of her divine espousal she is a light in the Lord, justified by faith, strong, clean, and virtuous in the Lord who frees and rescues our soul from death, our eyes from tears, our feet from the fall.[102] She should faithfully and constantly offer all these things, both the good and the bad, to the Creator through worthy consideration. As Bernard says [of the human person], "How lowly! How sublime! A tent of Kedar yet also a sanctuary of God, a terrestrial habitation yet a celestial palace, a house of clay yet also a royal apartment, a mortal body yet a temple of light, a source of contempt to the proud yet also a bride of Christ."[103]

Thus the godly spirit is the temple of God, the daughter of the prince; she is not only a dark wine cellar but a well-lit chamber. For in this stage a certain divine light reflects back to her and in its brilliance she sees well enough to walk in that state, to walk in the midst of her own gloom, indeed, sometimes, as we have said (III.7), to step beyond her gloominess until in that reflected light she can see the supreme and eternal light.[104]

Chapter Thirteen: An Exposition of the Apostle's Words: "We, with Unveiled Face, and So Forth"

Paul the Apostle seems to speak openly of this stage and of this light, which he calls glory,[105] and to describe this manner of speculative contemplation when he says, *For we, beholding with unveiled face the glory of God, are transformed into the same image from glory to glory, as by the Spirit of the Lord* (2 Cor 3:18).[106] *We,* he says, speaking in the guise of contemplatives, *with unveiled face,* that is, with our reason unpacked,[107] for at this stage this reason is unburdened, instructed, and taught to sniff out or perceive in advance what God is like by means of God's characteristics included in the divine subject matter, characteristics that have been chewed over inwardly for the sake of an inpouring of divine grace. He says, *the glory of God,* that is, the glorious God; *beholding,* that is, perceiving through the mirror of reason made fecund by divine gifts; *into the same image,* that is, Christ, who is the image of the Father;[108] *we are transformed,* that is, from a human frame of mind and from a weak animal nature, which for a short time is transcended by holy contemplation, *we are transformed,* I say, *into the same image,* that is, into the mind and knowledge of Christ, who is the image of the Father; and this *from glory to glory,* that is, from the glorious knowledge of this sapiential step to the glory of the highest step (the scintillating step); *as by the Spirit of the Lord,* because otherwise, as noted above, this cannot take place.

For our Creator himself has retained for himself authority over all of creation and over our redemption and our inward contemplation, and it is through himself that he desires and has desired to work. Hence it says in the *Book on the Solitary Life:* "Though men may teach how to seek God and angels may teach how to adore God, it is God himself who teaches how to find God."[109] Oh, happy souls who have such a teacher.

Chapter Fourteen: That the Cell Is the Most Suitable Workshop for Contemplation

One should also know that the most suitable workshop[110] for contemplation is the cell. For, although some of us who occupy it live there lazily, languidly, and in a manner unworthy of God, so too it is in the cell that those who busy themselves daily with holy leisure as they praise the Lord are made angels through their imitation of the angelic office—which is heavenly contemplation. For such men—the contemplatives—may justly be called either "heavenly men or, if it sounds better, earthly angels, whose dwelling place is in heaven,"[111] as is stated in the *Book on the Solitary Life*.[112] Nor is it absurd to say that every godly spirit of this sort is angelic, for such souls could in a certain sense rightly be called divine, not by nature but because of fellowship and participation. Such a spirit is indeed one spirit with the bridegroom, for *he who is joined to the Lord is one spirit [with the Lord]* (1 Cor 6:17).

Moreover, just as the Holy Spirit is the union of the Father and the Son, the love [*amor*], the nexus, the charity that binds or conjoins both of them, so the Holy Spirit himself joins that human spirit to God, as noted above (cf. III.7)—to the degree that the godly human spirit is willing to accept him spiritually. The Holy Spirit carries her and leads her until she is directly joined to her Savior himself, in fellowship with the holy angels. Hence, since the Holy Spirit himself makes the godly human spirit not merely angelic but even divine, it is not absurd to call her what the Lord has made her. But woe to us wretches whose actions will not permit us truly to be called by these names. For it is "the faithful soul," as the *Book on the Solitary Life* states, who "is frequently wedded to the word of God in the cell and shares as a bride the bridegroom's company as heavenly things are united with earthly and the divine joins the human."[113]

Chapter Fifteen: Third Degree of Divinely Infused Speculation: Inventive Contemplation

What follows is concerned with the third degree, which should be evaluated according to the following information. The third stage is contemplation that finds, since it begins there where the godly spirit is suddenly carried away to a vision of divine glory, as the preceding chapters have explained. The godly spirit herself, through the practices of the second stage, rarely but indeed occasionally catches sight of the flash of divine light as she is lit up by rays of divine grace. One may indeed frequently have the prospect of this envisioning contemplation in sight, when the godly favor of heavenly dignity smiles, but it seems that one rarely arrives at the aforementioned view of supreme Truth, since, if one attains a bit of it, one immediately slips back into what is darkness compared with the light just seen. This does not involve slipping back all the way to the situation of general human thoughts nor even as far as the first step mentioned above [attentive consideration], but it is a return and withdrawal to a certain lofty state between the sapiential stage [alluring meditation] and the scintillating stage. This third degree can be called the flashing [*scintillaris*] stage, not because the godly spirit sees the flash of truth but because she is very close to seeing it. Yet sometimes in this in-between state her eyes are indeed opened to catch a glimpse of the gleam of truth before she completely returns into herself.[114] One might also say—most accurately indeed—that this state has a view toward the lower, sapiential stage. For just as the godly spirit reaches the very threshold of the scintillating stage by ascending through the sapiential stage, so in retreating from the scintillating stage she descends to the very threshold of the sapiential stage.

This third state may most truly be called the "ornamented" stage, for there the godly spirit takes possession of golden jewelry chains inlaid, or filigreed, with silver[115] from messengers, who, to follow Saint Bernard's interpretation,[116] are the holy angels. Moreover, in this "ornamented" state, the godly spirit, somehow suspended in wonder[117] and suffused with a sort of fecundity and spiritual sweetness of heavenly dew, has a brief moment to think over what she has seen. Aided by the light she has seen, she is seized with the desire to recollect and retain more capacious and insightful similitudes and images granted her by those *ministering spirits sent to minister for them, who shall receive the inheritance of salvation* (Heb 1:14). Such are the thoughts of Saint Bernard.

There the godly spirit is captivated, as I have said, by a heavenly ecstasy and wonder as she reflects on the nature of the light she has seen. Certain spiritual images wondrous to behold pour into her from on high and flow out of her, functioning for her like a penumbra so that at least around the edges she might perceive a bit of the true rays of the sun she has seen, saying with unimaginable joy, *I sat down under the shadow of him whom I desired and his fruit was sweet to my mouth* (Ca 2:3), and *the light [of your countenance] has been signed above us* (Ps 4:7 [4:6]). The aforementioned images which bring knowledge of light itself into the soul are, as Bernard seems to think, the golden chains that the bride receives from among the Bridegroom's treasury when her enjoyment of the full vision is delayed for a while. Hence the bride herself, sighing and thirsting for a blessed sight of the Bridegroom but no longer according to the flesh, says *Tell me, you whom my soul loves, tell me where you pasture your flock, where you lie down at noon* (Ca 1:6). For when with much intimate sighing she has said this to the Bridegroom, just as it is being heard, the heavenly artisans are present, as Bernard says,[118] to moderate her desire to see the Bridegroom plainly, making a divine penumbra for her and saying, *We shall make for you chains of gold, inlaid with silver* (Ca 1:10).

As noted above, in this in-between stage, certain spiritual similitudes are powerfully and suddenly present in the godly spirit's imagination in order to moderate a splendor so intense as to be called golden—for, as the bride says, Christ's head is finest gold,[119] because *Christ's head is God.* These imaginings are present not only to moderate the intensity of the light but also to aid holy teaching,[120] which is called silver: *Your words, Lord, your pure words are silver refined by fire* (Ps 11:7 [12:6]). Through these images the godly spirit thus receives the impress of divine cognition and the ability, if she so desires, to declare to others what she has perceived from on high,[121] even if only stammeringly, since no one can fully explain these things in any way.[122] With respect to the former [the divine light of cognition from on high], the necklaces are of gold, with respect to the latter [the ability to teach others], they are of filigreed silver.

If you want to understand what has just been said, strive busily to cleanse your heart, for there is no other way to understand them: *Blessed are the pure in heart, for they shall see God* (Mt 5:8)—they shall see him in the present life as has been described[123] and shall see him in full view and perfectly, just as he is, in the future. This therefore is the form of divinely infused speculative contemplation which the good Lord grants to his servants to comfort them on their wanderings.

Chapter Sixteen: Saint Bernard's Comments on the Canticle as an Aid to Understanding What Has Just Been Said. What Are the Chains of Gold?

So that you might better understand the things just said, hear what Saint Bernard says about this passage from chapter one of the Canticle of Canticles: *We shall make for you chains of gold, inlaid with silver* (Ca 1:10) in sermon forty-one on the Canticle.[124]

Had he said "I shall make," in the singular, instead of "we shall make," in the plural, we could ascribe these words to the Bridegroom without hesitation. But as it is, we might more properly assign them to his companions, who promise to make beautiful and costly ornaments, i.e., earrings, for the bride as a way to comfort her until she has arrived at the vision of him for whom she longs so passionately. I say this because, since *faith comes by hearing* (Rom 10:17), as long as she walks by faith and not by sight,[125] she ought to work more at receiving with her ears than at casting her sight about her. The eye that is not cleansed by faith looks in vain, and abundant sight is promised only to those who are pure in heart.[126] Truly it is written in the Acts of the Apostles: *He purifies their hearts by faith* (Acts 15:9). Therefore, since faith comes by hearing and since sight is cleansed through hearing, it is right to focus on adorning her ears, for reason teaches us that hearing prepares the way for seeing. "You strain to gaze on the Beloved," they tell the bride, "but right now it is time for something else. For now we give you ornaments for your ears to serve as a consolation and to prepare you for the vision for which you beg." Their words to her recall those of the prophet: *Hear, daughter, and see* (Ps 44:11 [45:10])—you long to see, but first you must listen. Hearing is a step on the way to seeing. And therefore *listen and incline your ear* (*ibid.*) to receive the earrings we make for you, so that you might attain the glory of vision through the obedience of hearing. We shall make your listening joyful.[127] For it is not ours to give you the fullness of vision that would satisfy your yearning, rather, this belongs to him whom your soul loves.[128] The one who would reveal himself to you in order to make your joy full[129] will make your joy full by showing you his face.[130] In the meantime, accept these earrings from us as a consolation gift—the other delights he holds in his right hand will last to the end.[131]

One should pay attention to the sort of jewelry they offer her: chains made of *gold and inlaid with silver.* Gold is the flash of divinity, the gold of wisdom from on high.[132] The heavenly artisans commissioned with this task promise to fashion gleaming tokens of truth out of this gold, and to insert them in the inward ears of the soul. I think this can mean nothing else than to weave spiritual imagery that brings the purest insights of divine wisdom to the sight of those who contemplate so that they might at least see in a mirror obscurely (1 Cor 13:12) what they cannot see face-to-face.

The things we speak of are divine and remain unknown except to those who have experienced them. Although the substance of the clear inward light is not yet spread out, because we have faith, we can enjoy in advance partial contemplation of aspects of pure truth while still in this mortal body. Any one of us to whom the gift from on high has been given[133] can make his own the words of the Apostle Paul: *Now I know in part* (1 Cor 13:12) and *we know in part and we prophesy in part* (1 Cor 13:9). But when something heavenly shines into the human spirit instantly, like lightning, carrying her beyond herself in rapture, certain earthly images immediately appear—from I know not where. Whether they arise in order to tone down the overpowering splendor or for the sake of teaching, they are well suited to the insights poured out from on high. For they, as it were, overshadow the purest and most splendid ray of truth and make it bearable for the soul and more readily communicable to those with whom she wishes to share it. I personally think this imagery is formed in us by the suggestions of holy angels, just as no one doubts that contrary and evil suggestions can be thrust upon us by evil angels.[134]

Perhaps this is that mirror, as I said, with which the Apostle Paul saw darkly—by means of these pure and beautiful images fashioned by angelic hands. Although in his pure being God would have to be discerned without any physical imagery, these angelically fashioned images somehow are of God, for by what we consider to be an angelic ministry, these elegant images worthily clothe God's appearing.[135] This is stated more distinctly by another translation of our text, which says, *We shall make for you images of gold with markings of silver* (Ca 1: 10 according to the Septuagint). "With markings of silver" and "filigreed with silver" are the same. To me they mean not only that this imagery is suggested within us by angels but that through this imagery the beauty of the words we speak to others is suitably and delightfully enhanced so that it can be more readily received. Should you ask, "What does speech have to do with silver," let the prophet tell you: *Your words, Lord, your pure words are silver refined by fire* (Ps 11:7 [12:6]). Thus do these heavenly ministering spirits[136] make golden ornaments filigreed with silver for the pilgrim spouse on earth.

See too how she wants one thing and receives another. For the toil of preaching is laid upon the one straining for the repose of contemplation and upon the one who thirsts for the Bridegroom's presence is enjoined the responsibility for giving birth to and nurturing the Bridegroom's children. Nor is this the only time this has occurred, for once before, as I recall, as she sighed for the Bridegroom's embrace and kisses, she was told: *For your breasts are better than wine* (Ca 1:1). From this she was to understand that she is a mother and is recalled to the task of nursing her infants with her milk and nurturing her children. Unless you are too lazy to look, you may come across other instances of this elsewhere in the Canticle. Was not something like this prefigured in the holy patriarch Jacob, when, cheated out of the long-awaited embraces of Rachel, he unknowingly and against his will took to hand the fertile and weak-sighted Leah in place of the charming and sterile Rachel? So it is that golden ornaments inlaid with silver are brought to the bride eagerly seeking to know where her Beloved pastures his flock and takes his rest at noon,[137] i.e., she is given wisdom and eloquent words—undoubtedly for the work of preaching.

From this we are taught that we ought to interrupt sweet kisses for the sake of breasts that yield milk [of doctrine]. No one ought to live for himself, but all should live for the sake of him who died for all.[138] Woe to those who have been given the ability to think and speak of God if they should think godliness a means of profit,[139] if they turn to vainglory what has been paid out to them for the sake of making profit for God, if in tasting lofty things they refuse to agree with the lowly.[140] Let them quiver at what one reads in the Prophet, speaking for the Lord: *I gave them my gold and my silver; they have used my gold and my silver to serve Baal* (Hos 2:8).[141]

These are Bernard's words in the aforementioned sermon on the Canticle.

Chapter Seventeen: First Mortify Vices if You Wish to Rise to Contemplation; an Enumeration of Manifold Sins

Furthermore, if you long to receive the gift of this contemplation from the Lord, be diligent about mortifying [killing off] the old man and building up [*reparationem*] the inner man.

First, be careful to kill off—to the degree that God works in you—the vices within you. For as a certain wise man says, those who are proud, swelled up, slandering, cruel and malicious, or crafty; those who try to outwit their brother in business[142] or eagerly pursue vainglory;

those who are envious, impatient, irritable, habituated to flattery or grumbling, gluttonous, greedy, or covetous; those who are given to ease, listlessness, idle talk, or vain curiosity; those who are restless, who delight in running to and fro, who delight in seeking entertainment; those who are concerned only for themselves and not for their brothers' affairs or for that which pertains to Christ; those who voluntarily involve themselves in external concerns—these will not attain contemplation.

Strive to despise these things and others like them so that the faults that weigh a man down to destruction and perdition may not reign within you—things like ill-will, enticing delights, disobedience, despising of others, giving offense to or causing someone else to stumble, hatred, strife, trying to outdo another, disagreement, bragging, hypocrisy, impetuosity, indignation, hard-heartedness, presumption, rebellion, obstinacy, culpable shame, rash judgment, false accusation, bad excuses, ingratitude, cupidity (the root of all evils),[143] inordinate fear and love, reproachfulness, depravity, revenge, murder, outcry, blasphemy, spiritual listlessness, indolence, carelessness, spiritual timidity, breaking of vows, precipitateness, impenitence, infidelity, ignorance, melancholy, vain confidence, vain curiosity, vain leisure, a wandering heart, lack of discipline in apparel, gestures, speech, or table manners,[144] keeping good things from others, pillage, usury, theft, simony, sacrilege, fortune-telling, idolatry, maintaining things as one's own, including one's own will, freely accepting gifts, false oaths, cheating, giving false testimony.[145]

Whoever sighs from his heart of hearts for knowledge and love of his most merciful Creator should, from time to time, take a look at these and similar things, in order to be thankful for having escaped the more grave faults or for having been freed from them by the Lord. Likewise, he should have an eye for his failings, for human life cannot be lived without falling into them—one can only walk away from them repentantly. Of the vices just now enumerated, some do not at all bother and disturb the soul called to celestial life by the voice of the Holy Spirit, while others disturb her a little.

Chapter Eighteen: The First of the Three Vices That Particularly Attack the Soul: Pride

Three vices in particular busily attack the soul: pride, vainglory, and immoderate eating and drinking.[146]

Chief among all vices,[147] pride is the first to invade a man and the last to lay down its arms. Therefore the Psalmist says, *They shall have no dominion over me* (Ps 18:14 [19:13]), and the gloss comments, "Pride is the last vice to leave those returning to God and the first to greet those leaving God behind."[148] Someone has put it well: Although you are fighting well and think you have uprooted everything, pride still threatens to recontaminate you and must therefore be conquered. For the proud enemy uses pride from the start to make a man who is eager to hurry to heaven think that he amounts to something in the Lord's eyes or in the eyes of certain men, to think that he is more virtuous and less given to vices than he really is—and to have just the opposite opinion of others. In this light *it is a great grace to steady the heart* (Heb 13:9) and, by steady humility, to acquiesce to the word of God that says, *When you are invited to a wedding feast, sit down in the lowest place* (Lk 14:10) and *Esteem others better than yourself* (Phil 2:3). Let us then humbly and pragmatically put into practice the advice Saint Bernard rightly gives in his sermon on the Canticle, "I do not want you to compare yourself to those greater or lesser than you, to a particular few, not even to a single person, etc."[149] For we do not even know for sure what state we are in or what shall become of us tomorrow—much less can we know the truth about others. We are all created by one Creator, who establishes the members of the Body of Christ not according to our judgments but according to his own knowledge.

Chapter Nineteen: The Second Vice: Vainglory and Praise

Vainglory too is not slack in pursuing those servants of God who desire to progress in spiritual exercises. It frequently prompts them to do things out of eagerness to please men, for example, to make a show of virtuousness worthy of imitation for the sake of setting a good example—doing or feigning publicly the good things that one might fail to do privately in God's presence. Regardless how much one's highest intention aims at God, sometimes through carelessness or lack of foresight or forethought, vainglory sneaks up and mixes with good intentions. If, for example, someone who feels disdained by others silently indulges in inward self-pity—as long as it is not involuntary sadness[150]—this is a sign of vainglory. As Jerome says, "Seek not vainglory and you will not suffer when you are treated ingloriously; he who desires not praise does not feel the force of insults."[151] As Gregory says, "It is foolish to seek what passes away when we are able to possess what lasts forever."[152] Without a doubt, as Scripture says, contempt for vainglory is a great help in doing away with other vices. Hence John Chrysostom says, "Take away this vice so that men no longer wish to make an impression on men and all the other vices are cut off."[153] And conversely, as Bernard says, "Humility is a glorious thing—even pride tries to clothe itself in humility to avoid being despised."[154]

Since this vice pounds spiritual men in various ways, as daily experience proves, it must be fought by opposing to it a variety of virtues. Some people find, by the love of God and long habituation to virtue and good works, that vainglory not only does not bother the servants of God, but it is not even felt. These are truly worthy of praise. Sometimes indeed, by God's just judgment, it thoroughly attacks the weakest, especially when they let everyone know about their recent good works—works which in fact were freely given them by God. *He who boasts should boast in the Lord* (1 Cor 1:31), offering all his praise and glory to the majesty of him who made all things, frequently repeating in his heart and with his mouth: *Not to us, Lord, not to us, but to your name give glory* (Ps 113b:1 [115:1]).

Chapter Twenty: The Third Vice, Gluttony, and Its Cure, Temperance

The vice of gluttony is a daily malady and restless evil, a guest in one's own house that tries to trip up spiritual men. Hence Gregory says in book nine of the *Moralia*, "Much of the time the mind girded for the path of righteousness shakes off his torpor and is carried off into the heavens by such great longing that he appears to leave nothing of himself behind here below. Yet, when he is brought back to the concerns of the flesh without which the present life simply cannot be lived, that torpor keeps him weighed down so low that it seems as if he had never grasped the heights."[155] The testimony of the saints and of Holy Scripture assures us that the virtue of moderation, abstinence, and virile austerity is of great merit and wide-ranging usefulness. Hence John Chrysostom comments on the passage in Hebrews, "Nothing makes for health and sharpened senses, nothing chases away sickness as well as temperateness in eating";[156] and the preface to the Lenten observance also says, "When you restrict vices through corporal fasting you elevate the spirit and increase strength and reward."[157]

So too, moderation in eating is an especially powerful preparation for the delights of spiritual contemplation. In the third book of his *Moralia* Gregory says, "If we cut off that which pleases us in the flesh, we soon find that which delights us in the spirit"[158]—unless some other vice blocks the way. And conversely, as Jerome says, "Nothing so overwhelms understanding as dissipation in eating and drinking."[159] Thus the virtue of abstinence is clearly great in the Lord's eyes, worthy of praise, honor, and reward. In reading the lives of the holy confessors of Christ we seldom find one who achieved a lofty life who did not really possess great strength of abstinence. And in the fortieth chapter of the Rule of Saint Benedict we find, "Those to whom God grants the capacity to endure abstinence should know that they shall have their own reward." Those to whom the Lord, the giver of the various graces, grants this gift should shower him with gratitude. Those who truly sense that they lack the power or perhaps the strict will to embrace with virile vigor this ancient and holy simplicity should love it and honor it in others and strive to make up for this not inconsiderable loss (whether it be voluntary or involuntary) with humility and other virtues. They should at least not depart from the norm of moderate sobriety set forth by the Lord, as recounted by Luke: *Take care that your hearts be not weighed down in intoxication and drunkenness and with the cares of this life* (Lk 21:34). Cicero too says much the same: "Those full of food and drink cannot make right use of the spirit."[160] Likewise Jerome: "A fat stomach does not give birth to taut thinking."[161]

Chapter Twenty-One: Moderate Sobriety and Indiscretion; Virtue and Ways to Acquire It

The elect are commanded to give themselves to the pursuit of charity, for, as Gregory says in his homily *Because far from the city*, "The only sacrifice God accepts is that which is kindled by the flame of charity on the altar of good works."[162] What is true for all the elect is even more true for contemplatives—they should concentrate on the charity of God. Those who are drawn by inward yearning toward the divine work of godliness but who lack the gift of strict discipline should regulate their bodies as best they can by the grace of moderate sobriety, depending on the condition of their health. They should do this in light of conscience and of their experience, which teaches them well what to do and when to do it—so that it serves the spirit without exhausting or disgusting her. The *Book on the Solitary Life*, chapter nine, applies here: "The body should be dealt with more severely so that it does not rebel nor become impudent, yet in such a way that it can serve, for it has been given us in order to serve the spirit."[163] The same book admonishes that the beginner "must be taught to treat his body like a sick person entrusted to his care, denying it many of the unprofitable things it desires and forcing upon it many useful things it desires not, dealing with it not as his own but as belonging to him by whom *we have been bought at great cost so that we might glorify God in our bodies* (1 Cor 6:20)."[164] So too, in book ten of his *Confessions*, Augustine says that "food should be taken like medicine."[165] Spiritual exercises are better and have higher priority than physical exercise, as the Apostle Paul testifies in his first letter to Timothy: *Become well-practiced in godliness, for physical training benefits a bit but godliness is beneficial for everything and carries with it the promise of both this present life and the life to come* (1 Tm 4:7–8). Thus it is foolish for servants of God to be so burdened by their own beast of burden that they cannot make it tractable for spiritual service. The *Book on the Solitary Life* says "Such corporal exercises as vigils and fasts, . . . if undertaken without discernment to the point that they exhaust the spirit or make the body sick, become spiritual obstacles. Whoever does this robs his body of the effect of good works, his spirit of its *affectus*, his neighbor of an example, and God of honor. Such a person is sacrilegious and is accountable to God for all these sins."[166]

The faithful and prudent servant[167] ought to walk a path midway between the two extremes of weakness due to overwork and repugnance. The first of these two vices opposed to each other results from a zeal untempered by discretion, while the second results from corporal laxity. The wise servant follows a discerning regimen of virtue that strives to attain the middle way between these two contrary vices. As Master William of Auxerre says regarding virtue in his *Summa*, "Every virtue is a middle way between two vices. The more one keeps to the middle, the greater is the virtue; the more one slips to one side or the other, the more one approaches vice."[168] So too Albert [Hugo Ripelin of Strasbourg] says, "Since virtue falls into the middle, note that this middle takes three forms, namely, in action it is midway between the highest and lowest way (Romans: *your reasonable service* [Rom 12:1]), while in possession it is midway between excess and indigence (Proverbs: *Give me neither riches nor poverty* [Prv 30:8]), and in maintenance it is midway between riding high in prosperity and being bowed down under adversity (*you shall neither turn aside to the right nor to the left* [Dt 5:32]). Moreover, there are three conditions favorable to virtue: distance from temptation, repeated acts, and a delight in the good. The first of these roots virtue firmly, the second makes it blossom beautifully, the third gives it a delicious taste."[169]

In his book on the *Morals of the Church,* Augustine says [in effect] that all virtue is ordered love [*amor*][170] and, elsewhere, he says that "virtue is the charity by which that which ought to be loved is loved [*diligitur*]."[171] In his letter to Macedonius he adds, "In this life virtue is to love [*diligere*] what ought to be loved" and "To love is prudence, not to be turned away from love by any sort of affliction is fortitude, not to be turned away by any sort of enticement is temperance, not to be turned away by any sort of pride is justice [righteousness]."[172] Likewise Albert [Hugo Ripelin of Strasbourg] says, "Virtue is called by that name because it is an inward power, a force of aggressive response to difficulties, of endurance in adversity, of abstinence from pleasant things."[173] *Above all things, have charity, which is the bond of perfection* (cf. Col 3:14), about which [Pseudo] Ambrose comments, "The virtue that is greater than all others ought to be more sought after,"[174] and the gloss says, "Charity binds all things so that they cannot slip away."[175] Regarding the four virtues, Augustine says that "prudence knows what ought to be desired or avoided, temperance restrains desire from the things that give temporal delight, fortitude is a firm resolve in the face of things that cause temporal affliction, justice diffuses love [*dilectio*] of God and neighbor by means of all the other virtues."[176] [Pseudo-] Jerome tells us that when vices become routine, the path of virtues becomes arduous and rough, but if one looks at it from the other side, as the Scriptures say, *the path of righteousness is found to be easy* (Prv 3:20 in the Septuagint).[177] One ought therefore to develop good routines to combat bad routines and good attachments to counter evil attachments, as the *Letter to the Brethren of Mont Dieu* says.[178]

Near the beginning of his *Book on the Patriarchs,* Richard says, "For indeed virtue is nothing else than an ordered and controlled affectedness. It is ordered when directed toward that which should be its object, it is controlled when it is as great as it ought to be."[179] In his book on contemplation he speaks in a similar vein: "Since virtue is nothing other than an ordered and controlled affectedness, it acts out of a good intention so that it might be ordered, and it is accomplished by discernment so that it might be controlled. Moreover, we should constantly concentrate our effort and deliberation on this task and keep at it firmly as well as frequently so that all our affectedness moves by licit means away from illicit earthly concerns, preserving a sober even-handedness even in those desires that are permissible. Is it not true that an affectedness toward evil is restrained, diminished, and destroyed daily by force of deliberation? Is not an affectedness toward good steadily nourished, advanced, and consolidated by force of deliberation? Is it not the task of such deliberation to assail carnal desires with powerful reprimands, to repress forcefully the tumultuous fluctuations of thoughts, and to prepare oneself daily for spiritual battle?"[180] Moreover, concerning the acquisition of virtue, note carefully what Seneca says: "Virtue is impossible without zeal for virtue."[181] The *Book on the Solitary Life* also says, "Although talent, skill, understanding and the like may indeed be had gratuitously, virtue is acquired in a different way. For it wishes to be taught by humility, to be sought by hard work, and to be possessed through love [*amor*]—since it is worthy of all this effort, it can be taught, sought, and possessed in no other way."[182]

Chapter Twenty-Two: Fasting; Avoidance of Outward Concerns and Excessive Distraction (a Common Source of Straying); the Dangers of Bodily Necessities

Favored by Christ's grace, the faithful servant of Christ should apply himself carefully to the task of making the body obey the spirit as she thirsts for heavenly things in the course of her training in godliness, making these preparations at appropriate times. For, as far as the mortification of the flesh, the manifestation of bodily obedience, and the sacrificing of natural forces are concerned, both body and spirit, like two morsels, are better and more faithfully sacrificed to the Lord through exercising godliness than through daily fasting. Exercising godliness is indeed the fast that the Lord has chosen.

The godly spirit ought to fast from worldly cares and joys so that, in the battle in which she seeks God, she might abandon all wickedness that hinders the practice of holy godliness—since wickedness certainly is contrary to godliness. Hence the Lord, the true judge of corporeal and spiritual disciplines, utters this verdict: *Do not fast as you have done until now in order to make your outcry heard on high. Is this the sort of fast that I have chosen: that a man should afflict his soul for a day? Does it consist in twisting his head in a circle and spreading sackcloth and ashes? Is this what you call a fast and a day acceptable to the Lord? Is not this the greater fast that I have chosen:*[183] *untie the bonds of wickedness, undo the oppressive burdens* (Is 58:4–5 [4–6])?

Furthermore, since leisure for divine exercise should not be a soft or idle affair, rather should be the activity of activities, and since the inner disposition of a man is much obliged to follow the exterior disposition, as experience often shows, the servant of God would seem to profit greatly by prudently avoiding not only outward cares and activities but also any sort of excessive distraction or annoyance he is able to single out. In this way he is better able to implement his vows more freely and integrally. Likewise, in the fear and love of God, which gives better light to the eyes, he ought to consider what he does and what he uses out of necessity, utility, or slippery pleasure. He should also consider how often we go astray through ignorance, negligence, hurry, secret love, or even a passionate spirit, how *a man's path is not in himself* (Jer 10:23) *but in the Lord. A man born of woman lives for a short time filled with many miseries; he comes forth like a flower and is crushed; he flees like a shadow and never stays the same* (Jb 14:1–2). Hence our charity waxes and wanes like the moon. At one moment we are willing, at the next moment unwilling, but we never remain in the same state. Therefore we necessarily cry to the Lord that he might see fit to deliver us from our necessities.

Thus Gregory says, "Bodily necessities carry with them this danger—that one scarcely distinguishes which of them involves vice or which involves profitable pursuits."[184] The Psalmist wished to escape these necessities, knowing that many faults of the will erupt out of carrying out such obligations.[185] Yet, for healing from these and other failings that abound in this valley of misery, we must return constantly to that same Lord's mercy: we must return, in the righteousness and abundant peace that shall pour over us from the Lord until the moon disappears,[186] to the mercy that never fails those who seek it.[187]

Chapter Twenty-Three: Avoidance of Rash Judgment

Anyone who wishes to make progress in what we have just discussed should carefully avoid rash judgment, as the Scriptures say: *Judge not* (Mt 7:1). People who are themselves slow to speak may think that others are loquacious,[188] likewise those who eat moderately charge others with voraciousness—accusing another of the very fault one is particularly scrupulous about. Yet, as Gregory says in a homily on Ezekiel, "The virtue of abstinence is a great one, but if anyone abstains from food in order to pass judgment on others who eat and thereby condemns the nourishment *God created to be received with thanksgiving* (1 Tm 4:3), has not the virtue of abstinence become a sinful snare to him?"[189] Therefore join the Apostle Paul in saying, *Let him who eats not despise him who eats not, and let him who eats not, not judge him who eats. He who eats, eats in honor of the Lord while he who abstains, abstains in honor of the*

Lord (Rom 14:3, 6). It is in this manner that many who abstain from doing something are really judging others.

Chapter Twenty-Four: How to Keep Busy Outside the Brief Times of Contemplation Permitted by Human Weakness

To put the matter briefly, vices stemming from carnal desires make war[190] against the celibate life, and human weakness, as Gregory says,[191] will not permit one to remain in contemplation for a long time. Thus it is necessary, lest one be ensnared by leisure, to keep busy with the things mentioned in the first stage (namely reading, prayer, meditation, etc.), or to do other good works, so that the devil may always find the servant of God busy.[192] One should ask God for and, when received, practice the various virtues necessary to avoid idleness: *charity, joy, peace, patience, forbearance, goodness, kindness, gentleness, faithfulness, modesty, self-control, chastity* (Gal 5:22–23). Would that *we might show ourselves in all things to be ministers of God: in great patience, in tribulations, in times of need, in distresses, in beatings, in prison, in civil strife, in labors, in vigils, in fasts, in chastity, in knowledge, in forbearance, in sweetness, in the Holy Spirit, in unfeigned charity, in the word of truth, in the power of God, with the armor of righteousness on the right hand and on the left, . . . as sorrowful yet always rejoicing, . . . as having nothing yet possessing all things* (2 Cor 6:4–7, 10). And, as James, chapter one, says, *The wisdom that comes from above is first chaste, then peaceable, modest, ready to be persuaded, agreeable to good things, full of mercy and good fruits, judging without dissimulation* (Jas 3:17).[193] These and similar things renew the spirit.

Chapter Twenty-Five: How the Soul That Yearns to Contemplate God Should Behave

When the servant of God has attained the things discussed above, when he wishes to be by himself, to sit down silently and alone[194] so that he may lift himself above himself, let him be most vigilant about the clouds of images that bubble up abundantly. He should employ lively discernment to drive them away from his meditation, so that he might not cling to them, since they are almost always present at this stage. As Gregory says, "Those who strive to grasp the peak of perfection, who long to take hold of the citadel of contemplation, should first test themselves through training on the field of works, carefully examining themselves to see if they have done anything against their neighbors, whether they have borne patiently anything their neighbors might have done against them; to see whether they have rejoiced inordinately when receiving temporal goods, whether being deprived of temporal goods has wounded them with deep sorrow. Then, let them consider whether, when they return to their inner selves, they carry the shadows of corporal things with them into the place where they mine spiritual things, whether, having perchance dragged corporal things in, they have swept them away with the hand of discretion. Let them also consider whether, in their desire to see uncircumscribable light, they have repressed all their own circumscribed imagery, whether they have conquered the things that are in their hunger to reach what lies above."[195]

Thus, seeing by means of the phantasms that Gregory here calls shadows, the godly spirit passes through the second stage, as noted above (III.7), striving to penetrate to the pure ray of truth.[196] But let her beware of clinging to these phantasms themselves, as common as they may be in this life. Instead she should strive to contemplate the truth of the fabric of divine properties that clothes these images. For Saint Thomas says, "Human contemplation, given the situation of this present life, is not possible without phantasms, because it is part of human nature to see intelligible representations in phantasms, as Aristotle says in the third book *On the Soul*.[197] Yet intellectual cognition does not consist in these phantasms; rather, the purity of intelligible truth is contemplated in them. And this not only in natural contemplation, but also in the things revealed by revelation; hence Gregory says that contemplative men do not carry with them the shadows of corporal things."[198] What Thomas says here applies to the second step [of speculative contemplation], namely alluring meditation. In the third step one proceeds without any images at all. Having repelled phantasms all around, one sees the ray of divine brilliance, since the impediments to all intelligible forms[199] have been removed. Thomas seems to express this thought elsewhere, for in the course of giving his conclusion to several points, he says that "a man cannot see the divine essence in any other cognitive way than by the intellect; moreover, the human intellect cannot be directed toward things perceptible by the senses except through the medium of phantasms which it receives from sense-perceptible things through intelligible forms. By considering these phantasms, the intellect evaluates and analyzes sense-perceptible things, and thus abstraction from sense-perceptible things is necessary in every operation by which our intellect abstracts from phantasms. The human intellect, so long as it is found in this present life, must proceed by abstraction from images if it is to see God's essence. Moreover, God's essence cannot be seen through any phantasm, nor through any created intelligible form, for the essence of God infinitely exceeds not only all bodies to which phantasms belong but even all intelligible creatures. Therefore, when the human intellect is raised to the loftiest vision of the divine essence, the spirit must be entirely focused therein and perceive nothing from the phantasms anymore, being completely transported into God. Hence it is impossible that a man here on earth could see God in his essence without abstraction from things perceptible by the senses."[200] This conclusion agrees partially or completely with the contemplation and vision by which God is seen fleetingly. However, since I speak specifically about the vision of God that occurs through total overpowering of the spirit, such as happened to Paul (as discussed above [II.10; III.8], cf. 2 Cor 12:4), nothing that has been proposed here regarding the nature of ascending or descending speculations is suited to that vision of Saint Paul. All one can do is to agree with the decree of Sacred Scripture: *Seek not after lofty things and do not scrutinize things that are too great for you* (Sir 3:22).

Chapter Twenty-Six: Three Things That Must Be Done When Divine Grace Is Withdrawn—How to Handle Spiritual Listlessness (Acedia)

When, as happens frequently, grace is withdrawn from the servants of God, there would seem to be two[201] things that one specifically ought to do, namely, endure God's decision with humble patience and beware lest through dryness of heart the humble spirit be drawn to love of visible things.

To do the first, God's servant does what Bernard describes in the twenty-first sermon on the Canticle: "As long as grace is present, enjoy it in such a way that you do not come to think confidently that you possess God's gift by hereditary right, lest God perchance suddenly remove his hand and retract his gift, making you more depressed and unhappy than you should be under those circumstances. And, while flushed with success, do not say *I shall never be moved* (Ps 29:7 [30:6]), lest you be compelled by what follows to groan, *To my dismay you have turned your face away* (Ps 29:8 [30:7]). Instead, if you are wise, you will take care to heed the counsel of the wise: *In adversity do not forget the good times; in prosperity remember adversity* (Sir 11:27). When you feel strong, do not become carefree, but cry aloud to God with the prophet,

251

When my strength fails me, do not forsake me (Ps 70:9 [71:9]). Then in trying times you can console yourself by saying with the bride, *Draw me, we will run after you in the fragrance of your perfumes* (Ca 1:2–3 [1:4]). Thus hope shall not abandon you in bad times nor shall foresight be absent in good times. Amid the adversities and prosperities of changing times, you will hold fast to a view of eternity and possess a steady, inviolable, and unassailable equanimity, thanking God at all times. Likewise, you thus lay claim to a perennial steady state in the midst of the doubtful events and the certain failings of this changing world as you begin to renew and reform yourself into the ancient and distinguished likeness of the eternal God in whom there is no change or shadow of vicissitude.[202] For even in this world you will become as he is, neither fearful in adversity nor wanton in prosperity."[203] Likewise Augustine says, "Lord, you empty out those whom you fill; and since I am not full of you, I ought to be given a burden to bear."[204]

In the second place, the servant of God does what Gregory mentions in the homily, *Because far from the city:* "Everything that we have received for use in this life we turn to sinful uses. We use the tranquillity of human concord in the form of vain unconcern, we love this life's pilgrimage on earth as if it were a dwelling-place in heaven, we apply bodily health to the service of vices, and we invert rich abundance so that it serves perverse pleasure rather than the needs of the flesh."[205]

Third, the servant of God should observe what Bernard says, as quoted above, namely that a man should strive for spiritual exercise: "Do you see that the one who walks in the Spirit[206] never remains in one state[207] nor does he always advance with the same facility? For a man does not know his own way[208] but the Spirit who governs deploys him as he pleases so that he might forget what lies behind and reach toward what lies ahead,[209] sometimes slowly, sometimes with alacrity. Therefore, when you sense that you are taken by torpidity, listlessness, or boredom, do not become timid or abandon your spiritual pursuit, but seek out a helping hand, begging like the bride to be pulled along, until revived by grace you run with rapid pulse, saying, *I ran in the path of your commandments, when you have enlarged my heart*" (Ps 118:32 [119:32]).[210]

Chapter Twenty-Seven: Examination of Conscience, Venial Sin, and Idle Words

As far as examination of conscience is concerned—something no part of the day should be free of[211]—beware of two things in particular.

First, the spirit should not be permitted to cling to any fault, no matter how small, because, as Augustine says, any venial sin can become a mortal sin if you take pleasure in it.[212] Likewise, be careful not to waste good efforts or godly works by scattering them among thorns.[213] Furthermore, always consider yourself in your heart of hearts to be a beginner, as Ecclesiasticus says, *When a man has finished, then he shall begin* (Sir 18:6 [7]).

Second, strive to avoid idle words. "An idle word is one said neither out of necessity nor godly motive," as Gregory says in one of his homilies.[214] And Bernard's [William of Saint-Thierry's] letter says, "Something is idle if it has no usefulness and serves no useful purpose."[215] So too, Isidore [of Seville]: "It does no good to do some good thing intermingled with evil; first restrain the evil and then practice the good. For Isaiah says, *Cease to do perversely, learn to do well* (Is 1:16–17). Vices must first be rooted out before virtues can be planted."[216] The Psalmist too says, *Depart from evil* and so forth (Ps 33:15 [34:14]).

Having said something about speculative contemplation, it remains to see to anagogical contemplation. If you wish to see something about it, you will find material about it in the second book on contemplation, chapter ten.[217]

Here Ends the Book on Contemplation Put Together by Dom Guigo, Monk of the Chartreuse. Thanks be to God.

Notes

Introduction

1. Rosemary Ann Lees, *The Negative Language of the Dionysian School of Mystical Theology: An Approach to the "Cloud of Unknowing,"* 2 vols. (1983); James J. Walsh, " 'Sapientia Christianorum': The Doctrine of Thomas Gallus Abbot of Vercelli on Contemplation" (Ph.D. diss., Pontifical Gregorian University, Rome, 1957).

2. Hugh's relationship to the Pseudo-Dionysian revival will be considered below, as part of the discussion of the relative roles of knowledge and love in mystical union.

3. James Walsh, ed. and trans., *The Pursuit of Wisdom and Other Works by the Author of the Cloud of Unknowing,* Classics of Western Spirituality (New York: Paulist Press, 1988), esp. 68–73; idem, *The Cloud of Unknowing,* Classics of Western Spirituality (New York: Paulist Press, 1981), pp. 5–9, 19–26.

4. Perhaps most useful is the study by Gordon Mursell, *The Theology of the Carthusian Life in the Writings of St. Bruno and Guigo I,* Analecta Cartusiana, 127 (Salzburg: Institut für Anglistik und Amerikanistik, 1988), drawing on earlier work by Gaston Hocquard.

5. ". . . libro fundamental en la historia de nuestra espiritualidad"; "Realmente Balma es una de las claves de la espiritualidad peninsular," in *Los Recogidos: Nueva vision de la mistica española (1500–1700)* (Madrid: Fundacion Universitaria Española Seminario "Suarez," 1975), pp. 48, 75.

6. The chronology of events surrounding Bruno's departure from Reims ca. 1082 and his subsequent movements before settling at what became the Grande Chartreuse cannot be reconstructed with complete precision. See Gerardo Posada, *Der heilige Bruno, Vater der Kartäuser, ein Sohn der Stadt Köln,* trans. Hubertus Maria Blüm, with contributions by Adam Wienand and Otto Beck (Cologne: Wienand, 1987), pp. 72–75, 95–98.

7. Not to be confused with Bruno, the Archbishop of Cologne, brother to Otto I, whom he served as chancellor. He died in 965. His feast day is October 11; Bruno the Carthusian is honored on October 6.

8. The texts have been collected by Bernard Bligny, ed., *Recueil des plus*

NOTES TO INTRODUCTION

anciens actes de la Grande-Chartreuse (1086–1196) (Grenoble: Imprimerie Allier, 1958).

9. Mursell, *Theology of the Carthusian Life*, p. 175, citing Hans-Jakob Becker's studies of Carthusian liturgy.

10. There were at this time many eremitical and monastic movements involving men and women seeking to live the "apostolic life" in its supposed primitive simplicity. See Marie-Dominique Chenu, *Nature, Man, and Society in the Twelfth Century*, trans. Jerome Taylor and Lester K. Little (Chicago: Univ. of Chicago Press, 1968); Lester K. Little, *Religious Poverty and the Profit Economy in Twelfth-Century Europe* (Ithaca, N.Y.: Cornell Univ. Press, 1978); Henrietta Leyser, *Hermits and the New Monasticism: A Study of Religious Communities in Western Europe 1000–1150* (New York: St. Martin's, 1984); Carole Hutchison, *The Hermit Monks of Grandmont*, CS 118 (Kalamazoo: Cistercian Publications, 1989), esp. pp. 1–25; Jacques Dubois, "Quelques problèmes de l'histoire de l'ordre des Chartreux à propos de livres recents," *Revue d'histoire ecclésiastique* 63 (1968): 27–54, a critique of the work of Maurice Laporte, the Carthusian editor of an unpublished six-volume study of Carthusian origins produced for the internal use of the order, "Aux Sources de la vie cartusienne." Some of Laporte's conclusions are accessible in the introduction to Guigo I, *Coutumes de Chartreuse [Consuetudines Cartusienses]*, ed. and trans. by a Carthusian, SC, 313 (Paris: Du Cerf, 1984), and *Lettres des premiers Chartreux*, 2 vols, SC 88, 274 (1962, 1980). See James Hogg's defense of Laporte's interpretations in "The Carthusians and the 'Rule of St. Benedict,' " in *Itinera Domini: Gesammelte Aufsätze aus Liturgie und Mönchtum*, Festschrift Emmanuel von Severus O.S.B. (Münster: Aschendorff, 1988), pp. 281–318.

11. For instance, the mid-thirteenth century *Statuta Antiqua* reduced the required bread and water abstinence to a minimum of one day per week, while encouraging the original practice. See *Statuta Antiqua*, par. II, ch. 14 (Basel: Amerbach, 1510; reprinted in *The Evolution of the Carthusian Statutes*, AC 99: Documents, vol. 2, p. 192).

12. Heinrich Rüthing has written a fine study of how this system worked. See "Die Wächter Israels: Ein Beitrag zur Geschichte der Visitationen im Kartäuserorden," in *Die Kartäuser: Orden der schweigenden Mönche*, ed. Marijan Zadnikar and Adam Wienand (Cologne: Wienand, 1983), pp. 169–83.

13. A popularly written overview in English is found in Robin Bruce Lockhart, *Halfway to Heaven: The Hidden Life of the Sublime Carthusians* (New York: Vanguard Press, 1985). No thorough scholarly survey exists in any language. One of the finest illustrated overviews is that by Gabriel le Bras, "Les Chartreux," in *Les Ordres religieux: La vie et l'art*, ed. Gabriel le Bras, illus. Paul Hartmann and Madeleine Hartmann (Paris: Flammarion, 1979–1980), vol. 1, pp. 562–653. See also Thomas Merton, *The Silent Life* (New York: Farrar, Straus, and Cudahy, 1957), and E. Margaret Thompson, *The Carthusian Order in England* (London: S.P.C.K.; New York: Macmillan, 1930). A variety of studies have appeared in various languages, including English, in the series Analecta Cartusiana (Salzburg: Institut für Anglistik

NOTES TO INTRODUCTION

und Amerikanistik, 1970–), ed. James Hogg. Zadnikar and Wienand, *Kartäuser,* offers a helpful, illustrated, survey in German.

14. Mursell, *Theology of the Carthusian Life,* pp. 15, 17.

15. One of Guigo I's proverbs is "Nusquam ergo era secura anima Christiana nisi in adversis" ["Therefore, only in adversity will a Christian soul ever be carefree" (my translation)]. See Guigo I, *Les méditations,* ed. by a Carthusian, SC, 308 (Paris: Du Cerf, 1983), no. 76b; cf. ET by Jolin, p. 16, and by Mursell, p. 79.

16. Mursell, *Theology of the Carthusian Life,* p. 165. The concluding quotation is from Guigo I, *Meditations,* no. 471; cf. ET by Jolin, p. 82, and Mursell, p. 189.

17. Definition from *A Latin Dictionary,* first published in 1850 by Ethan Allen Andrews, rev. in 1879 by Charlton T. Lewis and Charles Short (Oxford: Clarendon Press, 1962).

18. Mursell, *Theology of the Carthusian Life,* pp. 213–15. Cf. Dennis D. Martin, *Fifteenth-Century Carthusian Reform: The World of Nicholas Kempf,* Studies in the History of Christian Thought, 49 (Leiden: Brill, 1992), ch. 4.

19. *Sermones,* 117.7 (PL 38:665D; ET in *The Works of St. Augustine: A Translation for the Twenty-First Century,* vol. III, pt. 4: *Sermons 94A–147A,* trans. Edmund Hill, O.P., ed. John E. Rotelle, O.S.A. (Brooklyn, N.Y.: New City Press, 1992), p. 214. My attention was drawn to this by Henry Chadwick, *Augustine* (New York: Oxford University Press, 1986), p. 48.

20. James Hogg has summarized what is known in "Hugh of Balma and Guigo du Pont," in *Kartäuserregel und Kartäuserleben,* AC 113.1 (1984), pp. 61–88, at 71–73. Patricia Guinan's dissertation ("Carthusian Prayer and Hugh of Balma's *Viae Sion Lugent,*" Medieval Institute, University of Notre Dame, 1985) offers nearly verbatim summaries of the French lexicon entries by Autore, Sochay, and Stoelen that are the definitive treatments at present, pending the appearance of the introduction to Ruello's Sources Chrétiennes edition. The most important archival work was by Artaud M. Sochay in the Archives of Ain, where the Meyriat archives are now found. See "Hughes de Balma," *Catholicisme,* 5:1028.

21. Charles Le Couteulx, *Annales ordinis cartusiensis ab anno 1084 ad annum 1429,* 8 vols. (Montreuil-sur-Mer, 1887–1891), 1:214.

22. See Jacques Dubois, "Le Domaine de la chartreuse de Meyriat: Histoire d'un désert cartusien," *Le Moyen Age Latin* 74 (1968): 459–93.

23. Stanislaus Autore, in *DSAM,* refers to unpublished research by Dom Thomasson de Gournay, O.S.B. (d. 1928) and Ambroise Mougel, a Carthusian of Parkminster in England (d. 1925).

24. These are Sochay's conclusions, modifying the earlier claims for a priorate between 1295 and 1304.

25. Harald Walach, *Notitia experimentalis Dei—Erfahrungserkenntnis Gottes: Studien zu Hugo de Balmas Text "Viae Sion lugent" und deutsche Übersetzung,* Analecta Cartusiana, 98, pt. 1 (Salzburg: Institut für Anglistik und Amerikanistik, 1994).

26. One branch of the family that had founded Meyriat carried the name "de Balmeto"; another was known as "de Dorchiis" based on property in the village of Dorche.

27. Walach, *Notitia*, p. 219.

28. I expect to give a detailed account of problems with Walach's argumentation in a review essay to be published elsewhere. Walach is aware of the incompleteness of his research, referring to his book as a call for further study. Unfortunately, he constructs a very detailed portrait of the author of the *Viae Sion* on the basis of an extended network of highly speculative assumptions.

29. Walach, *Notitia*. In one instance (p. 88), a quotation from Thomas Aquinas that Walach offers as evidence of Hugh of Balma's acquaintance with Aquinas's writings itself asserts that Thomas drew the ideas in question from Augustine. Walach nonetheless insists that Hugh could only have had this idea from Thomas. In another instance (p. 152), Walach attributes the theme of "amor est pondus mentis et origo omnis affectionis mentalis" to Bonaventure, apparently unaware of the classic passage from Augustine's *Confessions*, XIII.9. It may indeed be true that Hugh has this idea directly from Bonaventure, but given Augustine's widespread influence in the Middle Ages, to prove the influence of Bonaventure on Hugh of Balma one would have to do a thorough search of other sources. Likewise, on p. 237, Walach suggests Hugh of Balma may have been a source for Eckhart in his emphasis on the soul as the image of the entire Trinity, completely overlooking this theme in Augustine.

30. For instance, on pp. 79–81, 71, 88, 180, Walach (*Notitia*) interprets the central theme of *desiderium* in Hugh of Balma solely against a scholastic background. Hugh thus becomes unique and innovative in making *desiderium* his central principle, which then indicates that Hugh was a source for Olivi. Had Walach studied Augustine and the monastic tradition, he would see how eminently traditional Hugh was on this point.

31. See John Cassian, *Conferences*, IX.15, 25 (SC 54:52, 61–62; ET by Luibheid in CWS, pp. 109–10, 116; NPNF-2, 11:392, 396), on aspirative prayer, and IX.18–23 (SC 54:55–60; ET by Luibheid in CWS, pp. 111–16; NPNF-2, 11:393–96) for the exposition of the Our Father. Even the shift from third person to second person direct address that characterizes Hugh's shift from the longer to the shorter exposition of the Lord's Prayer is found in John Cassian (IX.17), as is the emphasis on importunate prayer (IX.34). For Augustine on arrow-like aspirative prayers, see *De diversis quaestionibus ad Simplicianum*, II.4.4 (CCSL 44:87), cited by Henry Chadwick, *Augustine*, Past Masters series (New York: Oxford Univ. Press, 1986), p. 74.

32. Walach, *Notitia*, pp. 89–90.

33. See the illuminative way, par. 5, note 5.

34. Walach notes (pp. 59–60) that par. 82–115 of the *via unitiva*, which constitute a commentary on Pseudo-Denis's *Mystical Theology*, are not cited in the "Difficult Question," which implies that this commentary was not yet written when

the *quaestio* was composed. Almost all of Walach's claims for cross-references from one part of *Viae Sion* to another are "indirect" or approximate. The clearest of the cross-references is an explicit reference to the "short exposition of the Our Father" in par. 40 of the *quaestio*. To preserve priority of composition for the *quaestio*, Walach argues that the expositions of the Our Father existed as separate treatises before or at the same time as the *quaestio* was being written. In general, one must say that the cross-references and other arguments for the priority of the *quaestio* do not definitively exclude the possibility of the *quaestio* being written last, unless one places more weight on the argument from silence than that argument will bear.

35. Guigo II, *Scala Claustralium*, ch. 2–7, SC 163 (Paris: Du Cerf, 1970), pp. 82–96. ET by James Walsh and Edmund Colledge, *The Ladder of Monks* by Guigo II (Garden City, N.Y.: Doubleday Image, 1978); reissued with different pagination (Kalamazoo: Cistercian Publications, 1981), CS 48.

36. These terms are used here in the same sense as set forth by Jean Leclercq in his famous *Love of Learning and Desire for God*, trans. Catherine Misrahi (New York: Fordham University Press, 1961; 3rd ed., 1982; originally *L'Amour des lettres et le désir de Dieu* [Paris: Editions du Cerf, 1957]). Although the distinction between monastic and scholastic theology has been challenged and certainly can be abused, I believe it remains useful (Martin, *Fifteenth-Century Carthusian Reform*, esp. p. 49).

37. Francis Ruello, after a study of 59 out of approximately 100 full and partial copies of *Viae Sion lugent*, concludes that the work originated in a general treatise on mystical theology, to which the scholastic *quaestio* was later added. A final revision intended by the author was never finished, and the work was published at some later point. Ruello sets forth these findings in his introduction to the new Sources Chrétiennes edition.

38. *S. Bonaventurae Opera Omnia*, 10 vols., ed. by the Franciscans at Quarracchi (Rome: 1882–1902), vol. 8 (1898), Prolegomena, c. 3, a. 2, n. 11 (p. CXI), and vol. 10 (1902).

39. Dubourg, "La Date de la *Theologia Mystica*," *Revue d'ascetique et de mystique* 8 (1927): 156–61.

40. Lists are found in all the lexicon entries; Hogg has summarized these in English, and a new list will undoubtedly appear in the introduction to the Sources Chrétiennes edition. My summary is based on the lexicon entries, not on an independent examination of these scarcely accessible early editions.

41. The following summary is based on the article by Faustino de Pablo Maroto, "Amor y Conocimiento en la Vida Mística según Hugo de Balma," *Revista de espiritualidad* 24 (1965): 399–447, at 404–5. Details on the Spanish "reception" of *Viae Sion lugent* can also be found in Jean Krynen, *Saint Jean de la Croix et l'aventure de la mystique espagnole*, Collection "Thèses et recherches," 20 (Toulouse: Presses universitaires du Mirail, 1990); Jean Orcibal, *La Rencontre du Carmel Thérésien avec les mystiques du nord*, Bibliothèque de l'école des hautes études, section des sciences religieuses, 70 (Paris: Presses universitaires de France, 1959); and Andrès Martín, *Recogidos*.

NOTES TO INTRODUCTION

42. See the text of the title page in Andrès Martín, *Recogidos*, p. 71. This publication described itself as a revised edition. Since Bernardino de Laredo referred to an earlier edition attributed to Henrique de Balma, some have speculated Laredo might have published it before 1514, perhaps in 1513. See the discussion of its impact in *Recogidos*, pp. 48, 70–76.

43. Ibid., pp. 241–43.

44. Ibid., p. 274; and Pablo-Maroto, "Amor y conocimiento," p. 404.

45. The various listings by Pablo-Maroto and Andrès Martín do not agree about this edition. See *Recogidos*, p. 71.

46. See Orcibal, *Rencontre*, p. 25. Orcibal devotes careful study to Gracian's work and the larger controversies about the nature of mystical theology in Carmelite circles. Hugh of Balma and Hendrik Herp were two leading and controversial authorities in these debates. Gracian thought the work was by Bonaventure, but also voiced some doubts about this attribution.

47. Andrès Martín, *Recogidos*, pp. 70–71.

48. Werner Höver lists the manuscripts in his article in the *Verfasserlexikon:* excerpts from Hugh's prologue, his treatment of the *via purgativa* and *via illuminativa*, and the prologue of the discussion of the *via unitiva* are found in Salzburg St. Peter b VI 15, 203r–204v, 228r–244v, 251r–278v, while ch. III, particula 1–2.4, and the "quaestio difficilis" are found in Munich, Universitätsbibliothek, 4o cod. Ms. 477, 60r–90v, a manuscript that comes from the Franciscan convent at Landshut. Excerpts are also found in Munich, Bayerische Staatsbibliothek, cgm 839, 116r–136v, from the Benedictine monastery at Tegernsee in southern Bavaria, probably translated from the Latin text found in Munich, Staatsbibliothek clm 18590. The Salzburg excerpts were published in a modern edition for students of German literature; see Höver, "Hugo von Balma," in *Verfasserlexikon*, rev. ed. edited by Kurt Ruh, Franz-Josef Worstbrock, and others (Berlin: de Gruyter, 1983), vol. 4, cols. 225–26, with references to Höver's 1971 study, *Theologia Mystica in altbairischer Übertragung.*

49. Arnold, *Historia . . . theologiae mysticae* (Frankfurt, 1702), 384. Regarding Arnold's life and works, see Peter C. Erb, *Pietists, Protestants, and Mysticism: The Use of Late Medieval Spiritual Texts in the Work of Gottfried Arnold (1666–1714)*, Pietist and Wesleyan Studies, 2 (Metuchen, N.J.: Scarecrow Press, 1989).

50. Thierry Mertens, "Hugo de Balma in het Middelnederlands," in *Codex in Context: Studies over Codicologie, kartuizergeschiedenis en laatmiddeleeuws geestesleven aangeboden aan Prof. Dr. A. Gruijs*, ed. Chr. de Backer, A. J. Geuirts, and A. G. Weiler (Nijmegen: Uitgeverei Alfa, 1985), pp. 249–61. The Berlin manuscript is Staatsbibliothek Preußischer Kulturbesitz, Hs. germ. quart. 1084, 154r–161r.

51. Walsh, "The Ascent to Contemplative Wisdom," *The Way* 9 (1969): 243–50, at 244–50, republished in revised form in *The Pursuit of Wisdom*, CWS (1988), pp. 302–10.

52. Lees, *Negative Language*, pp. 289–90. The catalogue is the *Catalogus*

NOTES TO INTRODUCTION

Manuscriptorum Codicum Bibliothecae Uffenbachianae (Frankfurt, 1747), pp. 302–4. The next item in the catalogue is a copy of the *Cloud of Unknowing.*

53. They formed an appendix to Hopkins, *Nicholas of Cusa's Dialectical Mysticism: Text, Translation, and Interpretive Study of De Visione Dei* (Minneapolis: Arthur J. Banning Press, 1985, 1988), pp. 369–92.

54. He is most commonly referred to in English publications as "Guigo du Pont," which combines French and Latin orthography. I have chosen to use an entirely Latin form: Guigo de Ponte. The term *Dom* in the title line of the prologue is an abbreviated form of *Dominus/Domnus*, a title of respect given to monks in the Benedictine, Cistercian, and Carthusian traditions.

55. Le Couteulx, *Annales* 4:439. Dupont gives the Latin text of Couteulx's entry in the introduction to his edition, p. 3. For the reference by Denis of Rijkel, see *Dionysii Cartusiani Opera Omnia* (Tournai: Charterhouse of Notre Dame de Près, 1912), 41:252–53.

56. Gourdel, "Chartreux," in *DSAM* 2 (1953): 739; and Hogg, "Hugh of Balma and Guigo du Pont."

57. The list of seventeenth-century scholars who made this attribution is given by Dupont in his introduction. The authorship question was dealt with in some detail by J. P. Grausem, "Le *De contemplatione* de Guiges du Pont," *RAM* 10 (1929): 259–89, at 264–67; cf. Philippe Dupont, "L'ascension mystique chez Guigues du Pont," in *Kartäusermystik und -mystiker*, Dritter Internationaler Kongress über die Kartäusergeschichte und -spiritualität 1, AC 55.1 (Salzburg: Institut für Anglistik und Amerikanistik, 1981): 47–80, and the introduction to his critical edition; Artaud M. Sochay, "Guigue du Pont," *Catholicisme, hier, aujourd'hui, demain*, ed. G. Jacquemet (Paris: Letouzy et ané, 1947–), vol. 5 (1962): 374–75; and Hogg, "Hugh of Balma and Guigo du Pont."

58. Guigo du Pont, *Della contemplazione*, trans. and intro. Emilio Piovesan, Analecta Cartusiana, 45 (Salzburg: Institut für Anglistik und Amerikanistik, 1979).

59. Indeed, 60 percent, if one includes under the unitive way the scholastic question with which the work concludes. The ratios of the parts are interesting: The prologue and the purgative way occupy about one-eighth of the total in the Peltier edition (6.5 pp.), the illuminative way occupies one-fourth (13 pp.), the unitive way occupies one-half (25.5 pp.), and the *quaestio difficilis* occupies one-eighth (7.5 pp.).

60. For the later Spanish and French reception of *The Roads to Zion*, see the works by Andrès Martín, Orcibal, and Krynen, cited above.

61. Edmond Vansteenberghe, *Autour de la docte ignorance* (1915), outlined the controversy and edited most of the primary texts that had not already been published in Bernhard Pez and Philibert Hueber, eds., *Codex diplomatico-historico-epistolaris* (= vol. 6 of *Thesaurus anecdotorum novissimus*) (Augsburg, Graz: Philip, Johannes, Martin Veit, 1729), pp. 327–56. For the letter referred to here, see Vansteenberghe, pp. 109–11. See also Jasper Hopkins, *Nicholas of Cusa's Dialectical Mysticism* (Minneapolis: Arthur J. Banning Press, 1985, 1988), pp. 3–25; Margot Schmidt, "Nikolaus von Kues im Gespräch mit den Tegernseer Mönchen über

NOTES TO INTRODUCTION

Wesen und Sinn der Mystik," in *Das Sehen Gottes nach Nikolaus von Kues* (Trieri Paulinus Verlag, 1989), pp. 25–49; Heribert Roßmann, "Die Stellungnahme des Kartäusers Vinzenz von Aggsbach zur mystischen Theologie des Johannes Gerson," in *Kartäusermystik und -mystiker*, vol. 5, Analecta Cartusiana, 55.5 (Salzburg: Institut für Anglistik und Amerikanistik, 1982), pp. 5–30; idem, "Leben und Schriften des Kartäusers Vinzenz von Aggsbach," in *Die Kartäuser in Österreich*, vol. 3, Analecta Cartusiana, 83.3 (Salzburg: Institut für Anglistik und Amerikanistik, 1981), pp. 1–20; idem, "Der Magister Marquard Sprenger in München und seine Kontroversschriften zum Konzil von Basel und zur mystischen Theologie," in *Mysterium der Gnade*, Festschrift J. Auer, ed. H. Roßmann and J. Ratzinger (Regensburg: Pustet, 1975), pp. 350–411; Alois Haas, "Schools of Late Medieval Mysticism," 165–73; and Pauline Moffitt Watts, *Nicolaus Cusanus: A Fifteenth-Century Vision of Man*, Studies in the History of Christian Thought, 30 (Leiden: E. J. Brill, 1982), pp. 154–71. See also Franz Hubalek, "Aus dem Briefwechsel des Johannes Schlitpacher von Weilheim (der Kodex 1767 der Stiftsbibliothek Melk)" (D. Phil. diss., Univ. of Vienna, 1963), pp. 93–120, 151ff.

62. In Benedictine monasteries, the prior is the assistant to the head of the monastery, the abbot. In Carthusian monasteries, the prior is the head of the monastery and is assisted by a vicar and procurator.

63. *Verfasserlexikon*, 2nd ed., col. 226.

64. Found in Munich, Bayerische Staatsbibliothek, clm 18150.

65. Gerson was chancellor of the University of Paris, a conciliar reformer, and a writer of devotional literature in Latin and French. For his use of Hugh see the index to André Combes, ed., *Ioannis Carlerii de Gerson de Mystica Theologia* (Lugano: Thesaurus Mundi, 1958); Combes, *La théologie mystique de Gerson: Profil de son évolution*, 2 vols., Spiritualitas, 1–2 (Rome: Desclée, 1963), esp. 1:90, 102; 2:401 ff., 671; and Colledge and Marler in *Mediaeval Studies* 41 (1979): 354–86.

66. This is my tentative conclusion based on a survey of some of the manuscripts in Munich and Melk during the years 1976–1977.

67. This copy is now found in Vienna National Library codex 1727.

68. Text in Vansteenberghe, *Autour de la docte ignorance* (1915), pp. 189–201; cf. idem, "Un écrit de Vincent d'Aggsbach contre Gerson," in *Studien zur Geschichte der Philosophie* (Festgabe Clemens Baeumker), Beiträge zur Geschichte der Philosophie des Mittelalters, Supplement-Band, 1 (Münster: Aschendorff, 1913), pp. 357–65.

69. The publication of Mark Burrows's study of the later career of Jean Gerson, building on the earlier work of André Combes, leads one to suggest that Vincent may have discovered the "early Gerson" of the *De mystica theologia speculativa* and *De mystica theologia practica* only after he had become acquainted with Gerson's later writings.

70. Joachim W. Stieber, *Pope Eugenius IV, the Council of Basel, and the Secular and Ecclesiastical Authorities in the Empire*, Studies in the History of Christian Thought, 13 (Leiden: E. J. Brill, 1978). Cusanus had played a key role as an ambas-

sador for the pope, 1438–1448, and was rewarded with a cardinal's hat in December 1448.

71. See his letter of 1453 to Schlitpacher in Pez and Hueber, *Cod. dip.-hist.-epist.* (1729), pt. III, p. 328, where he angrily tells Schlitpacher, "Thanks, but no thanks" for the copy of Cusanus's general church reform proposal written for Pope Nicholas V and sent to Vincent by Schlitpacher and then excoriates Cusanus's efforts at monastic reform, saying in effect: If this is the same Nicholas of Cusa who betrayed the council, then I expect nothing out of his reform efforts. Note, however, Vincent's reply to Bernard of Waging's *Defensorium impugnatorii laudatorii Doctae Ignorantiae* of 1459 (Pez and Hueber, pp. 343–46, at 344A: "I would not want you to think, friend, that I despise the teachings of your master the Cardinal. For I have copied his book titled *On the Icon* [= *De Visione Dei*], which I have indeed read carefully many times and find to be good and delightful.").

72. Gerson, *De vita spirituali animae*, near the end of the lectio prima, *Oeuvres complètes*, vol. 3, ed. Palémon Glorieux (Paris: Desclée, 1962), p. 127.

73. "Si fuissem praesens, dum praemissa verba dictavit, ego dixissem sibi: Insanis, Gerson, multae te litterae ad insaniam perducunt [cf. Acts 26:24]; mirabiliter enim involvis materias, et vere ex tuis scriptis nunquam aliquis fiet bonus contemplator aut mysticus discipulus" (Vansteenberghe, *Docte ignorance*, p. 199).

74. Pez-Hueber, *Cod. dip.-hist.-epist.* (1729), pt. III, p. 329.

75. See Hopkins, *Nicholas of Cusa's Dialectical Mysticism*, p. 16.

76. "Admonuit me quidam nobilis et religiosus Praelatus in terra nostra dicens: 'Pater, ego dico vobis, quod frater iste in periculo stat, quia in spiritu meridiano, id est, superbiae laborat, et vos tenemini sibi dicere tanquam pastor'" (Pez and Hueber, *Cod. dipl.-hist.-epist.* [1729], letter 20, p. 357).

77. As Vansteenberghe points out, the Tegernsee Benedictines and Johannes Schlitpacher at Melk provided two centers for the exchange of information, with Conrad of Geisenfeld, a monk of Melk who eventually transferred to Tegernsee, acting as intermediary. The Tegernsee monks sent Vincent's attack on Gerson to Cusanus and to Sprenger for "expert" evaluation. Cusanus provided this in letters and in his *De Visione Dei* and *De Beryllo*. When Bernard of Waging and his abbot, Gaspar Aindorffer, misinterpreted Cusanus's *De Visione Dei* by reading it in too affective a manner, Cusanus set him straight, but otherwise stayed out of the controversy. See Vansteenberghe, *Autour de le docte ignorance*, pp. 44–45.

78. My reading of Hugh of Balma was arrived at independently of Vincent's writings on mystical theology. Only after translating Hugh did I realize how much Vansteenberghe had been prejudiced against Vincent. That realization led me to a reassessment of Vincent and to the discovery that Vincent had not misunderstood Hugh—a fault I was still laying at Vincent's feet as late as September 1993 in a paper read at the Patristics, Medieval and Renaissance conference at Villanova University.

79. "Whether the soul in her affectus can, *by aspiration and yearning*, be moved into God without any of the intellect's cogitation leading the way or keeping her company." Cf., e.g., "Difficult Question," par. 32, 33.

NOTES TO INTRODUCTION

80. See his letter of September 1455 to Conrad of Geissenfeld in response to Marquard Sprenger's *Elucidatorium*, printed in Vansteenberghe, *Autour de le docte ignorance*, p. 215: "Hence the entire controversy has to do solely with the timing of cognition, for in the gift of wisdom, cognition precedes or at least accompanies the affectus, but in mystical theology, in fact, the affectus surges up without advance or concomitant cognition, yet not without subsequent cognition."

81. Vincent, letter to Conrad of Geissenfeld, Sept. 1455, printed in Vansteenberghe, *Autour de le docte ignorance*, p. 215.

82. "Hugo de Palma in libello suo allegat aliqua de septimo capitulo *De divinis nominibus*, que Mar[quardus] asserit suo proposito non servire. In fine addidit unam questionem cum sua solucione, quam eciam item Mar[quardus] multum impugnat. Dato autem quod utrobique victor existat, tamen civitatem mistice theologie per hoc non cepit, sed quedam eius suburbia solum vastavit civitate ipsa omnino manente illesa secundum exposiciones Vercellinco [Thomas Gallus of Vercelli and Robert Grosseteste, bishop of Lincoln]" (Vincent, letter presumably sent to Johannes Schlitpacher, printed in Vansteenberghe, *Autour de le docte ignorance*, p. 217).

83. A more detailed discussion of this question is found below, under the topic "Hugh and the Affective Taming of Pseudo-Denis."

84. Johannes Schlitpacher defended Vincent on this point—Schlitpacher, as requested by the Tegernsee Benedictines and Marquard Sprenger, had done his own research on the subject. Schlitpacher had lived a long time in the religious life without really understanding the term: He found it occurring once in Richard of Saint-Victor's *Benjamin major* but had misunderstood it to apply to Noah's Ark rather than the Ark of the Covenant (Letter to Marquard Sprenger, Sept. 1450, Vansteenberghe, *Autour de le docte ignorance*, p. 76).

85. Like Schlitpacher, Vincent noted that Richard of Saint-Victor used the term "mystical ark" as a title for one of his two treatises on contemplation. See the letter to Conrad of Geissenfeld, Sept. 1455, in Vansteenberghe, *Autour de le docte ignorance*, p. 215.

86. See, for example, Vansteenberghe's summary of Bernard of Waging's next-to-last salvo against Vincent, the *De cognoscendo Deum* of 1459 (Vansteenberghe, *Autour de le docte ignorance*, p. 95): Bernard glimpsed in Vincent a reprise of the extreme positions of some of the Free Spirit sectarians of the fourteenth-century.

87. Vansteenberghe, *Autour de le docte ignorance*, p. 101: "Bien autrement absolue et intransigeante est la position de Vincent d'Aggsbach. L'affection pure n'est pas pour lui l'exceptionnel, mais l'ordinaire; elle n'est pas l'anormal, mais la regle; elle est l'idéal, qu'il croit voir tracé dans les traités du pseudo-Aréopagite."

88. See Hogg, "Hugh of Balma and Guigo du Pont," p. 68.

89. See the letter of Sept. 1455 to Conrad of Geissenfeld, Vansteenberghe, *Autour de le docte ignorance*, p. 214. Sprenger had dismissed Vincent's affective "mystical theology" in its narrow application as suitable only to the simple; Vincent responded that it is indeed particularly accessible to the simple but not limited to them.

NOTES TO INTRODUCTION

90. See p. 27: "Mais, sur l'interpretation du 'bienheureux Denys,' notre chartreux [Vincent of Aggsbach] a des idées qui lui sont personnelles; et, avec son hu-
meur combative et son tempérament entier, il prend à partie les auteurs, si vénerables
soient-ils, qui paraissent les contredire."

91. Letter of Sept. 1460, to Marquard Sprenger, Vansteenberghe, *Autour de
le docte ignorance*, p. 76.

92. Endre von Ivánka, "Zur Überwindung des neuplatonischen Intellektualismus in der Deutung der Mystik: Intelligentia oder principalis affectio," *Scholastik*
30 (1955): 185–94, summarized in Lees, *Negative Language*, pp. 282–90. See also
Pablo-Maroto's summary of Spanish interpreters of Hugh, "Amor y Conocimiento," p. 426. In sixteenth-century Spain a number of Spanish interpreters understood Hugh to be teaching a totally affective ascent (Suárez, the Carmelite José
del Espiritu Santo) but various nineteenth- and twentieth-century interpreters say
he was not so anti-intellectual; Pablo Maroto seeks a moderate interpretation
(426–44).

93. Ivánka probably represents the most extreme position, but for decades
he was virtually alone in having studied Hugh of Balma and his viewpoint was widely
accepted. Walsh challenged him in his dissertation, but that study has remained unpublished (not even available in the microfilm network), although it is found in some
research library collections. An example of the "reception" of Ivánka's assessment
of Hugh of Balma is found in Barbara Faes de Mottoni, *Il Corpus Dionysianum nel
Medioevo: Rassegna di studi: 1900–1972* (Milan: Societá editrice il Mulino, 1977), p.
143, summarizing Ivánka, "Was heißt eigentlich 'Christlicher Neuplatonismus'?"
Scholastik 31 (1956): 31–40, reprinted in *Plato Christianus* (Einsiedeln: Johannes
Verlag, 1964), pp. 373–85. According to this author, from Thomas Gallus one ends
up "con la concezione dell'ultimo grado della contemplazione come *purus affectus*
sostenuta da Ugo di Balma." Here Balma is already a "name"; that his "purely affective" upsurge does *not* pertain to the ultimate stage of contemplation in a linear sense
is simply lost. Cf. Ivánka, "Apex mentis: Wanderung und Wandlung eines stoischen
Terminus," *Zeitschrift für katholische Theologie* 72 (1950): 129–76, at 169–72. Ivánka
badly distorts Hugh, asserting that Hugh taught that the "exclusion of every cogitative activity, from the very beginning onward is a prerequisite to mystical knowledge" (170: "ja das Ausschließen jeder gedanklichen Tätigkeit, von allem Anfang
an, ist eine Vorbedingung der mystischen Erkenntnis"). The quotes from Hugh in
the footnote for this statement say nothing about "from the very beginning." Nearly
all of Ivánka's quotations are drawn from the end of the *via unitiva* and the "Difficult
Question."

94. Even James Walsh, by far the most knowledgeable student of the impact
of Hugh of Balma on the English spiritual writers, comments in an otherwise discerning study that Hugh "is at pains to demonstrate the inferiority of speculative to
anagogical contemplation." Technically Walsh has not misrepresented Hugh here.
Unless one immediately adds, however, that speculative contemplation gives way to
affective upsurge, which in turn gives way to knowledge of God left behind in the

soul, such a comment might be read by the uninitiated as implying that Hugh's affective upsurge was the end of the mystical process. See Walsh, introduction to *Pursuit of Wisdom and Other Works by the Author of the Cloud of Unknowing*, CWS (New York: Paulist Press, 1988), p. 68.

95. *Nicholas of Cusa's Dialectical Mysticism* (1985, 1988), p. 389, n. 7.

96. *On the Divine Names*, ch. 7 (*Dionysiaca*, I:406; Luibheid translation), p. 109.

97. *On the Divine Names*, ch. 7; *Dionysiaca*, 386–87; Luibheid, p. 106. Hugh repeats this quotation in the "Quaestio difficilis" (par. 15).

98. "Primo oportet, quod considerationem et amorem sensibilium derelinquat, et contemplationem omnium intelligibilium, et purus consurgat affectus, sine admixtione intellectus, in illum, quem in sua tendentia cognoscit quietativum desiderii, ut ipsi intimius uniatur."

99. Referring to "Letter Five, to Dorotheus," *Dionysiaca*, 1:620; PG 3: 1073A; Luibheid, p. 265.

100. See the entire text, below, for context. Bernard McGinn, "Love, Knowledge, and Mystical Union in Western Christianity: Twelfth to Sixteenth Centuries," *Church History* 56 (1987): 7–24, at 12–13, summarizing the work of Robert Javelet, notes that Thomas Gallus distinguished first between the theoretical intellect and mystical theology, subdividing mystical theology into *theorica* (= the negative, abandonment ascent of Pseudo-Denis) and *practica* (the affective love theology of the medieval commentators on the Song of Songs). Hugh may well have been drawing on this in his quadripartite division here. Elsewhere, however, Hugh simply uses *practica* and *theoria* much as we would. For instance, in the "Difficult Question," par. 16: "Therefore one ought first to surge up in the movement of love before intellectually pondering in order to know the hidden God. For this is the general rule in mystical theology: One ought have practice before theory, that is, one ought to be well practiced in the heart before one has knowledge of the things said about it." Note also the discussion of the practical and theoretical in par. 9 of the Prologue and at various points in the illuminative way.

101. The longer but nonetheless anagogic exposition of the Our Father.

102. In the "Difficult Question," par. 34 and 40, Hugh finally clarifies that the proficients' affectivity is the same as no. 3 in our schematic and the perfected affectivity is the same as no. 4, rather than a subdivision of our no. 4 into 4a and 4b.

103. There is precedent for this: Medieval writers on the psychology of the human soul frequently reminded their listeners at the outset that the human soul is indivisible and that the distinctions between the various powers (potencies might be a better translation) of the soul are for the sake of analysis only.

104. Guigo II, *Scala Claustralium*, ch. 2–7, SC 163 (Paris: Du Cerf, 1970), pp. 82–96.

105. This is particularly characteristic of Walach, *Notitia*, e.g., pp. 119–20, 130–34.

106. Cf. the discussion of "Rapture and Presence" in Guigo de Ponte, below.

107. In the light of Hugh's teaching, one can greet the initial volume of Bernard McGinn's study of Western Christian mysticism with enthusiasm because it prefers the language of presence to the language of union. See *The Foundations of Mysticism*, vol. 1 of *The Presence of God: A History of Western Christian Mysticism* (New York: Crossroad, 1992). For other Carthusian expositors of "union" as a foretaste of the beatific vision rather than some return to God's utter essence, see Martin, *Fifteenth-Century Carthusian Reform*, ch. 5.

108. "One should not understand this to mean that this [second kind of] contemplation [from on high] does not terminate in the *affectus*, otherwise there would be no contemplation."

109. "It is something like the building of a bridge. A framework of wood supports the stones during the earliest stage of building, but after the edifice is constructed and the stone walls have been completely fixed in place, the entire wooden framework is removed, since the structure of stone can stand immovably without the service provided by the wood. That is how cogitation is employed as a vanguard during the stage of gaining proficiency; when love's affection is perfectly attained, all the faithful service provided by reflection and meditation up to and through the proficients' stage is removed." "Difficult Question," par. 40. Hugh uses the same analogy in par. 5 of the Prologue.

110. Walach interprets the bridge metaphor as proof of a sequentially ordered treatise on p. 130, but backs away from this interpretation on pp. 131–34. Cf. p. 238 where he cautiously suggests that Eckhart's metaphor of a ladder that is kicked away once one has climbed to one's destination might be derived from Hugh of Balma's bridge metaphor.

111. See the stimulating exploration of love as "lacking" in William of Saint-Thierry by Kurt Ruh, "*Amor deficiens* und *amor desiderii* in der Hoheliedauslegung Wilhelms von St. Thierry," in *Spiritualia Neerlandica*. [Albert Ampe Festschrift] (= *Ons geestelijk Erf*, 63.2–4, 64.1–3 [1989–1990]), ed. Elly Cockx-Indestege et al., pp. 70–88.

112. This unity of mundane monastic structure (liturgy, active discipline, asceticism, observance of the rule) with the rare glimpses of contemplative sweetness is clear from the writings of all the great contemplatives. For our purposes, it is perhaps enough to refer to Mursell's effort to demonstrate this unity within the early Carthusian tradition.

113. Significantly, Guigo de Ponte, *De Contemplatione*, II.10–13, does not interpret Hugh as "totally affective."

114. See letters no. 9, 8, 10, 15, and Vansteenberghe's commentary, *Autour de la docte ignorance*, pp. 44–48.

115. Cf. Kempf, *Tractatus de mystica theologia*, II.21, ed. Karl Jellouschek, Francis Ruello, Jeanne Barbet, AC 9 (Salzburg: Institut für englische Sprache und Literatur, 1973), pp. 172–77. See the discussion in Martin, *Fifteenth-Century Carthusian Reform*, ch. 5.

116. See Vansteenberghe, *Autour de le docte ignorance*, p. 46, referring to Bernard's letter to Cusanus of March 1454 (Vansteenberghe, pp. 130–33).

266

NOTES TO INTRODUCTION

117. Martin, *Fifteenth-Century Carthusian Reform*, ch. 5.

118. Bk. II.21, see also IV.1.

119. See bk. III.13; IV.1–2, V.2.

120. This is by far the most important work that has not seen any sort of printed edition. In addition to the various materials on Vincent of Aggsbach and Bernard of Waging available in the eighteenth-century collections by Bernhard and Hieronymus Pez (Pez and Philibert Hueber, *Codex diplomatico-historico-epistolaris* [= vol. 6 of *Thesaurus anecdotorum novissimus* (Augsburg and Graz, 1729)]); Bernard Pez, *Bibliotheca ascetica antiquo-nova* [1724–1740]), Edmonde Vansteenberghe produced transcriptions of the letters exchanged between Cusanus and the Tegernsee monks as well as some of Vincent of Aggsbach's polemics and some of Bernard of Waging's relevant writings, but the rest of Bernard of Waging's corpus and that of Marquard Sprenger and Johann Schlitpacher still await critical editing.

121. See Martin Grabmann, "Die Erklärung des Bernhard von Waging O.S.B. zum Schlußkapitel von Bonaventuras *Itinerarium mentis in Deum*," *Franziskanische Studien* 8 (1921): 125–35. See also Marianne Schlosser, *Cognitio et amor: Zum kognitiven und voluntativen Grund der Gotteserfahrung nach Bonaventura*, Veröffentlichungen des Grabmann-Institutes, 35 (Paderborn: Schöningh, 1990), and Timothy Johnson, *Iste Pauper Clamavit: Saint Bonaventure's Mendicant Theology of Prayer*, European University Studies, series 23, Theology, vol. 390 (Frankfurt a. M.: Peter Lang, 1990), pp. 218–36.

122. E.g., Walach, *Notitia*, p. 168, refers to the goal of the mystical ascent in *Viae Sion* as a "Dauerspannung" and "Dauersehnsucht" ("lasting tension" and "lasting yearning"). Significantly, in his entire monograph, he pays very little attention to the aspirative upsurge that so interested James Walsh in his translation of the *Cloud of Unknowing*.

123. Once more, one of the central sources for the Western monastic tradition on this point was John Cassian, who, in turn, was summarizing the Desert tradition. See *Conferences*, IX.26–29 (SC 54:62–65; ET by Luibheid in CWS, pp. 116–19; NPNF-2, 11:396–97). See also Bernard of Clairvaux's sermons on the Canticle, nos. 10–12 on the perfumes or ointments of the Bride(groom), and Aelred, *Mirror of Charity*, II.7–16. Cf. the theme of judgment and mercy that runs throughout the sermons on the Canticle as well as Bernard's *Steps of Humility and Pride*. For the infrequency with which Aelred refers to "mystical" or "contemplative union," see the various articles by John R. Sommerfeldt, e.g., "The Vocabulary of Contemplation in Aelred of Rievaulx's On Jesus at the Age of Twelve, A Rule of Life for a Recluse, and On Spiritual Friendship" in *Heaven on Earth*, ed. E. Rozanne Elder, Studies in Medieval Cistercian History, 9/Cistercian Studies series, 68 (Kalamazoo: Cistercian Publications, 1983), pp. 72–89; "The Vocabulary of Contemplation in Aelred of Rievaulx' Mirror of Love, Book 1," in *Goad and Nail*, ed. E. Rozanne Elder, Studies in Medieval Cistercian History, 10/Cistercian Studies series, 84 (Kalamazoo: Cistercian Publications, 1985), pp. 241–50.

124. See above on John Cassian's role in this. He specifically says that totally

affective aspirative prayer can be found as part of any of his four types of prayer (*Conferences*, IX.15). For the Carthusian tradition, see the fundamental legislation of the order: Guigo I, *Consuetudines*, 29.3 (*Coutumes de Chartreuse*, p. 228); cited by Walsh, ed., *Pursuit of Wisdom*, p. 72.

125. Ruh, "*Amor deficiens*," p. 87, with citations to William of Saint-Thierry, *On the Nature and Dignity of Love* and *Exposition on the Song of Songs*, p. 77.

126. In par. 45, the words *sine omni cogitatione praevia vel concomitante* are expressly used to describe the short exposition and its aspirative upsurge.

127. See the conclusion to par. 47: The aspirative method is a way "anagogice transferendo [a means for moving anagogically]," which is the same terminology Hugh used for the long exposition of the Our Father.

128. Anagogy is, in one sense, simply a rhetorical device for Hugh. See the discussion of par. 24 of the *via illuminativa* below under "Rhetoric and Language in Hugh." At the same time, anagogy is a spiritual reality. As modern people we tend to dismiss rhetorical devices as "mere" rhetorical devices. For Hugh, especially when dealing with inspired Scripture, but also with any spiritual text, rhetorical devices were marvelous means, not mere devices.

129. For an exposition of a fifteenth-century Carthusian method based on the principle that everything must be transported into the *affectus*, see Martin, *Fifteenth-Century Carthusian Reform*, ch. 3.

130. See John Cassian, *Conferences*, IX.17.

131. See Ruh, "*Amor deficiens*," p. 83, for a similar point with regard to William of Saint-Thierry.

132. Andrès Martín, *Recogidos*, pp. 386, 392–93, with citations to other literature. For the accusations of quietism that surrounded Jerónimo Gracian, see Orcibal, *Rencontre*, pp. 139, 153, 159, 218. Orcibal himself simply reduces Hugh to "voluntarism" (p. 48). Krynen, *L'Aventure*, assumes a famous debate took place already in the thirteenth century (p. 76).

133. The urgent need for a critical edition of Gallus's writings as a tool for understanding late medieval spirituality can scarcely be overemphasized. James Walsh and G. Théry have done much preliminary work, but since their time little has been done, apart from the critical edition of Thomas's commentaries on the Song of Songs by Jeanne Barbet (*Thomas Gallus: Commentaires du Cantique des Cantiques*, Textes philosophiques du Moyen Age, 14 [Paris: J. Vrin, 1967]). John P. H. Clark's work on the sources of the *Cloud of Unknowing* will be helpful to a future editor of Thomas Gallus. See Clark, "Sources and Theology in the 'Cloud of Unknowing,' " *Downside Review* 89 (1980): 83–109. Clark has promised an interpretive volume to accompany his editions of the Latin version of the *Cloud*, all to be published as segments of *The Latin Versions of the Cloud of Unknowing*, Analecta Cartusiana, 119 (Salzburg: Institut für Anglistik und Amerikanistik, 1989–).

134. See the summary in Rorem, *Pseudo-Dionysius: A Commentary* (1993), pp. 214–25, building on the fundamental research of James Walsh, "Sapientia Christianorum." A fund of information on the reception of the Dionysian corpus is found in Clark, "Sources and Theology in the 'Cloud of Unknowing.' "

NOTES TO INTRODUCTION

135. See Maika J. Will, "Dionysian Neoplatonism and the Theology of the *Cloud* Author," *Downside Review* 379 and 380 (April and July 1992): 98–109, 184–94, at 99 and 106, n. 5. The anonymous translator of *On Mystical Theology* and author of the *Cloud of Unknowing*, probably following Thomas Gallus, employed "affeccyon" in his translation, *Dionise Hid Divinitie* at several places, even though none of the Latin translations nor the Greek original strictly warranted this translation. See Will, citing the critical edition of the *Cloud* by Frances Hodgson, p. 99, and 107, n. 6.

136. Francis Ruello, "Statut et rôle de l'*intellectus* et de l'*affectus* dans la *Théologie Mystique* de Hughes de Balma," in *Kartäusermystik und -mystiker,* vol. 1, Analecta Cartusiana, 55.1 (Salzburg: Institut für Anglistik und Amerikanistik, 1981), pp. 1–46; James J. Walsh, " 'Sapientia Christianorum': The Doctrine of Thomas Gallus Abbot of Vercelli on Contemplation" (Dissertatio ad Lauream in Facultate Theologica, Pontifical Gregorian University, Rome, 1957); Lees, *Negative Language.* For Thomas Gallus in general, see the recent survey by Jeanne Barbet, "Thomas Gallus," *Dictionnaire de spiritualité ascétique et mystique,* vol. 15 (Paris: Beauchesne, 1991), cols. 800–16. Since Walsh's dissertation is not readily accessible, one might consult "Thomas Gallus et l'effort contemplatif," *Revue d'histoire de la spiritualité* 51 (1975): 17–42. For Thomas Gallus, God can be known either by the intellectus or by the *principalis affectio* (*synderesis, summus affectionis apex*). He bases this on Isaiah's vision in the temple (i.e., the human soul). The soul has three dwellings (*mansiones*), each of which has three further subdivisions corresponding to the nine choirs of angelic beings. The first has to do with nature, the second with human striving (*industria*), and the third is totally beyond both industry and nature. Both the *affectus* and *intellectus* are born in the first mansion (nature), and, aided by grace, they grow in the second mansion. They are perfected in the third by grace alone. In the third mansion are found the Thrones, Cherubim, and Seraphim. The *synderesis* or summit of the affective power forms the floor of the third dwelling and intellection plays no structural role. Since God's light comes from on high, it strikes the affective mansion first. Even if one starts from below (as Hugh does when he uses the analogy of the Trinity: The Holy Spirit, who proceeds from Father and Son, is closest to us and we thus begin with him, i.e., with love ["Difficult Question," par. 5, 42]), one starts all over after crossing the threshold between the eighth and ninth orders (between the Cherubim and Seraphim; the Thrones represent hope, the Cherubim faith, and the Seraphim love). From that point onward there is no more intellection. Obviously, Thomas Gallus has an "affective" epistemology, but it rests on a large substructure in which knowledge is a load-bearing element.

137. Walsh, " 'Sapientia Christianorum,' " p. 103.

138. Ibid., p. VI.

139. Walsh, *Pursuit of Wisdom,* p. 310, n. 5, points out that Hugh's Latin is "often clumsy."

140. Cf. the beginning of par. 45, regarding the transferral of "proprietates vocabuli ad sensum anagogicum" as a way of summarizing the method of meditation outlined in par. 14–44.

141. Many, but not all of these, have been pointed out in the notes to the translation, below. See, for example, *via unitiva,* par. 29.

142. For instance, the illuminative path (ch. 2) has five columns (Peltier, 8b–11a) of "theory" followed by eighteen columns of "praxis" (Peltier 11b–20a).

143. Within the Carthusian tradition they are found in Guigo I, but are common to the monastic tradition reaching all the way back to the Egyptian Desert Fathers and their Western interpreter, John Cassian.

144. In this regard, Walach is completely off the mark when he asserts that Augustine and Bonaventure had room for a purely literal reading of Scripture and creation, whereas Hugh sees an anagogy lurking everywhere. Nothing could be more Augustinian and Bonaventurian than to see every created thing and every creature as an anagogic signpost to God. See Walach, *Notitia,* pp. 148–52.

145. Guigo II, *Lettre sur la vie contemplative (L'échelle des moines); Douze Meditationes,* ed. Edmund Colledge and James Walsh, trans. by a Carthusian, SC 163; ET by Edmund Colledge and James Walsh, *Ladder of Monks: A Letter on the Contemplative Life, and Twelve Meditations* (Garden City, N.Y.: Doubleday-Image, 1978; reprinted Kalamazoo: Cistercian Publications, 1981), ch. 4–7.

146. The threefold metaphor of farmer, merchant, and soldier is taken from John Cassian, *Conferences,* Conference I.2 (SC 42:79; ET by Luibheid in CWS, p. 38; NPNF-2, 11:295).

147. See the discussion of *amor, caritas, gratia,* and *industria* in Johnson, *Iste Pauper Clamavit,* p. 219.

148. "How unitive wisdom disposes every contemplative affection for merit is plain, since, as often as the human spirit moves directly into God, she merits [*promeretur*] eternal life. As often as the soul disposed by wisdom wishes, she can actually be swept up by rapid movements that are more fleeting than tongue can tell. By merit she is thus raised up in glory by one of these surging motions. Since each merit corresponds to a particular glory (except for the essential crown, the crown of the vision of divine beauty), this confirms that the soul accumulates innumerable crowns through this wisdom" (*via unitiva,* par. 27). See Dieter Mertens, "Jakob von Paradies (1381–1465) über die mystische Theologie," in *Kartäusermystik und -mystiker,* vol. 5, Analecta Cartusiana, 55.5 (Salzburg: Institut für Anglistik und Amerikanistik, 1982), pp. 31–46, at pp. 41–43. Heiko A. Oberman, "Das tridentinische Rechtfertigungsdekret im Lichte spätmittelalterlicher Theologie," *Zeitschrift für Theologie und Kirche* 61 (1964): 251–82, expanded version in *Concilium Tridentinum,* ed. R. Bäumer (Darmstadt: Wissenschaftliche Buchgesellschaft, 1979), 301–40, has argued that some late medieval theologians made a distinction between *promereri* and *mereri,* reserving the former for merit in a strict sense (*meritum de condigno*). Even Oberman points out that evidence for this distinction is ambiguous in the late Middle Ages. Hugh of Balma does not appear to use *promereri* (see *via unitiva,* par. 72, 79, 107) in any specific sense as distinct from *mereri.*

149. See Heiko A. Oberman, *The Harvest of Medieval Theology* (Cambridge, Mass.: Harvard University Press, 1963; 3rd ed. Durham, N.C.: Labyrinth Press,

NOTES TO INTRODUCTION

1983), pp. 47–49, 131–45; Berndt Hamm, *Pactum, Promissio, Ordinatio: Freiheit und Selbstbindung Gottes in der scholastischen Gnadenlehre*, Beiträge zur historischen Theologie, 54 (Tübingen: J. C. B. Mohr, 1977). See also Burrows, *Jean Gerson*.

150. Geoffrey Koziol, *Begging Pardon and Favor: Ritual and Political Order in Early Medieval France* (Ithaca: Cornell, 1992), is a rich resource for beginning to understand the symbolism of supplication in medieval culture, including monastic culture.

151. For further development of this theme in Carthusian theology, see Martin, *Fifteenth-Century Carthusian Reform*, ch. 4.

152. See Kurt Ruh, "*Amor deficiens* und *amor desiderii*."

153. On importunate prayer, see John Cassian, *Conferences*, IX.34 (SC 54: 66–71; ET by Luibheid in CWS, p. 120–23; NPNF-2, 11:398–400).

154. Guigo de Ponte makes much the same point, calling on the soul to be *improbus* and citing Virgil (via Bernard of Clairvaux) as corroboration. *On Contemplation*, I.13.

155. For a discussion of the monastic tradition and Protestant misunderstandings of it, see Martin, *Fifteenth-Century Carthusian Reform*, ch. 4; cf. Karlfried Froehlich, "Justification Language and Grace: The Charge of Pelagianism in the Middle Ages," in *Probing the Reformed Tradition: Historical Studies in Honor of Edward A. Dowey, Jr.*, ed. Elsie Ann McKee and Brian G. Armstrong (Louisville, Ky.: Westminster/John Knox, 1989), pp. 21–47.

156. " 'Sapientia Christianorum,' " 30: "Et hec est portio Marie, que nemo novit nisi qui accipit: sapientia Christianorum, quam apostolos loquebatur inter perfectos: in cor nullum ascendit, sed descendit: sapientia celestis, que de sursum est." [And this is Mary's portion, which no one can know without receiving it: the wisdom of Christians which the apostles proclaimed in the midst of the perfected. It does not ascend in any heart, rather, it descends, for it is a celestial wisdom that comes from above.] These phrases occur so frequently in Gallus's writings that Walsh does not give a specific citation for this particular quotation. Cf. Walsh, "Thomas Gallus et l'effort contemplatif."

157. The following outline is based on Dupont's summary in the introduction to his critical edition; another summary is found in Walsh, *The Cloud of Unknowing*, CWS (1981), pp. 23–26. Denis of Rijkel also summarized it in his own book *De contemplatione*, bk. 2, ch. 11.

158. Hogg, "Hugh of Balma and Guigo du Pont," p. 84.

159. Moreover, Guigo may have initially intended to write only what is now book one, as the concluding paragraph to chapter seven hints. Three of the five manuscripts give this paragraph more tentativeness than do the other two: "There is another manner, or rather, another type, of being affected toward God, which takes place almost daily in an anagogically uplifted soul. You may *perhaps* find fuller truth about this elsewhere, *perhaps* in one of the two books that follow." What may have originally been a reference to other people's writings about contemplative union could have been altered later to become a cross-reference to the two subsequently composed books.

160. Summarized most helpfully by Hogg, p. 87. The scholastic sources include Peter Lombard, William of Auxerre, William Perauldus, Hugo Ripelin of Strasbourg, Bonaventure, Thomas Aquinas.

161. Walach, *Notitia*, pp. 210–15.

162. See Martin, *Fifteenth-Century Carthusian Reform*, pp. 113–34.

163. "These things also apply to the ninth step (constant meditation), where the godly spirit is already for the most part free from pressing and oppressive thoughts and experiences purity and tranquillity of heart. She is thus suited in a certain sense for steady meditation on the divine will and sometimes can taste and attain the affected, clinging fruition of God that most properly belongs to the eleventh step" (I.8, Dupont ed., p. 146).

164. Guigo I, *Meditationes*, nos. 16, 19, SC 308: 108; ET by Jolin, pp. 8–9, modified; cf. ET by Mursell pp. 66–67.

165. Dupont, p. 152.

166. In what follows I am dependent on the exhaustive manuscript researches of Kent Emery, Jr., now published as *Dionysii Cartusiensis Opera Selecta*, vol. 1: *Prolegomena: Bibliotheca manuscripta*, in 2 vols., CCCM 121A, 121B (Turnhout: Brepols, 1991), vol. 2, pp. 589–702. Page numbers refer to specific portions of this lengthy discussion.

167. Ibid., vol. 2, p. 591.

168. For a close comparison of Hugh of Balma (based on the Peltier edition) and this anonymous treatise, which considerably augments and expands Hugh's purgative section, see ibid., pp. 602–5.

169. Ibid., pp. 606–14.

170. Mertens, "Jakob von Paradies," and Johann Auer, "Die *Theologia Mystica* des Kartäusers Jakob von Jüterbog (+ 1465)," in *Die Kartäuser in Österreich*, vol. 2, ed. James Hogg, Analecta Cartusiana, 83.2 (Salzburg: Institut für Anglistik und Amerikanistik, 1981), pp. 19–52. The treatise was included in Jacob de Paradiso, *Opuscula inedita*, ed. Stanislaw A. Porebski, Textus et studia historiam theologiae in Polonia excultae spectantia, 5 (Warsaw: Akademia theologii Katolickiej, 1978), pp. 251–312.

171. Kleineidam, pp. 188–89.

172. For Kempf's writings, see Martin, *Fifteenth-Century Carthusian Reform*, appendix A, cf. pp. 314, 405.

173. A quick glance at the appendix in Jellouschek, Ruello, Barbet, eds., *Tractatus de mystica theologia* (1973), listing parallels and sources for Kempf, pp. 423–71, might imply that Kempf depended heavily on Hugh of Balma. Many of the references, however, have to do with parallels, rather than dependence.

174. See Robert Ritter von Srbik, *Maximilian I. und Gregor Reisch*, ed. Alphons Lhotsky, Archiv für österreichische Geschichte, 122.2 (Vienna: Böhlau, 1961), p. 21.

175. In addition to Emery's detailed discussion of the purgative way, see B. Spaapen's thorough, though perhaps overdrawn, summary of Denis's use of the

NOTES TO INTRODUCTION

seven industries found in the unitive way: "Kartuizer-Vroomheid en Ignatiaanse Spiritualiteit," *Ons geestelijk Erf* 30 (1956): 339–66. For the passages see Denis of Rijkel, *De contemplatione*, I.21, 24 (*Doctoris Ecstatici D. Dionysii Cartusiensis Opera Omnia*, 41 [1912]: 157B, 162B), III.11 (41:266A), III.14–15 (41:270AD, 271–74); *De fonte lucis ac semitis vitae*, art. 4–5, 25 (*Opera*, 41:99C, 101B, 130C).

176. This text is from the conclusion to Denis's *De contemplatione* (*Opera*, 41: 274), quoted by Emery in *Dionysii Cartusiensis Opera Selecta*, p. 710; cf. the discussion in Emery, "Twofold Wisdom," 129–33.

177. Walsh, *Cloud*, CWS, pp. 19–23.

178. *Notitia*, pp. 157–84.

179. Ibid., pp. 185–99. Walach believes Hugh of Balma may even be the author of interpolations in the longer version of the *Stimulus amoris*.

180. Ibid., pp. 200–6.

181. Ibid., pp. 206–9.

182. Ibid., pp. 236–39: Hugh is a "Vorbild" for Eckhart, even if Eckhart did not know Hugh's treatise.

183. Ibid., pp. 230–33, based largely on the fact that Hugh of Balma represents a non-Thomist, intuitive epistemology.

184. Ibid., pp. 239–40. Walach points to the commonplace "If you lack sorrow for sin, at least beg God for sorrow at your lack of sorrow" as evidence of John of Kastl's use of *Viae Sion*.

185. Walsh, ed., *The Cloud of Unknowing*, CWS (1981), introduction passim; Walsh, ed., *The Pursuit of Wisdom*, CWS (1988), pp. 310–13, documents some direct quotes; Lees, *Negative Language*, pp. 308–60, argues that Hugh is an even more important parallel than Thomas Gallus.

186. Clark, "The *Cloud of Unknowing* and the Contemplative Life," in *Die Kartäuser und ihre Welt: Kontakte und gegenseitige Einflüsse*, Analecta Cartusiana, 63.1 (Salzburg: Institut für Anglistik und Amerikanistik, 1993), pp. 44–65, at 53–54.

187. Hogg, "Hugh of Balma and Guigo de Ponte," p. 69.

188. For recent summaries see Mark S. Burrows, *Jean Gerson and "De Consolatione Theologiae (1418)"* (Tübingen: J. C. B. Mohr, 1991), pp. 23–27, 143–48, 191. Cf. Edmund Colledge and J. C. Marler, "*Tractatus Magistri Johannis Gerson de Mistica Theologia:* St. Pölten Diözesanarchiv MS. 25," *Mediaeval Studies* 41 (1979): 354–86.

189. Brian Patrick McGuire, "Loving the Holy Order: Jean Gerson and the Carthusians," in *Die Kartäuser und ihre Welt: Kontakte und gegenseitige Einflüsse*, Analecta Cartusiana, 63.1 (Salzburg: Institut für Anglistik und Amerikanistik, 1993), pp. 100–39.

190. See Th. Mertens, "Het aspirative gebed bij Hendrik Mande: Invloed van Hugo de Balma?" *Ons geestelijk Erf* 58 (1984): 300–21.

191. Krynen, *L'Aventure*, p. 105. See the brief quotations in English in E. Allison Peers, *The Mystics of Spain* (London: Allen and Unwin, 1951), pp. 46–48.

NOTES TO INTRODUCTION

192. Described by Walsh in *The Pursuit of Wisdom*, pp. 287–96, with a transcription of the Hugh of Balma excerpt and another excerpt from an anonymous tract on repentance and grace. Cf. Lees, *Negative Language*, pp. 191–92.

193. See Margot Schmidt's discussion of Rudolf in "Nikolaus von Kues im Gespräch mit den Tegernseer Mönchen über Wesen und Sinn der Mystik," in *Das Sehen Gottes nach Nikolaus von Kues*. Akten des Symposions in Trier vom 25. bis 27. September 1986, ed. Rudolf Haubst (= *Mitteilungen und Forschungsbeiträge der Cusanus-Gesellschaft*, 18) (Trier: Paulinus-Verlag, 1989), pp. 25–49. In her article "de Biberach, Rodolphe," *DSAM* 13 (1987): 846–50, she omits significant discussion of Hugh of Balma's influence.

194. *DSAM*, col. 872.

195. Alois Haas in *Christian Spirituality*, vol. 2: *High Middle Ages and Reformation*, ed. Jill Raitt et al. (New York: Crossroad, 1987), pp. 162–63, says "Harphius tried to translate Ruysbroeck's speculative mysticism into an affective mysticism, and in doing so he frequently followed Hugh of Balma. The mystical vision of the divine essence as the third step beyond the active and contemplative life is designated as *superessentialis* (*overweselic*); it is characterized as pure gift and by passivity. The way to it is shown through affective love and the imitation of Christ" (*Christian Spirituality: High Middle Ages and Reformation* [New York: Crossroad, 1987], pp. 162–63). See also the assessment by Emery, *Dionysii Cartusiensis Opera Selecta*, pp. 705: "The foundation of Herp's writing, however, . . . is the mystical theology of Hugh of Balma." Emery's assessment is based on fairly general criteria; we still lack an adequately detailed study of the relationship between Herp and Balma.

196. See Pablo-Maroto; Guinan, "Carthusian Prayer," pp. 314–16, 371ff.; Hogg, "Hugh of Balma and Guigo du Pont," p. 69; Andrès Martín, *Recogidos*, pp. 70–76. See also the detailed, careful study by Jean Orcibal, *Saint Jean de la Croix et les Mystiques Rhéno-flamands*, Présence du Carmel, 6 (Bruges, Paris: Desclée de Brouwer, 1966), citing the even more thorough work of Jean Krynen in his unpublished 1955 Paris dissertation. Krynen has since published a book on the same subject (*L'aventure*, 1990). I have not seen the dissertation.

197. ". . . libro fundamental en la historia de nuestra espiritualidad"; "Realmente Balma es una de las claves de la espiritualidad peninsular." *Recogidos*, pp. 48, 75.

198. "Hugo de Balma es matizado y desintelectualizado por el traductor y educido a su esencia en los recolectorios franciscanos." *Recogidos*, p. 75. The later Spanish versions, beginning in 1543, were attributed entirely to Bonaventure and offered a more loosely paraphrased version.

199. See Andrès Martín, *Recogidos*, p. 119; Orcibal, *Jean de la Croix* (1966), notes that it is difficult to distinguish Herp and Hugh of Balma in Osuna's work. See pp. 25–30. See also Fidèle de Ros, *Un maître de sainte Thérèse, le P. François d'Osuna: Sa vie, son oeuvre, sa doctrine spirituelle* (Paris: Beauchesne, 1936), p. 361.

200. Translated and introduced by Mary Giles, but without any direct reference to Hugh of Balma.

NOTES TO INTRODUCTION

201. Andrès Martín, *Recogidos*, p. 174.

202. Andrès Martín, *Recogidos*, pp. 212ff. "No es tarea fácil distinguir si las citas implícitas que señala T. Martín como de Herp en Osuna son del franciscano de los Países Bajos o del cartujo Hugo de Balma, en quien se inspira tantas veces." Krynen, *L'aventure*, pp. 176–77, thinks the influence of Herp was paramount, and that Herp gives a "curious interpretation" of Hugh of Balma in arriving at his idea of a "path of perfect repose." The relevant passage in which Bernardino cites Hendrik Herp and Hugh of Balma by name (Henry, rather than Hugh) is available in English in Peers, *The Mystics of Spain*, p. 50: "Our own part in this sovereign operation is difficult in the beginning, but if we persevere in this upraising of our affective nature with all our might, we reach that degree of facility of which high contemplatives say that the well-schooled soul can rise to it in a moment, almost as often as it will, and become united with Him through love. And concerning this St. Denis says (and Herp and Henry of Balma, both contemplatives, confirm it) that in the practised soul this happens as often as it pleases, and with such facility that they cannot predict it."

203. Andrès Martín, *Recogidos*, pp. 282, 289–90. See the excerpts on aspirative prayer in Peers, *Mystics of Spain*, pp. 106–8.

204. Andrès Martín, *Recogidos*, p. 341.

205. Ibid., p. 71.

206. Ibid., pp. 392–93, 443–49.

207. Krynen, *L'aventure*, pp. 166–67: "Nul doute, Nadal connaît bien son Balma et son Gerson. . . ." See also William V. Bangert, S. J., *Jerome Nadal, S. J., 1507–1580: Tracking the First Generation of Jesuits*, ed. and completed by Thomas M. McCoog (Chicago: Loyola University Press, 1992).

208. Andrès Martín, *Recogidos*, pp. 459, 483. For other religious orders, see ibid., pp. 538, 584.

209. See Ignatius of Loyola, *The Autobiography*, ch. 1, par. 12, trans. in *The Spiritual Exercises and Selected Works*, ed. George E. Ganss, S. J., CWS series (New York: Paulist Press, 1991), p. 72. Cf. Jean Beyer, "Saint Ignace de Loyola chartreux," *Nouvelle revue théologique* 78 (1956): 937–51.

210. Spaapen, "Kartuizer-Vroomheid," part 1.

211. Orcibal, *Rencontre;* Andrès Martín, *Recogidos*, pp. 652, 658.

212. See Orcibal, *Saint Jean de la Croix*, p. 163, n. 1; pp. 180–81; cf. Hogg, "Hugh of Balma and Guigo du Pont," pp. 69–70, for additional names and literature on Hugh's impact in Spain.

213. Andrès Martín, *Recogidos*, pp. 72, 212–27.

214. Literature is cited in ibid., p. 73.

215. Hogg, "Hugh of Balma and Guigo du Pont," p. 70.

216. Hugh of Balma, 16 citations; Gerson, 16; Bernard of Clairvaux, 9; Denis the Carthusian 8; Hendrik Herp, 3. Statistics from Erb, *Arnold*, pp. 132–43.

217. See Walter Baier, *Untersuchungen zu den Passionsbetrachtungen in der*

NOTES TO INTRODUCTION

Vita Christi des Ludolfs von Sachsen, 3 vols., AC, 44 (Salzburg: Institut für Anglistik und Amerikanistik, 1977), pp. 292-95, 339-61.

218. See Emmerich Raitz von Frentz, "Ludolphe le Chartreux et les exercices de S. Ignace de Loyola," *Revue d'ascetique et de mystique* 25 (1949): 375-88; cf. Baier, *Untersuchungen*, pp. 172-86.

219. For the general influence of Ludolf's work, see Baier, 165-91.

220. Ignatius of Loyola, *The Spiritual Exercises and Selected Works*, p. 21. The quotations from Ludolf's preface on p. 22 are, in contrast, indeed Ludolf's own words, not Guigo's.

221. See above, p. 15.

222. Emery, *Dionysii Cartusiensis Opera Selecta*, p. 27, n. 59.

223. *On Contemplation*, III.6, Dupont ed., pp. 282-83. Cf. III.2 (p. 262) and III.5 (p. 277), and my comments on Dupont's notes in my notes to the translation of these passages in Guigo.

224. Walsh in his introduction to his translation of *The Cloud*, pp. 23-26, says Methley knew Guigo's work. See "Hugh of Balma and Guigo du Pont," 88, citing his own published work on the Latin *Cloud*.

225. See the summary by François Vandenbroucke in Jean Leclercq, François Vandenbroucke, and Louis Bouyer, *A History of Christian Spirituality*, vol. 2, trans. by the Benedictines of Holme Eden Abbey (New York: Seabury, 1968), pp. 536-41.

226. Note the section from Hugh of Balma, *Roads to Zion*, trans. James Walsh in *The Pursuit of Wisdom*, CWS, pp. 302-10, constituting most of par. 82-112 of the *via unitiva* section in the present translation; cf. the translation of the prologue and "Difficult Question" by Jasper Hopkins, *Nicholas of Cusa's Dialectical Mysticism*, pp. 369-92.

227. When the present volume went to press, the Sources Chrétiennes volume had been announced for publication late in 1995. I have not seen the critical apparatus.

228. Even then, one would have to reconstitute it from the critical apparatus.

229. A list of errata uncovered in the process and corrected in this translation was published in *Spiritualität Heute und Gestern*, vol. 13, Analecta Cartusiana, 35 (Salzburg: Institut für Anglistik und Amerikanistik, 1991), pp. 125-26.

230. See Virgil, *Aeneid*, VIII. 109: "terrentur visu subito cunctique relictis consurgunt mensis" ("with terrorstruck visage, they all jumped up from the abandoned tables").

231. Ruh, *Amor deficiens*, p. 88.

232. Walsh, *Pursuit of Wisdom*, p. 310, notes that *speculatio* can vary in meaning depending on whether one derives it from *specula* (a watchtower) or *speculum* (mirror).

The Roads to Zion Mourn: Prologue

1. A passage in David of Augsburg, *De exterioris et interioris hominis compositione secundum triplicem statum; incipientium, proficientium, et perfectorum libri tres*, II.5, ed. by the College of St. Bonaventure (Quaracchi: Collegium S. Bonaven-

276

turae, 1899), pp. 85–87, resembles Hugh's opening lament here: Having abandoned the pursuit of virtues, the perfection of holiness and of wisdom and *pietas* (the worship of God), which are most useful and free of anxiety, a man, especially someone in a religious order, pursues less useful things that excite the curiosity and make one troubled over many things (Lk 10:41). It includes a definition of *pietas* as worship of God by which we "seek to know, love, have, and please God." David of Augsburg (ca. 1200–1272) was a Franciscan whose writings were very popular in the late Middle Ages.

2. The word used here is *curiosius*, an adverbial form in the comparative that can mean anything from "more carefully" to "more fussily." Hugh here indulges in a wordplay on the "vain curiosity" he has been deploring.

3. The last sentence in par. 3 is not found in the Peltier edition.

4. Cf. Bernard of Clairvaux, *Sermons on the Song of Songs*, sermons 3–8, trans. Kilian Walsh in CF 4: 16–52.

5. In Latin, *superenatat*. Cf. the "Difficult Question," par. 43, below, for the return of this imagery.

6. Note that both paths, the shorter and longer exposition of the Our Father, are examples of anagogy, i.e., both of them deal with the spiritual sense beyond the literal.

7. Antiphon from Sir 24:5 [24:3], the first of the great "O Antiphons" that precede the *Magnificat* at Vespers in the week before Christmas.

8. This corresponds to *via unitiva*, part A (par. 1–29), below.

9. See *via unitiva*, part B (esp. par. 38–54) below.

10. *Quasi infinita*, cf. "*almost* countless number of lines," below.

11. This corresponds to *via unitiva* part D (par. 82–115), below, the commentary on Pseudo-Denis's *Mystical Theology*, rather than part C. The fact that the prologue places this commentary ahead of the section on the eight *industriae* (*via unitiva*, part C), an inversion of the order these two sections occupy in the body of the work, is a key argument in Harald Walach's claim that *Viae Sion* was compiled from several separate treatises.

12. This corresponds to *via unitiva*, part C (par. 58–81), below.

13. This corresponds to the "Difficult Question" with which the treatise concludes.

The Roads to Zion Mourn: Concerning the Path of Cleansing

1. The clause "since both . . . same wisdom" is missing in the Peltier edition.

2. The Peltier edition adds here: "As Blessed Denis says in the *Angelic Hierarchy*." Omission of the names of authorities is characteristic of the group B (Austrian) manuscripts followed by Ruello in his edition.

3. The Peltier text has "to the highest bread."

4. The Peltier text has "to a practical rather than a theoretical illumination,"

which does not conform to Hugh's repeated insistence elsewhere that praxis must precede theory.

5. Cf. Wis 7:27.

6. The Peltier edition adds: "or yearning" (*divino subsidio vel desiderio*).

7. The Peltier text, based on the Franciscan editions, substitutes "ad religionem Fratrum Minorum" for "ad religionem Carthusii Ordinis." It also drops the reference to the priestly office. In subsequent lines, the Franciscan interpolator failed to remove the reference to the *columba in deserto*, a telltale reference to the Carthusians, but tried to make it applicable to the mendicants by adding "in deserto, *videlicet secessum contemplationis*," i.e., making the explicit reference to the Carthusian "desert" a mere metaphor for contemplative withdrawal. This strategy was not unusual in late medieval mendicant and lay spirituality. See Thomas J. Renna, "Wyclif's Attacks on the Monks," in *From Ockham to Wyclif*, ed. Anne Hudson and Michael Wilks, Studies in Church History, Subsidia 5 (Oxford: Basil Blackwell for the Ecclesiastical History Society, 1987), pp. 267–80.

8. *Segregati a via saeculari, veluti columba vel turtur in deserto.* "Segregati" is not found in the Peltier edition.

9. A theology of meekness was characteristic of monastic spirituality, but meekness, based on Christ's kenotic example (Phil 2:6–111), was not the unremittingly shameful thing it has become in a modern world based on sheer power. Some understanding of these dynamics is essential to an understanding of the typically Carthusian theology enunciated here. See Dennis D. Martin, *Fifteenth-Century Carthusian Reform: The World of Nicholas Kempf*, Studies in the History of Christian Thought, 49 (Leiden: E. J. Brill, 1992). See also Ruh, "*Amor deficiens*," of which I was unaware when I published my book on Kempf.

10. The Franciscan editor whose text is represented in the Peltier edition interpolates here, alongside the clear references to the Carthusian charism of the eremitical life in imitation of John the Baptist and Jesus Christ, two characteristics of mendicant spirituality: "et in maxima paupertate per mundum praedicavit, et saluti omnium ardentissime intendit." Together, they constitute a polemical attack on Carthusian contemplative withdrawal into the desert, asserting that the mendicant charism of public preaching seeks the salvation of all, thus implying that the Carthusian flight into the wilderness abandons the mass of sinners to damnation. For a discussion of this polemic in late medieval monastic and secular clergy circles, see Martin, *Fifteenth-Century Carthusian Reform*, ch. 6; see also the note to *via unitiva*, par. 69, below.

11. "Sed si hoc [i.e., to destroy me] tuae benignitati non placet," i.e., "should it not please your kindness to destroy me"—the language here is that of a king issuing a decree: *placet* ("it pleases [the king to decree thus]") was a technical term in ancient and medieval government.

12. "Qui de me vindictam accipiat"—*vindicta* can refer to the rod used in a ceremony of manumission of a slave, a sign of defense and protection, or simply a word meaning revenge or punishment. Although medieval use tended toward the

idea of punishment, the most plausible sense here is that he is handing over to the angel his own liberty and self-defense, i.e., entering into a servile relationship to God. The angel could scarcely be receiving the rod of punishment from the sinner.

13. "Tamen hoc quod in me est faciam," a reference to the well-known phrase "facere quod in se est," i.e., doing what one can to save oneself, which, in this instance is to enter humbly, like a worthless thief, as a slave, into God's service. It was common in the ancient and medieval world for pardoned criminals to be considered slaves and servants of the person who had pardoned them.

14. See par. 2, above, where humility is offered as a remedy for the sinner's contempt for God, and bitter sorrow for sins is a remedy for the sinner's former delight in sins.

15. Here Hugh enunciates the classic Latin Christian soteriology of a restoration not only to the lost innocence of paradise, as taught so clearly by the Greek patristic tradition, but a *restoration* to something greater, a *renovatio in melius*. On this subject see Gerhart B. Ladner, *The Idea of Reform: Its Impact on Christian Thought and Action in the Age of the Fathers* (Cambridge, Mass.: Harvard University Press, 1959; reprinted Harper Torchbooks, 1967), esp. pp. 153–62.

16. "Sufficit quando homo facit quod in se est"—another instance of the "facere quod in se est" theology.

17. Vulgate: *decora*; Douay-Rheims: "comely."

18. *Vestigia*, footsteps, tracks, traces. Hugh draws on the very Augustinian tradition, which is common to much of patristic theology, of the entire creation as a forest of signs pointing to God. For a discussion, see Ladner, *Idea of Reform*; for a contemporary parallel, see Bonaventure, *The Soul's Journey to God* (*Itinerarium Mentis in Deum*), available in various translations, including the Classics of Western Spirituality Bonaventure volume (1978), ed. Ewert Cousins.

19. For the Carthusian role in the origin of the Rosary, see Herbert Thurston, "Our Popular Devotions II: The Rosary IV, The Rosary amongst the Carthusians," *The Month* 96 (1900): 513–27; Karl-Josef Klinkhammer, *Adolf von Essen und seine Werke: Der Rosenkranz in der geschichtlichen Situation seiner Entstehung und in seinem bleibenden Anliegen; Eine Quellenforschung*, Frankfurter theologische Studien, 13 (Frankfurt a. M.: Josef Knecht, 1972), cf. Klinkhammer, "Zur ursprünglichen Spiritualität des Rosenkranz-Betens," in *Spiritualität Heute und Gestern*, vol. 2, Analecta Cartusiana, 35.2 (Salzburg: Institut für Anglistik und Amerikanistik, 1983), pp. 143–59; [A Carthusian], *El Santo Rosario en la Cartuja*, Analecta Cartusiana, 103 (Salzburg: Institut für Anglistik und Amerikanistik, 1983). Although the "invention" of the Rosary has been ascribed to the Carthusian Dominic of Prussia (d. 1460) at Trier since the work of Thurston and Klinkhammer, a key development came with Heinrich Egher von Kalkar (d. 1408), who combined the idea of meditating on mysteries in the life of Christ and the Virgin Mary with the division of the Rosary into decades. Hugh, a century earlier than Heinrich Egher von Kalkar, represents the general stage of development for his time. In 1977, Andreas Heinz discovered a manuscript with a Rosary text composed of meditations on the life of Christ that

was a century older than that of Dominic of Prussia. See Andreas Heinz, "Die Zisterzienser und die Anfänge des Rosenkranzes," *Analecta Cisterciensia* 33 (1977): 262–309; summarized in Anne Winston, "Tracing the Origins of the Rosary: German Vernacular Texts," *Speculum* 68 (July 1993): 619–36. Cf. André Fracheboud, "Les antécédents cisterciens du Rosaire," *Collectanea Cisterciensia* 56.2 (1994): 153–70. Less developed forms of the devotion are found in manuscripts as old as the twelfth century. Scholars still agree, however, that Dominic of Prussia deserves credit for establishing the number of mysteries at fifty and that his Rosary text was disseminated in thousands of copies made by Carthusians.

The Roads to Zion Mourn: Concerning the Illuminative Way

1. *Ascensiones* in the Gallican Psalter on which the Vulgate known to Hugh was based is *sacra itinera* in the twentieth-century revised Vulgate, based on the Hebrew text. In the modern Revised Standard Version the latter yields "highways of Zion," i.e., a close parallel to the verse in Lamentations from which Hugh took his title.

2. If one thinks of a window as consisting of panes of glass, an open window would be one in which the glass has been opened to let air through. Translucent coverings of glass or mica were not unknown even in the Roman Empire, but translucent windows that admitted light even when closed were the exception rather than the rule. Thus, in employing this metaphor Hugh probably had in mind an opening in a wall that could not let light in when covered. Even the Latin word *fenestra*, in its root meaning, refers to an opening, not to glass or anything else that fills the space. We still preserve this meaning in the English verb *to fenestrate*.

3. *De divinis nominibus*, ch. 1; *Dionysiaca*, 1:18; PG 3:589B; CWS trans. by Colm Luibheid and Paul Rorem, *Pseudo-Dionysius: Complete Works* (New York, Paulist Press, 1987), pp. 50–51. *Letter Nine to Titus* is also generally relevant here. See Luibheid, pp. 280–88; PG 3:1104–1113.

4. Cf. *Letter Nine to Titus*, par. 1; *Dionysiaca*, 1:626–27; PG 1104C; Luibheid, p. 281.

5. The manuscripts on which the Ruello text is based include a direct reference to *Letter Nine to Titus* here; the Peltier edition notes it in a footnote. Hugh's precise words ("verte te ad radium") are not found in any of the Latin versions of the letter, not even in Thomas Gallus's paraphrase. However, the general point he is making here is found in par. 1; *Dionysiaca*, p. 715, par. 637ff.; PG 3:1105Dff.; Luibheid, p. 283. Walach, *Notitia*, pp. 128–29, has located this quote in Bonaventure, *De triplici via*, although he does not give an exact citation. See Bonaventure, *De triplici via*, ch. 1, par. 4, in *Doctoris Seraphici S. Bonaventurae Opera Omnia*, vol. 8: *Opuscula varia ad theologiam mysticam* (Quaracchi: Collegium S. Bonaventurae, 1898), pp. 2–27, at p. 4. The Quaracchi editors note that some manuscripts of *De triplici via* attribute the quotation to Pseudo-Denis's letter to Timothy; others attribute it to the letter to Titus.

6. Peltier: mercy (*clementia*); Ruello: wisdom (*sapientia*).

7. "Goodness" (*bonitas*) is omitted in the Peltier edition.

8. "Unitive" is omitted in the Peltier edition.

9. *De mystica theologia*, ch. 1; *Dionysiaca*, 568.1 [Sarracenus translation], cf. the paraphrase by Thomas Gallus, ibid., 709, par. 568; PG 3:997B; Luibheid trans., 135. This passage is cited throughout part D of the *via unitiva* section and the "Difficult Question," below.

10. Ibid. Here Hugh clearly is following the Sarracenus translation, which is close to that of Eriugena at this point, but quite different from Thomas Gallus's paraphrase. See *Dionysiaca*, 568.2 to 569.1, cf. 709, par. 569; PG 3:1000A; Luibheid, p. 135.

11. The manuscripts on which the Ruello edition is based have *apparet* here; the Peltier edition has the more tentative subjunctive form, *appareat* ["might shine forth"], with *apparet* noted as a variant.

12. The Austrian manuscripts followed by Ruello have *vita* here; the Peltier edition has *via*. Subsequent references could refer to either the path or the life, since they use adjectival forms or pronouns rather than repeating the noun. Practically speaking, *via* and *vita* are virtually equivalent here, and a scribal variant is not at all surprising. I have employed both nouns in my translation.

13. This phrase appears in Peltier, even though the initial reference to the illuminative life corresponding to the Cherubim was omitted in the edition, whether out of an intention to streamline the text or out of oversight.

14. The Peltier edition has *theoricae* here; Ruello has *theologicae*.

15. Here Hugh applies the fourfold exegetical scheme common in the Middle Ages: literal, moral (tropological), allegorical, and anagogic. Note that, in his second form of anagogy, he combines the moral and allegorical sense to yield a threefold division. His point here is that all the senses beyond the literal are anagogy. Although the fourfold division is well known to modern students, a simple twofold division—literal and spiritual (mystical, anagogical)—was also common among medieval exegetes. See Henri de Lubac, *Exégèse médiéval: Les quatre sens de l'Ecriture*, 2 parts in 4 vols. (Paris: Aubier, 1959–1964), part 1; Beryl Smalley, "Use of the 'Spiritual' Senses of Scripture in Persuasion and Argument by Scholars in the Middle Ages," *Recherches de Théologie ancienne et médiévale* 52 (1985): 44–63.

16. The Peltier edition has *Church Triumphant* here, which makes little sense.

17. Here Hugh combines moral and allegorical senses.

18. The Ruello edition has *sed* here; the Peltier edition has *secundo*, which makes more sense, since a third interpretation of Jerusalem follows below.

19. The Latin term here is *captatur benevolentia infundentis*, referring to the *captatio benevolentiae*, the beginning of a speech or letter that aims at capturing the reader's or listener's goodwill.

20. Note the layering of divisions here: the *captatio benevolentiae* as three parts, three commendations. We are presently in the third, which in turn has three

parts—heaven has three things to commend it. Each of the three is anagogically effective.

21. Cf. Mt 19:7

22. "In odorem unguentorum suorum," literally "her perfumes," but, given the carelessness with which medieval writers observed the distinction between "suus" and "eius," the phrase could be read as "in the odor of his perfumes," i.e., the Bridegroom's perfumes, which would then fit the text of the Canticle.

23. Mt 15:27.

24. Rv 3:20, cf. 3:8, 4:1; Ca 5:2–3.

25. In ecclesiastical Latin, *obfuscantia* meant "degradation, vilification," but, in this context, it also carries inverse overtones of the thought in Ca 5:2–3, where the bride does not open the door to her Lover because she has washed her feet and does not want to sully them.

26. Rv 3:20.

27. Cf. Gn 29:17–28: Leah was *lippos oculos*, "blear-eyed," presumably from a medical condition.

28. 2 Cor 6:14.

29. The Ruello text has *placidam conspectionem* for the Bridegroom in the preceding sentence and *placitam in conspectu* with regard to the human spirit in the present sentence. The difference (*placidus*: peaceful, gentle; *placitus*: pleasant) is slight, and the Peltier edition simply assimilates *placitam* to *placidam*. I have followed the Ruello text here.

30. Cf. Gn 29:17, 28.

31. Cf. Lk 14:10; Mt 20:22–23.

32. *Peccato levitatis*, a play on words, since *levis* can mean both "smooth, delicate, soft" and "light, flexible, trivial, nimble, easy," depending on whether the first vowel is pronounced long or short.

33. Literally, "precious and ponderous gold" (*pretiosissimi et ponderosissimi amoris auro contextis vestimentis*); to translate Hugh's alliteration in Latin into English requires using a word that carries negative connotations and is not normally applied to gold (ponderous). Thus I have opted to sacrifice the alliteration for readability.

34. The Peltier edition has *aspectantes* here: "catching sight of" rather than *acceptantes* as in the Ruello text, which I have followed.

35. Hugh did not quote the last part of this verse, since he assumed that his readers would have completed it effortlessly from memory. It has been supplied here to indicate how it applies to the basic theme of the third part of the *captatio benevolentiae*: adorned with a *variety* of constellations and to the immediately preceding reference to a sinner sullied by a *variety* of vices and now adorned with lovely colors.

36. Hugh uses the word *flesh* in its biblical and patristic sense—the human person's turning, in both body *and* soul, from God toward the creatures. It does not refer merely to physicality.

37. The word *rubigo* normally means "rust," and is often so used by spiritual writers to refer to sin. However, it can mean any kind of blight, scale, tarnish, or excrescence on a variety of substances. The reference to *rubigo* being consumed by fire, rather than grated away by a file, leads to the translation employed here. Cf. Ez 24:11; Mt 6:19–20; Heb 12:29.

38. Cf. Is 25:6; Ps 65 [66]:15; Ps 19:4 [Vulgate only].

39. Cf. Ps 90:1 [91:1], in variant readings.

40. Cf. Rv 19:16.

41. Note how Hugh simply inserts here the anagogical meaning for "heaven" that he had arrived at above, indicating that "anagogical sense" has a certain fixed, metonymic implication for Hugh.

42. The term used here is *proprie*, which has a technical meaning within medieval semantics, of "in a strict sense" or "literally."

43. *Defectus*, i.e., an unmaking, an undeed—in keeping with the Christian tradition that evil is a lack of potential good, a perversion of good. See the discussion of presence and absence, below.

44. The portion in brackets is included in the Peltier edition but not in the manuscripts on which Ruello based his edition. Medieval scribes assumed the readers could complete the quotation on their own. The quotation has been extended here for the convenience of readers.

45. Cf. *via unitiva*, par. 114, below.

46. Cf. Ca 7:11.

47. Reading *specialis* with Ruello rather than *spiritualis* with Peltier.

48. Hugh's comments here would seem to support the main thesis of Bernard McGinn, *The Foundations of Mysticism*, vol. 1 of *The Presence of God: A History of Western Christian Mysticism* (New York: Crossroad, 1992), namely, that Western Christian mysticism, at least, is better understood under the language of presence than of union. See the discussion in the introduction, above.

49. *Hierarcha*, a medieval Latin term for religious leader, sacral leader. Hugh's use of it here may be derived from Pseudo-Dionysius.

50. "Dwelling-place" translates *conversatio*, which produced the now archaic English translation, "our conversation is in heaven," in the Douay-Rheims and King James versions.

51. This paragraph introduces the three final petitions, which, as Hugh pointed out in paragraph 19, above, are requests to be preserved from bad things. Hugh applies "forgive us our debts" to the request to be freed from all venial sin and "lead us not into temptation" to freedom from the *malo periculi*, the danger of temptation. "Deliver us from evil" (petition seven), which one might otherwise interpret as the umbrella for the other two, is here applied by Hugh to a desire to be freed from the penalty of sin.

52. The Peltier edition has *ardentissime* here; Ruello has *adtentissime*.

53. This particular sentence is badly garbled in the Peltier edition.

54. Here, as elsewhere, Hugh plays on ad*ficio* and *facies*.

55. For a discussion of interpretations of this phrase in medieval commentaries, see Martin, *Fifteenth-Century Carthusian Reform*, ch. 4.

56. ". . . et tunc per istam rectificationem et consurrectionem adfectus venialis culpa tanquam gutta aquae cadens in ignem per suam concrescentiam vel adunationem nullo modo importunum sibi valet ingerere nocumentum." We, of course, would say that the drop of water is evaporated, rather than congealed, in order to make it disappear into the fire, but the metaphor works either way.

57. Para. 32 and 33a deal with a commonplace of monastic spirituality. For one example, see Aelred of Rievaulx, *Speculum caritatis* [*Mirror of Charity*], esp. I.27–30, II.1–6.

58. To Hugh's readers, this image would have been clear: To bow the neck low is a reference to being vanquished, humiliated, disgraced, conquered, subjected, whether it is a domesticated animal broken to the plow or a captive at the feet of his conqueror. The image is at least partially lost on modern Westerners, who must therefore make a special effort to grasp its implications.

59. Cf. Eph 2:19.

60. On this commonplace of monastic tradition, see Karl Suso Frank [*Angelikos Bios*]: *Begriffsanalytische und begriffsgeschichtliche Untersuchung zum 'engelgleichen Leben' im frühen Mönchtum*, Beiträge zur Geschichte des alten Mönchtums, 26 (Münster i. Westfalen: Aschendorff, 1964).

61. Hugh's emphasis on separation of body and soul differs from Bernard's insistence that the human soul achieves only imperfect bliss so long as the body is separated from her; after the resurrection of the body, the reembodied human person finally enjoys total beatitude. See *De diligendo Deo*, XI.30–33 [*Bernardi Opera*, 3: 144–47; CF 13, pp. 121–25]. Note the frequent references to the sweet yoke and light burden found in the preceding paragraphs of Bernard's treatise.

62. The Peltier edition has *carnem pinguem* (juicy meat), while the Ruello text has *avem pinguem* (fat fowl).

63. Hugh's language here ("frigoris egestas vel aestus vel calor importunus non sibi ingerant aliquod nocumentum") recalls that of the end of paragraph 31 ("per suam concrescentiam vel adunationem nullo modo importunum sibi valet ingerere nocumentum").

64. On confidence in the mercy of God, see, among others, Bernard of Clairvaux, *Sermons on the Canticle*, e.g., sermon 3, par. 5 (*Bernardi Opera*, 1:17; ET in CF. 14, p. 19).

65. These two verses have subjects in the singular in the Vulgate; Hugh changed the first one to plural in order to fit his context, but left the other in the singular (Ruello text); the Peltier edition assimilated the second to the first.

66. Cf. Rv 3:20.

67. The Peltier edition has a line here that is missing in the Ruello edition. It consists of a series of adjectives expanding on the idea of "endless battle," and thus may well be an editorial interpolation.

68. Based on Peltier, which supplies *dividitur*, here.

69. See par. 2 of the *via purgativa* for this basic medical principle cited by Hugh.

70. Cf. 1 Jn 1:7; Rom 13:13; Jn 11:9, 12:35.

71. Cf. Rom 13:11–14.

72. *De sponsi et sponsae colloquiis vel eorum altercationibus*; "altercatio" can mean a scholastic disputation or some other form of interlocution.

73. *Quaecumque sint ab ultimo centro inferni*; "infernus" can mean simply the place of the dead, the netherworld, or hell. That Hugh means by it "hell" is evident from his comments in par. 54, below, where he clearly distinguishes *infernus* and *purgatorium*.

74. The first few lines in the Peltier edition have been omitted here. They do not appear in the Austrian manuscript tradition and consist of introductory material for the illuminative path in general, repeating some of the themes found at the beginning of the illuminative path. The presence or absence of these sentences is one of the main distinguishing marks of the two main text families discussed by Ruello in the introduction to his Sources Chrétiennes edition.

75. For the monastic roots of this aspirative method in John Cassian and others, see the introduction, above.

76. The reference here is to the second of three stages in a common alternative schema to Pseudo-Denis's cleansing, illuminative, and unitive paths: beginners, those making progress, those who have arrived (incipientes, proficientes, perfecti).

77. This key sentence is missing in the Peltier edition.

78. *Proprietatem vocabuli.*

79. Item one would seem to have to do with the discursive anagogy of par. 13–44; items two and three would seem to have to do with the aspirative anagogy of par. 45–54, below.

80. Note the shift from third person, which characterized the "theoretical" discussion of anagogical hermeneutics in part two, to a first- and second-person dialogue in the "practical" application of those hermeneutics in part three.

81. The classical meaning of *accendo*, the word used here, is to kindle from on top so that the fire might burn downward, in contrast to *succendo*, meaning to kindle from below. The distinction was not always maintained in medieval usage.

82. *Stuppa* [= tow], the coarse, short fibers of flax, used for candle wicks, rope, yarn, etc.

83. A repetition of the section on Our Father, dealt with in par. 46, that is found in the Peltier edition, is omitted in the Austrian text family used by Ruello. It has been omitted in this translation.

84. Cf. par. 18 above, where the same theme occurs. Hugh's aspirative method does not differ in content from the longer, discursive anagogy of par. 13–44. It merely differs in rhetorical style—the aspirative method is of short duration, gasping, direct address. Respect for this style difference has led to longer, more paratactic sentences in the English translation that follows. In paragraphs 48–54, the many phrases missing in the Peltier text yet found in the Austrian manuscripts suggest that

Hugh originally left this section very brief and suggestive; the Austrian copyists then embellished them.

85. See par. 20, above, for the same content in different style.

86. This sentence is missing in the Peltier edition.

87. *Advenias* carries the overtones of a triumphal ceremonial royal entry.

88. *Consentire*, to think together, know together, be of one mind—but not in a purely intellectual or rational way: *Sentire* is to sense, to know experientially.

89. Cf. 2 Cor 3:18.

90. This sentence is missing in the manuscript tradition on which the Peltier text is based, possibly as the result of an eyeskip from "cognoscam" to "cognoscerem."

91. The Peltier edition has "touch."

92. The Peltier text has here "make you, who were once an offense, pleasing to me." This is precisely the great discovery that Martin Luther made in relation to God's righteousness. The Ruello text inverts the phrase at first (make me pleasing to you), then reverses it in the next sentence. For a discussion of the monastic tradition and Protestant misunderstandings of it, see Martin, *Fifteenth-Century Carthusian Reform*, ch. 4.

93. ". . . a malo non tantum poenae infernalis, sed et purgatorii." Hugh uses the term *purgatorium* here, not the more general, abstract concept of purgation (*purgatio*).

94. Cf. 1 Pt 1:12.

The Roads to Zion Mourn: Concerning the Unitive Way

1. "Quae sit" (what it is like, what its nature is) is missing in the Peltier text. This leads to confusion about the illuminative way. As it turns out, the "quae sit" is the long meditative method of anagogy and the practical climbing is the short aspirative anagogy.

2. Hugh does not give the fourth topic, which concludes the unitive way section: how unitive wisdom is taught by God alone (par. 82–115). This is the "theoretical" part of the practice of mystical wisdom, according to par. 18, below, and is in fact a commentary on Pseudo-Denis's *Mystical Theology*, the most clearly distinct portion of *The Roads to Zion*. See the introduction to this volume for the origins of *Roads to Zion* in two or more distinct treatises.

3. Hugh will expand on nearly every word of this text in the first two parts of the unitive way section. The antiphon, based on Sir 24:5ff. [24:3ff.], is the first of the "great O Antiphons" sung before and after the Magnificat at Vespers in the week before Christmas.

4. *On the Divine Names*, ch. 7.3; *Dionysiaca* 1:406; PG 3:872B; Luibheid, p. 109.

5. *Promeretur.* Heiko Oberman has argued that "promereri" meant "to merit fully" in comparison with "mereri," meaning "to merit congruently," for

some fourteenth-century theologians and was thus employed at the Council of Trent. The evidence for this technical theological distinction is ambiguous in the later Middle Ages, and there is no particular reason to think that Hugh was using it in this technical sense here. See the discussion in Heiko A. Oberman, "Das Tridentinische Rechtfertigungsdekret im Lichte spätmittelalterlicher Theologie," *Zeitschrift für Theologie und Kirche* 61 (1964): 251–82, esp. 269–73. Except where noted otherwise, the verbs "deserve" and "merit" are employed in the present translation to denote *promereri*.

6. ". . . *omnia suis rationibus aeternis . . . regulantur.*" The root meaning of *ratio*, conventionally translated as "reason," is "order" or "relation," as is evident from the mathematical term in English, "ratio." Thus this phrase might also be translated more literally as "regulated in an unshakable ordering by his eternal arrangements," or "eternal governance."

7. Here Hugh employs "*in suis ordinibus conquiescant,*" making the meaning of "*in suis aeternis rationibus*" clear.

8. We must keep in mind that *concordia* still meant, for Hugh, "of one heart," and had not yet become a pale synonym for agreement.

9. The reference here is to the conventional medieval understanding of gravity as the tendency of objects to seek their natural place, the place to which they belong. Although medieval scholars spoke of the stone seeking the place it desires or belongs to, they were fully aware that stones are insensate creatures that do not "seek" or "long" in the same sense that a human being does. Cf. par. 24, below.

10. For this common theme in monastic spirituality, see above, *via illuminativa*, par. 32–33, with references to Aelred of Rievaulx's *Mirror of Charity*.

11. Cf. Bonaventure, *Itinerarium mentis in Deum*, VI.6; ET in CWS, *Bonaventure: The Soul's Journey into God; The Tree of Life; The Life of St. Francis*, intro. and trans. by Ewert Cousins (New York: Paulist Press, 1978), p. 115.

12. The Peltier edition follows the Vulgate here with *nidulo* (nest), whereas the Austrian manuscripts followed by the Ruello edition have modified this to *lectulo* (couch).

13. The meaning of the medieval technical theological and psychological term *habit* is difficult to convey succinctly in English. It refers to an established character-attitude-disposition in the human person, whether a "habit of grace" poured into the person at baptism or a capability belonging to a person by nature or acquired by long practice or formation. The essential point is that it has some degree of fixed, established character and is not easily or quickly changed. Such habit-character in the human soul or psyche then underlies the human will, intellect, and other powers. To avoid confusion with the more common meaning of the English word "habit," the Latin *habitus* has been retained in this translation.

14. Peter Lombard, *Sentences*, bk. III, dist. 26. Cf. Walach, *Notitia*, 69.

15. Here Hugh is talking about what we would call the (natural) *sciences*. He assumes that knowledge of the depths of the human psyche belongs to a category of inquiry distinct from the natural sciences, as, indeed, psychology has come to be

reckoned to the social sciences under most modern schematizations. Only those things that can be known by sense perception, i.e., known empirically, belong to the (natural) philosopher's inquiry.

16. What Hugh refers to as "metaphysical" would correspond to what we would now call "philosophical." The Peltier edition has "theoretical" rather than "theological" at this point, two words frequently confused owing to their similarity when abbreviated in medieval manuscripts.

17. *In theorica huius practicae ostenditur.* "Theorica," a transliteration of the Greek word for "gaze" or "contemplation," was used by Thomas Gallus to distinguish the mystical path of negation from the mystical path of affective longing. See McGinn, "Love and Knowledge," pp. 12–13. In the section Hugh refers to, par. 82–115, below, he conflates these two into one abstractive affective upsurge. Cf. par. 27, 29, and 31, below, for a usage of "theorica" closer to our modern understanding. The reader should remember, however, that even this more familiar understanding of the word "theoretical" did not, for medieval writers, carry with it the implication that something is "airy" or "irrelevant."

18. Cf. Ps 31:9 [32:9].

19. The Peltier edition identifies this as part of the antiphon to the *Benedictus* (the "Canticle of Zechariah" from Lk 1:68–79, sung every day at morning prayer in the liturgy of the hours). The phrase is also found as an antiphon at Terce for the Feast of SS Peter and Paul (June 29) and in the Common of Apostles. See the modern (1879) Carthusian Breviary, as now readily available in *The Evolution of the Carthusian Statutes from the Consuetudines Guigonis to the Tertia Compilatio,* ed. James Hogg, Analecta Cartusiana, 99 (Salzburg: Institut für Anglistik und Amerikanistik, 1989ff.; Lewiston: Edwin Mellen, 1991ff.), Documents, parts 21–25: *Brevarium Sacri Ordinis Cartusiensis* (1993), part 24, p. 845.

20. Par. 21 marks the transition from prudence to fortitude, by way of shrewd struggle against the wiles of the devil.

21. *Iucunditas,* replacing *delectio* as used up to this point.

22. Here Hugh explicitly links the technical theological virtue of *caritas* with *amor,* his preferred term in the mystical upsurge. He makes the linkage more explicit in the next paragraph.

23. Cf. par. 79, below.

24. The Peltier edition has *theologicam affectionem* here; the Austrian manuscripts on which the Ruello edition is based have *theoricam affectionem.* "Theoricam" has been rendered "contemplative," in keeping with the original Greek meaning of the word, which figures in Pseudo-Denis.

25. *Promereatur.*

26. "Merit" is used here in the medieval Catholic sense: By God's grace humans do things that deserve the reward of eternal life; salvation is by grace alone, but eternal life is truly merited. See the *via purgativa* section, above.

27. The words translated as "completion" and "complete" here are *perficitur, perfecta.*

28. Once again, Hugh concludes a section with a peroration.

29. Much of what Hugh says about prudence here was transmitted under the rubric of *discretio* in the monastic tradition. For the earlier monastic tradition on discernment as the mother and moderator of all virtues (John Cassian) and the transition to prudence in the twelfth and thirteenth centuries, see F. Dingjan, *Discretio: Les origines patristiques et monastiques de la doctrine sur la prudence chez saint Thomas d'Aquin* (Assen, 1967); Pierre J. Payer, "Prudence and the Principles of Natural Law," *Speculum* 54 (1979): 55–70; Martin, *Fifteenth-Century Carthusian Reform*, pp. 113–33.

30. The sentence that follows is omitted in the Ruello edition. It is supplied here on the basis of the Peltier edition. Apparently it was omitted in the Austrian manuscript tradition because of an eyeskip from *quia* to *quia*.

31. See unitive way, par. 1, above.

32. Another sentence found in the Peltier edition is missing from the manuscripts on which the Ruello edition is based. It appears to be an editorial interpolation, purporting to outline the subjects of the next section, but it does not fit the contents of the next section, although it might fit the last section (par. 82–115). It reads: "A description of the threefold way follows, a path by which anyone, no matter how unlearned, can gain from on high the use of this heavenly rather than human doctrine."

33. Hugh's final sentence, convoluted in Latin as well as in English, has been left as a single sentence in order to indicate something of the rhetorical flourish with which he ends this section.

34. The Peltier text includes a verbatim repetition of the outline of the unitive way that appears in par. 1 above. It has been omitted here.

35. The following three examples are found, partly verbatim, in John Cassian, *Conferences*, Conference I.2 (SC 42:79; ET by Luibheid in CWS, p. 38; NPNF-2, 11:295).

36. At the end of his first persuasive reason, Hugh has placed a long and involved sentence intended as a rhetorical climax. Because it is part of his rhetorical strategy, I have not broken it up in translation.

37. The Latin text adds a second image here, that of the marrow, or inner core, of the human person being covered with dew. Since the two images clash for modern readers and since the image of dew recurs in the next clause, the latter metaphor has been suppressed. These two metaphors would not have clashed for ancient and medieval readers, since both refer to refreshment. Oil has become largely a negative image for modern Westerners, although something of the ancient role played by oil would be apparent to those who have applied soothing lotion to dry or chapped skin.

38. Reading *uniens* with Peltier rather than *unicus* with Ruello.

39. Ruello: *Ignita desideria*; Peltier: *ignota desideria*.

40. The Peltier edition adds: "or a well-crafted mortise-and-tenon joint."

41. *Dionysiaca*, 1:406; PG 3:872B; Luibheid, p. 109.

42. In the Latin original this passage is obscurely written and has been expanded in translation.

43. *Divinam influentiam provocando ipsius dono gratuito pervenire ad maiora et copiosiora praemia praehabitis promeretur.* Here Hugh articulates the medieval Catholic doctrine of human free will made to merit eternal life by the free gift of grace. But note the next paragraph, which makes clear that there can be no question of "works righteousness" here.

44. Cf. Ca 2:8.

45. A sentence found in the Peltier edition is omitted in the Austrian manuscripts used by Ruello: "This is understood through the following saying: *Inspectress of divine wisdom.*"

46. In the paragraphs that follow, Hugh gives a total of seven human exercises or efforts. Only the first four are mentioned here and not in exact sequence.

47. Cf. Mt 15:27; Mk 7:28.

48. Again, I have not broken this passage up into many discrete sentences, in order to retain something of the style of Hugh of Balma—the long chains of relative clauses that are his rhetorical attempt to underscore the majesty of the celestial scene he is describing.

49. The manuscripts on which the Ruello text is based refer to the gospel of John here.

50. The Peltier text omits the actual description of Christ's posture, which is supplied here on the basis of the Austrian manuscripts employed by Ruello. The posture given here conflates descriptions from both Matthew (Christ was prostrate on the ground) and Luke (Christ fell to his knees).

51. Reading *cassaretur* with Ruello rather than *cessaret* with Peltier.

52. Reading *ipsam* with Ruello, instead of *ipsum* with Peltier.

53. *De mystica theologia*, ch. 1 (Sarracenus version): "Tu autem, O amice Timothee, circa mysticas visiones forti contritione et sensus derelinque, et intellectuales operationes, et omnia sensibilia et intelligibilia, et omnia non exsistentia et exsistentia; et sicut est possibile, ignote consurge ad ejus unitionem *qui est super omnem substantiam et cognitionem.* Etenim excessu tui ipsius et omnium irretentibili et absoluto munde, ad supersubstantialem divinarum tenebrarum radium, cuncta auferens et a cunctis absolutus *sursum ageris.*" *Dionysiaca*, 1:567–69; ET by Luibheid in CWS, p. 135. Cf. Augustine, *De doctrina Christiana*, I.7; ET in NPNF-1, vol. 2: 524.

54. This sentence does not entirely make sense. Hugh seems to intend to say that, as long as the face is pointed upward in congruence with the spirit's attitude, either of two postures for the rest of the body is acceptable: kneeling or standing erect.

55. Ruello adds a line missing in the Peltier text, where it may have been removed because of redundancy.

56. Reading *specialia* with Ruello rather than *spiritualia* with Peltier.

57. This indicates clearly that Hugh assumes a monastic context for his read-

ers. The twelfth-century Carthusians normally ate only twice a day and, during the long period of fasting from September to Easter, they ate only once a day, supplemented by a bit of bread. See Guigo I, *Consuetudines cartusienses,* ed. by a Carthusian as *Coutumes de Chartreuse,* Sources chrétiennes, 313 (Paris: Editions du Cerf, 1984) [= PL 153:635–758], ch. 33; confirmed in the mid-thirteenth century *Statuta Antiqua,* pars. II, ch. 14 (Basel: Amerbach, 1510; reprinted in *The Evolution of the Carthusian Statutes,* AC 99: Documents, vol. 2, p. 192). Although it would be mistaken to assume that medieval people always ate "three square meals a day" (those who worked at hard physical labor may have eaten—very simply, to be sure—more than three times a day), "once or twice" would hardly have been typical of lay society.

58. I.e., it would be a shame if our soul, the mistress of the body, remained spiritually unfed while we regularly see to it that our body, the garrulous maidservant, is fed with material food.

59. Cf. 1 Pt 5:8.

60. Cf. Rom 8:29.

61. Here Hugh addresses the quintessential temptation for a Carthusian, one that was repeatedly cast at them by the more active mendicant religious orders and by devout lay people: We all agree that you live an exemplary life of devotion, but why do you hide it from everyone else? The world needs your example and the world cannot know it unless you make it available. By the later Middle Ages some Carthusians had become convinced of this reasoning and had begun to engage the surrounding world in a variety of ways, all of which they were convinced remained eminently faithful to the Carthusian vision. This development has been called a "Copernican shift" in Carthusian history. Where this trajectory would have ended had it not been interrupted by the Protestant and Catholic Reformations, no one can say. Some Carthusians opposed it and even those who accepted aspects of it, notably the London or Basel Carthusians, proved in the fire of the Protestant Reformation that the Carthusian life still burned fiercely in their hearts. Hugh's words here show that this was a problem not merely for late medieval Carthusians, after they began to found monasteries near large cities in response to enthusiastic patronage from the highest levels of society; rather, it was a problem even during the first two centuries of Carthusian existence, when they were patronized largely by the rural nobility. Hugh is writing just as the shift in locations began (about 1250), when bishops and urban patricians began to found charterhouses. For previous literature and a discussion of these issues, see Martin, *Fifteenth-Century Carthusian Reform,* esp. ch. 6, and idem, " 'The Honeymoon Was Over': Carthusians between Aristocracy and Bourgeoisie," in *Die Kartäuser und ihre Welt: Kontakte und gegenseitige Einflüsse,* Analecta Cartusiana, 63.1 (Salzburg: Institut für Anglistik und Amerikanistik, 1993; Lewiston, N.Y.: Edwin Mellen Press, 1993), pp. 66–99.

62. Hugh has conflated the opening of the Lord's Prayer with the verse from Mt 6: "When you shall pray . . . pray to your Father in secret."

63. Cf. Eph 6:11, 16.

64. *Promereatur.*

65. Cf. Jb 2:7; Is 52:14.

66. Hugh could assume that his readers knew the rest of the verse: "For he that has suffered in the flesh, has ceased from sins."

67. In the Peltier edition, this is labeled the third aspect; Ruello's edition calls it the second. Hugh is not entirely clear in these paragraphs as to the progression of his thought. If meditation on the Passion of our Lord is the first, main dish, one could expect two side dishes to follow, but Hugh seems to have abandoned his metaphor at some point.

68. *Mereatur*, rather than *promereatur*.

69. Referring to the judgment, as described in the following sentences.

70. In what follows it is not immediately clear what the two aspects are, although at the end of par. 79 and in par. 80 Hugh seems to say that the punishment of sinners serves two purposes: to convict a person of his own sin and thus escape damnation, and to expend oneself for the salvation of others. These are two fruits of compassion, i.e., two things inspired by observing and sharing the suffering of others. We should not confuse this, however, with the two repasts of par. 73, which are (1) meditation on Christ's Passion and (2) meditation on the suffering of sinners.

71. Hugh quotes only the first half of this verse but indicates with "etc." that he expected his readers to be able to complete it.

72. Hugh's quotation here follows the Septuagint, the Greek translation of the Hebrew Scriptures made before the time of Christ. The Vulgate and all modern English versions follow the slightly different Hebrew text. Presumably Hugh's source was either one of the Church Fathers or ancient liturgical elements based at least indirectly on the Septuagint. In all likelihood Hugh had no direct access to the Greek Septuagint.

73. This is not characteristically Carthusian, but it is not an interpolation by the later Franciscan editors; rather, it is present in the Austrian Carthusian manuscripts used by Ruello.

74. The redundant use of "true" is present in the Latin: ". . . sic ad veram veritatis cognitionem adtingat."

75. Reading *claritatis* with the Ruello edition rather than *caritatis* with Peltier.

76. Cf. par. 26, above.

77. The following interpolation is found in the Peltier edition but not in the manuscripts used by Ruello: "who was only a man, and though mild among his people and seemingly gentler than others."

78. *Promeruit*.

79. Reading *Dominum* with Peltier rather than *Deus* with Ruello, since the nominative form makes little sense in the absence of a passive verb.

80. *Condigna*.

81. Reading *ordinatum* with Peltier rather than *inordinatum* with Ruello typescript draft edition.

82. Reading *forti contritione* with the Sarracenus translation and Ruello, instead of *forti concertatione* in the Peltier text.

83. Hugh repeats this quotation in par. 12 of the "Difficult Question," below.

84. Pseudo-Denis, *De mystica theologia*, ch. 1.1–2; *Dionysiaca*, 1:567–69, Sarracenus translation; PG 3:998B–999A; Luibheid translation, 135–36.

85. See PL 196: 63–202; ET by Grover A. Zinn, *Richard of St. Victor: The Twelve Patriarchs, The Mystical Ark, Book Three of the Trinity*, Classics of Western Spirituality (New York: Paulist, 1979). Cf. "Difficult Question," par. 25, below.

86. "*Habitus gratum faciente*," given in the sacraments of baptism and penance.

87. "*Habitus gratis dato.*"

88. *On the Divine Names*, ch. 7. The Peltier text has "Sapientia est Dei divinissima cognitio per ignorantiam cogniti" but notes that some editions have "cognita" as the last word—which is the form given by Sarracenus (*Dionysiaca*, 1: 406; PG 3:872B; Luibheid translation, p. 109; cited in expanded quotation in the "Difficult Question," par. 31, below) and in the Ruello edition.

89. I have translated *mens* as "mind" here because the context is the intellectual continuum set out by Pseudo-Denis, rather than the mixture of affective and intellective powers of the soul assumed by much of the Latin tradition.

90. *On the Divine Names*, ch. 7.1; *Dionysiaca*, 1:386–87, Sarracenus translation; PG 3:868A; Luibheid, p. 106. Hugh cites this passage again in par. 15 and 46 of the "Difficult Question," below.

91. In the Peltier text this would seem to be a reference to the way that Pseudo-Denis understands hierarchy: Each of the triads of heavenly powers involves a higher one that is already something (perfected, illuminated, purified) and a middle one that is being made (perfecting, illuminating, purifying) into what the higher one already is, in turn serving as something already accomplished (perfected, illuminated, purified) toward the one below it, which is being perfected, illuminated, purified. See *Celestial Hierarchy*, ch. 3, par. 2 (PG 3:173C–175A; Luibheid translation, p. 154). The Ruello text replaces *perficiens* with *proficiens*, which places the human spirit in two different triads rather than on the top two rungs of the highest triad.

92. Cf. Lk 10:42.

93. Thomas Gallus of Vercelli (d. 1246). See Jeanne Barbet, "Thomas Gallus," *DSAM*, vol. 15 (Paris: Beauchesne, 1991), cols. 800–16; M. Capellino, *Tommaso di San Vittore* (Vercelli: Abbey of S. Andrea, 1978); Rosemary Ann Lees, *The Negative Language of the Dionysian School of Mystical Theology: An Approach to the "Cloud of Unknowing,"* 2 vols., Analecta Cartusiana, 107 (Salzburg: Institut für Anglistik und Amerikanistik, 1983), pp. 181–94, 270–308, for the most recent survey of literature.

94. A technical term for the highest part of the human person—for some medieval writers it is intellective, for others, including Hugh and Thomas Gallus, it is affective.

95. Here Hugh extracts the heart of Gallus's "affective" reading of Pseudo-Denis. Pseudo-Denis operated with a continuum from knowing to unknowing; affectivity and love played no role. For a summary of how the affective powers came to be viewed as equivalent to Pseudo-Denis's "unknowing," see Paul Rorem, *Pseudo-Dionysius: A Commentary on the Texts and an Introduction to their Influence* (New York: Oxford University Press, 1993), pp. 214–22, with summaries of previous literature. On Gallus's use of the term *principalis affectio*, see Endre von Ivánka, "Zur Überwindung des neuplatonischen Intellektualismus in der Deutung der Mystik: Intelligentia oder principalis affectio," *Scholastik* 30 (1955): 185–94; reprinted in *Plato Christianus*, pp. 352–63; reprinted in *Platonismus in der Philosophie des Mittelalters*, pp. 147–60.

96. Reading *caeci* with Ruello, rather than *caeteri*, with Peltier.

97. This refers to Thomas Gallus's paraphrase/translation found in *Dionysiaca*, 1:709–12, at 710, corresponding to the end of chapter one of Denis's *De mystica theologia*, ibid., p. 578. Hugh repeats this quotation in par. 13 of the "Difficult Question," below.

98. See par. 89, above.

99. Cf. Lk 10:42.

100. Hugh follows the Sarracenus translation, which has here *invisibilia* for *noeta*—all other medieval Latin translations give *intelligibilia* or *intellecta*.

101. The Sarracenus version reads: *sed nos ipsos totos extra nos ipsos statutos*, instead of the rather garbled version in both Peltier and Ruello editions: "*non secundum nos ipsos sed totos nos ipsos statutos.*" I have translated here by supplying the missing idea of *extra*.

102. *Dionysiaca*, 1:385, Sarracenus version; PG 3:865D–868A; cf. Luibheid, p. 106. Walsh, *Pursuit of Wisdom*, p. 311, cites the *Cloud of Unknowing*, ch. 4 (pp. 122–23 in the Walsh CWS translation), as a simpler and clearer statement of the affective epistemology involved here. Hugh quotes this in par. 14 of the "Difficult Question," below.

103. See par. 82, above.

104. Cf. par. 9, above.

105. The Peltier edition is badly garbled here and makes little sense: *Omnino autem ignorata notatio omnis cognitionis;* Ruello: *Omnino autem ignota vacatione omnis cognitionis.*

106. *Dionysiaca*, 1:590–91, Sarracenus translation; PG 3:1033B; Luibheid, p. 139. Walsh, *Pursuit of Wisdom*, p. 312, n. 31, cites Thomas Gallus's *Explanatio* on Pseudo-Denis's *Mystical Theology* in the very rare G. Théry edition, pp. 89–90, as a parallel here.

107. Walsh, *Pursuit of Wisdom*, p. 312, n. 32, cites the *Cloud of Unknowing*, ch. 26 (pp. 174–75 in CWS edition), as a parallel here.

108. Hugh's quotation departs from the Vulgate text: "By strength I trod the hearts of all the lofty and humble"; which in turn differs from modern translations

made from the original language. The textual history of the Wisdom of Sirach [Ecclesiasticus] is very problematic.

109. Cf. Is 29:14.

110. The redundancy is present in the original: *desideriis sursumactione consurrectionis.*

111. The reference is to the quotation from *On Mystical Theology*, ch. 1, as quoted in par. 82.

112. *Dionysiaca* 1:7–8; PG 3:588A; Luibheid, p. 49.

113. *On Mystical Theology*, ch. 1.1; *Dionysiaca* 1:568; PG 3:1000A; Luibheid, p. 135.

114. *Promeretur.*

115. On this twofold cleansing, see the parallel ascetic theology of Nicholas Kempf, as outlined in Martin, *Fifteenth-Century Carthusian Reform*, ch. 5.

116. "Than at the outset of the work of surging up" is omitted in the Peltier edition.

117. Walsh, *Pursuit of Wisdom*, cites Thomas Gallus's *Explanatio* commentary on Pseudo-Denis's *Mystical Theology*, in the Théry edition, p. 44, as a parallel.

118. Reading *extensivum amorem* with Ruello rather than *excessivum amorem* with Peltier.

119. The reference seems to be to *On Mystical Theology*, ch. 1.1 (*Dionysiaca* 1:596: "et a cunctis absolutus." Hugh quotes this as "cuncta auferens").

120. Walsh, *Pursuit of Wisdom*, cites Thomas Gallus's *Explanatio* commentary on Pseudo-Denis's *Mystical Theology* in the Théry edition, p. 49: Temporal cares, or any obstacle to receptivity, are the restraining force.

121. Reading *quae pro experimentali notitia sursumactivae consurrectionis relinquitur* with Ruello. *Pro* is missing in the Peltier edition.

122. Note that Hugh qualifies what he says about receiving ("being conceded") the beatific vision in this life. This was a controversial issue among Latin Christian spiritual writers. Hugh here qualifies it with "for the short time" and "according to her capacity," but he still strikes James Walsh as less sophisticated on the matter than the anonymous author of the *Cloud of Unknowing*. See Walsh, *Pursuit of Wisdom*, p. 313, n. 51. Of course, the *Cloud* author was writing after the papal pronouncement on the beatific vision in 1336 [which, however, dealt primarily with the blessed in heaven, not with the question of whether that vision is somehow accessible in rapture to people still in this present life]. Cf. Martin, *Fifteenth-Century Carthusian Reform*, pp. 173–74, for Nicholas Kempf's discussion of whether the rapture out of the body in which the extraordinary visions granted Moses, Paul, or the Virgin Mary took place within this life. Specifically for the context for Hugh of Balma, see H. F. Dondaine, "L'object et le' 'medium' de la vision béatifique chez les théologiens du XIIIe siècle," *Recherches de théologie ancienne et médiévale* 19 (1952): 60–130.

123. "Letter Five, to Dorotheus," *Dionysiaca*, 1:620; PG 3:1073A; Luibheid, p. 265. For Thomas Gallus's gloss, see James J. Walsh, ed., "The Expositions of

NOTES TO HUGH, DIFFICULT QUESTION

Thomas Gallus on the Pseudo-Dionysian Letters," *Archives d'histoire doctrinale et littéraire du Moyen Age* 38 (1964): 199–220, at 215.

124. Cf. par. 82, above.

125. *Dionysiaca* 1:55; PG 3:597C; Luibheid, pp. 57–58.

126. See above, par. 35.

127. Cf. *via illuminativa*, par. 24, above.

128. *In demonstratione a Spiritu motae theologorum virtutis;* using the technical term for scientific proof (demonstration) and referring to Scripture writers as "theologues"—drawing on the underlying assumptions of Pseudo-Denis's Greek.

129. *On the Divine Names*, ch. 1 (*Dionysiaca*, 1:5–7; PG 3:588A; Luibheid, p. 49).

130. Reading *levissime* with Ruello, rather than *levissima*, with Peltier.

The Roads to Zion Mourn: A Difficult Question

1. Cf. unitive way, par. 57, above.

2. This is not a direct quote from Augustine. Walach, *Notitia*, 89–90, has traced it to Pseudo-Thomas Aquinas (Helwicus Teutonicus), *De dilectione Dei et proximi*, ch. II, in Thomas Aquinas, *Opera Omnia*, ed. Fretté (Paris: Vives, 1875), vol. 28, pp. 324–94, at 324, 333. I have not been able to verify this citation. Cf. Augustine, *On the Trinity*, X.1.1; XIV.9 (CCSL 50:311–12; 50A: 432–33); ET in *Augustine: Later Works*, ed. John Burnaby, Library of Christian Classics, 8 (Philadelphia: Westminster Press, 1955), pp. 73, 106–7; Augustine, *Sermo* 117.7 (PL 38: 665D; ET in *The Works of St. Augustine: A Translation for the Twenty-First Century*, vol. III, part 4: *Sermons 94A–147A*, trans. Edmund Hill, ed. John E. Rotelle (Brooklyn, N.Y.: New City Press, 1992), p. 214; and Gregory the Great, *XL Homiliarum in Evangelia*, hom. 11.1 (PL 76:1115A = homily 9 in ET in CS 123, p. 62). The phrase employed by Hugh is quoted verbatim by Jean Gerson in *Elucidatio scolastica mysticae theologiae*, consideratio 8.5 (Combes ed., p. 229).

3. *On the Divine Names*, 7.1; *Dionysiaca* 1:386; PG 3:868A; Luibheid, p. 106.

4. The entire section from "in his procession binding" to "precedes the procession of the Holy Spirit, who is true love" is missing in the Peltier edition but present in the Austrian manuscripts on which the Ruello edition is based. Presumably a copyist's eyeskip from "who is true love" lies behind the omission.

5. *Celestial Hierarchy*, 6.2; *Dionysiaca*, 2:830–34; PG 3:200D, 201A; Luibheid, p. 161.

6. The section from "Third must come" to "means 'ardent,' 'burning' " is missing in the Austrian manuscripts on which Ruello based his edition. Presumably an eyeskip from "postea" to "postea" caused this omission.

7. In the repetition of this quote (cf. unitive way, par. 82, above), the Peltier edition has *forti contritione*, instead of *forti concertatione*, thus agreeing with the Sarracenus translation.

8. Pseudo-Denis, *De mystica theologia*, ch. 1.1–2; *Dionysiaca*, 1:567–69, Sarracenus translation; PG 3:998B–999A; Luibheid translation, pp. 135–36.

9. Thomas Gallus's paraphrase of Denis, *On Mystical Theology*, at the end of ch. 1 (*Dionysiaca* 1:710 at 578). Hugh has already cited the first part of this passage in unitive way, par. 95, above.

10. At the earlier quotation of this passage, we find simply *melior* here, which agrees with Thomas Gallus; in this second instance it has become *melior nobiliori* in the manuscripts on which the Ruello edition is based and simply *nobiliori* in the Peltier edition.

11. Cf. unitive way, par. 97, above.

12. Reading *tactum* with Ruello and the variant given in Peltier, instead of *actum*.

13. *Dionysiaca*, 1:385–86, Sarracenus version; PG 3:868A; cf. Luibheid, p. 106. Hugh has already quoted this in unitive way, par. 97, above. See the textual notes accompanying that instance. The translation there and here reflects other differences in the Latin original, stemming, undoubtedly, from the fact that Hugh was quoting from memory. Hugh's quotation is obscure, apparently a conflation of the Eriugena and Sarracenus translations. The Peltier edition added an alternative reading from a seventeenth-century version of Denis for clarification. Luibheid's translation reads: "What we should really consider is this. The human mind has a capacity to think, through which it looks on conceptual things, and a unity which transcends the very nature of the mind, through which it is joined to things beyond itself. And this transcending characteristic must be given to the words we use about God. They must not be given the human sense. We should be taken wholly out of ourselves and become wholly of God."

14. *On the Divine Names*, ch. 7.1; *Dionysiaca*, 1:386–87 in Sarracenus translation; PG 3:868A; Luibheid, p. 106. Hugh has cited this in unitive way, par. 86, above, with slight variations.

15. Reading *intelligimus* with Ruello, rather than *diligimus*, with Peltier.

16. The quotation is obscure. It is not from Thomas Gallus's paraphrase (the *Extractio*) of Denis's *On Mystical Theology* (printed in *Dionysiaca*, 1:709–12), but is undoubtedly found in the *Explanatio super Mysticam Theologiam*. See Walsh, " 'Sapientia Christianorum,' " pp. 23–27. The edition of Thomas Gallus's commentary by Gabriel Théry, *Thomas Gallus: Grand Commentaire sur la Theologie Mystique* (Paris: Haloua, 1934), is extremely rare and I have not seen it.

17. The phrase about the Father being the highest power is missing in the Ruello edition and has been supplied from Peltier.

18. This last sentence is missing in the Ruello edition and is supplied from the Peltier edition.

19. Reading *ardentius* with Ruello, rather than *attentius* with Peltier.

20. "Philosopher" meant a person of wide scientific, moral, and theological learning in Hugh's day and context and did not yet have the restricted scope that a student of "philosophy" has today.

21. Cf. Lk 10:42.

22. Hugh may be referring to Jn 20:11.

23. Cf. unitive way, par. 84, above, for this reference.

24. Walach, *Notitia*, pp. 139–42, rightly identifies Bonaventure's *Itinerarium mentis in Deum* as a parallel to Hugh here. However, Walach's claim that Hugh is criticizing Bonaventure here and may have actually held a disputation on this topic in response to Bonaventure, ca. 1259–1260, would mean that Hugh was a regent master at the university. It seems more likely to me that Hugh agrees with Bonaventure.

25. An interpolation found in the Peltier edition, "where the primordial foundation of the creatures is left behind," has been omitted here.

26. I have not been able to identify the phrase attributed to Augustine. What Hugh describes here would seem to be the first affective method, from lower to higher, terminating in the *affectus*.

27. *Adficiatur*, i.e., affected, moved, impacted into God.

28. *Dionysiaca*, 1:406; PG 3:872B; Luibheid translation, p. 109; Hugh has quoted the first phrase of this definition and summarized the rest of it in unitive way, par. 85.

29. *Dionysiaca*, 1:567; PG 3:997B; Luibheid, p. 135; quoted with different wording in unitive way, par. 82, above, and elsewhere.

30. An interpolation found in the Peltier edition, apparently an attempt to specify the "aforementioned path" ("through humility, knowledge, and illumination gained in prayer"), has been omitted here. It is not found in the Austrian manuscripts on which Ruello's edition is based.

31. Reading *originis* with Ruello, rather than *ordinis* with Peltier.

32. Cf. 1 Cor 2:4.

33. Hugh has alluded to this passage from the opening of *On the Divine Names* in unitive way, par. 115. Here he quotes it more directly, but it is garbled badly in the Peltier edition. See *Dionysiaca*, 1:5–6; 5–7; PG 3:588A; Luibheid, p. 49.

34. Reading *effectiva* with Ruello, rather than *affectiva* with Peltier.

35. The quotation, with its characteristic use of *unitio*, is actually from Thomas Gallus's paraphrase, rather than from the Sarracenus translation. See *Dionysiaca*, 1:710, at 577. The Ruello text gives an additional clause not found in the Peltier edition.

36. Hugh's use of *meditando* here only illustrates the intimate interconnection between affective and cogitative. Here he uses it to refer to the point of departure for the aspirations of the short exposition. Strictly speaking, only the aspiration is purely affective, thus he can refer to the base from which the aspiration thrusts off as "meditation." See the introduction for more extended discussion of the outline of Hugh's various types of cogitative and affective ascent.

37. See the Prologue, par. 5, above, for this analogy.

38. Hugh cites this verse in par. 3 and 40 of the present question, in the unitive way, par. 57, and in par. 45 of the illuminative way, above.

39. I.e., the sequence: Father (power), Son (knowledge), Holy Spirit (love).

40. The Peltier edition makes this the response to the fourth proposition. It is clearly a continuation of the response to the third proposition. Four and five are then combined in par. 43.

41. In other words, Hugh is pointing out an ancient principle of Christian faith in the incarnation: Because of the limits of human beings as embodied souls, God must come to us via a mixture of sense-perceptible and intellectual perception.

42. The Peltier edition here has "Even if love and illumination from on high." The editor's error misreading *majorem* as *amorem* led to a significant shift in emphasis, combining love and intellect from on high.

43. The likely antecedent for *ipsam* would be *consurrectio*, leading to the rather odd statement that the mystical upsurge should be completely isolated from the *affectus*. Therefore we have taken the antecedent to be *cogitatio* in the preceding sentence.

44. Hugh uses the puzzling phrase *liber supernatans* (. . . *in tantum amoris affectio veluti liber supernatans citius quod desiderat apprehendit*). Literally, the image would be that of a book, piece of bark, or parchment (or a child, since in the nominative, *liber* can mean either), soaring above. Assuming a scribal error in which *libere* became *liber*, I have translated this to mean that the affection freely soars on high. Cf. the similar, but not identical, phrase in the Prologue, par. 7.

45. See par. 32, above.

46. Cf. illuminative way, par. 46; unitive way, par. 1.

47. *On the Divine Names*, ch. 7.1; *Dionysiaca*, 1:386–87 in Sarracenus translation; PG 3:868A; Luibheid, p. 106. Hugh cites this passage in par. 15, above, and in par. 86 of the unitive way, above.

48. *On Mystical Theology*, ch. 1; *Dionysiaca*, 1:569; PG 3:1000A; Luibheid, p. 136.

49. This does not seem to be a literal quotation.

50. *Dionysiaca*, 1:569–70; PG 3:1000A; Luibheid, p. 136.

51. The Ruello text has a slightly different arrangement of clauses in this passage.

52. Cf. 1 Cor 2:12–16.

On Contemplation: Prologue

1. The title to the prologue and each book of *De Contemplatione* begins, as many medieval manuscripts do, with *Incipit*. . . . The present translation reflects this discursive style for headings here and in subsequent books.

2. Compare this with the exordium to William of Saint-Thierry's *Epistola*, written to the Carthusians of Mont-Dieu, bk. I, ch. 3–4 (PL 184:310–11 [= par. 10–14 in SC 223:150–54; ET in CF 12:11–14]), where William asks the Carthusians not to pay attention to those who accused them of novelty. One encounters similar cautions in Hugh of Balma's *The Roads to Zion Mourn, via unitiva*, par. 112, "Diffi-

cult Question," par. 47. Cf. the *Cloud of Unknowing*, where the anonymous author specifies in the prologue that his work is not for the eyes of those who know nothing of the mystical life. See also Nicholas Kempf, *Tractatus de mystica theologia*, bk. I, ch. 1 (p. 15).
3. Cf. Rom 1:30.
4. Jerome, *Vita S. Hilarionis*, par. 1 (PL 23:29B, ET NPNF-2, 6:303).
5. See bk. 2, ch. 7, below.
6. Cf. Augustine of Hippo, *Sermo 90*, par. 2 (PL 38:559C).

On Contemplation: Book One

1. The chapter heading apparently was not intended to detail the four steps precisely. In the chapter itself, both steps one and two are related to "justification of the unrighteous," with step two being repentance and compunction. Step three involves the water of grace from the lower fountain, and step four includes both compassion and goodwill toward one's neighbor.
2. Ps 50:3 [51:1].
3. Rom 8:29.
4. Thomas Aquinas, *In Evangelium secundum Ioannem*, commentary on John, ch. 4, lectio 7, par. 4: "In justification of the unrighteous there are four things necessary, especially in adults: namely the infusion of grace and remission of guilt, the movement of the free will toward God, which is faith, and toward sin, which is contrition." *Super Evangelium S. Ioannis Lectura*, ed. Raphaelis Cai, 5th rev. ed. (Rome: Marietti, 1952), p. 129, par. 688; ET by James A. Weisheipl and Fabian R. Larcher, *Commentary on the Gospel of John* (Albany, N.Y.: Magi Books, 1980). Cf. *STh*, Ia IIae, q. 113, art. 8.
5. Cf. Ez 18:21–22; Prv 26:11.
6. Pseudo-Ambrose, *Sermo 25: De sancta quadragesima*, par. 2 (PL 17: 655A); Pseudo-Bernard, *Liber de modo bene vivendi*, ch. 27, par. 78 (PL 184:1247D).
7. Gregory the Great, *Homilia 33 in Evangelia*, no. 4 (PL 76:1241C; ET in CS 123:271); *Moralia*, bk. XXIII, ch. 6, par. 11 (PL 76:292B; CCSL 143B:1195).
8. William of Saint-Thierry, *Epistola*, bk. I, ch. 26 (PL 184:324D [= par. 99 in SC 223:222; ET in CF 12:45]). Guigo repeats this quotation in I.6, below.
9. Cf. Ps 38:5 [39:4].
10. Cf. Lk 13:8.
11. Guigo here cites two of the seven penitential psalms.
12. Ps 84:9 [85:8].
13. Cf. Jgs 1:15; Jos 15:19.
14. Cf. 2 Cor 6:1.
15. Bernard of Clairvaux, *Sermon 9 in Cantica*, par. 9 (PL 183:819A; *Bernardi Opera*, 1:47; ET in CF 4:59); Gregory the Great, *Dialogues*, bk. III, ch. 34 (PL 77:300D-301A; ET in FC 39:173–74); idem, *Letter 26* (PL 77:880C; bk. VII, no. 23 in CCSL 140:476).

NOTES TO GUIGO, BOOK ONE

16. Cf. Ca 4:5. Bernard of Clairvaux, *Sententiae,* ser. 1, nos. 9, 31 (PL 183:749D, 754C; *Bernardi Opera,* 6, pt. 2, pp. 9, 18); *Sermo 10 in Cantica,* par. 1 (PL 183:819D; *Bernardi Opera,* 1:49; ET in CF 4:61); *Sermo 9 in Cantica,* par. 5 (PL 183:817B; *Bernardi Opera,* 1:45; ET in CF 4:57).

17. The beatitudes pericope was read on the feast of St. Maurice, but not in Carthusian practice.

18. Bernard of Clairvaux, *Sermo 31 in Cantica,* par. 4 (PL 183:942B; EC 1:221; ET CF 7:127).

19. Augustine, *In prima epistola Ioannis,* tractate 4, ch. 2, par. 6 (PL 35:2008D; SC 75:230; ET NPNF-1 7:484; LCC 8:290). See also Gregory the Great, *Homilia 25 in Evangelia,* par. 2 (PL 76:1190C; ET in CS 123:189–90).

20. Three manuscripts have *ipsum* ["him"] here; two have *ipsam* ["her"]. I follow the former, departing from Dupont's choice of reading, since *ipsum* agrees better with the verse from Jeremiah that follows.

21. The application of the Holy Spirit to the south wind is made by Gregory the Great, *Homiliae in Hiezechielem,* bk. I, hom. 2, par. 9 (PL 76:799D; CCSL 142:22; ET by Theodosia Gray, *The Homilies of St. Gregory the Great on the Book of the Prophet Ezekiel,* ed. by Presbytera Juliana Cownie [Etna, Cal.: Center for Traditionalist Orthodox Studies, 1990], p. 25); bk. II, hom. 1, par. 6 (PL 76:939D-940A; CCSL 142:212; ET by Gray, p. 161). Cf. Bernard of Clairvaux, *Sermo in aquaductu* [*In nativitate Mariae*], par. 6 (PL 183:441B; *Bernardi Opera,* 5:279). The original context in Jeremiah is a negative one: A wild ass smells a female in heat, no male ass will turn her away, they all seek her out in her "monthly filth."

22. Ca 4:16.

23. Cf. Ps 71 [72]:6.

24. Hugh of Saint-Victor, *De arrha animae* (PL 176:970AB; ET by Kevin Herbert [1956], p. 35).

25. Cf. Ps 41:3 [42:2]. The Vulgate has "Deum fortem, vivum," although Jerome noted this as an uncertain passage textually.

26. Cf. Bernard of Clairvaux, *Sermo 31 in Cantica,* par. 6 (PL 183:943A; *Bernard Opera,* 1:223; ET in CF 7:129).

27. Cf. Ps 47:10 [48:9].

28. This is Guigo's eleventh degree, found in bk. I, ch. 10.

29. Cf. Ca 1:7.

30. On the process of introversion, see Gregory the Great, *Homiliae in Hiezechielem,* bk. II, hom. 5, par. 9 (PL 76:989D-990B; CCSL 142:281–82; ET by Gray, p. 209); Johannes of Kastl? (Pseudo-Albert the Great), *De adhaerendo Deo,* ch. 7 (*Alberti Magni Opera Omnia,* ed. August Borgnet [Paris] 37 [1898]: 529–30; ET by a Benedictine of Princethorpe Priory); Pseudo-Augustine, *De spiritu et anima,* ch. 2 (PL 40:781). See also Augustine, *Enarrationes in Ps. 41,* par. 7, 9 (PL 36:467–70; CCSL 38:464, 466); *Confessions,* bk. III, ch. 11; bk. X, ch. 38 (PL 32:688A, 795C; CCSL 27:32–33, 175).

31. Ps 147:14.

32. Cf. Wis 7:26.

33. Augustine, *De trinitate,* bk. XIV, ch. 8, par. 11 (PL 42:1044B–1045C; CCSL 50A:436; ET in NPNF-1, 3:189; LCC 8:108-9).

34. Gn 1:26.

35. Cf. Ez 1:13.

36. Guigo here has enumerated the three parts of the image of God in human beings: memory, understanding, will.

37. Guigo employs the term *vacare,* drawing on the contemplative monastic tradition of "busy leisure" (*otium negotiosum*). See Jean Leclercq, *Otia monastica* (1963).

38. Cf. Bar 2:18. The word *incurvata* used here literally means crooked or bent, but also connotes cheating and wrongfulness, just as in a "crooked deal." It was used by monastic spiritual writers to refer to the human will curved in upon itself in sin.

39. Cf. Jas 1:5.

40. "Decies millies centena millia" ("ten thousand times hundred thousand"; Dn 7:10 in the Vulgate) = ten thousand times ten thousand (KJV).

41. Cf. Mt 15:27. This prayer expands on that found in Guigo II, *Scala claustralium,* ch. 4, par. 5, in PL 184:478D; ch. 6 in SC 163:94; ET in CS 48:73/Doubleday ed., p. 87.

42. Reminiscent of Augustine, *De trinitate,* bk. XV, ch. 28, par. 51: "meminerim tui, intelligam te, diligam te" (PL 42:1098A-B; CCSL 50A:534; ET in NPNF-1, 3:227; LCC 8:179–80).

43. Cf. Ps 64:11. See Guigo II, *Scala claustralium,* ch. 10 in PL 184:481C, ch. 12 in SC 163:108; ET in CS 48:79/Doubleday ed. p. 93: "haec adveniens praedictorum trium laborem renumerat, dum caelestis rore dulcedinis animam sitientem inebriat" ["Contemplation when it comes rewards the labors of the other three; it inebriates the thirsting soul with the dew of heavenly sweetness."].

44. Cf. 1 Jn 2:27.

45. *Ad salutem,* for salvation, for spiritual health.

46. Cf. Rom 8:26.

47. *Cognoscit per experientiam,* literally, "knows by experience," although the English word "experience" does not fully express the meaning here.

48. *Calculus,* i.e., a small stone used in games or as a counting piece.

49. The Tortosa manuscript glosses: "shining stone, that is the Eucharist, and on the stone is written a name, that is, the reality [*res*] of the sacrament by which the person who receives it is renewed day-by-day."

50. Cf. 1 Cor 11:29.

51. Cf. Rom 2:5; Jas 5:3.

52. Gregory, *Homilia 37 in Evangelia,* par. 7 (PL 76:1279A; ET in CS 123:333).

53. On tears see John Cassian, *Collationes,* IX, ch. 29 (PL 49:805–806; SC 54:64–65; ET in NPNF-2, 11:397). See also Guigo II, *Scala claustralium,* ch. 7 (PL

NOTES TO GUIGO, BOOK ONE

184:479; ch. 8 in SC 163:98; ch. 8 in ET CS 48:74–75/Doubleday ed., pp. 88–89). On the two types of compunction, see Gregory the Great, *Dialogorum libri*, bk. III, ch. 34 (PL 77:300A–301A; ET in FC 39:173–74).

54. 1 Sm 24:17.

55. Gregory the Great, *Homiliae in Hiezechielem*, bk. II, hom. 8, par. 17 (PL 76:1038B–C; CCSL 142:349; ET by Gray, p. 255). While modern diet-conscious people would consider a lean sacrifice superior, traditional societies with subsistence-level diets valued fatty foods high in calories simply for the sake of survival. Thus the fattened animal was the richest animal and the proper sacrifice to God. Cf. Ps 65 [66]:15.

56. This quotation has not been identified.

57. This quotation, not identified in the Dupont edition, comes from Jerome, *Epistolae*, letter 11 (CSEL 54:40; ET in NPNF-2, 6:12).

58. Gregory the Great, *Moralia*, bk. V, ch. 7–8 (PL 75:686BC). See also Guigo I, *Consuetudines*, ch. 80, par. 11: baptisma[ta] lacrimarum (PL 153:758; SC 313:292), and Guigo II, *Scala claustralium*, ch. 13 in PL, ch. 15 in SC: oculos qui modo sacris lacrimis baptisati erant . . . (PL 184:484B; SC 163:120; ET CS 48:85/Doubleday ed., p. 98).

59. The identity of this quotation from Gregory is uncertain; cf. *Moralia*, bk. IX, ch. 62, par. 94 (PL 75:911C; CCSL 143:523), and *Homiliae in Hiezechielem*, bk. II, hom. 10, par. 20 (PL 76:1070B; CCSL 142:395; ET by Gray, p. 285).

60. William of Saint-Thierry, *Epistola*, bk. 1, ch. 26 (PL 184:324D [= par. 99 in SC 223:222; ET in CF 12:45]), already cited in ch. I.1, above. The Tortosa manuscript adds quotations from Richard of Saint-Victor, *Benjamin major* [*The Mystical Ark*], bk. IV, ch. 6 (PL 196:139D; ET in CWS, *Richard of Saint Victor: The Twelve Patriarchs, The Mystical Ark, Book Three of the Trinity*, trans. by Grover Zinn [New York: Paulist Press, 1978], pp. 265–66); Gregory the Great, *Super Cantica*, ch. 1, par. 5 in PL 79:481A, par. 18 in CCSL 144:21, and *Homilia 20 in Evangelia*, par. 15 (PL 76:1169A; ET [= homily 6] in CS 123:48); and Cassiodorus, *Expositio Psalmorum 6*, verse 7 (PL 70:63C; CCSL 97:75).

61. Gregory, *Homiliae in Hiezechielem*, bk. I, hom. 1, par. 15 (PL 76:792A, CCSL 142:12; ET by Gray, p. 19). The Tortosa manuscript adds a reference to Basil the Great, *Homilia in Psalmum 1*, par. 2 (PG 29:214A).

62. Bernard of Clairvaux, *Sermo 15 in Cantica*, par. 6 (PL 183:847B; *Bernardi Opera*, 1:86; ET in CF 4:110).

63. William of Saint-Thierry, *Epistola*, bk. I, ch. 22 (PL 184:322C [= par. 86 in SC 223:210; ET in CF 12:40]).

64. The Vulgate has "fountain of living waters" [*fons aquae vivae*].

65. Cassiodorus, *Expositio Psalmorum*, preface (PL 70:11B; CCSL 97:5).

66. Prv 28:14.

67. Bernard of Clairvaux, *Sermo 54 in Cantica*, par. 9 (PL 183:1042D; *Bernardi Opera*, 2:108; ET in CF 31:78).

68. Cf. Hugh of Balma, *Roads to Sion, via purgativa*, par. 14.

69. Bernard of Clairvaux, *Sermo in aquaductu* [*In nativite Mariae*], par. 5 and 9 (PL 183:440C, 443A; *Bernardi Opera*, 5:277–78, 281).

70. Gregory the Great, *Dialogorum libri*, bk. III, ch. 34 (PL 77:300C; ET in FC 39:174).

71. Gregory the Great, *Homilia 33 in Evangelia*, par. 1 (PL 76:1239B; ET in CS 123:269).

72. Cf. Col 3:9.

73. This citation has not been identified.

74. Gregory the Great, *Super Cantica*, ch. 1, par. 5 in PL 79:480BC; par. 18 in CCSL 144:19.

75. Richard of Saint-Victor, *Benjamin major* [*The Mystical Ark*], bk. IV, ch. 15 (PL 196:153BC; ET by Zinn in CWS, p. 285).

76. Cf. Ps. 38:4 [39:3].

77. Cf. Lk 12:49.

78. Cf. Ps 75:11.

79. Cf. Sir 23:22 [23:16].

80. Cf. Is 58:13.

81. Cf. Ps 65 [66]:15: *holocausta medullata*.

82. The Tortosa manuscript adds a gloss explaining that this refers to Ca 4:9: *Vulnerasti cor meum soror mea*, a "wounding" that consists in touching and pushing toward God, a clinging to God while covered with dew, as the *Glossa ordinaria* says in regard to Tobit 3:11.

83. See the discussion of "anagogical" in the introduction to this volume.

84. See Bernard, *Sermo 7 in Cantica*, par. 7 (PL 183:809D; *Bernardi Opera*, 1:35; ET in CF 4:43). Although he obviously had a text from Bernard's sermon in mind, Guigo erroneously attributed it to William of Saint-Thierry's *Golden Epistle*. One passage from William's letter bears some resemblance to the quotation from Bernard of Clairvaux: "It is for others to serve God—it is for you to cling. It is for others to believe, to know [*scire*], to love and venerate—it is for you to taste, understand, know intimately [*cognoscere*], and enjoy." William, *Epistola*, bk. I, ch. 5 (PL 184:311C [= par. 16 in SC 223:154, 156; ET in CF 12:14]).

85. Cf. William of Saint-Thierry, *Epistola*, bk. II, ch. 14 (PL 184:347A [= par. 249 in SC 223:342; ET in CF 12:92]).

86. The etymology deriving *sapientia* from *sapere* was a commonplace of Latin Christian spiritual writers. See Guigo II, *Scala claustralium*, ch. 3, par. 4 in PL 184:478B, ch. 5 in SC 163:92; Adam of Dryburgh, *De quadripartito exercitio cellae*, ch. 17 (PL 153:830C); Hugh of Balma, *Roads to Zion*, passim; Bonaventure, *In IIIa Sententiarum*, dist. 35, a. unic., qu. 1; Thomas Aquinas, *STh*, IIa IIae, qu. 45, art. 2, obj. 2.

87. The Tortosa manuscript adds a passage from Richard of Saint-Victor, *Benjamin major* [*The Mystical Ark*], bk. III, ch. 9 (PL 196:119A; ET by Zinn in CWS, pp. 234–35), here.

88. Cf. Augustine, *De trinitate*, bk. XIV, ch. 3, par. 5 (PL 42:1039; CCSL

50A:426–27; ET in NPNF-1, 3:185); Bernard of Clairvaux, *Sermo 11 in Cantica*, par. 5 (PL 183:826B; *Bernardi Opera*, 1:57; ET in CF 4:73).

89. Cf. Prv 31:21.

90. Cf. Mt 11:25.

91. Bernard of Clairvaux, *Sermo 85 in Cantica*, par. 14 (PL 183:1194C; *Bernardi Opera*, 2:316; ET in CF 4:210).

92. Ps 33:9 [34:8].

93. Cf. bk 2, ch. 10. See the discussion of Guigo's process of composition of the three books in the Introduction.

94. On the vision beyond the cloud see bk. III, ch. 10, note 80, below.

95. Cf. Ex 13:21–22.

96. The Latin term used here is *obliquus*, which was used by the Latin translators of Pseudo-Dionysius to translate the Greek *helikoeidso*, meaning "spiral." See Pseudo-Dionysius, *De divinis nominibus*, ch. 4, par. 8 (PG 3:703D; *Dionysiaca*, I: 189–93; ET by Luibheid in CWS, p. 78). Cf. Thomas Aquinas, *STh*, IIa IIae, qu. 180, art. 6. See also E. Hugueny, "Circulaire, rectiligne, hélicoïdal: les trois degrés de la contemplation," *Revue des Sciences Philosophiques et Théologiques*, 13 (1924): 327–31, and A. Gardeil, "Les mouvements direct, en spirale et circulaire de l'âme et les oraisons mystiques," *Revue Thomiste*, 30 (1925): 321–40.

97. Cf. Eph 4:7.

98. Cf. Jn 3:8.

99. Cf. Thomas Aquinas, *STh*, IIa IIae, qu. 180, art. 6, ad 2ndm.

100. Note the shift to the passive voice, which is found in the Latin text, here. It constitutes the main distinction between the two forms of the second, circular, movement. The description of both forms is otherwise quite similar.

101. On this cloud, see, e.g., Gregory of Nyssa, *Homilia in Cantica 11* (PG 44:999C; ET by Casimir McCambley, *Commentary on the Song of Songs*, Archbishop Iakovos Library of Ecclesiastical and Historical Sources, 12 [Brookline, Mass.: Hellenic College Press, 1987], p. 202).

102. I.e., abandoning—see bk. II, ch. 10, below, for Guigo's definition, based on Hugh of Balma.

103. Cf. Ps 83:6–7 [84:5–6].

104. Cf. 1 Jn 3:2.

105. Cf. 1 Cor 13:12.

106. The same image of the sun appears in Ambrose, *Sermo 19 in Psalmum 118*, par. 38 (PL 15:1481A).

107. Cf. Ex 3:2.

108. Cf. Is 6:1.

109. Cf. Gal 5:6.

110. Cf. bk. I, ch. 10, below.

111. Gregory the Great, *Homiliae in Hiezechielem*, bk. II, hom. 2, par. 14 (PL 76:956B; CCSL 142:234; ET by Gray, p. 177).

112. Cf. Pseudo-Dionysius, *Epistola 1 to Gaius* (PG 3:1066A; *Dionysiaca*, pp.

605-7; ET by Luibheid in CWS, p. 263), and *Epistola 5 to Dorotheus* (PG 3:1074A; *Dionysiaca*, pp. 620-23; ET in CWS, p. 265). This phrase is taken up by Denys of Rijkel in *De contemplatione*, bk. III, art. 8 (*Opera* 41:264).

113. Sir 24:12 [24:8].

114. Cf. 1 Tm 6:16.

115. The Tortosa manuscript adds a gloss from Bernard of Clairvaux, *Liber Sententiarum*, 2nd series, par. 27 (PL 184:1141B; *Bernardi Opera*, vol. 6, pt. 2, pp. 31-32).

116. Cf. 1 Cor 10:4. See also Augustine, *Sermon 13* [76] *de verbis Domini*, par. 1 (PL 38:479D).

117. Cf. Ps 44:8 [45:7].

118. Cf. Ca 5:16.

119. Cf. Dt 4:24.

120. See the hymn, *Veni creator*, attributed to Rabanus Maurus (ninth century).

121. An expression favored by Gregory the Great, e.g., *Dialogi*, bk. III, ch. 37, par. 20 (PL 77:313B; SC 260:424, 426; ET in FC 39:184), and even before that by Augustine (see *Epistola 130*, par. 28 [PL 33:505C]).

122. Pseudo-Dionysius, *De divinis nominibus*, ch. 7, par. 3 (PG 3:871B; *Dionysiaca*, p. 406; ET by Luibheid in CWS, p. 109).

123. Cf. Rv 21:6.

124. The Tortosa manuscript refers this passage to "Bernard," referring in actuality to Guigo II, *Scala claustralium*, ch. 3 (PL 184:477B-D [= ch. 5 in SC 163: 88-90]; ET in CS 48:70-72/Doubleday ed., pp. 83-86).

125. A gloss added in the Charleville manuscript makes it clear that step ten ends here. It emphasizes that step ten is a step of darkness and shadow in the inner chamber of the heart. Step eleven, the direct movement to God in higher things, emphasizes light. See p. 150 of the DuPont edition.

126. Cf. Lk 2:27.

127. Guigo is careful here to say "with the same sort" (*ad instar*), rather than with a vision identical to that of the saints in heaven.

128. *Benjamin major*, bk. V, ch. 14 (PL 196:187B; ET by Zinn in CWS, pp. 335-36).

129. Cf. Ca 3:2.

130. The text adds a parenthetical comment here that has been removed for the sake of readability: "Saint Augustine says that no one is so clean that he might not still be cleansed more." Augustine, *Tractatus 80 in Ioannem*, par. 2 (PL 35:1840A; CCSL 36:528-29; ET in NPNF-1, 7:344).

131. *Sermon 41 in Cantica*, par. 2 (PL 183:985B-D; *Bernardi Opera*, 2:29; ET in CF 7:205-6). The Tortosa manuscript adds a gloss from Ps 4:7 and Jn 16:22. Guigo returns to this theme at length in III.15-16.

132. The Tortosa manuscript adds a gloss from Augustine's *Enarrationes in psalmum 30* (par. 6 in PL 36:253D; par. 10 in CCSL 38:219-20), which defines the

term "excessus mentis" as "the elevation of the pure heart to see and enjoy God above the measure of human weakness through fecund and aroused affections, as it is said in this passage."

133. Cf. *Sermo 49 in Cantica*, par. 4 (PL 183:1018B; *Bernard Opera*, 2:75; ET in CF 31:24–25). The Tortosa manuscript adds a quotation from this sermon.

134. Cf. Thomas Aquinas, *STh*, Ia, qu. 12, art. 11.

135. *Benjamin major*, bk. V, ch. 19 (PL 196:192B; ET by Zinn in CWS, p. 343).

136. DuPont notes that this phrase seems to have been invented by Guigo himself.

137. The Tortosa manuscript adds a gloss based on Gregory the Great, *Moralia*, bk. XVIII, ch. 54, par. 88–89 (PL 76:92B–93A; CCSL 143A: 950–53), dealing with the matter of seeing God face-to-face and purity of heart required for the vision of God. Dom DuPont offers additional references to Augustine, Nicholas of Lyra, and Ambrose.

138. *Sermo 70 in Cantica*, par. 2 (PL 183:1117B; *Bernardi Opera*, 2:208; ET in CF 41:38).

139. Cf. Gregory the Great, *Moralia*, bk. XVIII, ch. 54, par. 88 (PL 76:92A–D; CCSL 143A:950–52).

140. Cf. Gn 18:23; Ambrose, *De fide*, bk. I, ch. 13, par. 80 (PL 16:547B; CSEL 78:35); and idem, *De excessu fratris*, bk. II, par. 96 (PL 16:1342D; CSEL 73:302).

141. The Tortosa manuscript adds a reference to Bernard on the Canticle; cf. *Sermo 33 in Cantica*, par. 3 (PL 183:952C; *Bernardi Opera*, 1:235; ET in CF 7:146–47).

142. Cf. Rv 1:12–16.

143. Cf. Ps 26:13 [27:13] and 114:9 [116:9].

144. Cf. Mt 25:21.

145. Cf. Hugo Ripelin of Strassburg, *Compendium theologicae veritatis*, bk. I, ch. 16, on the incomprehensibility of God, and bk. VII, ch. 31, on the enumeration of celestial joys. See *Alberti Magni Opera*, ed. Borgnet, 34:17–19, 260–61.

146. On this commonplace of medieval theology, see Tertullian, *De paenitentia*, ch. 4 and 12 (PL 1:1343B and 1360A; CCSL 1:326, 340; ET in ANF 3:708–9, 714–15); Pacian of Barcelona, *Epistola 1*, par. 5 (PL 13:1056A); Jerome, *Commentarium in Isaiam*, bk. II, ch. 3, par. 8 (PL 24:65D; CCSL 73:51); Jerome, *Epistola 130*, par. 9 (PL 22:1115B).

147. Par. 2–3 (PL 183:820; *Bernardi Opera* 1:49–50; CF 4:63).

148. Gregory, *Moralia*, bk. XXII, ch. 17, par. 43 (PL 76:238C; CCSL 143A: 1122).

149. Denys of Rijkel, *De contemplatione*, bk. II, ch. 2; *Opera*, 41:234, points to Origen as the source of this passage.

150. Ca 2:3.

151. *De consolatione philosophiae*, bk. I, metrum 1, lines 14–15 (PL 63:585A; CCSL 94:1).

152. Guigo is actually referring to bk. II, ch. 7 and 10.

153. Guigo is actually referring to bk. II, ch. 6–8.

154. The Tortosa manuscript adds a gloss based on the *Glossa Ordinaria* on Mt 5:8.

155. This quotation from Bernard has not been located among his writings or among the works commonly attributed to him.

156. Cf. *De vera religione*, ch. 34, par. 64 (PL 34:150C; CCSL 32:229; CSEL 77, pt. 5:46; ET in LCC 6:257).

157. Gregory the Great, *Homiliae in Hiezechielem*, bk. I, hom. 4, par. 5 (PL 76:817D–818A; CCSL 142:50–51; ET by Gray, p. 43).

158. The Tortosa manuscript adds a gloss referring to Gregory the Great's *Moralia*, bk. XXIV, ch. 6, par. 12 (PL 76:292D–293A; CCSL 143B:1196); cf. Jerome, *Adversus Pelagianos*, bk. III, par. 12 (PL 23:582CD); Jerome, *Commentarium in Isaiam*, bk. III, ch. 6, par. 1 (PL 24:93A; CCSL 73:85).

159. Bernard, *De consideratione*, bk. V, ch. 14, par. 32 (PL 182:806C; *Bernardi Opera*, 3:493; CF 37:178–79). Guigo refers to the second, rather than fifth, book of this treatise.

160. "*Noli cessare, labor improbus omnia vincit.*" Virgil, *Georgics*, bk. I, line 145. The Tortosa manuscript adds a second proverb adapted from Ovid: "Water hollows out a stone," which the glossator applies to Christ, since the import of Ovid's imagery (a ring worn away by long use, a plough worn thin by long use) is that the water accomplishes its work not by main force but by frequent falling, just as a man is made wise not by force but by constant study. See Ovid, *Epistolae ex Ponto*, bk. IV, epist. 10, lines 5–8 (text and ET by Arthur Leslie Wheeler in Loeb Classics, pp. 464–65).

On Contemplation: Book Two

1. Augustine, *Soliloquia*, bk. I, par. 3 (PL 32:869; ET in NPNF-1, 7:537–38; LCC 6:24–25).

2. The first five chapters of book two were taken up, often word-for-word, in Ludolf of Saxony's *Vita Christi*. See Walter Baier, *Untersuchungen . . . Vita Christi des Ludolfs von Sachsen*, 3 vols., AC, 44, 292–95.

3. Augustine, *Confessiones*, bk. I, ch. 1 (PL 32:661A; CCSL 27).

4. Is 58:13.

5. The Tortosa manuscript adds a gloss on the meaning of confession, consisting of Ps 105:3 [106:3] plus quotations attributed to but not verifiable in Cassiodorus, the *Glossa Ordinaria*, and Jerome.

6. Cf. Dt 4:24; Heb 12:29; Mt 3:12.

7. Jn 1:5.

8. The Tortosa manuscript adds an extensive gloss on true and false joys of contemplation.

NOTES TO GUIGO, BOOK TWO

9. Cf. Ca 1:15; and Pseudo-Gregory the Great [Robert of Tombelaine], *Super Cantica*, ch. 3 (on Ca 3:1) (PL 79:502).

10. Cf. Ca 3:1.

11. Cf. Eph 2:19. See also the earlier references to the city of supernal citizens (*civitatem civium supernorum*) and fellowship of holy saints above (*sanctorum civium supernorum consortio*) in I.8, movement three, and I.11, step eleven.

12. Cf. Ps 93:10 [94:10].

13. Lk 10:42.

14. Gregory the Great, *Homiliae in Hiezechielem*, bk. II, hom. 2, par. 9 (PL 76:954A; CCSL 142:230–31; ET by Gray, p. 175).

15. Cf. the postcommunion prayer, *Deus, auctor pacis*, for the votive mass for peace, P. Bruylants, ed., *Les oraisons du missel romain* (Louvain: Centre de Documentation et d'Information Liturgiques, 1952), vol. 2, p. 64, par. 204. This prayer is found already in the eighth-century Gelasian and Gregorian sacramentaries. The formula *cui servire regnare est* (whom to serve is to reign) is found in various ecclesiastical authors, e.g., in the *Vita sancti Henrici* [Life of Saint Henry, the German Emperor, Henry II (972–1024)], par. 3. See Adalbert, *Vita Sancti Henrici*, ed. Georg Heinrich Pertz, *Monumenta Germaniae Historica, Scriptorum*, vol. 4 (Hanover: Hahn, 1841), p. 792.

16. The Tortosa manuscript adds "idle" [*otiosum*] here; it is not in the Vulgate, but the Hebrew text permits this translation, as, e.g., in the RSV; the Tortosa glossator undoubtedly drew his translation from a patristic source.

17. The Tortosa manuscript adds a gloss quoting this verse together with cross-references to Dt 33:12 and Mt 12:50 and to commentary by Ambrose (PL 15:1561D–1562A; SC 45:82, 84).

18. Cf. Lk 10:42.

19. Cf. Mt 25:21.

20. Cf. Jn 5:24.

21. *Sermo 24 in Cantica*, par. 8 (PL 183:899A; *Bernardi Opera*, 1:162; CF 7:49).

22. The Tortosa manuscript adds the long gloss "good for maintaining humility or fear or love" assembled from Augustine's letter 167 to Jerome (PL 33:739BC), and Anselm of Canterbury, *Meditatio* 2 (PL 158:722-23; ET by Benedicta Ward, *The Prayers and Meditations of St. Anselm* [Harmondsworth: Penguin, 1973], 225–28).

23. Cf. Mt 25:14–30.

24. Ps 142:2a [143:2a]; cf. Jb 9:3.

25. Mt 9:13.

26. Cf. Guigo I, *Meditationes*, nos. 16, 19, SC, 308:108; ET by Jolin, pp. 8–9: "By this alone are you just, that you acknowledge and proclaim you should be damned on account of your sins. If you say you are just, you are a liar, and are condemned by the Lord, the truth, as being contrary to Him. Say that you are a sinner, so that speaking the truth you may agree with the Lord, the truth, that you

need liberation." "When you are charming to your praiser, it is not really to your praiser that you are charming, for it is no longer you who are being praised. So vain are you. When one says: 'How good, how just he is,' the one who is such is praised, not you who are not such. Rather, you are no little blamed, so bad and so unjust are you. For the praise of the just is blame for the unjust. Therefore [it is] blame for you, an unjust man. When, therefore, you applaud the just man's praiser, you are applauding your truest blamer, because you are unjust. For he is not just who thinks himself just. Not even [if he be] an infant of one day." See also the editor's note regarding Guigo's understanding of liberty in the SC edition, pp. 312–14.

27. The word translated "service" here is *officium*, a voluntary or obligatory service. Guigo would have had in mind the "work of God" (*opus Dei*), i.e., the psalmody and liturgical services carried out by monks.

28. Cf. Evagrius Ponticus, *De oratione*, ch. 113 (PG 79:1191–92D; ET in CS 4:74).

29. Cf. Jn 15:5. The Tortosa manuscript adds a gloss based on the Rule of Benedict, ch. 20; Pseudo-Augustine, *De spiritu et anima*, ch. 50 (PL 40:816B); and Ps. 101:18 [102:17].

30. Cf. Mt 6:7.

31. Cf. Ca 3:6.

32. Cf. Mt 11:29.

33. Cf. Ps 102:8 [103:8].

34. Cf. Prv 8:31.

35. William of Saint-Thierry, *Epistola*, bk. I, ch. 14, par. 44 (PL 184:337A [= par. 179 in SC 223:288; CF 12:71]).

36. See bk. III, ch. 6–15, for a fuller discussion of these three steps. The Tortosa manuscript adds a long gloss here based on Gregory the Great's *Homilia 24 in Evangelia*, par. 6 (PL 76:1188AB; ET in CS 123:185); Bernard of Clairvaux, *De consideratione*, bk. V, ch. 11, par. 24 (PL 182:802B; *Bernardi Opera*, 3:486; ET in CF 37:169).

37. Bernard of Clairvaux, *De consideratione*, bk. II, ch. 2, par. 5 (PL 182:745B; *Bernardi Opera*, 3:414; ET in CF 37:52).

38. Richard of Saint-Victor, *Benjamin major*, bk. I, ch. 4 (PL 196:67D; ET in CWS, p. 157).

39. Cf. Richard of Saint-Victor, ibid.; idem, *De exterminatione mali*, tractatus 2, ch. 15 (PL 196:1102C); ET by Clare Kirchberger, *Richard of St Victor: Selected Writings on Contemplation* (London: Faber and Faber, 1957), pp. 244–45.

40. Richard of Saint-Victor, *Benjamin minor* [*The Twelve Patriarchs*], ch. 86 (PL 196:61D; ET in CWS, p. 145).

41. Guigo repeats this paragraph largely verbatim in III.6 below; this translation omits the second instance.

42. Gregory's text has *interna*, i.e., inward things, here. Three of the manuscripts of Guigo's treatise have *caelestia*, one (Paris) has *aeterna*, i.e., heavenly things and eternal things, respectively. The fifth manuscript, Tortosa, follows Gregory in

inserting *interna*. Dom Dupont is probably correct to follow the majority reading here—if Guigo was quoting Gregory from memory, he may have made the leap from Gregory's "inward things" to "heavenly things" quite easily, since he and the spiritual tradition he represents understood the two to be intimately interrelated.

43. Gregory the Great, *Moralia*, bk. V, ch. 31, par. 55 (PL 75:709D; CCSL 143:257).

44. Wis 1:1.

45. Cf. Gregory of Nyssa, *Vita Moysis*, pt. 2, par. 162 (PG 44:376D–77A; SC 1:81; ET in CWS, pp. 94–95).

46. The Tortosa manuscript adds texts from Augustine, *Soliloquia*, bk. I, ch. 13, par. 22 (PL 32:881BC; CSEL 89:34; ET in NPNF-1, 7:545; LCC 6:37); Pseudo-Denis, *Epistola 1 ad Gaium* (PG 3:1065–66, 1069–70; ET in CWS, p. 263); Gregory the Great, *Moralia*, bk. V, ch. 36, par. 66 (PL 75:716A; CCSL 143:265), and bk. XVIII, ch. 54, par. 88–93 (PL 76:91–96; CCSL 143A:950–55).

47. Cf. 1 Tm 6:16.

48. Cf. Mt 11:25–26.

49. Paterius, *Expositio super Genesim*, ch. 68 (PL 79:717C), quoting Gregory the Great, *Moralia*, bk. XXIV, ch. 6, par. 11 (PL 76:292BC; CCSL 143B:1195). Guigo quotes the same passage in III.8, below.

50. Gregory the Great, *Moralia*, bk. V, ch. 36, par. 66 (PL 75:716A; CCSL 143:265). The phrase could also be translated: "we know something of God when we fully sense that we are unable to know anything."

51. Cf. 1 Cor 13:12.

52. Cf. Ez 44:23.

53. William of Saint-Thierry, *Epistola*, bk. II, ch. 3, par. 18 (PL 184:349C–350A [= par. 267-70 in SC 223:356–60]; ET in CF 12:97). Guigo has omitted several short clauses.

54. Gregory of Nazianzus, *Oratio 45 in sanctum Pascha* [formerly Oratio 42], par. 3 (PG 36:626D–627A; ET in NPNF-2, 7:423–24). The Tortosa manuscript adds a long quotation from Gregory the Great, *Homilia 36 in Evangelia*, par. 1–2 (PL 76:1266AD; ET in CS 123:312–13).

55. Cf. Mal 4:2.

56. For Gregory this imperfect vision is involved in everything here below. See *Homilia 30 in Evangelia*, par. 10 (PL 76:1227A; ET in CS 123:246–47); *Moralia*, bk. IV, ch. 24, par. 45, and bk. V, ch. 30, par. 53 (PL 75:659A, 708A: CCSL 143: 190, 255). The Tortosa manuscript adds a quotation from Bernard of Clairvaux, *Sermo 31 in Cantica*, par. 2–3 (PL 183:941AD; *Bernardi Opera*, 1:220–21; ET in CF 7:125–26).

57. William of Saint-Thierry, *Epistola*, bk. II, ch. 2, par. 6 (PL 184:342D–343A [= par. 217 in SC 223:320; CF 12:84]).

58. Cf. bk. I, ch. 8–10, above.

59. Cf. 2 Cor 1:3.

60. Cf. Lam 3:25.

NOTES TO GUIGO, BOOK TWO

61. Cf. Gregory the Great, *Homiliae in Hiezechielem*, bk. II, hom. 5, par. 18 (PL 76:995C; CCSL 142:289; ET by Gray, p. 214); *The Cloud of Unknowing*, ch. 26 (ed. by Phyllis Hodgson, Early English Text Society, 218 [London: H. Milford for the Early English Text Society, 1944], p. 62; modern ET in CWS by James Walsh [New York: Paulist Press, 1981], p. 174).

62. Cf. Sir 35:17.

63. Most of the manuscripts have *promovet* here, but the Tortosa manuscript adds *cooperando*, thus modifying the *sola gratia* emphasis of the other two.

64. Sir 50:8; Ca 2:1.

65. Sir 39:17.

66. Cf. Ps 83:6–7 [84:5–6].

67. The Latin text here reads: "ascendens adhaerendo in Deum sitibunde affici et afficiendo Deo sitibundius adhaerere," a complex play on words that defies facile translation.

68. "Qui cathedram habet in caelo et in terris," together with the phrase "docet hominem sanctam scientiam" that follows, this concluding sentence links the offices of king, bishop, and university professor in a *sola gratia* statement: One must be taught even to know what one needs to pursue, seek, and study.

69. William Peraldus, *Summa virtutum*, tractate 2, part 7, ch. 10 (Cologne ed. 1629, p. 264).

70. Cf. Eph 2:19, and II.3, above.

71. The Tortosa manuscript adds a rather tangential gloss here on the meaning of *mysticus*, as derived from *mysterium*.

72. See Pseudo-Denis, *Theologia mystica*, ch. 5 (PG 3:1045D–1048B; ET in CWS p. 141); Gregory the Great, *Moralia*, bk. V, ch. 7–8, par. 13–15; bk. VI, ch. 37, par. 58; bk. X, ch. 8, par. 13 (PL 75:686BC, 762D–763A, 927D–928A; CCSL 143:227, 328, 545–46); idem, *Homiliae in Hiezechielem*, bk. II, hom. 2, par. 13, and bk. II, hom. 5, par. 14 (PL 76:955D–956A and 993D–994; CCSL 142:233–34, 286–87; ET by Gray, p. 177, 212–13); Bernard of Clairvaux, *Sermo 31 in Cantica*, par. 4 (PL 183:943BC; *Bernardi Opera*, 1:221–22; CF 7:127), and *Sermo 9 de diversis*, par. 1 (PL 183:565; *Bernardi Opera*, 6, pt. 1, p. 118).

73. The Tortosa manuscript adds the essential gloss here, explaining that *anagogica* is derived from *ana*, meaning "above" (sursum) and *gogos*, meaning "head" (*caput*) or "leading" (*ductio*). See Garnier de Rochefort [late twelfth-century Abbot of Clairvaux], *Sermo 31* (PL 205:766B). Thus any contemplation in a general sense is anagogical. The specific meaning of "uplifting by means of renunciation" that Guigo bases himself on here was developed by the authors cited in the preceding note.

74. In order to explain the vision of St. Paul, Augustine devotes book 12 of *De Genesi ad litteram* to these three types of seeing. See ch. 6, par. 15, and ch. 7, par. 16 (PL 34:458–459; CSEL 28, pt. 1, pp. 386–89). See also Augustine, *Contra Adimantum*, ch. 28, par. 2 (PL 42:171B; CSEL 25:188–90); and Peter Lombard's commentary on 2 Cor 12:2–4 (PL 198:80BC).

75. The Tortosa manuscript makes it clear that this vision was had by Abraham (Gn 18:2) and Moses at the burning bush (Ex 3:2).

76. The Tortosa manuscript refers to John's Apocalypse on Patmos (Rv 1:13).

77. Cf. 2 Cor 12:2–4.

78. The work now attributed to Hugh of Balma but transmitted largely anonymously in Guigo's day.

79. Cf. 1 Cor 6:17. The Tortosa manuscript adds a reference to Pseudo-Denis, *De divinis nominibus*, ch. 4, par. 15 (PG 3:714A; ET in CWS, p. 83).

80. Cf. Mt 11:29.

81. Cf. Ps 118:116 [119:116].

82. Cf. Ca 6:9 [6:10].

83. The Tortosa manuscript adds a long gloss here based on Ps 41:5 [42:4]; Gregory the Great, *Moralia*, bk. V, ch. 8, par. 14 (PL 75:686C: CCSL 143:227); Rv 3:20; Bernard of Clairvaux, *Sermo 15 in Cantica*, par. 6 (PL 183:847A; *Bernardi Opera*, 1:86; ET in CF 4:110): "To me, Christ is honey in the mouth, music in the ear, a song in the heart."

84. Jgs 13:20.

85. Cf. Eph 2:19.

86. Cf. bk. I, ch. 7.

87. The Tortosa manuscript adds a gloss based on Augustine, *De civitate Dei*, bk. X, ch. 6 (PL 41:283BC; CCSL 47:278).

88. Ex 33:11.

89. The Tortosa manuscript adds a gloss here explaining the nature of the soul's colloquy with God.

90. Ps 35:7 [36:6].

91. Rom 11:33.

92. Gregory the Great, *Homilia 9 in Evangelia*, par. 1 (PL 76:1106A; ET [homily 18] in CS 123:127).

93. Cf. Ca 1:7.

94. For this chapter, cf. Guigo II, *Scala Claustralium*, ch. 9–11 (PL 184:480–81; SC 163:100–106; ET in CS 48:76–79/Doubleday ed., pp. 89–92).

95. Cf. Jn 3:8.

96. Cf. Bernard of Clairvaux, *Sermo 17 in Cantica*, par. 1 (PL 183:855D; *Bernardi Opera*, 1:98; ET in CF 4:126). See also Gregory the Great, *Moralia*, bk. XXVI, ch. 19, par. 13 (PL 76:369A; CCSL 143B:1291); bk. V, ch. 4, par. 6 (PL 75:683A; CCSL 143:223), and *Homilia 25 in Evangelia*, par. 2 (PL 76:1190C; ET in CS 123:189–90): "Holy desires increase when their fulfillment is delayed."

97. The Tortosa manuscript adds a gloss based on Bernard of Clairvaux, *Sermo 17 in Cantica*, par. 2 (PL 183:856AB; *Bernardi Opera*, 1:99; ET in CF 4:127).

98. Ibid.

99. Cf. Heb 5:12–14.

100. The Tortosa manuscript adds a gloss based on Gregory the Great,

NOTES TO GUIGO, BOOK TWO/BOOK THREE

Homilia 33 in Evangelia, par. 4 (PL 76:1241C; ET in CS 123:271): "The rust of sin is all the more consumed when the heart of the sinner is burned up with a great fire of love."

101. The Tortosa manuscript adds a gloss here explaining the symbolism of *face*.

102. Cf. bk. II, ch. 8, above.

On Contemplation: Book Three

1. Augustine, *Tractatus 124 in Ioannem*, par. 5 (PL 35:1974B; CCSL 36:685; ET in NPNF-1, 7:450).

2. This describes the sequence of characterizations found in Ecclesiastes, e.g., in ch. 10:12-20.

3. A phrase used often by Gregory the Great. See *Moralia*, bk. X, ch. 29, par. 48 (PL 75:947A; CCSL 143:570-71).

4. The reference is to Mt 25:35-36, although these verses do not mention burial of the dead. Thomas Aquinas, *STh*, IIa IIae, qu. 32, art. 2, explains the absence by referring to Mt 10:28.

5. These activities would encompass the seven spiritual works of mercy: admonishing sinners, instructing the ignorant, counseling the doubtful, consoling the sorrowful, bearing wrongs, forgiving injuries, praying for the living and the dead.

6. On the "mixed life" of prelates and pastors, see Gregory the Great, *Moralia*, bk. XXXI, ch. 25, par. 49 (PL 76:600BC; CCSL 143B:1584-85); Augustine, *De civitate Dei*, bk. XIX, ch. 19 (PL 41:647AC; CCSL 48:686); Bernard of Clairvaux, *Sermo 9 in Cantica*, par. 8, and *Sermo 12*, par. 1 (PL 183:818C, 828; *Bernardi Opera*, 1:47, 60; CF 4:59, 77); Thomas Aquinas, *STh*, IIa IIae, qu. 182, art. 1 ad tertium, and art. 2, also qu. 188, art. 6, and IIIa, qu. 40, art. 1, ad secundum; *idem, Opusculum 18 de perfectione vitae spiritualis*, ch. 23, no. 5 (Leonine edition, vol. 41 [Rome, 1969]; ET in three unpublished MA dissertations at St. Louis University, 1942-1944—see James A. Weisheipl and Fabian R. Larcher, *Commentary on the Gospel of John* [Albany, N.Y.: Magi Books, 1980], p. 384). See also Claude Dagens, *S. Grégoire le Grand: Culture et expérience chrétiennes* (Paris: Etudes Augustiniennes, 1977), pp. 158-63.

7. Cf. Thomas Aquinas, *STh*, IIa IIae, qu. 180, art. 2.

8. Thomas Aquinas, *STh*, IIa IIae, qu. 180, art. 5 ad secundum.

9. Gregory the Great, *Moralia*, bk. VI, ch. 37, par. 59 (PL 75:763C; CCSL 143:329), a text cited by Thomas Aquinas, *STh*, IIa IIae, qu. 180, art. 5, obj. 2.

10. Thomas Aquinas, *STh*, IIa IIae, qu. 180, art. 5, ad secundum. The Stonyhurst manuscript adds a cross-reference to a fuller discussion of this topic in ch. 25 below.

11. Gregory the Great, ibid.

NOTES TO GUIGO, BOOK THREE

12. Gregory the Great, *Homiliae in Hiezechielem*, bk. II, hom. 2, par. 8 (PL 76:953A; CCSL 142:230; ET by Gray, p. 183).

13. Ibid.

14. Ibid., par. 11 (PL 76:954D–955A; CCSL 142:232).

15. Gregory the Great, *Homiliae in Hiezechielem*, bk. II, hom. 2, par. 8 (PL 76:953AB; CCSL 142:230; ET by Gray, pp. 174–75).

16. This citation has not been identified.

17. Cf. Thomas Aquinas, *In Evangelium secundum Ioannem*, commentary on John, ch. 11:3, lect. 6 (Marietti edition, p. 290, par. 1555; no ET); Peter Lombard, *Sermo 12* (PL 171:395B). This is one of a set of sermons attributed to Hildebert of Lavardin, Bishop of Tours, but actually by several other medieval personages, in this case, Peter Lombard. See André Wilmart, "Les sermons d'Hildebert," *Revue Bénédictine* 47 (1935): 1–51, at 12, 20, with references to work by B. Hauréau and others. Other references to the adage about Christ's exemplarity are found in Philippe Dupont, ed., *Sermons capitulaires de la Chartreuse de Mayence du début du XVe siècle*, AC 46 (1978): 86, n. 9.

18. Mt 17:1–9.

19. Cf. Nicholas Kempf, *De mystica theologia*, bk. IV, ch. 15 (AC ed., p. 321). Kempf's comments need not have been drawn from Guigo. Kempf simply mentions Jesus' own admonition to the three disciples not to tell anyone about what they had seen. Guigo makes no direct reference to Jesus' warning. Kempf's comment is shorter and could have been suggested by the Scripture text itself or by other commentators relating the same passage to mystical thology.

20. The Tortosa manuscript adds a long gloss here about hiding things from and revealing things to the proper people on the proper occasion.

21. Citation not identified. The Tortosa manuscript adds a gloss about the role of prelates, with citations to Scripture and Augustine.

22. Ps 83:8 [84:7].

23. Mt 13:46.

24. Cf. Lk 24:13–25.

25. Cf. Gregory the Great, *Moralia*, bk. XXXII, ch. 3, par. 4 (PL 76:636A; CCSL 143B:1629). The Tortosa manuscript adds a quotation from Isidore of Seville, *Libri sententiarum*, bk. III, ch. 15, par. 1 (PL 83:690A).

26. Lk 10:42.

27. *Moralia*, bk. VI, ch. 37, par. 61 (PL 75:764B; CCSL 143:330).

28. Guigo II, *Scala claustralium*, ch. 3–7 (PL 184:477–80; SC 163:84–96); Adam of Dryburgh (Adam of Witham), *De quadripartito exercitio cellae*, ch. 17 (PL 153:829–30).

29. Cf. Ex 26:34.

30. Richard of Saint-Victor, *Benjamin major*, bk. III, ch. 3, 6 (PL 196:113A, 116D–117A, 118A; ET in CWS, pp. 225, 231). Cf. idem, *Benjamin minor*, ch. 71 (PL 196:51C; ET in CWS, p. 129).

31. The Latin word translated *thanksgiving* here is *confessiones* in the Vul-

gate. Its English cognate is misleading—what is confessed is faith and gratitude toward God, hence the translation as "thanksgiving."

32. Bernard of Clairvaux, *Sermo 11 in Cantica*, par. 1 (PL 183:824B; *Bernardi Opera*, 1:54–55; ET in CF 4:69).

33. Cf. Ca 4:3. On the scarlet color of twin charity, see Pseudo-Gregory the Great [Robert of Tombelaine], *Expositio super Cantica*, par. 4 (PL 79:508C); Gilbert of Hoyland, *Sermo 24 in Cantica*, par. 3–4 (PL 184:127–28; ET in CF 20:297–303); William of Saint-Thierry, *Excerpta ex libris Sancti Gregorii Papae super Cantica Canticorum* (PL 180:457B).

34. Guigo II, *Scala claustralium*, ch. 2 (PL 184:467B; SC 163:84; ET in CS48: 68/Doubleday ed., p. 82).

35. This citation has not been located.

36. Hugh of Balma, *Roads to Zion*, unitive way, par. 84, "Difficult Question," par. 26–31, and illuminative way, par. 4–7.

37. Thomas Aquinas, *Super libros Sententiarum*, bk. I, dist. 3, qu. 1, art. 3, and qu. 2, art. 1–3 (no ET). Cf. Nicholas Kempf, *Mystica theologia*, bk. IV, ch. 3 (AC 9:265–67).

38. Cf. Thomas Aquinas, *Super libros Sententiarum*, bk. I, dist. 3, qu. 1, art. 4.

39. Augustine, *De vera religione*, ch. 29, par. 52 (PL 34:145B; CCSL 32:221; ET in LCC 6:251).

40. Cf. bk. II, ch. 7, above.

41. Cf. Gregory the Great, *Moralia*, bk. XXX, ch. 16, par. 54 (PL 76:554A; CCSL 143B:1428): "We by no means attain the summit of contemplation unless we cease from all exterior concerns" ["nequaquam culmen contemplationis attingimus si non ab exterioribus curare oppressione cessemus"].

42. Cf. Nicholas Kempf, *Mystica theologia*, bk. I, ch. 11 (AC 9:69–72).

43. Augustine, *Epistola 166*, par. 4 (PL 33:722A; CSEL 44:550–51).

44. This citation has not been located.

45. Peter Lombard, *Libri Sententiarum*, bk. I, dist. 3, ch. 12, par. 41 (PL 192:531D).

46. Hugo Ripelin of Strassburg, *Compendium theologicae veritatis*, bk. II, ch. 31, 62 (*Alberti Magni Opera*, 34:62, 84–85). See also Augustine, *De trinitate*, bk. X, ch. 11, par. 18 (PL 42:983A; CCSL 50:330–31; ET in NPNF-1, 3:142–43; LCC 8:88–89); Bernard of Clairvaux, *Sermo 11 in Cantica*, par. 5 (PL 183:826B; *Bernardi Opera*, 1:57; ET in CF 4:73); Thomas Aquinas, *In Evangelium secundum Iohannem*, commentary on John ch. 6:58, lect. 2 (Marietti edition, pp. 184–85, par. 977; ET by Weisheipl and Larcher, pp. 388–89).

47. Augustine, *De trinitate*, bk. XV, ch. 7, par. 11 (PL 42:1065B; CCSL 50A:474–75; ET in NPNF-1, 3:204–5; LCC 8:138).

48. Peter Lombard, *Libri Sententiarum*, bk. I, dist. 3, par 11 (PL 192:531D).

49. Est 13:9 (Vulgate).

50. Hugh of Saint-Victor, *Summa Sententiarum*, tractatus 3, ch. 8 (PL

NOTES TO GUIGO, BOOK THREE

176:101D–102A), and *De sacramentis*, bk. I, part. 5, ch. 21 (PL 176:255C; ET by Deferrari, p. 83).

51. Bernard of Clairvaux, *Sermo 81 in Cantica*, par. 5–6 (PL 183:1173C; *Bernardi Opera*, 2:287; ET in CF 40:162). Cf. Adam of Dryburgh (Adam of Witham), *De quadripartito exercitio cellae*, ch. 27 (PL 153:849D).

52. The Tortosa manuscript adds a quotation attributed to the *Glossa Ordinaria*, regarding creation in the image and likeness of the Trinity. The quotation has not been located.

53. Dom Dupont cites a variety of possible sources for this passage: Alain of Lille (PL 210:762D), Pseudo-Augustine, *Liber de spiritu et anima*, ch. 10 (PL 40:786A); Isaac of Stella, *Sermo 16* (PL 194:1744AB); Anselm of Laon, *De natura et libero arbitrio hominis*, in O. Lottin, *Psychologie et morale au XIIe et XIIIe siècles* (Louvain: Abbaye du Mont César, 1952), vol. 5, p. 345. Cf. Peter Lombard, *Libri Sententiarum*, bk. II, dist. 16 (PL 192:684), and Robert Javelet, *Image et ressemblance au XIIe siècle* (Paris: Letouzy et Ané, 1967), ch. 6, pp. 212–24.

54. Pseudo-Bernard, *De humana conditione*, ch. 4, par. 11 (PL 184:493A).

55. Richard of Saint-Victor, *Benjamin major*, bk. IV, ch. 17–18 (PL 196:156–60: ET in CWS, pp. 289–95) offers the properties of the divine essence and the concepts of the three Persons as material for reflection in the fifth and sixth steps of contemplation. The Tortosa manuscript adds a reference to this passage.

56. Cf. Ca 5:2.

57. Cf. Ps 62:6 [63:5].

58. Cf. 1.7 above.

59. Cf. Wis 1:1.

60. On withholding or restraining of grace, see II.11, above.

61. Gregory the Great, *Moralia*, bk. XXXI, ch. 51, par. 101 (PL 76:629A; CCSL 143B:1619–20).

62. Cf. Is 55:9.

63. Bernard of Clairvaux, *Sermo 41 in Cantica*, par. 3 (PL 183:986B; *Bernardi Opera*, 2:30; CF 7:207).

64. Cf. Ps 45:5 [46:4].

65. See I.9, I.10. To be completely separated from the senses would be to die.

66. Nicholas of Lyra, *Biblia postillata*; cf. Pseudo-Denys, *De caelesti hierarchia*, ch. 6–7 (PG 3:202A–205B), and Peter Lombard, *Commentarium in 2 Cor.* (PL 192:82D). Once more, citing from memory, Guigo errs, citing to ch. 13 rather than ch. 12 of the *Gloss*.

67. Nicholas of Lyra, *Biblia postillata*, which recalls words of John Chrysostom. Cf. Peter Lombard, *Commentarium in 2 Cor.* (PL 192:82BC).

68. Gregory the Great, *Moralia*, bk. XXIV, ch. 6, par. 11 (PL 76:292B; CCSL 143B:1195). The same citation is found in II.8, above.

69. Gregory the Great, *Moralia*, bk. XVIII, ch. 54, par. 89 (PL 76:93A; CCSL 143A:952).

70. Omitted in the PL edition of the *Glossa Ordinaria* (PL 114:90C), found in Nicholas of Lyra, *Biblia postillata*. Cf. Augustine, *De doctrina Christiana*, bk. II, ch. 7, par. 11 (PL 34:40A; CCSL 32:38; ET in NPNF-1, 2:538).

71. Nicholas of Lyra, *Biblia postillata*. Cf. Gregory the Great as cited above.

72. Cf. Eph 2:14.

73. Cf. Ps. 115:16 [116:16].

74. Cf. Ps 76:3 [77:2].

75. Cf. II.8.

76. Cf. 1 Cor 13:12.

77. The Tortosa manuscript adds a gloss regarding the absence of any veil that might cloud the vision of a soul in rapture, citing Augustine in *Soliloquia*, bk. I, ch. 13, par. 22 (PL 32:881B; CSEL 89:34; ET in NPNF-1, 7:545; LCC 6:37).

78. For the vision of Paul and Moses, see Augustine, *De videndo Deo* (= *Epistola 147 ad Paulinum*), ch. 13, par. 31–32 (PL 33:610–11; CSEL 44:305–7; ET in FC 20:199–200), and *De Genesi ad litteram*, bk. XII, ch. 26, par. 53, and ch. 28, par. 56 (PL 34:476, 478; CSEL 28:418–23; ET ACW 42:216–17, 219–20); Gregory the Great, *Moralia*, bk. XXIV, ch. 11, par. 34 (PL 76:306CD; CCSL 143B: 1213); Richard of Saint-Victor, *Benjamin major*, bk. IV, ch. 22 (PL 196:164–66; CWS, p. 302–4); Bernard of Clairvaux, *Sermo 32 in Cantica*, par. 9, and *Sermo 33*, par. 6 (PL 183:950A, 954C; *Bernardi Opera*, 1:231, 238; CF 7:141, 149–50), *Sermo 9 de diversis*, par. 1 (PL 183:565D; *Bernardi Opera* 6:118, referring to the vision of St. Benedict); William of Saint-Thierry, *Epistola*, bk. II, ch. 3, par. 18 (PL 184:350A [= par. 268 in SC 223:358]; CF 12:97); Hugh of Balma, *Roads to Zion*, via unitiva, par. 84; Albert the Great, *Summa theologica*, Ia, tr. 3, qu. 15, m. 1 ad 3um; Thomas Aquinas, *STh*, Ia, qu. 12, art. 11, ad secundum; IIa IIae, qu. 175, art. 3, and qu. 180, art. 5. For the Greek Fathers see Gregory of Nyssa, *Tractatus 2 in Psalmos*, ch. 14 (PG 44:577B), *Homilia 10 in Cantica* (PG 44:989D–992A; ET by McCambley, 193–95), and *Vita Moysi*, bk. II, par. 162–64 (PG 44:376D–377B; SC 1:80–82; ET in CWS, pp. 94–95); Pseudo-Denis, *Theologia mystica*, ch. 1, par. 3 (PG 3:1000C; ET in CWS, pp. 136–37). See also L. Reypens, "Dieu," in *DSAM* 3:883–929, and L. Malevez, "Essence de Dieu" in *DSAM* 4:1333–45.

79. These authors (including some already mentioned in the preceding note) would say that this vision of God in his essence is exceptional and limited to those in extraordinary rapture. See Gregory the Great, *Moralia*, bk. V, ch. 29, par. 52, and bk. XVIII, ch. 54, par. 88, etc. (PL 75:707A, PL 76:92D; CCSL 143:253–54, 143A:950–52), and *Homiliae in Hiezechielem*, bk. I, hom. 8, par. 30, and bk. II, hom. 2, par. 14 (PL 76:868C, 956B; CCSL 142:118–19, 234–35; ET by Gray, pp. 92, 177–78); Bernard of Clairvaux, *Sermo 31 in Cantica*, par. 2, *Sermo 34*, par. 1, *Sermo 41*, par. 3, *Sermo 18*, par. 6 (PL 183:941A, 960A, 986A–B, 862C; *Bernardi Opera*, 1:220, 245, 107, 2:30; CF 7:125, 160, 206-7, CF 4:138), and *Sermo 41 de diversis*, par. 11–12 (PL 183:659–60; *Bernardi Opera*, 6:252–53); Thomas Aquinas, *In Evangelium secundum Ioannem*, commentary on John ch. 1:18, lect. 11 (Marietti edition, pp. 42–43, par. 209–214; ET by Weisheipl and Larcher, pp. 101–4); Bonaventure,

NOTES TO GUIGO, BOOK THREE

Commentarium in IV Libros Sententiarum, bk. II, dist. 23, art. 2, qu. 3 (Quaracchi *Opera Omnia*, 2:544B); Bonaventure, *Hexaëmeron*, ch. 3, par. 30 (*Opera*, 5:348).

80. Cf. 1 Cor 13:12. See Gregory the Great, *Moralia*, bk. XVII, ch. 27, par. 39, bk. XVIII, ch. 54, par. 90, bk. XXIII, ch. 20, par. 39 (PL 76:29A, 93D–94A, 274C; CCSL 143A:873–74, 953; 143B:1173–74), cf. idem, *Homilia 30 in Evangelia*, par. 10 (PL 76:1226D; CS 123:246).

81. Cf. Num 12:8: "With him I speak mouth to mouth and plainly, and not by riddles and figures does he see the Lord."

82. All authors say that the vision can only be fleeting, furtive, transitory. See Augustine, *Enarratio in Psalmum 41*, par. 10 (PL 36:471C; CCSL 38:468); Gregory the Great, *Moralia*, bk. V, ch. 33, par. 58, bk. VIII, ch. 30, par. 49–50, bk. XXIV, ch. 6, par. 12 (PL 75:711C, 832B–833C, PL 76:292D; CCSL 143:259–60, 420–22, 143B:1196); idem, *Homiliae in Hiezechielem*, bk. I, hom. 5, par. 12 (PL 76:825D–826C; CCSL 142:62–64; ET by Gray, p. 51–52); Bernard of Clairvaux, *Sermo 23 in Cantica*, par. 15, *Sermo 32*, par. 2 (PL 183:893A, 946A; *Bernardi Opera*, 1:149, 227; CF 7:39, 135); Thomas Aquinas, *STh*, IIa IIae, qu. 174, art. 5 ad primum, qu. 175, art. 3 ad secundum, qu. 180, art. 8; Bonaventure, *In IV Libros Sententiarum*, bk. IV, dist. 6, part. 2, dub. 1 (Quaracchi *Opera* 4:160).

83. *De trinitate*, bk. I, ch. 2, par. 4 (PL 42:822A; CCSL 50:31; ET in NPNF-1, 3:19).

84. Ibid., bk. I, ch. 6, par. 11 (PL 42:826C; CCSL 50:40; ET in NPNF-1, 3:22).

85. Gregory the Great, *Moralia*, bk. X, ch. 8, par. 13 (PL 75:928B; CCSL 143:546); cf. *Homiliae in Hiezechielem*, bk. II, hom. 2, par. 14 (PL 76:956B; CCSL 142:234; ET by Gray, p. 177). Gregory does say that compunction permits one to fix this gaze—see *Moralia*, bk. XXIII, ch. 21, par. 42 (PL 76:277A; CCSL 143B:1176).

86. Cf. Lk 12:49.

87. Cf. Heb 12:29, which cites Dt 4:24.

88. Bernard of Clairvaux, *Sermo 15 de diversis*, par. 4 (PL 183:578C; *Bernardi Opera*, 6:142).

89. Cf. I.7, with citations to the literature.

90. *De trinitate*, bk. XII, ch. 15, par. 25 (PL 42:1012B; CCSL 50:379; ET in NPNF-1, 3:165).

91. Guigo's referents are not entirely clear here. If the *donum intellectus* ("gift of understanding") here refers to the "attentive consideration" of ch. 6 and the opening line of the present chapter, then "the other two" would refer to "alluring meditation" and "inventive contemplation" of ch. 11–14, and 15. This seems a more likely explanation than the possibility that he is referring to distinctions among the three divisions of the second stage (which is supposed to be entirely sapiential) dealt with in the present chapter alone. If the latter reference is intended, then "cognition of things by true taste of them" would involve a "knowing as if by seeing" and "the

other two" means of knowing "as if by tasting" would refer to "knowledge of eternal things" and "experiential knowledge of divine sweetness".

92. *Confessions*, bk. X, ch. 40 (PL 32:807B; CCSL 27:191).

93. Cf. Rom 8:13.

94. Cf. Bernard, *Sermo 12 in Cantica*, par. 9 (PL 183:832C; *Bernardi Opera*, 1:66; CF 4:84–85). See the discussion of late medieval use of this unusual verse in Martin, *Fifteenth-Century Carthusian Reform*, 215–19.

95. Cf. Odo of Cluny, *Vita Geraldi Auriliacensis*, bk. II, ch. 8 (PL 133:675B; ET by Gerald Sitwell, *St. Odo of Cluny, Being the Life of St. Odo of Cluny by John Salerno and the Life of St. Gerald of Aurillac* [London: Sheed and Ward, 1958], p. 139); Thomas Aquinas, *STh*, IIa IIae, qu. 184, art. 8, obj. 3: "a bad monk is a good cleric."

96. The citation has not been located. The three components (obedience, steadiness, and patience) recall but do not precisely repeat the main elements of monastic life: obedience, stability, conversion of life. See *Rule of St. Benedict*, ch. 58. These were integrated with the three evangelical counsels: poverty, celibacy, and obedience in medieval monasticism. See the discussion in Timothy Fry et al., eds., *RB 1980: The Rule of St. Benedict in Latin and English with Notes* (Collegeville, Minn.: Liturgical Press, 1981), pp. 457–59.

97. Cf. Is 46:8.

98. The two best manuscripts (Stonyhurst, Tortosa) have *sperma* here, a medieval equivalent for the Latin *semen*, which can mean a variety of forms of seed, both animal and vegetable. Three manuscripts have *spina*, i.e., "thorns" or "brambles" (also backbone, spigot, etc.).

99. This citation has not been located.

100. Cf. Mt 22:21.

101. Cf. Ca 1:4 [1:5].

102. Cf. Ps 114:8 [116:8].

103. Bernard of Clairvaux, *Sermo 27 in Cantica*, par. 14 (PL 183:920D; *Bernardi Opera*, 1:191; CF 7:86).

104. Cf. Ps 35:10 [36:9].

105. The Latin term *claritas* used here, quoting from the Vulgate, carries as its primary connotation brightness, splendor, but can also connote glory and renown. The Greek word *doxa* that Jerome rendered as *claritas* was translated as "glory" in the Authorized version.

106. Cf. William of Saint-Thierry, *Epistola*, bk. I, ch. 5, par. 12 (PL 184:316B [= par. 45 in SC 223:180]; CF 12:27); cf. *Meditation III*, par. 8 (PL 180:213B; SC 324:70; CF 3:104, 106).

107. The Latin term used here is *expedita ratione*, which can mean either "free," "disentangled," or "unpacked," "light of foot," i.e., "expedited" in one of its two meanings in English: "made easy." But it can also mean "sent hurriedly on its way," "sent packing," "sent off on a journey," i.e., "expedited" in another sense in English. The context argues for the former connotations, although given the em-

phasis on reason being surpassed and in some sense left behind in favor of affective ascent, the second sense of sending reason packing may perhaps lurk under the surface here.

108. Cf. 2 Cor 4:4.

109. William of Saint-Thierry, *Epistola*, bk. II, ch. 3, par. 17 (PL 184:349C [= par. 266 in SC 223:356; CF 12:96]).

110. Cf. *Rule of Saint Benedict*, ch. 4: "The workshop where we carefully work at these things is the enclosure of the monastery and our stable commitment to the community." See also Adam of Dryburgh (Adam of Witham), *De quadripartito exercitio cellae*, ch. 15 (PL 153:826D).

111. Cf. Phil 3:20.

112. William of Saint-Thierry, *Epistola*, bk. I, ch. 13, par. 38 (PL 184:333A [= par. 158 in SC 223:268]; CF 12:62). Cf. bk. I, ch. 4, par. 10 (PL 184:314A [par. 31 in SC 223:168]; CF 12:20), where William plays with the similarity between *cella* (cell) and *caelum* (heaven).

113. William of Saint-Thierry, *Epistola*, bk. 1, ch. 4, par. 11 (PL 184:314D [= par. 35 in SC 223:172]; CF 12:22).

114. See Gregory the Great, *Moralia*, bk. XXIV, ch. 6, par. 12 (PL 76:292D; CCSL 143B:1196).

115. Cf. Ca 1:10. The RSV translates the Hebrew here as "studded with silver"; the present translator prefers "inlaid" or "filigreed," because it better captures the sense of the Vulgate term "murenulas vermiculatas."

116. Bernard of Clairvaux, *Sermo 41 in Cantica*, par. 4 (PL 183:986C; Bernardi Opera, 2:31; CF 7:207).

117. Cf. Richard of Saint-Victor, *Benjamin major*, bk. 1, ch. 4 (PL 196:67D; ET in CWS, p. 157).

118. Bernard of Clairvaux, *Sermo 41 in Cantica*, par. 3 (PL 183:986AB; Bernardi Opera, 2:30; CF 7:206–7).

119. Cf. Ca 5:11. There is, of course, no direct reference to Christ in this passage, and one MS, Parkminster, substitutes "Word" here for "Christ."

120. Cf. Bernard of Clairvaux, *Sermo 41 in Cantica*, par. 3, as cited above.

121. Cf. Gregory the Great, *Moralia*, bk. V, ch. 36, par. 66 (PL 75:715C; CCSL 143:264–65); Peter Lombard, *Libri Sententiarum*, bk. I, dist. 9, ch. 10, par. 94 (PL 192:547D).

122. Cf. Gregory of Nyssa, *Homilia 3 in Cantica* (PG 44:820D; ET by McCambley, pp. 82–83).

123. Cf. I:2, 10; III:10.

124. Guigo is quoting paragraphs 2–6a of the sermon (PL 183:985–87; Bernardi Opera, 2:29–32; CF 7:205–8).

125. Cf. 2 Cor 5:7.

126. Cf. Mt 5:8.

127. Cf. Ps 50:10 [51:8, drawing on the alternate reading in RSV: "Make [me] to hear"].

128. Cf. Ca 1:6.
129. Cf. Jn 16:24.
130. Cf. Ps 15:11 [16:11].
131. Cf. 1 Cor 13:12.
132. Cf. Jas 1:7.
133. Cf. Jn 19:11.
134. Cf. Ps 77:49 [78:49].
135. For the doctrine that images of terrestrial reality obscure the eye in contemplation, see Gregory, *Moralia,* bk. VIII, ch. 6, par. 9 (PL 75:806D; CCSL 143:387).
136. Cf. Heb 1:14.
137. Cf. Ca 1:6.
138. Cf. 2 Cor 5:15.
139. Cf. 1 Tm 6:5.
140. Cf. Rom 12:16.
141. The Vulgate text is worded slightly differently: "I gave her corn and wine and oil, and multiplied her silver, and gold, which they have used in the service of Baal."
142. Cf. 1 Thes 4:6.
143. Cf. 1 Tm 6:10.
144. Cf. Hugh of Saint-Victor, *De institutione novitiorum,* ch. 10 (PL 176:935D): "Four things are to be kept well-disciplined: clothing, gestures, speech, and table [i.e., food]."
145. Cf. the list of vices given by Gregory the Great, *Moralia,* bk. XXXI, ch. 45, par. 87–88, bk. XXX, ch. 3, par. 13 (PL 76:621AB, 530C; CCSL 143B:1610, 1499–1500).
146. The Latin term used here, *gula,* refers to intemperance in a wide variety of things, especially in food and drink.
147. Cf. Gregory the Great, *Moralia,* bk. XXXI, ch. 45, par. 87 (PL 76:621A; CCSL 143B:1610).
148. Cf. Augustine, *Enarratio in Psalmos,* 18:14 [19:14] (PL 36:156D; CCSL 38:104); Nicholas of Lyra, *Postilla.*
149. Bernard of Clairvaux, *Sermo 37 in Cantica,* par. 7 (PL 183:974B; *Bernardi Opera,* 2:13; CF 7:186).
150. Guigo here distinguishes between self-pity and what might today be called clinical depression.
151. *Commentarium in Matthaeum,* bk. 1, citing Ecclesiastes 9:16 (CCSL 77:26; PL 26:35B).
152. This citation has not been located.
153. This citation has not been located.
154. Bernard of Clairvaux, *De gradibus humilitatis et superbiae,* ch. 18, par. 47 (PL 182:967C; *Bernardi Opera,* 3:52; CF 13:74).

155. Gregory the Great, *Moralia*, bk. IX, ch. 66, par. 105 (PL 75:916D–917A; CCSL 143:530–31).

156. John Chrysostom, *Homilia 29 in Hebraeos*, par. 7 (PG 63:426B; ET NPNF-1, 14:502).

157. Roman missal, preface for Lent.

158. Gregory the Great, *Moralia*, bk. XXX, ch. 10, par. 39 (PL 76:546C; CCSL 143B:1519–20).

159. *Adversus Jovinianum*, bk. 2, ch. 12 (PL 23:302A; ET NPNF-2, 6:397). Cf. Jerome, *Epistola 52*, par. 11 (PL 22:537A; CSEL 54:434; NPNF-2, 6:94–95).

160. Source not located.

161. Source not located.

162. Gregory the Great, *Homilia 35 in Evangelia*, par. 4 (PL 76:1262A; ET in CS 123:305).

163. William of Saint-Thierry, *Epistola*, bk. I, ch. 18 (PL 184:320C [= par. 74 in SC 223:200; CF 12:36]). Guigo's numbering does not correspond either to PL or SC numberings.

164. Ibid. (PL 184:320B [= par. 72 in SC 223:200; CF 12:36]).

165. Augustine, *Confessions*, bk. X, ch. 31, par. 44 (PL 32:797D; CCSL 27:178).

166. William of Saint-Thierry, *Epistola*, bk. I, ch. 11, par. 32 (PL 184:328C [= par. 126 in SC 223:242; CF 12:53]). Guigo gives "chapter twenty-four" as the reference.

167. Cf. Mt 24:45.

168. William of Auxerre, *Summa aurea* [*Summa super quatuor sententiarum*], ed. Ribaillier (1980–1987).

169. Hugo Ripelin of Strassburg, *Compendium theologicae veritatis*, bk. V, ch. 6 (*Alberti Magni Opera* 34:136); cf. Gregory the Great, *Moralia*, bk. XX, ch. 7, par. 17 (PL 76:147; CCSL 143A:1015–16).

170. Augustine, *De moribus Ecclesiae*, bk. I, ch. 15, par. 25 (PL 32:1322A; ET in NPNF-1, 4:48), cf. *De civitate Dei*, bk. XV, ch. 22 (PL 41:467D; CCSL 48:488): "a good, short definition: 'virtue is the order of love.' "

171. Augustine, *Epistola 167*, par. 15 (PL 33:739B; CSEL 44:602; ET in FC 30:44).

172. Augustine, *Epistola 155*, par. 13 (PL 33:671D–672A; CSEL 44:443; ET in FC 20:314). Augustine is citing the four cardinal virtues here.

173. Hugo Ripelin of Strassburg, *Compendium theologicae veritatis*, bk. V, ch. 5 (*Alberti Magni Opera* 34:136). Hugh is playing on the similarity of *vires* (strength, power) and *virtutes* (virtues) here.

174. Ambrosiaster, *Commentarium in Epistolam ad Colossenses*, 3:14 (PL 17:437B; CSEL 81, pt. 2, p. 198).

175. Nicholas of Lyra, *Postilla*.

176. Augustine, *De diversis quaestionibus 83 liber*, bk. I, qu. 61, par. 4 (PL 40:51C; CCSL 44A:127; ET in FC 70:121). Carthusians read this on the seventh

Sunday in Pentecost season. See R. Etaix, "L'homiliaire cartusien," *Sacris Erudiri* 13 (1962): 67–112, at 76.

177. Pseudo-Jerome, *Epistola 148*, par. 10 (PL 22:1209A).

178. William of Saint-Thierry, *Epistola*, bk. I, ch. 8, par. 24 (PL 184:323C [= par. 92 in SC 223:214: CF 12:42]).

179. Richard of Saint-Victor, *Benjamin minor*, ch. 7 (PL 196:6B; ET in CWS, p. 60).

180. Richard of Saint-Victor, *Benjamin major*, bk. III, ch. 23 (PL 196:132BD; ET in CWS, p. 254).

181. Seneca, *Epistles to Lucilius*, no. 89, par. 8 (Loeb Classics, Seneca, *Ad Lucilium Epistulae Morales*, vol. 2:382–83).

182. William of Saint-Thierry, *Epistola*, bk. I, ch. 6, par. 17 (PL 184:319D [= par. 69 in SC 223:198; CF 12:35]).

183. All manuscripts except the Tortosa copy repeat this sentence, with the addition of "and day acceptable to the Lord."

184. Gregory the Great, *Moralia*, bk. XX, ch. 14, par. 28 (PL 76:154B; CCSL 143A:1024).

185. Cf. Ps 24:17 [Vulgate].

186. Cf. Ps 71:7 [72:7].

187. Cf. Ps 9:11 [9:10].

188. Cf. Jas 1:19.

189. Gregory the Great, *Homiliae in Hiezechielem*, bk. I, homily 8, par. 8 (PL 76:857D-858A; CCSL 142:106; ET by Gray, pp. 81–82).

190. Cf. 1 Pt 2:11; Gal 5:17.

191. Gregory the Great, *Moralia*, bk. X, ch. 15, par. 31 (PL 75:938C; CCSL 143:559). Cf. ibid., bk. V, ch. 32, par. 57 (PL 75:711B; CCSL 143:259).

192. The Charleville manuscript attributes this thought to Jerome. It is from *Epistola* 125, par. 11 (CSEL 56:130; ET NPNF-2, 6:248). Cf. Bernard of Portes, *Letter to Raynaud the Hermit*, par. 3 (PL 153:893B; SC 274:54).

193. The Vulgate has "without judging, without dissimulation" instead of "judging without dissimulation." Guigo has once more cited incorrectly from memory.

194. Cf. Lam 3:28.

195. Gregory the Great, *Moralia*, bk. VI, ch. 37, par. 59 (PL 75:763BC; CCSL 143:329).

196. Cf. Gregory, *Moralia*, bk. IV, ch. 24, par. 45 (PL 75:659A; CCSL 143:190–91).

197. Aristotle, *De anima*, bk. III, ch. 7, par. 3.

198. Thomas Aquinas, *STh*, IIa IIae, qu. 180, art. 5 ad 2um. The quotation from Gregory is from *Moralia*, bk. VI, ch. 37, par. 59 (PL 75:763C; CCSL 143:329).

199. The Latin term used here, *species intelligibilis*, is a technical term describing the way many medieval natural philosophers understood the process of physical

vision: an intelligible form, or representation (*species*), provided a physical medium between the object seen and the inner senses of the mind in which perception was completed. See the summary of this view and critiques of it by late medieval natural philosophers in Katherine H. Tachau, *Vision and Certitude in the Age of Ockham: Optics, Epistemology, and the Foundations of Semantics*, Studien und Texte zur Geistesgeschichte des Mittelalters, 22 (Leiden: E. J. Brill, 1988), with citations to earlier secondary literature, including the important work of David Lindberg.

200. Thomas Aquinas, *STh*, IIa IIae, qu. 174, art. 4.

201. All manuscripts say "duo" here, but Guigo proceeds to enumerate three—the third is to undertake spiritual exercises.

202. Jas 1:17.

203. Bernard of Clairvaux, *Sermo 21 in Cantica*, par. 5–6 (PL 183:874; *Bernardi Opera*, 1:125; CF 7:7–8). Cf. Guigo II, *Scala Claustralium*, ch. 8 (PL 184:480C [= ch. 10 in SC 163:102, ET in CS 48:77/Doubleday ed., p. 90]): "For this grace the spouse bestows when He pleases and to whom He pleases; it is not possessed as though by lawful title."

204. Augustine, *Confessions*, bk. 10, ch. 28, par. 39 (PL 32:795D; CCSL 27:175).

205. Gregory the Great, *Homilia 35 in Evangelia*, par. 1 (PL 76:1260B; ET in CS 123:302–3).

206. Cf. Gal 5:25.

207. Cf. Jb 14:2

208. Cf. Jer 10:23.

209. Cf. Phil 3:13.

210. Bernard of Clairvaux, *Sermo 21 in Cantica*, par. 4–5 (PL 183:874; *Bernardi Opera*, 1:124–25; CF 7:7).

211. Cf. William of Saint-Thierry, *Epistola*, bk. I, ch. 10, par. 28–29 (PL 184:325D–326D [= par. 107-8 in SC 223:228–30; CF 12:47–48]).

212. This quotation has not been located in Augustine, but is attributed to Augustine by Hugh Ripelin of Strasbourg in *Compendium theologicae veritatis*, bk. III, ch. 12 (*Alberti Magni Opera* 34:102).

213. Cf. Jer 4:3 and Mt 13:7.

214. Gregory, *Moralia*, bk. VII, ch. 37, par. 58 (PL 75:800C; CCSL 143:379). Cf. *Homilia 6 in Evangelia*, par. 6 (PL 76:1098D; ET [hom. 5] in CS 123:33), and *Regula pastoralis*, part 3, ch. 14 (PL 77:74A; NPNF-2, 12:38).

215. William of Saint-Thierry, *Epistola*, bk. I, ch. 8, par. 21 (PL 184:321D [= par. 82 in SC 223:206; CF 12:39]).

216. Isidore of Seville, *Sententiae*, bk. II, ch. 36, par. 5–6 (PL 83:637D).

217. The text actually says "in the first tractate" on contemplation but gives the opening words of the intended section ("scilicet alia"), which appears to refer to II.10, where Guigo discusses anagogical contemplation.

Bibliography

For editions and translations of Hugh of Balma and Guigo de Ponte, see the Introduction.

Primary Sources

Adam of Dryburgh (Adam of Witham). *De quadripartito exercitio cellae.* PL 153:830C.

Aelred of Rievaulx. *Speculum caritatis.* Edited by A. Hoste and C. H. Talbot, *Aelredi Rievallensis Opera Omnia,* vol. 1: *Opera ascetica,* CCCM, 1. Turnhout: Brepols, 1971. ET as *The Mirror of Charity,* by Elizabeth Connor, O.C.S.O., CF 17. Kalamazoo: Cistercian Publications, 1990.

Albert the Great. *Alberti Magni Ratisbonensis episcopis ordinis praedicatorum opera omnia.* Edited by Augustus Borgnet and Emile Borgnet. 38 vols. Paris: Vivés, 1890–1899. See Hugo Ripelin of Strassburg and Johannes von Kastl below.

Ambrose of Milan. *De excessu fratris.* PL 16. CSEL 73.

———. *De fide.* PL 16. CSEL 78.

Anonymous. *The Cloud of Unknowing.* Edited by Phyllis Hodgson. Early English Text Society, 218. London: H. Milford for the Early English Text Society, 1944. Modern ET by James Walsh as *The Cloud of Unknowing.* New York: Paulist Press, 1981.

BIBLIOGRAPHY

Anonymous. *The Pursuit of Wisdom and Other Works by the Author of the Cloud of Unknowing.* Edited and translated by James Walsh. CWS. New York: Paulist Press, 1988.

Anselm of Canterbury. *Meditationes.* PL 158. ET by Benedicta Ward as *The Prayers and Meditations of St. Anselm.* Harmondsworth: Penguin, 1973, pp. 221–37.

Augustine, *Confessiones.* PL 32. CSEL 33. CCSL 27. Various English translations as *Confessions.*

————. *De civitate Dei.* PL 41. CCSL 47–48. Various English translations as *On the City of God.*

————. *De doctrina Christiana.* PL 34:15–122. CSEL 89:3–169. CCSL 32:1–167. Various English translations, including NPNF-1, vol. 2; FC, vol. 2.

————. *De moribus Ecclesiae.* PL 32. No modern edition. ET by Richard Stothert in NPNF-1, 4:48.

————. *De trinitate.* PL 42. CCSL 50–50A. ET by Arthur West Haddan and W. G. T. Shedd as *On the Trinity* in NPNF-1, vol. 3, and LCC, vol. 8 (excerpts). Complete translation by Edmund Hill, *The Trinity.* The Works of St. Augustine, part I, vol. 5. Brooklyn, N.Y.: New City Press, 1991.

————. *De vera religione.* PL 34. CCSL 32. CSEL 77, pt. 5. ET by J. H. S. Burleigh as *On True Religion* in LCC, vol. 6. Philadelphia: Westminster, 1953.

————. *Enarratio in Psalmos.* PL 36. CCSL 38. Partial ET by A. Cleveland Coxe, *Expositions on the Book of Psalms,* in NPNF-1, vol. 8.

————. *In prima epistola Ioannis.* PL 35. SC 75. ET by H. Brown and Joseph H. Meyer as *Ten Homilies on the Epistle of John to the Parthians* in NPNF-1, vol. 7. ET by John Burleigh in LCC, vol. 8. Philadelphia: Westminster, 1955.

BIBLIOGRAPHY

Bernard of Clairvaux. *De diligendo Deo.* PL 182:973–1000; *Bernardi Opera* 3:119–54. ET in *Treatises II: The Steps of Humility and Pride; On Loving God.* CF 13. Translated by M. Ambrose Conway and Robert Walton. Kalamazoo: Cistercian Publications, 1980. Reprinted in separate booklets as CF 13A and 13B.

————. *De gradibus humilitatis et superbiae.* PL 182:941–972; *Bernardi Opera* 3:13–59. ET as above.

————. *Sermo in aquaductu* [*In nativitae Mariae*]. PL 183. *Bernardi Opera* 5.

————. *Sermones in Cantica Canticorum.* PL 183. *Sancti Bernardi Opera* 1–2. Edited by Jean Leclercq, H. M. Rochais, and C. H. Talbot. Rome: Editiones Cistercienses, 1957, 1958. ET by Kilian Walsh and Irene Edmonds as *On the Song of Songs I–IV.* CF 4, 7, 31, 40. Kalamazoo: Cistercian Publications, 1971, 1976, 1979, 1980.

Biblia Sacra cum glossis, Interlineari et Ordinaria, Nicolai Lyrani Postilla, etc. 6 vols. Venice, 1588.

Bonaventure. *Itinerarium Mentis in Deum.* ET in *The Soul's Journey into God; The Tree of Life; The Life of St. Francis.* Introduction and translation by Ewert Cousins. CWS. New York: Paulist Press, 1978.

————. *S. Bonaventurae Opera Omnia.* Edita studio et cura PP. Collegii S. Bonaventurae. 10 vols. Rome: Ad Claras Aquas [Quaracchi], 1882–1902. Vol. 8 (1898) and 10 (1902).

Cloud of Unknowing. See Anonymous, above.

Denis of Rijkel. *Doctoris Ecstatici D. Dionysii Cartusiensis Opera Omnia.* 42 vols. Montreuil-sur-Mer, Tournai, Parkminster: Charterhouse of Notre Dame des Près, 1896–1913, 1935.

Evagrius Ponticus. *De oratione.* PG 79. ET by John Eudes Bamberger as *Praktikos; Chapters on Prayer.* CS 4. Kalamazoo: Cistercian Publications, 1981.

BIBLIOGRAPHY

Gerson, Jean. *Elucidatio scolastica in theologiae mysticae.* Edited by André Combes in *Ioannis Carlerii de Gerson de Mystica Theologia.* Lugano: Thesaurus Mundi, 1958, pp. 221–34.

Gilbert of Hoyland. *Sermons on the Song of Songs I–III.* Translated by Lawrence Braceland. CF 14, 20, 26. Kalamazoo: Cistercian Publications, 1978–1979.

Glossa Ordinaria. PL 113–14n (abbreviated). See Nicholas of Lyra, under Abbreviations, and *Biblia sacra,* above.

Gregory of Nyssa. *Homiliae in Cantica.* PG 44. SC 314. ET by Casimir McCambley as *Commentary on the Song of Songs.* Archbishop Iakovos Library of Ecclesiastical and Historical Sources, 12. Brookline, Mass.: Hellenic College Press, 1987.

———. *Vita Moysis.* PG 44:376D–77A. SC 1. ET by Everett Ferguson and Abraham J. Malherbe as *The Life of Moses.* New York: Paulist Press, 1978.

Gregory the Great. *Dialogorum libri.* PL 77. SC 251, 260, 265. ET by Odo John Zimmermann as *Dialogues* in FC 39. Washington, D.C.: Catholic University of America, 1959.

———. *XL Homiliarum in Evangelia libri duo.* PL 76. ET by David Hurst as *Forty Gospel Homilies.* [The PL numbering of the first twenty homilies has been rearranged.] CS 123. Kalamazoo: Cistercian Publications, 1990.

———. *Homiliae in Hiezechielem.* PL 76. CCSL 142. Translated by Theodosia Gray as *The Homilies of St. Gregory the Great on the Book of the Prophet Ezekiel.* Edited by Presbytera Juliana Cownie. Etna, Cal.: Center for Traditionalist Orthodox Studies, 1990.

———. *Moralia in Job.* PL 76. SC 32, 212, 221. CSL 143–43B. ET by J. Bliss as *Moralia on in Book of Job,* Library of the Fathers of the Church, 18, 22, 23, 31. Oxford: J. H. Parker, 1844–1850.

Guigo I. *Consuetudines cartusienses.* Edited by a Carthusian. *Coutumes de Chartreuse.* Sources chrétiennes, 313. Paris: Editions du Cerf, 1984.

BIBLIOGRAPHY

Cf. PL 153:635–758. Reprinted in *The Evolution of the Carthusian Statutes from the Consuetudines Guigonis to the Tertia Compilatio, Documents,* vol. 1. AC 99, Documents, 1. 1989. Pp. 7–56.

———. *Les méditations: Recueil de pensées.* Edited by a Carthusian. SC 308. Paris: Du Cerf, 1983. ET by John J. Jolin, Mediaeval Philosophical Texts in Translation, 6. Milwaukee: Marquette University Press, 1951. ET by A. Gordon Mursell, *The Meditations of Guigo I, Prior of the Charterhouse.* Cistercian Studies series, 155. Kalamazoo: Cistercian Publications, 1995.

Guigo II. *Scala Claustralium.* PL 40 and PL 184. Edited by James Walsh and Edmund Colledge. SC 163. Paris: Editions du Cerf, 1970. ET refers to James Walsh and Edmund Colledge translation with dual pagination from Doubleday edition: *The Ladder of Monks: A Letter on the Contemplative Life; and Twelve Meditations,* by Guigo II (Garden City, N.Y.: Doubleday Image, 1978) and the reissue with different pagination (Kalamazoo: Cistercian Publications, 1981), CS 48. This work was included in Migne's *Patrologia* twice because it has been attributed both to Augustine and to Bernard of Clairvaux.

Hopkins, Jasper. *Nicholas of Cusa's Dialectical Mysticism: Text, Translation, and Interpretive Study of De Visione Dei.* 2nd ed. Minneaplis: Arthur J. Banning Press, 1988, first published 1985. Contains translation of Hugh of Balma, *The Roads to Zion,* Prologue and Quaestio Difficilis, pp. 369–92.

Hugh of Saint-Victor. *De arrha animae.* PL 176. ET by Kevin Herbert as *Soliloquy on the Earnest Money of the Soul.* Milwaukee: Marquette University Press, 1956. ET by F. Sherwood Taylor, *The Soul's Betrothal Gift.* Westminster, England: Dacre Press, 1945.

———. *De sacramentis.* PL 176. ET by Roy J. Deferrari as *Hugh of Saint Victor on the Sacraments of the Christian Faith (De Sacramentis).* Cambridge, Mass.: Mediaeval Academy of America, 1951.

Hugo Ripelin of Strassburg. *Compendium theologicae veritatis.* In *Alberti Magni Ratisbonensis episcopis ordinis praedicatorum opera omnia.* Edited by Augustus Borgnet and Emile Borgnet. Paris: Vivés, 1895, Vol. 34,

BIBLIOGRAPHY

pp. 1–261. This work is also found in vol. 8 of the Peltier edition of Bonaventure's *Opera Omnia*, pp. 60–246.

Ignatius of Loyola. *The Spiritual Exercises and Selected Works.* Edited by George E. Ganss, S. J. CWS. New York: Paulist Press, 1991.

Johannes von Kastl? (Pseudo-Albertus Magnus). *De adhaerendo Deo.* In *Alberti Magni Opera Omnia.* Edited by Augustus Borgnet. Paris: Vivés, 1898. Vol. 37, pp. 523–42. ET by a Benedictine of Princethorpe Priory as *On Union with God (De Adhaerendo Deo).* London, 1911.

John Cassian, *Conlationes [Conferences].* PL 49. SC 42, 54, 64. ET by Edgar C. S. Gibson. NPNF-2, vol. 11. Partial ET by Colm Luibheid as *John Cassian: Conferences.* CWS. New York: Paulist Press, 1985.

John Chrysostom. *Homiliae in Hebraeos.* PG 63:426B. ET in NPNF-1, vol. 14.

Kempf, Nicholas. *Tractatus de mystica theologia.* Edited by Karl Jellouschek, Francis Ruello, and Jeanne Barbet. AC 9. Salzburg: Institut für englische Sprache und Literatur, 1973.

Nicholas of Lyra. See Abbreviations.

Odo of Cluny. *Vita Geraldi Auriliacensis.* PL 133. ET by Gerald Sitwell, *St. Odo of Cluny, Being the Life of St. Odo of Cluny by John of Salerno and the Life of St. Gerald of Aurillac.* London: Sheed and Ward, 1958.

Peter Lombard. *Libri Sententiarum.* PL 192.

Pez, Bernhard, and Hueber, Philibert, eds. *Codex diplomatico-historico-epistolaris* (= vol. 6 of *Thesaurus anecdotorum novissimus*). Augsburg, Graz: Philip, Johannes, Martin Veit, 1729; letters of Vincent of Aggsbach, Johannes Schiltpacher and others, pp. 327–56.

Pseudo-Dionysius. *De divinis nominibus; De mystica theologia; Epistolas; De coelestia hierarchia; De ecclesiastica hierarchia.* In *Dionysiaca. Recueil donnant l'ensemble des traductions latines des ouvrages attribués au Denys l'Aréopagite.* 2 vols. Edited by Ph. Chevallier et al. Paris: Desclée de Brouwer, 1937, 1950. PG 3. SC 58 (*Celestial Hierarchy*). ET by Colm

BIBLIOGRAPHY

Luibheid and Paul Rorem as *The Divine Names; The Mystical Theology; The Letters; The Celestial Hierarchy; The Ecclesiastical Hierarchy* in *Pseudo-Dionysius: Complete Works*. CWS. New York: Paulist Press, 1987.

Richard of Saint-Victor. *Benjamin major* [*The Mystical Ark*]. PL 196. ET by Grover Zinn as *Richard of Saint Victor: The Twelve Patriarchs, The Mystical Ark, Book Three of the Trinity*. CWS. New York: Paulist Press, 1978.

―――. *Benjamin minor* [*The Twelve Patriarchs*]. PL 196. ET by Grover Zinn as above.

―――. *De exterminatione mali* (*On Destroying Evil*). PL 196. Excerpts translated by Clare Kirchberger in *Richard of Saint Victor: Selected Writings on Contemplation*. London: Faber and Faber, 1957, pp. 244–45.

[Carthusian Order.] *Statuta Antiqua* (1259). Basel: Amerbach, 1510. Reprinted in *The Evolution of the Carthusian Statutes from the Consuetudines Guigonis to the Tertia Compilatio, Documents*, vols. 1–2. AC 99, Documents, 1–2. 1989. Pp. 57–269.

Tertullian. *De paenitentia*. PL 1. CCSL 1. SC 310. ET by A. Cleveland Coxe as *On Patience* in ANF 3:707–17. New York: Scribner's, 1899.

Thomas Aquinas. *Super Evangelium S. Ioannis Lectura*. 5th rev. ed. Edited by Raphaelis Cai. Rome: Marietti, 1952. ET by James A. Weisheipl and Fabian R. Larcher, *Commentary on the Gospel of John*. Albany, N.Y.: Magi Books, 1980.

Thomas Gallus. *Commentaires du Cantique des Cantiques*. Edited by Jeanne Barbet. Textes philosophiques du Moyen Age, 14. Paris: J. Vrin, 1967.

―――. *Grand commentaire sur la Théologie Mystique*. Edited by G. Théry. Paris: Haloua, 1934 [very rare].

The Way of Silent Love: Carthusian Novice Conferences. Translated by an Anglican Solitary. CS 149. Kalamazoo: Cistercian Publications, 1993.

BIBLIOGRAPHY

William of Auxerre [Guillelmus Altissidorensis]. *Summa aurea* [*Summa super quatuor sententiarum*]. Edited by Jean Ribaillier. Spicilegium Bonaventurianum, vol. 16–20. Paris: Centre Nationale de Recherches Religieuse, 1980–1987. Rome: Quaracchi, 1980–1987.

William of Saint-Thierry. *De contemplatione.* SC 61. ET by Sr. Penelope C.S.M.V. as *On Contemplating God; Prayer; Meditations.* CF 3. Kalamazoo: Cistercian Publications, 1977.

⸻. *Epistola ad Fratres de Monte Dei.* PL 184. SC 223. ET by Theodore Berkeley as *The Golden Epistle.* CF 12. Kalamazoo: Cistercian Publications, 1971.

The Wound of Love: A Carthusian Miscellany. CS 157. Kalamazoo: Cistercian Publications, 1994.

Secondary Sources

Carthusians

Hocquard, Gaston. "Les idées maîtresses des *Meditations* du Prieur Guiges Ier." In *Historia et Spiritualitas Cartusiensis.* Acta Colloquii Quarti Internationalis, Ghent-Antwerp-Bruges, 16–19 Septembre 1982. Edited by Jan de Grauwe. Destelbergen: de Grauwe, 1983, pp. 247–56.

le Bras, Gabriel. "Les Chartreux." In *Les Ordres religieux: La vie et l'art.* Edited by Gabriel le Bras, illustrations by Paul Hartmann and Madeleine Hartmann. Paris: Flammarion, 1979–1980. Vol. 1, pp. 562–653.

Martin, Dennis D. *Fifteenth-Century Carthusian Reform: The World of Nicholas Kempf.* Studies in the History of Christian Thought, 49. Leiden: E. J. Brill, 1992.

⸻. "The Honeymoon Was Over": Carthusians between Aristocracy and Bourgeoisie." In *Die Kartäuser und ihre Welt: Kontakte und gegenseitige Einflüsse,* vol. 1, Analecta Cartusiana, 62.1. Salzburg: Institut für Anglistik und Amerikanistik, 1993, pp. 66–99.

333

BIBLIOGRAPHY

Mursell, Gordon. "Love of the World in the *Meditations* of Guigo I." In *De Cella in Seculum: Religious and Secular Life and Devotion in Medieval England.* Edited by Michael G. Sargent. Cambridge, England: D. S. Brewer, 1989, pp. 59–65.

———. *The Theology of the Carthusian Life in the Writings of St. Bruno and Guigo I.* AC, 127. 1988.

HUGH OF BALMA

Andrès Martín, Melquíades. *Los Recogidos: Nueva vision de la mistica española (1500–1700).* Madrid: Fundacion Universitaria Española Seminario "Suarez," 1975.

Auer, Johann. "Die *Theologia Mystica* des Kartäusers Jakob von Jüterbog (+1465)." In *Die Kartäuser in Österreich,* vol. 2. Edited by James Hogg, Analecta Cartusiana, 83.2. Salzburg: Institut für Anglistik und Amerikanistik, 1981, pp. 19–52.

Autore, Stanislaus. "Hughes de Balma." In *Dictionnaire de théologie catholique.* Edited by A. Vacant and E. Mangenot. Paris: Letouzy et ané, 1922, vol. 7, pp. 215–20.

Dubois, Jacques. "Le Domaine de la chartreuse de Meyriat: Histoir d'un désert cartusien." *Le Moyen Age Latin* 74 (1968): 459–93.

Dubourg, Pierre. "La Date de la *Theologia Mystica.*" *Revue d'ascetique et de mystique* 8 (1927): 156–61.

Emery, Kent, Jr. "The Cloud of Unknowing and Mystica Theologia." In *The Roots of the Modern Christian Tradition.* The Spirituality of Western Christendom, vol. 2. Edited by E. Rozanne Elder. CS 53. Kalamazoo: Cistercian Publications, 1984, pp. 46–70.

———. *Dionysii cartusiensis opera selecta,* vol. 1: *Prolegomena: Bibliotheca manuscripta,* in 2 parts. CCCM 121A, 121B. Turnhout: Brepols, 1991.

BIBLIOGRAPHY

———. "Twofold Wisdom and Contemplation in Denys of Ryckel (Dionysius Cartusiensis, 1402–1471)." *Journal of Medieval and Renaissance Studies* 18 (1988): 99–134.

Erb, Peter C. *Pietists, Protestants, and Mysticism: The Use of Late Medieval Spiritual Texts in the Work of Gottfried Arnold (1666–1714).* Pietist and Wesleyan Studies, 2. Metuchen, N.J.: Scarecrow Press, 1989.

Guinan, Patricia A. "Carthusian Prayer and Hugh of Balma's Viae Sion Lugent." Ph.D. diss., Medieval Institute, University of Notre Dame, 1985.

Haas, Alois M. "Schools of Late Medieval Mysticism." In *Christian Spirituality: High Middle Ages and Reformation.* Edited by Jill Raitt, Bernard McGinn, and John Meyendorff. World Spirituality: An Encyclopedic Quest, 17. New York: Crossroad, 1987, pp. 140–75.

Hogg, James. "Hugh of Balma and Guigo du Pont." In *Kartäuserregel und kartäuserleben.* Internationaler Kongress vom 30. Mai bis 3. Juni 1984, Stift Heiligenkreuz. AC 113.1. Salzburg: Institut für Anglistik und Amerikanistik, 1984, pp. 61–88.

Höver, Werner. "Hugo von Balma." In *Die deutsche Literatur des Mittelalters: Verfasserlexikon.* Rev. ed. Edited by Kurt Ruh, Franz-Josef Worstbrock, and others. Berlin: de Gruyter, 1983, vol. 4, cols. 225–26.

———. *Theologia Mystica in altbairische Übertragung: Bernhard von Clairvaux, Bonaventura, Hugo von Balma, Jean Gerson, Bernhard von Waging und andere: Studien zum Übersetzungswerk eines Tegernseer Anonymus aus der Mitte des 15. Jarhunderts.* Münchener Texte und Untersuchungen zur deutschen Literatur des Mittelalters, 36. Munich: C. H. Beck, 1971.

Kleineidam, Erich. "Die Spiritualität der Kartäuser im Spiegel der Erfurter Kartäuser-Bibliothek." In *Die Kartäuser: Der Orden der schweigenden Mönche.* Edited by Marijan Zadnikar and Adam Wienand. Cologne: Wienand Verlag, 1983, pp. 185–202. Originally published as separate booklet in the series Miscellanea Erffordiana. Leipzig: Benno Verlag, 1962.

BIBLIOGRAPHY

Krynen, Jean. "La Pratique et la theorie de l'amour sans connaissance dans le Viae Sion lugent d'Hughes de Balma." *Revue d'ascetique et de mystique* 40 (1964): 162–83.

————. *Saint Jean de la Croix et l'aventure de la mystique espagnole.* Collection "Thèses et recherches, 20. Toulouse: Presses Universitaires du Mirail, 1990.

Le Couteulx, Charles. *Annales ordinis cartusiensis ab anno 1084 ad annum 1429,* 8 vols. Montreuil-sur-Mer, 1887–1891.

Mertens, Dieter. "Jakob von Paradies (1381–1465) über die mystische Theologie." In *Kartäusermystik und -mystiker.* Dritter Internationaler Kongress über die Kartäusergeschichte und -spiritualität. Vol. 5. AC 55.5. Salzburg: Institut für Anglistik und Amerikanistik, 1982, pp. 31–46.

Mertens, Thierry. "Het aspirative gebed bij Hendrik Mande: Invloed van Hugo de Balma?" *Ons geestelijk Erf* 58 (1984): 300–21.

————. "Hugo de Balma in het Middelnederlands." In *Codex in Context: Studies over Codicologie, kartuizergeschiedenis en laatmiddeleeuws geestesleven aangeboden aan Prof. Dr. A. Gruijs.* Edited by Chr. de Backer, A. J. Geuirts, and A. G. Weiler. Nijmegen: Uitgeverei Alfa, 1985, pp. 249–61.

Orcibal, Jean. *La Rencontre du Carmel Thérèsien avec les mystiques du nord.* Bibliothèque de l'école des hautes études, section des sciences religieuses, 70. Paris: Presses Universitaires de France, 1959.

Pablo Maroto, Faustino de. "Amor y Conocimiento en la Vida Mística según Hugo de Balma." *Revista de espiritualidad* 24 (1965): 399–447.

Ruello, Francis. "Statut et rôle de l'*intellectus* et de l'*affectus* dans la *Théologie Mystique* de Hughes de Balma." In *Kartäusermystik und -mystiker.* Dritter Internationaler Kongress über die Kartäusergeschichte und -spiritualität, 1. AC 55.1. Salzburg: Institut für Anglistik und Amerikanistik, 1981, pp. 1–46.

BIBLIOGRAPHY

Schmidt, Margot. "Nikolaus von Kues im Gespräch mit den Tegernseer Mönchen über Wesen und Sinn der Mystik." In *Das Sehen Gottes nach Nikolaus von Kues*. Akten des Symposions in Trier vom 25. bis 27. September 1986. Edited by Rudolf Haubst (= *Mitteilungen und Forschungsbeiträge der Cusanus-Gesellschaft*, 18). Trier: Paulinus-Verlag, 1989, pp. 25–49.

———. "Rodolphe de Biberach." *DSAM* 13 (1987), cols. 845–50.

———, ed. *Rudolf von Biberach: Die siben strassen zu got: Die hochalemanische Übertragung nach der Handschrift Einsiedeln 278*. Spicilegium Bonaventurianum, 6. Quaracchi: Collegium S. Bonaventurae, 1969. Revised edition in the series Mystik in Geschichte und Gegenwart, Texte und Untersuchungen, I.2. Stuttgart-Bad Cannstatt, 1985.

Sochay, Artaud-M. "Hughes de Balma." In *Catholicisme: Hier et aujourd'hui, demain*. Edited by E. Jacqueme. Paris: Letouzy et ané, 1947– . Vol. 5 (1962), cols. 1028–29.

Spaapen, B. "Kartuizer-vroomheid en ignatiaanse spiritualiteit." *Ons geestelijk Erf* 30 (1956): 337–66.

Stoelen, Anselme. "Hughes de Balma." *DSAM* 7 (1969), cols. 859–73. Numerous additional references elsewhere in *DSAM* to Hugh of Balma are listed at the end of this article.

Walach, Harald. *Notitia experimentalis Dei—Erfahrungserkenntnis Gottes: Studien zu Hugo de Balmas Text "Viae Sion lugent" und deutsche Übersetzung*. AC 98.1. Salzburg: Institut für Anglistik und Amerikanistik, 1994.

GUIGO DE PONTE

Baier, Walter. *Untersuchungen zu den Passionsbetrachtungen in der Vita Christi des Ludolfs von Sachsen: Ein quellenkritischer Beitrag zu Leben und Werk Ludolfs und zur Geschichte der Passionstheologie*, 3 vols. AC 44. Salzburg: Institut für Englische Sprache und Literatur, 1977.

Dupont, Philippe. "L'ascension mystique chez Guigues du Pont." In *Kartäusermystik und -mystiker*. Dritter Internationaler Kongress über

BIBLIOGRAPHY

die Kartäusergeschichte und -spiritualität, 1. AC 55.1. Salzburg: Institut für Anglistik und Amerikanistik, 1981, pp. 47–80.

Grausem, J. P. "Le *De contemplatione* du Chartreux Guiges du Pont (+ 1297)." *Revue d'Ascetique et de Mystique* 10 (1929): 259–89.

Pawsey, Humphrey. "Guigo the Angelic." In *Spirituality through the Centuries: Ascetics and Mystics of the Western Church.* Edited by James Walsh. New York: P. J. Kenedy, 1964. Pp. 138–39 deal with Guigo de Ponte; the article itself deals with Guigo II, the author of the *Scala Claustralium.*

Raitz von Frentz, Emmerich. "Ludolphe le Chartreux et les exercices de S. Ignace de Loyola." *Revue d 'ascetique et de mystique* 25 (1949): 375–88.

Sochay, Artaud-M. "Guigues du Pont." In *Catholicism, hier, aujour-d'hui, demain.* Edited by G. Jacquemet. Paris: Letouzy et ané, 1947– . Vol. 5 (1962), pp. 374–75.

See also Hogg, James, "Hugh of Balma and Guigo du Pont," above.

Other Secondary Literature

[A Carthusian], *El Santo Rosario en la Cartuja.* Analecta Cartusiana, 103. Salzburg: Institut für Anglistik und Amerikanistik, 1983.

Bangert, William V. *Jerome Nadal, S.J., 1507–1580: Tracking the First Generation of Jesuits.* Edited and completed by Thomas M. McCoog. Chicago: Loyola University Press, 1992.

Barbet, Jeanne. "Thomas Gallus." *Dictionnaire de spiritualité ascetique et mystique.* Vol. 15. Paris: Beauchesne, 1991, cols. 800–16.

Beyer, Jean. "Saint Ignace de Loyola chartreux." *Nouvelle revue théologique* 78 (1956): 937–51.

Burrows, Mark S. *Jean Gerson and "De Consolatione Theologiae" (1418): The Consolation of a Biblical and Reforming Theology for a Disordered Age.* Beiträge zur historischen Theologie, 78. Tübingen: J. C. B. Mohr, 1991.

BIBLIOGRAPHY

Capellino, M. *Tommaso di San Vittore.* Vercelli: Abbey of S. Andrea, 1978.

Clark, John P. H. "The *Cloud of Unknowing* and the Contemplative Life." In *Die Kartäuser und ihre Welt: Kontakte und gegenseitige Einflüsse.* Analecta Cartusiana, 63.1. Salzburg: Institut für Anglistik und Amerikanistik, 1993, pp. 44–65.

————. *The Latin Versions of the Cloud of Unknowing.* AC 119. Salzburg: Institut für Anglistik und Amerikanistik, 1989–

————. "Sources and Theology in the 'Cloud of Unknowing.' " *Downside Review* 89 (1980): 83–109.

Colledge, Edmund, and Marler, J. C., "*Tractatus Magistri Johannis Gerson de Mistica Theologia:* St. Pölten Diözesanarchiv MS. 25." *Mediaeval Studies* 41(1979): 354–86.

Combes, André. *La théologie mystique de Gerson: Profil de son évolution.* 2 vols. Spiritualitas, 1–2. Rome: Desclée, 1963.

Dingjan, F. *Discretio: Les origines patristiques et monastiques de la doctrine sur la prudence chez saint Thomas d'Aquin.* Van Gorcum's Theologische Bibliothek, 38. Assen: Van Gorcum, 1967.

Faes de Mottoni, Barbara. *Il Corpus Dionysianum nel Medioevo: Rassegna di studi: 1900–1972.* Rome: Societá editrice il Mulino, 1977.

Frank, Karl Suso. [*Angelikos Bios*]: *Begriffsanalytische und begriffsgeschichtliche Untersuchung zum "engelgleichen Leben" im frühen Mönchtum.* Beiträge zur Geschichte des alten Mönchtums, 26. Münster i. Westfalen: Aschendorff, 1964.

Froehlich, Karlfried. "Justification Language and Grace: The Charge of Pelagianism in the Middle Ages." In *Probing the Reformed Tradition: Historical Studies in Honor of Edward A. Dowey, Jr.* Edited by Elsie Ann McKee and Brian G. Armstrong. Louisville, Ky.: Westminster/John Knox, 1989, pp. 21–47.

BIBLIOGRAPHY

Fry, Timothy, and others, eds. *RB 1980: The Rule of St. Benedict in Latin and English with Notes.* Collegeville, Minn.: Liturgical Press, 1981, pp. 3–151, 301–493.

Gardeil, A. "Les mouvements direct, en spirale et circulaire de l'âme et les oraisons mystiques." *Revue Thomiste* 30 (1925):321–40.

Hamm, Berndt. *Pactum, Promissio, Ordinatio: Freiheit und Selbstbindung Gottes in der scholastischen Gnadenlehre.* Beiträge zur historischen Theologie, 54. Tübingen: J. C. B. Mohr, 1977.

Hugueny, Etienne. "Circulaire, rectiligne, hélicoïdal: les trois degrés de la contemplation." *Revue des Sciences Philosophiques et Théologiques* 13 (1924):327–31.

Ivánka, Endre von. "Apex mentis: Wanderung und Wandlung eines stoischen Terminus." *Zeitschrift für katholische Theologie* 72 (1950): 129–76.

———. "Was heißt eigentlich 'Christlicher Neuplatonismus'?" *Scholastik* 31 (1956):31–40. Reprinted in *Plato Christianus.* Einsiedeln: Johannes Verlag, 1964, pp. 373–85.

———. "Zur Überwindung des neuplatonischen Intellektualismus in der Deutung der Mystik: Intelligentia oder principalis affectio." *Scholastik* 30 (1955): 185–94. Reprinted in *Plato Christianus,* pp. 352–63. Reprinted in *Platonismus in der Philosophie des Mittelalters,* pp. 147–60.

Johnson, Timothy. *Iste Pauper Clamavit: Saint Bonaventure's Mendicant Theology of Prayer.* European University Studies, series 23, Theology, vol. 390. Frankfurt a. M.: Peter Lang, 1990.

Klinkhammer, Karl-Josef. *Adolf von Essen und seine Werke: Der Rosenkranz in der geschichtlichen Situation seiner Entstehung und in seinem bleibenden Anliegen; Eine Quellenforschung.* Frankfurter theologische Studien, 13. Frankfurt a. M.: Josef Knecht, 1972.

Koziol, Geoffrey. *Begging Pardon and Favor: Ritual and Political Order in Early Medieval France.* Ithaca: Cornell University Press, 1992.

BIBLIOGRAPHY

Leclercq, Jean. *Otia monastica: Etudes sur le vocabulaire de la contemplation au moyen âge.* Studia Anselmiana, 51. Rome: Pontificum Institutum S. Anselmi, 1963; Rome: Herder, 1963.

Lees, Rosemary Ann. *The Negative Language of the Dionysian School of Mystical Theology: An Approach to the "Cloud of Unknowing."* 2 vols. AC 107. Salzburg: Institut für Anglistik und Amerikanistik, 1983.

Martín, Teodoro H. "Los misticos allemanes en la España del XVI y XVII." *Revista de Espiritualidad* 48 (1989): 111–28.

McGinn, Bernard. *The Foundations of Mysticism.* Vol. 1 of *The Presence of God: A History of Western Christian Mysticism.* New York: Crossroad, 1992.

———. "Love, Knowledge, and Mystical Union in Western Christianity: Twelfth to Sixteenth Centuries." *Church History* 56 (1987): 7–24.

Oberman, Heiko A. *The Harvest of Medieval Theology.* Cambridge, Mass.: Harvard University Press, 1963; 3rd ed. Durham, N.C.: Labyrinth Press, 1983.

———. "Das tridentinischen Rechtfertigungsdekret im Lichte spätmittelalterlicher Theologie." *Zeitschrift für Theologie und Kirche* 61 (1964): 251–82. Expanded version in *Concilium Tridentinum.* Edited by R. Bäumer. Darmstadt: Wissenschaftliche Buchgesellschaft, 1979, pp. 301–40.

Payer, Pierre J. "Prudence and the Principles of Natural Law." *Speculum* 54 (1979): 55–70.

Rorem, Paul. *Pseudo-Dionysius: A Commentary on the Texts and an Introduction to their Influence.* New York: Oxford University Press, 1993.

Ros, Fidèle de. *Un maître de sainte Thérèse, le P. François d'Osuna: Sa vie, son oeuvre, sa doctrine spirituelle.* Études de Théologie Historique. Paris: Beauchesne, 1936.

BIBLIOGRAPHY

Ruh, Kurt. "*Amor deficiens* und *amor desiderii* in der Hoheliedauslegung Wilhelms von St. Thierry." In *Spiritualia Neerlandica: Opstellen voor Dr. Albert Ampe, S.J., hem door vakgenooten en vrienden aangeboden uit waardering voor zijn wetenschappelijke werk.* Edited by Elly Cockx-Indestege, Jan Deschamps, Frans Hendrickx, and Paul Verdeyen, S. J. [= *Ons geestelijk Erf,* 63.2–4, 64.1–3 (1989–1990)], pp. 70–88.

Schlosser, Marianne. *Cognitio et amor: Zum kognitiven und voluntativen Grund der Gotteserfahrung nach Bonaventura.* Veröffentlichungen des Grabmann-Institutes, 35. Paderborn: Schöningh, 1990.

Sommerfeldt, John R. "The Vocabulary of Contemplation in Aelred of Rievaulx' Mirror of Love, Book 1." In *Goad and Nail.* Edited by E. Rozanne Elder. Studies in Medieval Cistercian History, 10/Cistercian Studies series, 84. Kalamazoo: Cistercian Publications, 1985, pp. 241–50.

———. "The Vocabulary of Contemplation in Aelred of Rievaulx's On Jesus at the Age of Twelve, A Rule of Life for a Recluse, and On Spiritual Friendship." In *Heaven on Earth.* Edited by E. Rozanne Elder. Studies in Medieval Cistercian History, 9/Cistercian Studies series, 68. Kalamazoo: Cistercian Publications, 1983, pp. 72–89.

Srbik, Robert Ritter von. *Maximilian I. und Gregor Reisch.* Edited by Alphons Lhotsky. Archiv für österreichische Geschichte, 122.2. Vienna: Böhlau, 1961.

Stieber, Joachim W. *Pope Eugenius IV, the Council of Basel, and the Secular and Ecclesiastical Authorities in the Empire.* Studies in the History of Christian Thought, 13. Leiden: E. J. Brill, 1978.

Vansteenberghe, Edmond. *Autour de la docte ignorance.* Beträge zur Geschichte der Philosophie und Theologie des Mittelalters, 14. Münster i. W.: Aschendorff, 1915. Reprinted as AC 35, pt. 17. Salzburg: Institut für Anglistik und Amerikanistik, 1992; Lewiston, N.Y.: Edwin Mellen Press, 1992, pp. 1–221.

Walsh, James J. " 'Sapientia Christianorum': The Doctrine of Thomas Gallus Abbot of Vercelli on Contemplation." Dissertatio ad Lauream in Facultate Theologica, Pontifical Gregorian University, Rome, 1957.

BIBLIOGRAPHY

———, ed. "The Expositions of Thomas Gallus on the Pseudo-Dionysian Letters." *Archives d 'histoire doctrinale et littéraire du Moyen Age* 38 (1964): 199–220.

———. "Thomas Gallus et l'effort contemplatif." *Revue d 'histoire de la spiritualité* 51 (1975): 17–42.

Watts, Pauline Moffitt. *Nicolaus Cusanus: A Fifteenth-Century Vision of Man*. Studies in the History of Christian Thought, 30. Leiden: E. J. Brill, 1982.

Index of Scriptural Citations
and Allusions

References for chapter and verse generally are to the Douay-Rheims Bible. References to the Old Testament books are given in the Vulgate numbering; references to the Hebrew Bible, when indicated, follow in parentheses.

344

INDEX OF SCRIPTURAL CITATIONS AND ALLUSIONS

INDEX OF SCRIPTURAL CITATIONS AND ALLUSIONS

Index of Subjects

Aristotle: on the intellect, 167, 250
Augustine: on Christ Jesus as
  foundation, 197; on cogitation, 156,
  163, 231; on compassion, 175; on
  contemplation, 221; on eating, 245;
  on life, 217; on repentance, 196; on
  soul, 223; on virtue, 246

Bernard of Clairvaux: on awe before
  God, 183; on the Blessed Virgin
  Mary, 183; on Canticles 1:10, 236,
  236–237, 237–240; on cleansing the
  spirit, 195–196; on contemplation,
  197; on humility, 243; on rapture,
  192, 227; on the soul, 223–224, 233;
  on spiritual listlessness, 251–252,
  252; on yearning for the Lord, 176
Book of Solitary Life. See William of St.
  Thierry (Bernard)

Carthusian Order: characteristics of
  spirituality, 5–8, 290–291 n. 57,
  291 n. 61; history of, 3–5; overview
  of, 255–256 n. 13
Cassiodorus: on tears, 183
Cogitation: and aspiration, 168; and
  love, 25–34, 161–166, 166–170; and
  movement into God, 155–158, 158–
  161. See also Contemplation: subject
  of; God: knowing

Contemplation: abandonment and,
  147–148, 152; alluring meditation
  and, 221, 225–228, 231–232, 250,
  319–320 n. 91; anagogical, 208–212,
  213; of Christ, 197–198, 198–199,
  199–201; circular movements of,
  187–190; comparison of types, 213–
  215; direct movement of, 190–192;
  exercising, 204–205; foundation of,
  195, 197; inventive, 235–237;
  knowledge and, 31–32, 51–52,
  272 n. 163, 231, 319–320 n. 91; as
  life for few, 216–218, 218; means of
  living life of, 218–220; requirements
  for, 196–197, 202–203; Scripture
  and, 219, 221; sins and, 240–241,
  253; speculative and anagogical
  movements of, 186–192, 195, 221–
  222; spiral movements of, 187; steps
  to prepare for, 174–176, 176–177;
  steps in speculative contemplation,
  203–204, 319–320; subject of, 72,
  75–76, 136, 166, 178–180, 184–186,
  194, 196–197, 202, 203, 221–224;
  summary of steps, 194–195; and
  support of saints, 177, 201–202;
  types of, 162–164, 220; types of
  speculative contemplation, 220–221;
  vices and, 240–241, 243–244, 249;
  vision revealed during, 153, 205–
  208, 295 n. 122; versus wisdom, 231;
  workshop for, 234–235; yearning

INDEX OF SUBJECTS

INDEX OF SUBJECTS

INDEX OF SUBJECTS

Other Volumes in this Series